The New
Moosewood
Cookbook

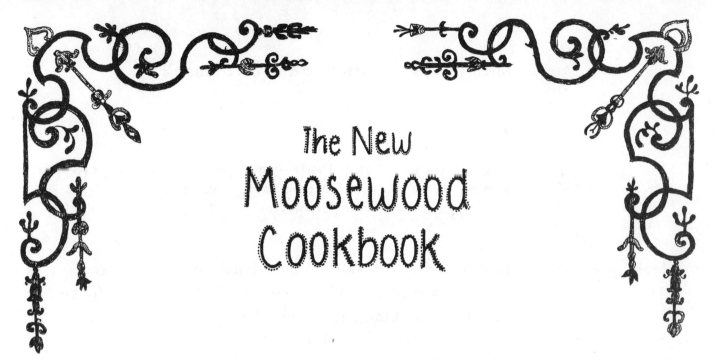

The New Moosewood Cookbook

by Mollie Katzen

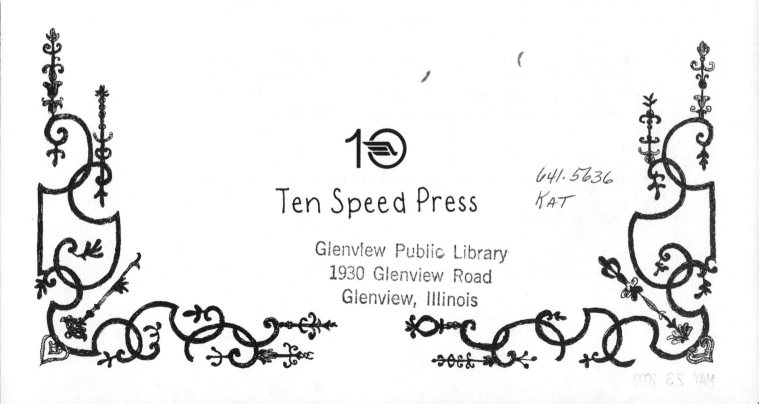

Ten Speed Press

Dedicated to Hal, with love and gratitude.

Cover design for original edition: Meredith Barchat and Mollie Katzen
Revised cover design: Fifth Street Design, Nancy Austin, and Mollie Katzen
Typesetting for revised edition: Star Type, Berkeley
Frontispiece and illustrations: Mollie Katzen
Food Photography: Richard Jung
Food Styling: Andrea Lucich
Prop Styling: Lorraine Battle
Author photo on back cover: Lisa Keating

Ten Speed Press
P. O. Box 7123
Berkeley, California 94707
www.tenspeed.com

Correspondence for the author can be sent to the above address, or visit
Mollie's web site at www.molliekatzen.com.

Distributed in Australia by Simon & Schuster Australia, in Canada by
Ten Speed Press Canada, in New Zealand by Southern Publishers Group,
in South Africa by Real Books, in Southeast Asia by Berkeley Books, and
in the United Kingdom and Europe by Airlift Books.

Library of Congress Cataloging-in-Publication Data is on file with publisher.

First printing, 2000

Printed in the United States of America

1 2 3 4 5 6 7 8 9 10 — 04 03 02 01 00

MAY 23 2000

❄ Contents ❄

ACKNOWLEDGEMENTS

I want to express my deepest appreciation for all the support and encouragement I receive, always, from the folks at Ten Speed Press. This includes Aaron Wehner, Nancy Austin, Hal Hershey, Lorena Jones, Phil Wood, Kirsty Melville, Dennis Hayes, Jo Ann Deck, Anna Erickson, Brook Barnum, Dave Pereira, Raúl Carrizales, and last but not least, George Young (who, although no longer at Ten Speed, is still one of my guardian angels). I am indebted, also, to Linda Davis, who organized the laying-out and pasting-up process for this new edition, and to Phil Gardner and Janet Fohner, who helped her.

Many thanks to Richard Jung, the very gifted photographer who shot the photos; to Andrea Lucich and her assitant, Elisabet der Nederlanden, who styled the food; to Lorraine Battle, who styled the props for both the photos and my T.V. show; and to Lissa Ivy and Diana Alexander, who assisted with the shoot. Props for the photos were generously loaned by Sur La Table, Sante Salvoni, and Cyclamen, among others.

I am grateful to Torri Randall for all her love and support over the years, and to the other producers of "Mollie Katzen's Cooking Show": Peggy Lee Scott, Tina Salter, and Kate Zilavy. I also want to acknowledge the show's food stylist, Heidi Gintner, as well as the wonderful crew. Vincent Nattress, the chef-supervisor of the back kitchen, was a great inspiration, as was Rich Hartwig and the other terrific folks at KTVU in Oakland, California, where the show is taped. Thanks, also, to everyone at Maryland Public Television, my partner station. I am deeply indebted to Boca Burger, Inc., not only for their delicious products, which often sustain me, but also for their generous underwriting of my show. I especially want to thank Katie Torres.

I couldn't do any of this without the rich love and encouragement I get from my husband, Carl, and my children, Sam and Eve. And last of all, thanks so much to all you readers out there for continuing to cook and enjoy the recipes. As always, this book is for you.

Welcome to the New Moosewood Cookbook!

I am very pleased to present this new edition of the Moosewood Cookbook, which I'm thrilled to say is still going strong well into its third decade. When Moosewood was first published by Ten Speed Press in 1977, vegetarian cuisine was still a fledgling concept to the general American population. Over time, however, many people have come to welcome meatless meals into their regular routines, whether they eat meat at other times or not. Loving vegetables and good meatless cuisine as I do, I am excited about this evolution. And needless to say, I'm so happy that the Moosewood Cookbook is still here, and that it continues to reach new generations of cooks, both young and old.

A few years back, to mark the fifteenth anniversary of the Moosewood Cookbook, I retested each recipe in the book to see if my culinary style had evolved enough to warrant some adjustments. Sure enough, I found that my cooking had changed over the years, becoming more streamlined in preparation – and lighter in "weight," while richer in flavor. So without altering the essential character of the book or the nature of the cuisine, which celebrates fresh vegetables, fruit, legumes, and whole grains, I rewrote many of the recipes. Some changed a little, some changed quite a bit, and others stayed exactly the same. I added twenty-five new recipes (make that thirty with this new edition), and worked to improve the organization of the text, so the book would be more accessible and user-friendly. And now, I've added a special visual treat as well: sixteen color photographs of some of the most popular recipes, for your view-ing enjoyment.

I hope you will find the recipes enticing, approachable, and easy to follow. And of course, I hope you and your loved ones will enjoy the food, and incorporate this kind of cooking and eating into your daily lives. Here's to our cooking adventures, and to great health and vibrancy for us all!

Mollie Katzen
Berkeley, California
1999

A Personal History of This Book

Fifteen years after the Ten Speed Press publication of the <u>Moosewood Cookbook</u>, I remain amazed and gratified by the response this book has received. I still ponder the reasons. What has happened to shift the culture, so that it is no longer considered fringe behavior to cut down on one's meat intake or to eat vegetarian meals at least a few times a week? Greater awareness of our bodies and our health has played a major role. People want to eat meals that are easy to prepare, nutritious, and relatively inexpensive. Also, as the world has gotten smaller and we've been more exposed to diverse cultures, there has been a growing openness to — and fascination with— various ethnic styles of cooking, many of which place far less emphasis on meat, and more on creative preparation of simple ingredients. In addition, concern about the environment has led many people to become more aware of the impact our food choices have on the health of the earth. This evolution toward reshaping and rethinking our eating habits has been gradual but steady. As meatless cooking is being welcomed more and more into the mainstream, and as the <u>Moosewood Cookbook</u> approaches its 15th birthday, I've been reflecting on my unexpected role in this movement, and have decided to share with you my personal story surrounding the creation of this book.

Although I always loved to cook, I never set out to write cookbooks, nor to be a food professional in any way. My earliest culinary exposure was to simple, largely processed foods. A child of the '50s and '60s, I was raised on Minute Rice, Campbell's soups, Velveeta cheese, and frozen vegetables — the miracle convenience foods of that era. We ate red meat about five nights a week; on the other two we ate chicken or fish. "Salad" meant iceberg lettuce, hothouse tomatoes, and mayonnaise. Cucumbers were sometimes included, but that was already edging toward the exotic. My biggest excitement came each Friday, when my mother would bake a challah (braided egg bread). I was enthralled, and would come in from wherever I was playing just in time to help her braid it. When she or my grandmother would bake desserts from scratch, I would be breathing down their necks with eagerness and fascination. My mother was tolerant and encouraging enough to allow me free run of the kitchen, and I learned early to prepare all the instant foods, but also to experiment and improvise. My focal point, at age 9 or 10, was chocolate desserts, and I invented several in earnest. I thank my mother for telling me she liked them.

My main interests, though, were art, music, and writing— I wanted to be an artist <u>and</u> a musician <u>and</u> a writer. I saw cooking as a trade that could be a source of income until my paintings were hanging in the Metropolitan Museum, my concerts sold out at Carnegie Hall, and my prize-winning novels and poetry published in many languages. I started cooking to earn money at age 16, flipping thin, grayish-colored hamburgers and deep-frying frozen potatoes in the coffee shop of a department store. Meanwhile, I drew, studied piano and oboe, and wrote umpteen tragic poems and humorous (at least, to me) stories in my room at night. It seemed a good strategy.

I continued to work at various food-related jobs, including bussing tables in my dorm at college. Yet I still didn't know very much about real food or cooking from scratch. I hadn't tasted a fresh green vegetable until the age of 12, when I was invited to dinner at the home of a friend whose mother had a vegetable garden. She picked fresh green beans for dinner, and served them lightly steamed in bowls, with a little warmed milk poured on top. I went wild! This was a radical new discovery for me! I kept thinking about those green beans long afterwards— until I had my second experience with fresh vegetables at age 18 in, of all places, the college cafeteria. The meat was uninviting, but the vegetables were fresh, wonderful, and abundant. After six months of ecstatically piling my plate high with freshly steamed broccoli, cauliflower, asparagus, etc., I realized I hadn't eaten any meat at all. I wondered if this made me a vegetarian, although at that time I didn't know anyone who was — and to be one was looked upon as a cross between an eccentricity and an affliction. Labels aside, my love of cooking and newfound infatuation with fresh vegetables led me to search for ways to cook interesting non-meat dishes. I found a job at a small macrobiotic restaurant, and there I discovered the beauty of simple legumes and grains. The year was 1970, and there were still no major vegetarian cookbooks in wide circulation yet, so this was largely uncharted territory. In addition to my personal journal of drawings and writing, I began an illustrated notebook filled with ideas for cooking with vegetables, grains, and legumes. I had no idea that this would ever coalesce into a cookbook, nor that I was in the thin of what would become the thick of a new lifestyle movement.

When I moved to San Francisco later that year to continue studying art, I discovered an exciting new restaurant that was serving fresh, creative, and sophisticated vegetarian food. The clientele was hip and fashionable, but I was drawn not by the "scene" but by the food. It was revelatory! Crêpes! Curries! Pesto! Stir-fries! Fresh fruit salads! This stuff was incredible! And the range of colors and textures of all the fresh fruits and vegetables added a visual component, providing a delightful bridge to my artistic impulses. I worked there for 1½ years and learned a great deal, not only about cooking but also about running a restaurant. My recipe notebook grew thick with ideas. During this time I received a visit from my brother and a friend, who were about to build a restaurant in Ithaca, New York, but didn't yet know what type of food they wanted to serve. When they dropped in on me at work and tasted the food, they knew this was what they were looking for. They invited me to join them in their project, and to bring this new cooking style with me. I hesitated, as I had planned to continue studying art. But the thought of starting a restaurant with unlimited creative freedom was too appealing to resist. After much thought, I decided to go for just three months, to help get things started. I did, and the result was the Moosewood Restaurant, opened by seven of us in January 1973.

Starting this restaurant was a labor of love. The kitchen was tiny, the storage facilities negligible. The wide variety of fresh produce, so readily available year-round in California, was a distant dream in upstate New York in January. The menu was minimal at first: simple soups, two regular salads (fresh fruit and raw vegetable, cut by hand), and two daily entrées (usually casseroles). Even though vegetarianism was gradually coming into its own — boosted tremendously by the publication in 1971 of Diet for a Small Planet, by Frances Moore Lappé, and The Vegetarian Epicure, by Anna Thomas, published in 1972 — we had no idea of how meatless cooking would be received. So we tried adding one meat entrée to the menu each night. Invariably it would be left over the next day, much to our surprise. The vegetarian dishes, on the other hand, were being ordered as fast as we could make them. Eventually, we dropped the meat, and with the exception of serving fish on weekends, the restaurant quietly and unofficially went vegetarian. The food, prepared with loving, sincere effort and served without dogma, must have spoken for itself. It seemed that our customers, whose numbers were swelling, and most of whom were neither vegetarians nor people we knew, just wanted some good homemade food.

We worked hard at the restaurant. I was there long hours every day, and pretty soon noticed I'd been there longer than three months. I didn't have a lot of time or energy left over to do ambitious art, music, or writing projects, but as I continued my illustrated recipe journals, the boundary between food and officially "creative" work began to blur. I loved being at the restaurant—it felt very challenging and fulfilling. The food was coming out better all the time. Some of the people who came to work there were innovative cooks, bringing with them their own ethnic backgrounds and personal styles. As most of us cooked by feel and not literally from recipes, I began to write down some version of what was being prepared, so we could standardize the cooking. At the same time, customers were asking for recipes, and I would often jot something down for them—on a napkin or whatever—after my shift. Eventually I put together a small, casual cookbook, for use both in the restaurant kitchen and in customers' homes. I handlettered the book because I intended it to be used by people I knew, or by acquaintances of acquaintances. It didn't occur to me that some day an expanded version, still in handlettered format, would be used by over a million strangers.

The first edition, funded by a small loan from a local bookstore, had 78 pages, spiral-bound. Eight hundred copies sold out in a week. Considering that Ithaca is a very small town, this was astonishing. No one was more astonished than I. I revamped it slightly, adding more drawings (a great excuse to do some art), and had it reprinted. Two thousand copies sold out in six months, followed by another printing the same size, which sold out just as quickly. Meanwhile, I had begun to receive mail orders—apparently from people who had passed through town, picked up a copy, and shared it with friends elsewhere. I couldn't handle the demand—I was still looking for time to paint, write, and practice music, and was spending too much time running to the post office to mail packages. People were encouraging me to seek national publication, but I was reluctant. It seemed too "commercial". Still, I approached a few publishers, and one major house was interested, but with a caveat: I would have to get rid of the whimsical drawings and the handlettering. Enter Ten Speed Press, a small, new outfit in Berkeley. I had no idea who they were, but was thrilled when they offered me complete artistic and editorial freedom. Their representative told me he thought this "natural-type" cooking was about to become a major trend, and that I could sell perhaps fifty thousand books over the next five years. (This was a huge number then.) Even though I didn't quite believe him, I decided to take the plunge. I signed on, spent most of the next year expanding and revising the book (still working shifts at the restaurant), and in the autumn of 1977 the Ten Speed edition was born. It caught on slowly. Meanwhile, I retired from the restaurant—the three months had become almost five years—and set out to find horizons beyond restaurant work. As of this writing, the Moosewood Restaurant is still going strong.

Now it is fifteen years later, and the Moosewood Cookbook's sales have exceeded the fifty thousand mark beyond anything I could ever have imagined. I live on the West Coast with my husband and children, and have a painting studio. I have published two more cookbooks, the most recent one illustrated with full-color still lifes. While the old fantasies of paintings hanging at the Met, recitals in major halls, and earth-shaking novels have faded, recently I spotted a familiar-looking marinated fresh vegetable salad at a food stand in the Pittsburgh airport. I remain overwhelmed by the enthusiasm with which my cookbooks have been received, and by the loving responses sent to me by readers. My ideas about what is important have changed. To be of use, to have the opportunity to impart information and skills that serve to enrich people's daily lives—this is what matters most to me. People have brought these books into their lives for the simple purpose of getting a few ideas for good things to cook and eat, and sometimes they have come out with more. I now realize that to have my work be broadly accessible and well embraced, and to have it contribute in any way to people's health and pleasure, has been the ultimate privilege.

Mollie Katzen
Berkeley, California
1992

⚜ MODIFICATIONS ⚘

A brief guideline to further reduce the fat, dairy, and egg content of these recipes:

LOWER-FAT COOKING:

Even though the oil content of these recipes has been pared down, you can reduce it still further by using <u>oil sprays</u>. These enable you to spray a mist of oil onto the food and/or the pan, instead of using oil by the tablespoon. Oil sprays are available commercially in many gourmet and natural foods stores. (The brands I know of are Pam, Bertolli, El Molino, and Trysons.) Used in combination with high-quality nonstick cookware, oil sprays can greatly reduce the fat content of your cooking without sacrificing flavor or texture.

DAIRY REDUCTION OR SUBSTITUTION:

Milk can be substituted with soy milk or rice milk, both of which are nondairy and can be found in natural foods stores.

There are some lowfat, low sodium cheeses — as well as nondairy soy cheeses — available. Be sure to taste these before using them in your cooking. They might taste perfectly fine to you, but then again, they might not. Remember, you can always cut down on the amount of cheese prescribed in a recipe and in many cases, you can omit it altogether. Whipped tofu (puréed in a blender or food processor — or simply mashed) can sometimes substitute for cottage or ricotta cheese in casseroles. You might want to adjust the salt.

EGG OPTIONS:

Of the approximately 60 entrées, only 15 contain eggs, and of these, many are egg- or yolk-optional. If you need to reduce this further, experiment with egg substitutes. There are also desserts made without eggs, or with egg whites only.

FOR LISTS OF LOWFAT AND EGGLESS RECIPES, SEE APPENDIX

🌾 PANTRY NOTES 🌿

In case you need a brief explanation of some of the ingredients used in this book:

BEANS & LEGUMES: Usually these recipes call for dry beans to be soaked and cooked. Occasionally, it's fine to substitute canned — individual recipes will indicate this. When you use dry beans or legumes, save money by buying in bulk.

BUTTER: Use unsalted or lightly salted.

FOOD FROM CANS OR JARS: These recipes use very few canned (or jarred) foods, with the following exceptions: artichoke hearts or crowns, beans or chick peas (on occasion), water chestnuts, pineapple-in-juice, and tomato products (paste, purée, whole tomatoes, etc.)

DAIRY PRODUCTS: You can use lowfat (and often nonfat) everything: milk, cottage cheese, ricotta, sour cream, evaporated milk, yogurt, etc. Soy or rice milk can frequently be substituted.

EXTRACTS (VANILLA, ALMOND, ETC.): Use pure only.

FLOURS: Unless otherwise specified, use unbleached white flour.

FROZEN FOODS: I frequently tested these recipes with frozen unsweetened fruit (berries, cherries, etc.) with great success, when fresh were unavailable. You can also use frozen peas, corn, cooked squash, and if you're in a pinch, a 10-oz. package of frozen chopped spinach can substitute for 1 large bunch fresh in cooked dishes. Defrost and drain thoroughly before using.

GARLIC: Use fresh only and buy it frequently. The fresher, the better.

HERBS: If it's not specified, the recipe was tested with dried herbs, as these are more readily available year-round. However, if you have access to fresh herbs, by all means use them! Here's the exchange rate: 1 tsp. dried approximately equals 1 Tbs. minced fresh.

JUICES: Use fresh-squeezed lemon, lime, or orange juice in these recipes whenever possible.

OILS: For sautéing vegetables, use peanut, corn, or pure olive oil. For salads, use virgin or extra virgin olive oil, canola oil, or nut oils (walnut or hazelnut). Use virgin or extra virgin olive oil for drizzling on pasta. For seasoning certain soups, salads, and stir-fries, use Chinese sesame oil (available in Asian groceries). For information about oil sprays, see p. XVI.

NUTS, SEEDS, NUT BUTTERS: Use unprocessed, available (often in bulk) at natural foods stores and at many grocery stores. Tahini (raw sesame paste) is available in natural foods stores, in some specialty groceries, and in the imported foods section of many grocery stores.

PASTA: The recipes in this book were tested with dried egg pasta of various shapes, but you can also use fresh. More details are on p. 75.

RICE: Short- and long-grain brown rice are interchangeable in these recipes. There is no nutritional difference, and the cooking method is the same. Short-grain is chewier; long-grain is fluffier. Buy either kind in bulk at natural foods stores.

SOY SAUCE: Japanese soy sauces (tamari or shoyu) have a deeper, slightly sweeter flavor than Chinese, which are thinner and saltier (and sometimes contain additives, so read the label). Whichever kind you prefer, you can find good soy sauce in natural foods stores and in Asian markets.

SWEETENERS: To varying degrees, sugar, brown sugar, honey, and real maple syrup are used in the desserts. In some cases they are interchangeable. This is indicated on individual recipes.

TOFU: Tofu is soybean curd, available in many forms. It is high in protein, low in price, and has no cholesterol. Buy it by the pound, packed in water in little plastic tubs, by the piece—out of large buckets of water, or vacuum-packed—either in plastic wrapping or in small boxes (see p. 91). Tofu is available in natural foods stores, in Asian markets, or in the produce department of the grocery store.

☆☆☆☆☆☆☆☆☆☆☆☆☆☆☆☆☆☆☆☆☆☆☆☆
SOME USEFUL TOOLS (HIGHLY RECOMMENDED)
☆☆☆☆☆☆☆☆☆☆☆☆☆☆☆☆☆☆☆☆☆☆☆☆

☆FOOD PROCESSOR~ for puréeing, grating, mincing, and mashing. For pie crusts, too. This time- and skin-saving device might turn out to be one of the best kitchen investments you'll ever make!

☆BLENDER~ It still does some things better than a food processor — it makes smoother purées and is good for processing medium-sized amounts.

☆MINI-PROCESSOR~ finely minces garlic and fresh herbs in seconds flat. It has about a 1-cup capacity.

☆CITRUS SQUEEZER~ manual or electric.

☆CUTTING BOARDS~ one for fruit, one for vegetables, and one for onions and garlic.

☆MICROWAVE OVEN~ for reheating with little or no cleanup. With a microwave, you'll be encouraged to do more cooking in advance.

☆ELECTRIC MIXER~ hand-held or larger. This is a must for baking, especially when beaten egg whites are featured.

☆WIRE WHISKS~ of varying sizes.

☆BOWLS~ of varying sizes.

☆SEVERAL COLANDERS~ including one big enough for pasta.

☆A FEW KNIVES THAT YOU JUST LOVE~ straight-edged and serrated, of various sizes, all of them very sharp.

☆SEVERAL SPOONS THAT YOU JUST LOVE~ including a large slotted one.

☆A SOUP POT ~ (kettle or Dutch oven)

☆A LARGE PASTA-BOILING POT

☆A LARGE (10- to 12-inch) SKILLET ~ for sautéing. Nonstick = ideal.

☆A MEDIUM TO LARGE WOK ~ for stir-fries. Nonstick, if possible.

☆A 6- TO 8-INCH CRÊPE OR OMELETTE PAN ~ Again, nonstick, if possible.

☆ SEVERAL SAUCEPANS WITH LIDS ~ various sizes.

☆ A TIMER WITH A BELL ~ So you can think about other things in the meantime.

☆ A GARLIC PRESS (optional) ~ I actually prefer to mince garlic in a mini-processor or on a cutting board with a sharp paring knife, but some people love to press their garlic.

☆ BAKING PANS AND CASSEROLES ~ of various shapes and sizes.

☆TONGS ~ (useful for spaghetti); PASTA SCOOP ~ (useful for other shapes)

☆SPATULAS ~ metal and rubber.

☆ ROLLING PIN

☆ "WAFFLE" ~ heat absorber, to place under pots for very slow simmering.

☆ VEGETABLE SCRUB BRUSH and /or PEELER

☆ VEGETABLE STEAMER ~ a little metal basket to fit into a saucepan, letting you cook vegetables over water.

☆ OVEN THERMOMETER ~ to help ensure the success of your baking.

❋ TABLE OF CONVERSIONS ❋

❋ DRY INGREDIENTS ❋

Beans (any type): ½ cup = 100 grams
Cornmeal, coarse (polenta): 1 cup = 170 grams
Cornmeal, fine: 1 cup = 150 grams
Herbs, dried = ¼ to ⅓ the amount of fresh herbs
Flour, white unbleached: 1 cup = 140 grams
Grains, dried (rice, bulgur, wheat berries, etc.): 1 cup = 200 grams
Sugar, brown: 1 cup (packed) = 200 grams
Sugar, powdered: 1 cup = 130 grams
Sugar, granulated: 1 cup = 200 grams

❋ BULK INGREDIENTS ❋

Cheese: 1 lb. = 4 to 5 cups (packed), grated
Nut butter (peanut, almond, etc. – or tahini): 1 cup = 250 grams
Nuts, chopped: ⅓ to ½ cup (2 oz.) = 50 grams
Onion: 1 small to medium-sized = approximately 1 cup, chopped
Raisins: ⅓ cup (2 oz.) = 50 grams
Sesame or sunflower seeds: ¾ cup = 100 grams

[1 lb. = 454 grams]

❋ LIQUIDS ❋

1 cup (8 oz.) = 250 ml.
1 Tbs. (½ fluid oz.) = 16 ml.
16 Tbs. = 1 cup

SOUPS

Many of these soups, which feature a variety of vegetables and legumes, can be the centerpiece of a meal, especially when served with rice or good bread and a light salad.

The hot soups can be made in advance and reheated gently on the stovetop or in a microwave. The cold soups that follow can be made up to several days in advance of serving. They keep very well if covered tightly and refrigerated.

Most of the soups from earlier editions of the Moosewood Cookbook are still here, many with only minor changes/improvements (most notably, the reduction of the butter or oil by as much as ½ to ⅔). You will find a few new recipes as well.

NOTE: Any soup containing milk can be converted to nondairy status by simply substituting soy milk. It will taste fine.

ABOUT STOCK:

I used water instead of stock in testing these recipes. But you can make your own stock and use it wherever water is indicated. Just be sure the stock is mildly flavored, so it won't dominate the soup.

To prepare a good, mild stock, add a variety of vegetables (or their parts) to a kettleful of boiling water, and simmer, partially covered, for about an hour. Let it cool, strain it, and give it a taste test before using, to be sure it's compatible with your intended soup.

Recommended for stock:

ONIONS	ZUCCHINI	MUSHROOMS	GREEN BEANS
GARLIC	POTATOES	APPLES	LETTUCE
CARROTS	SWEET POTATOES	TOMATOES	CORN
PARSNIPS	WINTER SQUASH		

TABLE OF CONTENTS: SOUPS

Cream of Asparagus

The original version called for 6 Tbs. butter. This new one has just 1½ Tbs.

Preparation time: 1 hour

Yield: 4 to 5 servings

2 lbs. fresh asparagus	2 cups water
1½ Tbs. butter	2 cups hot milk (lowfat ok)
2 cups chopped onion	2 tsp. dill
1½ tsp. salt	½ tsp. tarragon
3 Tbs. flour	white pepper, to taste

1) Break off and discard the tough asparagus bottoms. Slice off the tips and set them aside. Chop the remaining stalks into 1-inch pieces.

2) Melt the butter in a medium-sized skillet. Add onion, asparagus stalks, and salt. Sauté for about 10 minutes over medium heat. When the onions are clear and soft, sprinkle in 2 Tbs. flour, while constantly stirring. Continue to cook over the lowest possible heat, stirring frequently, another 5 to 8 minutes.

3) Add water, stirring constantly. Heat to a boil, then turn down to a simmer. After about 5 minutes, sprinkle in the remaining 1 Tbs. flour, mixing well. Cook another 8 to 10 minutes, stirring frequently.

4) Purée the soup with the milk, bit by bit, in a food processor or blender. Return the purée to a kettle or large saucepan, and season with dill, tarragon, and white pepper.

5) Cut the reserved asparagus tips into small pieces, and steam until just tender. Add these to the soup, heat very gently (don't cook or boil!), and serve immediately.

Spicy Tomato Soup

Preparation time:
50 minutes

1 Tbs. olive oil
1 Tbs. butter (optional)
1½ cups minced onion
3 to 4 cloves garlic, minced or crushed
½ tsp. salt
1 tsp. dill (or more, to taste)
lots of freshly ground black pepper
1 1-lb.,12-oz. can "crushed concentrated tomatoes"
2 cups water
1 Tbs. honey (optional)
1 Tbs. mayonnaise or sour cream (lowfat OK)
2 medium-sized fresh tomatoes, diced

for { yogurt
the { finely minced parsley and/or basil leaves
top { finely minced scallions or chives

1) Heat olive oil (plus or minus optional butter) in a kettle or a Dutch oven. Add onion, garlic, salt, dill, and black pepper. Stir over medium heat for about 5 to 8 minutes, or until the onions are translucent.

2) Add canned crushed tomatoes, water, and optional honey. Cover and simmer over low heat for 20 to 30 minutes.

3) About 5 minutes before serving, whisk in mayonnaise or sour cream, and stir in diced fresh tomatoes. Serve hot, topped with yogurt and freshly minced herbs.

Gypsy Soup

About 45 minutes to prepare

NOTE: chick peas need to be cooked in advance. (canned = ok)

...a delicately spiced Spanish-style vegetable soup....

Yield: 4 to 5 servings

The vegetables in this soup can be varied. Any orange vegetable can be combined with any green. For example, peas or green beans could replace- or augment- the peppers. Carrots, pumpkin, or squash could fill in for the sweet potatoes. Innovate!

2 medium-sized ripe tomatoes
2 Tbs. olive oil
2 cups chopped onion
3 medium cloves garlic, crushed
1 stalk celery, minced
2 cups peeled, diced sweet potato
1 tsp. salt
2 tsp. mild paprika

1 tsp. turmeric
1 tsp. basil
a dash of cinnamon
a dash of cayenne
1 bay leaf
3 cups water
1 medium bell pepper, diced
1½ cups cooked chick peas

1) Heat a medium-sized saucepanful of water to boiling. Core the tomatoes, and plunge them into the boiling water for a slow count of 10. Remove the tomatoes, and peel them over a sink. Cut them open; squeeze out and discard the seeds. Chop the remaining pulp and set aside.

2) Heat the olive oil in a kettle or Dutch oven. Add onion, garlic, celery, and sweet potato, and sauté over medium heat for about 5 minutes. Add salt, and sauté 5 minutes more. Add seasonings and water, cover, and simmer about 15 minutes.

3) Add tomato pulp, bell pepper, and chick peas. Cover and simmer for about 10 more minutes, or until all the vegetables are as tender as you like them. Taste to adjust seasonings, and serve.

Light Cream of Celery Soup

2 average person's fist-sized potatoes, peeled and diced
4 cups chopped celery (in 1-inch chunks) (you'll also need
     another cup a few ingredients from now)
3 cups water
1¼ tsp. salt (plus another ½ tsp. later)
1 to 2 Tbs. butter
a heaping cup finely minced onion
a heaping cup very finely minced celery (the innermost
     stalks work best for this)
1 tsp. celery seed
1 cup milk (can be lowfat), warmed
white pepper, to taste
4 to 5 Tbs. sour cream, half and half, or heavy cream
     (optional, for a richer tasting soup)
freshly minced chives and/or parsley for garnish (some-
     thing green to liven up the appearance)

1) Place potatoes, 4 cups of celery, water, and 1¼ tsp. salt in a medium-sized saucepan. Bring to a boil, turn the heat way down, and simmer, covered, for about 15 minutes ~ until everything is soft. Purée, and transfer to a larger saucepan or a kettle.

2) Melt butter in a small skillet. Add onion, finely minced celery, celery seed, plus ½ tsp. salt. Sauté about 8 to 10 minutes ~ until the vegetables are just tender. Add to purée.

3) Stir in remaining ingredients, except garnish. Heat gently (don't cook or boil), and serve topped with something minced and green.

Minestrone

About 1 hour
to prepare.
(Beans must be
cooked ahead.)

Yield:
6 to 8
servings

For a minestrone that is more a stew than a soup, use the larger amounts of beans and pasta.

NOTE: These instructions assume the beans or chick peas are already cooked. You can soak and cook your own, or use canned (well rinsed and well drained).

2 Tbs. olive oil
2 cups chopped onion
5 medium cloves garlic, minced
1½ to 2 tsp. salt
1 stalk celery, minced
1 medium carrot, diced
1 small zucchini, diced and/or
   1 cup diced eggplant
1 tsp. oregano
fresh black pepper, to taste
1 tsp. basil

1 medium bell pepper, diced
3 to 4 cups (or more) water
1 14½-oz. can tomato purée
   (approximately 2 cups)
1 to 1½ cups cooked pea beans,
   chick peas, or kidney beans
½ to 1 cup dry pasta (any shape)
1 or 2 medium-sized ripe tomatoes,
   diced (optional)
½ cup freshly minced parsley
parmesan cheese

1) Heat the olive oil in a kettle or Dutch oven. Add onion, garlic, and 1½ tsp. salt. Sauté over medium heat for about 5 minutes, then add celery, carrot, eggplant (if using zucchini, add it later, with the bell pepper), oregano, black pepper, and basil. Cover and cook over very low heat about 10 more minutes, stirring occasionally.

2) Add bell pepper, zucchini, water, and tomato purée. Cover and simmer about 15 minutes. Add beans and simmer another 5 minutes.

3) Bring the soup to a gentle boil. Add pasta, stir, and cook until the pasta is tender. Stir in the diced fresh tomatoes, and serve right away, topped with parsley and parmesan.

Hot & Sour Soup

1 oz. dried Chinese black mushrooms
8 cups water
3 Tbs. dry sherry or Chinese rice wine
¼ to ⅓ cup cider vinegar (to taste)
2 Tbs. soy sauce
1¾ tsp. salt
1 cake (¼ lb.) firm tofu, in thin strips
2 Tbs. cornstarch
2 beaten eggs (yolks may be omitted)
6 minced scallions (whites and greens)
¼ tsp. white pepper (to taste)
Chinese sesame oil (optional)

1) Place the dried mushrooms in a small bowl. Heat 2 (of the 8) cups of water to boiling; pour over the mushrooms. Cover with a plate, and let stand at least 30 minutes. (You can assemble the other ingredients in the meantime.) Drain the mushrooms, squeezing out and saving all the liquid. Slice the mushrooms, removing and discarding the stems.

2) In a kettle or Dutch oven, combine the remaining 6 cups of water, the reserved mushroom-soaking liquid, and the sliced mushrooms. Heat to a gentle boil.

3) Add sherry, vinegar, soy sauce, salt, and tofu. Lower the heat, and let simmer uncovered for about 10 minutes.

4) Place the cornstarch in a small bowl. Measure out about ¾ cup of the hot soup, and whisk it into the cornstarch. When the cornstarch is dissolved, stir this mixture back into the soup.

5) Drizzle the beaten eggs into the simmering soup, stirring constantly. Add scallions and white pepper. Cook only a few minutes more. Top each serving with a few drops of sesame oil, if desired.

MISO SOUP

~ almost instant soup! You can make an individual serving for your-self whenever the inspiration hits. Or you can multiply the amounts (simple math), do Step 1 in advance, and divide it into serving bowls, adding Step 2 just before serving.

Miso is a deep-flavored paste made from fermented soybeans and grains. There are several kinds available in the United States — usually in Japanese markets or in natural foods stores. The most common are red, white, Hatcho, and barley miso. Any one of them can be used to make this very simple and satisfying soup.

In traditional Japanese cooking, fish or vegetable stock (made from various kinds of seaweed) would be used to make Miso Soup. Water will also work very well, so you needn't do the extra work of making stock. But if you happen to have some good vegetable broth on hand, by all means use it.

NOTE: The optional wakame seaweed is available in Japanese markets and in some natural foods stores.

❀ PER SERVING (easily multiplied):

1 Tbs. (more or less) miso
1 cup (more or less) boiling water
a few tiny cubes of soft tofu
a few delicate slices of scallion greens
optional additions:
- 1 to 2 Tbs. dried wakame seaweed, soaked in water for 10 to 15 minutes, then drained
- tiny carrot sticks (matchstick-like), lightly steamed
- finely shredded cabbage, lightly steamed
- a few leaves of spinach

1) Place the miso in the serving bowl. Add about ¼ cup of the boiling water and stir to make a uniform paste.
2) Stir in remaining water plus all remaining ingredients. Serve immediately.

✺ Summer Vegetable Soup ✺

Ultralight, this features the best offerings from a summer garden; it's like a salad in soup form. Use the freshest vegetables available, and make substitutions wherever necessary.

This recipe contains no oil or fat. If you choose not to add the optional buttermilk, it can also be completely dairy-free.

2 medium potatoes, peeled or not,
      and diced
4 cups water
3 to 4 large cloves garlic
1 to 1½ tsp. salt
black pepper, to taste
½ lb. green beans, trimmed & cut
1 cup small broccoli florets
1 cup chopped cauliflower

1 medium carrot, diced
½ lb. sugar snap or snow peas
2 small zucchini or yellow squash, diced
1 medium red bell pepper, in strips

OPTIONAL {
1 cup fresh corn
a small bunch spinach, chopped
1 cup buttermilk, room temperature
freshly minced herbs, for the top
}

1) Place potatoes and water in a medium-sized saucepan. Bring to a boil, lower heat, and simmer until the potatoes are tender. Add the garlic (whole cloves, peeled) during the last few minutes of simmering.

2) Purée the potatoes and garlic in their cooking water. Add salt and pepper to taste. Set aside until just before serving time.

3) Meanwhile, steam the vegetables until just tender in the following groupings: ⓐ green beans ⓑ broccoli, cauliflower, carrot ⓒ peas, zucchini, bell pepper, corn, spinach. (NOTE: A microwave does a good, fast job of steaming, with no added water.) Set the vegetables aside.

4) Heat the potato purée shortly before serving. Stir in the steamed vegetables and optional buttermilk at the last minute. Optional: a light sprinkling of freshly snipped herbs (ideally: basil, dill, parsley, and / or chives).

Succotash Chowder

Preparation time:
30 minutes, at most,
after beans are cooked

Yield: 6 servings,
possibly more

PRELIMINARY: Soak 1 to 1½ cups dry baby lima beans in water for at least 4 hours. Cook in plenty of simmering – NOT rapidly boiling – water for 35 to 40 minutes, or until perfectly tender. Try not to overcook the beans, or the soup will become gluey and lose its textural charm.

1 medium potato (average fist-sized), diced (peeling = optional)
1 Tbs. butter
2 cups chopped onion
3 to 4 medium cloves garlic, crushed or minced
3 stalks celery, minced
1½ tsp. salt
1 tsp. basil
½ tsp. thyme
3 cups corn (fresh OR a 1-lb. bag frozen, defrosted)
2 to 3 cups cooked baby lima beans
4 cups milk (can be lowfat)
a generous amount of fresh black pepper
finely minced parsley and/or chives (optional)

1) Cook the diced potato in boiling water until just tender. Drain well, and set aside.

2) Meanwhile, melt the butter in a kettle or Dutch oven. Add onion, garlic, celery, salt, and herbs. Sauté over medium heat for about 10 minutes, or until the onion and celery are tender. Stir in the corn, and sauté for about 10 minutes more. Add the cooked beans.

3) OPTIONAL: Purée some of the sauté in a food processor or blender. Return to the kettle. (This will make a thicker soup.)

4) Add potatoes and milk. Season to taste with black pepper; correct salt. Serve very hot, topped with minced fresh herbs, if available.

VEGETABLE CHOWDER

Instead of ¼ cup butter and ½ pint heavy cream, as in the original version, this new light one has only 1 Tbs. butter, no cream, and the option of lowfat milk. It still tastes luxurious.

Try not to shy away from the full amount of garlic. It gives the soup a rich flavor and is surprisingly smooth and subtle.

1 Tbs. butter	1 medium potato, diced
2 cups chopped onion	2 medium stalks celery, diced
6 cloves garlic, minced	2 medium carrots, diced
2 tsp. salt	2 cups chopped broccoli
½ tsp. thyme	2 cups chopped cauliflower
2 tsp. basil	½ lb. mushrooms, chopped

2 cups corn (frozen-defrosted is fine)
lots of fresh black pepper
1½ cups water
1 quart milk (lowfat ok), heated
optional: minced fresh herbs
(chives, basil, marjoram)

1) Melt the butter in a kettle or Dutch oven. Add onion, half the garlic, salt, thyme, and basil. Sauté over medium heat 5 minutes. Add potato, celery, carrots, broccoli, and cauliflower. Sauté another 5 to 8 minutes. Add mushrooms and corn, plus lots of black pepper. Sauté another 8 to 10 minutes.

2) Add water, cover, and simmer about 15 minutes, or until everything is tender. (Make sure the potatoes are done.)

3) Stir in hot milk and remaining garlic. Remove from heat until about 10 minutes before serving time, then heat gently. Serve topped with freshly minced herbs.

Chinese Vegetable Chowder

Only 10 minutes to prepare after mushrooms are soaked

Yield: 4 to 6 servings

Simple and delicious ~ made with no dairy products, no eggs, no oil, no garlic, no onions!

The mushrooms need to soak for at least 30 to 40 minutes ahead of time, and this can be done a day or two in advance.

2 oz. dried Chinese black mushrooms
5 cups boiling water
a 1-lb. package frozen corn, defrosted
1 to 1½ tsp. salt
1 to 2 Tbs. soy sauce

black pepper, to taste
1 medium carrot, diced
1 stalk celery, minced
1 8-oz. can water chestnuts, minced

1) Place the mushrooms in a medium-large bowl, and pour in the boiling water. Cover with a plate and let stand for at least 30 to 40 minutes, or until the mushrooms are soaked through and very soft. Drain well, reserving both the mushrooms and the water, squeezing all the excess liquid from the mushrooms. Place the mushrooms on a cutting board and slice thinly, removing and discarding their tough stems.

2) Combine the mushroom water and the corn in a food processor or blender, and purée until as smooth as possible. (You will probably have to do this in more than one batch.) Transfer to a kettle or a large saucepan. (For a smoother soup, you can strain the purée on its way into the kettle.) Stir in salt, soy sauce, and black pepper to taste.

3) Lightly steam the carrot and the celery until just tender. (If you have one, a microwave oven will do this in 2 minutes.)

4) Add sliced mushrooms from Step 1, carrot, celery, and water chestnuts to the soup. Heat gently just before serving.

Cream of Broccoli

45 minutes
to prepare

Yield:
4 to 6
servings

2 Tbs. butter or margarine
1½ cups chopped onion
1 bay leaf
1 tsp. salt (more, to taste)
1 medium bell pepper, diced
4 cups chopped broccoli
2½ cups water
2 cups milk (lowfat ok)

½ cup sour cream (lowfat ok)
¼ tsp. allspice
black pepper ⎱ to taste
white pepper ⎰
a dash of thyme
½ tsp. basil
1 cup broccoli florets, sliced thin
    and lightly steamed

1) Melt butter or margarine in a kettle or Dutch oven. Add onion, bay leaf, and salt. Sauté over medium heat until the onion is translucent.

2) Add green pepper, chopped broccoli, and water. Cover, and cook over medium heat for 10 minutes, or until the broccoli is very tender.

3) Remove the bay leaf, and purée the soup little by little with the milk in a blender or food processor.

4) Whisk in the sour cream and remaining seasonings. Heat gently. Serve hot, topped with lightly steamed broccoli florets.

Gypsy Soup (page 5)

Crêpes with Asparagus-Mushroom Sauce (page 77, pages 142–143)

Strawberry-Rhubarb Crisp (page 201)

Polenta Pie (page 165)

Curried Squash & Mushroom Soup

Yield: 4 or 5 servings

Preparation time: 45 minutes. (Prepare other ingredients while squash bakes.)

NOTE: This soup can be made with no dairy products.

2 medium acorn or butternut squash
2½ cups water
1 cup orange juice
1 Tbs. butter or oil
1 cup chopped onion
2 medium cloves garlic, crushed
1¼ tsp. salt
½ tsp. ground cumin

½ tsp. coriander
½ tsp. cinnamon
1 tsp. ginger
¼ tsp. dry mustard
½ lb. mushrooms, sliced
a few dashes cayenne (to taste)
fresh lemon juice } optional
yogurt, for the top }

1) Preheat oven to 375°F. Split the squash lengthwise, remove seeds, and place face-down on a lightly oiled tray. Bake until soft (about 30 to 40 minutes). Cool, then scoop out the insides. Measure out 3 cups'-worth, place this in a food processor or blender with the water, and purée until smooth. (You may need to do this in batches.) Transfer to a kettle, and stir in the orange juice.

2) Heat the butter or oil in a skillet, and add onion, garlic, salt, and spices. Sauté over medium heat until the onion is very soft ~ about 8 minutes. (You may need to add a small amount of water to prevent sticking.) Add mushrooms, cover, and cook about 10 minutes over medium heat, stirring occasionally.

3) Add the sauté to the squash, scraping the skillet well to salvage all the good stuff. Add cayenne and heat gently. Once it is hot, taste it to correct the seasonings. This is a fairly sweet soup; you may choose to balance this by adding fresh lemon juice to taste and/or topping each bowlful with a small spoonful of yogurt.

Cauliflower-Cheese Soup

1 medium-large potato, peeled and diced
   (about 2 to 3 cups diced)
1 large cauliflower, cut or broken into
   florets (put aside 2 cups of florets)
1 medium carrot, peeled and chopped
3 medium cloves garlic, peeled
1½ cups chopped onion
1½ tsp. salt
4 cups water
2 cups (packed) grated cheddar (plus
   extra for garnishing each serving)
3/4 cup milk (lowfat OK)
1 tsp. dill
½ tsp. caraway seeds
black pepper, to taste

1) Place potato, cauliflower (except for the 2 cups reserved), carrot, garlic, onion, salt, and water in a large saucepan. Bring to a boil, then simmer until all the vegetables are very tender. Purée in a blender or food processor, and transfer to a kettle or Dutch oven.

2) Steam the reserved cauliflower pieces until just tender. Add these to the purée along with all remaining ingredients. Heat gently, and serve topped with a little extra cheese.

Instead of sautéing the vegetables, you add them directly to the simmering soup. Thus, with the exception of the optional sesame oil garnish, this soup is fat-free.

◊ Split Pea Soup ◊

3 cups dry split peas
about 7 cups of water (more, as needed)
1 bay leaf
2 tsp. salt
½ to 1 tsp. dry mustard
2 cups minced onion
4 to 5 medium cloves garlic, crushed
3 stalks celery, minced
2 medium carrots, sliced or diced
1 small potato, thinly sliced
lots of freshly ground black pepper
3 to 4 Tbs. red wine vinegar (to taste)
      Chinese sesame oil (optional)
TOPPINGS — a fresh, ripe tomato, diced
      freshly minced parsley

1) Place split peas, water, bay leaf, salt, and dry mustard in a kettle or Dutch oven. Bring to a boil, lower heat as much as possible, and simmer, partially covered, for about 20 minutes.

2) Add onion, garlic, celery, carrots, and potato. Partially cover, and leave it to simmer gently for about 40 more minutes with occasional stirring. If necessary, add some water.

3) Add black pepper and vinegar to taste. Serve topped with a drizzle of sesame oil, diced tomato, and minced parsley.

Hungarian Mushroom Soup

1 hour
to prepare

2 Tbs. butter
2 cups chopped onion
1½ to 2 lbs. mushrooms, sliced
1 tsp. salt
2 to 3 tsp. dried dill (or 2 to 3 Tbs. freshly minced)
1 Tbs. mild paprika
2 tsp. fresh lemon juice
3 Tbs. flour
2 cups water
1 cup milk (can be lowfat) ~ at room temperature
black pepper, to taste
½ cup sour cream (can be reduced-fat variety)
finely minced fresh parsley, for the top

1) Melt the butter in a kettle or Dutch oven. Add onions, and sauté over medium heat for about 5 minutes. Add mushrooms, salt, dill, and paprika. Stir well and cover. Let cook for about 15 more minutes, stirring occasionally. Stir in lemon juice.

2) Gradually sprinkle in the flour, stirring constantly. Cook and stir another 5 minutes or so over medium-low heat. Add water, cover, and cook about 10 minutes, stirring often.

3) Stir in milk; add black pepper to taste. Check to see if it needs more salt. Whisk in the sour cream, and heat very gently. Don't boil or cook it after this point. Serve hot, topped with freshly minced parsley.

The original version of this recipe called for 6 Tbs. butter, 3 cups whole milk, plus ½ pint heavy cream. This new one has only 1½ Tbs. butter, a little milk, and no cream.

Mushroom Bisque

... and it tastes equally good, if not better.

1 hour to prepare

Yield: a good 8 servings

```
2 medium potatoes (the size of an average person's fist)
1½ cups water
1½ Tbs. butter or margarine
2 cups chopped onion
1 small stalk celery, minced
1½ lbs. mushrooms
1½ to 2 tsp. salt
1 to 2 small cloves garlic, minced
¼ tsp. thyme
3 Tbs. dry sherry
2 tsp. soy sauce
fresh black pepper, to taste
1 cup milk (can be lowfat)
croutons (recipe on p.20)        } optional toppings
minced scallion greens or chives
```

1) Peel potatoes, chop into small pieces, and place in a small saucepan with the water. Cover, bring to a boil, and simmer until potatoes are tender.

2) Meanwhile, melt butter in a deep skillet or Dutch oven. Add onion and celery, and sauté over medium heat for about 5 minutes. Stir in mushrooms and salt, cover, and cook about 10 minutes, stirring occasionally. Somewhere in there, add garlic and thyme. (Adding garlic later keeps its flavor stronger.) Remove from heat; stir in sherry, soy sauce, and pepper.

3) Use a blender or food processor to purée both the potatoes in their cooking water and the mushroom sauté in its own liquid. (When you run out of the liquid, use the milk.) Combine the purées in a kettle or Dutch oven.

4) Stir, and heat gently; taste to adjust seasonings. Serve very hot, with optional but highly recommended toppings.

ONION SOUP

This soup is very, very simple and easy. Most of the preparation time, after the onions are sliced, is for simmering: slowly, thoroughly, deliciously. You can use this time to make the croutons and to prepare other components of the meal. The original recipe called for 6 Tbs. butter. I've reduced that amount to just 2 Tbs., yet the buttery flavor is still generously imparted.

2 Tbs. butter
4 large yellow onions, thinly sliced
1 tsp. salt
½ tsp. dry mustard
a dash or two of thyme
4 cups water
2 Tbs. soy sauce

2 to 3 Tbs. dry white wine (optional)
a few dashes of white pepper

TOPPINGS:
thin slices of Swiss cheese
croutons (recipe below)

1) Melt the butter in a kettle or Dutch oven. Add onions and salt, and cook over medium heat about 10 minutes, stirring occasionally.

2) Add mustard and thyme; stir and cover. Continue to cook very slowly for about 35 more minutes. The onions will be exquisitely soft and simmering in their own liquid.

3) Add water, soy sauce, optional wine, and white pepper. Simmer at least 10 minutes more. Taste to adjust seasonings. Serve topped with croutons and Swiss cheese. If you're serving the soup in ovenproof bowls, you can put them under the broiler briefly, to brown the cheese. Be careful handling the bowls!

HOMEMADE CROUTONS:

a) Sauté cubed bread in garlic butter for about 10 minutes, then transfer to a tray, and toast in a 300°F. oven until crisp. OR:

b) Brush thin slices of baguette on both sides with olive oil. (Optional: crush some garlic into the oil first.) Bake on a tray in a 350°F. oven until crisp (8 to 12 minutes, depending on thickness), but check on them frequently! They can look underdone one minute and burn the next.

Swiss Cheese & Onion Soup

2 Tbs. butter
2 medium onions, thinly sliced (about 4 cups)
1 to 2 medium cloves garlic, minced
1½ tsp. salt
2 tsp. dry mustard
1 to 3 Tbs. flour (depending on how thick you like your soup)
2 Tbs. dry sherry
2 cups water
1 tsp. prepared horseradish (the white kind)
1½ cups warmed milk (can be lowfat)
1½ cups (packed) grated Swiss cheese
white pepper
OPTIONAL TOPPINGS: croutons (see preceding page)
              paprika~ or some minced pimientos

1) Melt the butter in a kettle or Dutch oven. Add onions, garlic, salt, and dry mustard, and cook over medium heat 8 to 10 minutes, or until the onions are very soft.

2) Gradually sprinkle in the flour, stirring constantly, then add the sherry and mix well. Add water and horseradish. Stir and cook for about 5 more minutes.

3) Add warm milk and cheese. After adding the cheese, stir assiduously with a wooden spoon for a good few minutes. Much to your delight, everything will become remarkably smooth and well blended.

4) Add white pepper to taste, and while you're at it, adjust the other seasonings as well. You might wish to increase the mustard, sherry, or horseradish (too late to decrease). Serve hot ~ plain, or topped with croutons and/or a light dusting of paprika and/or a small amount of finely minced pimiento.

CARROT SOUP VARIATIONS

Each of the following Carrot Soup Variations is a thick, creamy purée that can be made with no dairy products. Each soup also keeps and freezes very well, and doesn't suffer from repeated reheatings.

❋ Gingered Carrot Soup ❋

Serve this as a thick sauce over rice for a simple supper. It also goes well with Samosas (p.170) and Raita (p.99).

2 lbs. carrots
4 cups water
1 Tbs. butter or oil
1½ cups chopped onion
2 medium cloves garlic, minced
2 Tbs. freshly grated ginger
1½ tsp. salt

¼ tsp. each: cumin
              ground fennel
              cinnamon
              allspice
              dried mint

3 to 4 Tbs. fresh lemon juice
1 cup lightly toasted cashews
OPTIONAL: buttermilk, to
          drizzle on top

1) Peel and trim carrots, and cut them into 1-inch chunks. Place in a medium-large saucepan with the water, cover, and bring to a boil. Lower the heat, and simmer until very tender (about 10 to 15 minutes, depending on the size of the carrot pieces).

2) Meanwhile heat the butter or oil in a small skillet. Add onions, and sauté over medium heat for about 5 minutes. Add garlic, ginger, salt, and spices. Turn heat to low, and continue to sauté for another 8 to 10 minutes, or until everything is well mingled and the onions are very soft. Stir in lemon juice.

3) Use a food processor or blender to purée everything together (including the toasted cashews). You will need to do this in several batches. Transfer the purée to a kettle, and heat gently just before serving. If desired, pass a small pitcher of buttermilk, for individual drizzlings.

Herbed Carrot Soup

You can make this with no oil. The onions and garlic can be cooked in the water with the carrots. Add the seasonings later, as the soup simmers.

2 lbs. carrots
1 medium potato (the size of a medium fist)
4 cups water
1 Tbs. butter or oil
1 cup chopped onion
1½ tsp. salt
2 medium cloves garlic, minced or crushed
½ tsp. thyme
½ tsp. marjoram or oregano
1 tsp. basil
1 to 2 Tbs. lemon juice (or, to taste)
optional: small amounts of finely minced
fresh mint,
chives,
and or
parsley,
for the top

1) Peel and chop the carrots and potato, and place them in a medium-large saucepan with the water. Bring to a boil, cover, and simmer until the vegetables are tender (10 to 15 minutes).

2) Meanwhile, heat oil in a small skillet. Add onions and salt, and sauté over medium heat for about 5 minutes. Add garlic and dried herbs, and sauté about 5 minutes more, or until the onions are soft. Stir in lemon juice.

3) Purée everything together in a blender or food processor, and transfer to a kettle or Dutch oven. Simmer gently 8 to 10 minutes. Serve hot, topped with a light sprinkling of fresh herbs.

White Bean & Black Olive Soup

NOTE: This recipe calls for 2 cups cooked white pea beans. Use 1 cup dry, and cook them, without prior soaking, in plenty of simmering (<u>not</u> rapidly boiling) water until tender (about 1¼ hours).

2 Tbs. olive oil
1 heaping cup chopped onion
1 stalk celery, diced
1 medium carrot, diced
1 to 1½ tsp. salt
1 tsp. oregano or marjoram
1½ tsp. basil
1 small (5 to 6 inches long) zucchini, diced
1 small bell pepper, chopped
3 to 4 medium cloves garlic, crushed
fresh black pepper
4 cups water
3 oz. (half a small can) tomato paste
¼ cup dry red wine (optional)
2 cups cooked white pea beans
1 cup sliced Kalamata (Greek) olives (or plain black ones)
1 Tbs. fresh lemon juice
finely minced fresh parsley ⎫
a ripe tomato, diced   ⎬ TOPPINGS

1) Heat the olive oil in a kettle or Dutch oven. Add onion, celery, carrot, salt, and herbs. Sauté over medium heat 8 to 10 minutes, or until the vegetables are just tender.

2) Add zucchini, bell pepper, and garlic. Sauté 5 minutes more. Grind in some black pepper.

3) Combine water and tomato paste. Add to vegetables, along with the remaining ingredients, except toppings. Cover and simmer over low heat for about 15 minutes. Serve hot, topped with parsley and diced tomato.

Lentil Soup

...... gentle.

This is a very easy fat-free lentil soup that just about cooks itself. Only one pot is needed, so cleanup is easy.

Preparation time: about 1 hour

Yield: 6 to 8 servings

3 cups dry lentils
7 cups water
2 tsp. salt
6 to 8 medium cloves garlic, crushed
2 cups chopped onion
2 stalks celery, chopped
2 medium carrots, sliced or diced
Optional: ½ to 1 tsp. basil
 ½ tsp. thyme
 ½ tsp. oregano
lots of freshly ground black pepper
2 to 3 medium-sized ripe tomatoes
red wine vinegar, to drizzle on top

1) Place lentils, water, and salt in a kettle. Bring to a boil, lower heat to the slowest possible simmer, and cook quietly, partially covered, for 20 to 30 minutes.

2) Add vegetables (except tomatoes), herbs, and black pepper. Partially cover, and let simmer peacefully another 20 to 30 minutes, stirring occasionally.

3) Heat a medium saucepanful of water to boiling. Drop in the tomatoes for 10 seconds, then take them out, peel off the skins, and squeeze out the seeds. Chop the remaining pulp and add to the soup. Let the soup cook for at least 5 minutes more.

4) Serve hot, with a drizzle of vinegar on top of each steaming bowlful.

Brazilian Black Bean Soup

New and Improved!
... and actually easier
than the original

PRELIMINARY: Soak 2 cups dry black beans in plenty of water for at least 4 hours (and preferably overnight.)

2 cups dry black beans, soaked
6 cups water
1 Tbs. olive oil
3 cups chopped onion
10 medium cloves garlic, crushed
2 tsp. cumin
2 to 2½ tsp. salt
1 medium carrot, diced

1 medium bell pepper, diced
1½ cups orange juice
black pepper, to taste
cayenne, to taste
2 medium tomatoes, diced (optional)

optional toppings: { sour cream
cilantro
salsa (recipe p. 96)

1) Place the soaked beans in a kettle or Dutch oven with 4 cups water. Bring to a boil, cover, and simmer until tender (about 1¼ hours).

2) Heat olive oil in a medium-sized skillet. Add onion, half the garlic, cumin, salt, and carrot. Sauté over medium heat until the carrot is just tender. Add remaining garlic and the bell pepper. Sauté until everything is very tender (another 10 to 15 minutes). Add the sautéed mixture to the beans, scraping in every last morsel.

3) Stir in orange juice, black pepper, cayenne, and optional tomatoes. Purée all or some of the soup in a blender or food processor, and return to kettle. Simmer over very low heat 10 to 15 minutes more. Serve topped with an artful arrangement of sour cream, cilantro, and salsa.

RUSSIAN CABBAGE BORSCHT

Preparation time: 1 hour

Yield: 4 to 6 servings

1½ cups thinly sliced potato
1 cup thinly sliced beets
4 cups water
1 to 2 Tbs. butter
1½ cups chopped onion
1 scant tsp. caraway seeds
1½ tsp. salt (or more, to taste)

1 stalk celery, chopped
1 medium-sized carrot, sliced
3 to 4 cups shredded cabbage
freshly ground black pepper
1 tsp. dill (plus extra, for garnish)
1 to 2 Tbs. cider vinegar
1 to 2 Tbs. brown sugar or honey
1 cup tomato purée

TOPPINGS { sour cream or yogurt
          { extra dill

1) Place potatoes, beets, and water in a medium-sized saucepan. Cover, and cook over medium heat until tender (20 to 30 minutes).

2) Meanwhile, melt the butter in a kettle or Dutch oven. Add onion, caraway seeds, and salt. Cook over medium heat, stirring occasionally, until the onions are translucent (8 to 10 minutes).

3) Add celery, carrots, and cabbage, plus 2 cups of the cooking water from the potatoes and beets. Cover and cook over medium heat until the vegetables are tender (another 8 to 10 minutes).

4) Add the remaining ingredients (including all the potato and beet water), cover, and simmer for at least 15 more minutes. Taste to correct seasonings, and serve hot, topped with sour cream or yogurt and a light dusting of dill.

Mushroom-Barley Soup

Preparation time: 1¼ hours

Yield: 6 to 8 servings

½ cup uncooked pearl barley
6½ cups water
1 to 2 Tbs. butter
1 medium onion, chopped (about 1½ cups)
2 medium cloves garlic, minced
1 lb. mushrooms, sliced
½ to 1 tsp. salt
3 to 4 Tbs. soy sauce
3 to 4 Tbs. dry sherry
freshly ground black pepper

1) Place the barley and 1½ cups of the water in a large saucepan or a Dutch oven. Bring to a boil, cover, and simmer until the barley is tender (20 to 30 minutes).

2) Meanwhile, melt the butter in a skillet. Add the onions and sauté for about 5 minutes over medium heat. Add garlic, mushrooms, and ½ tsp. salt. Cover and cook, stirring occasionally, until everything is very tender ~ about 10 to 12 minutes. Stir in soy sauce and sherry.

3) Add the sauté with all its liquid to the cooked barley, along with the remaining 5 cups of water. Grind in a generous amount of black pepper, and simmer, partially covered, another 20 minutes over very low heat. Taste to correct seasonings, and serve.

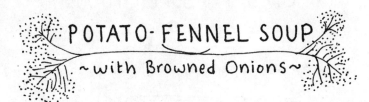

POTATO-FENNEL SOUP
~with Browned Onions~

This very simple and rich-tasting soup can be made with no dairy products.

Fennel is well known as a seasoning, particularly in seed form. It is less well known as a vegetable: a light green bulb that is crunchy, juicy, and deeply, though subtly, flavored.

1 Tbs. butter or oil
4 cups thinly sliced onions
2 tsp. salt
4 medium potatoes (average fist-size), not necessarily peeled, and sliced into thin pieces 1 to 2 inches long
1 cup freshly minced fennel bulb
½ tsp. caraway seeds
4 cups water
white pepper, to taste
OPTIONAL TOPPINGS:
~sour cream, thinned (by beating with a little whisk in a little bowl)
~the feathery tops of the fennel, well minced

1) Melt the butter (or heat the oil) in a kettle or Dutch oven. Add the onions and 1 tsp. salt. Cook over medium-low heat, stirring occasionally, for about 15 to 20 minutes, or until the onions are very, very soft and lightly browned.

2) Add the potatoes, another ½ tsp. salt, the minced fennel bulb, and the caraway seeds. Sauté over medium heat for another 5 minutes, then add the water. Bring to a boil, then partially cover, and simmer until the potatoes are tender (10 to 15 minutes).

3) Taste to adjust salt; add white pepper. Serve hot, topped with a decorative swirl of thinned sour cream and/or minced feathery fennel tops.

Cream of Spinach Soup

For a lowfat version, simply skip Step 2.

Preparation time:
20 to 30 minutes

1 large onion, chopped
2 medium potatoes, peeled and chopped
3 cups water
2 tsp. salt
1 lb. spinach, cleaned and stemmed
5 medium cloves garlic, peeled only
optional { 1½ to 2 Tbs. butter
{ 3 Tbs. flour
1½ cups hot milk (may be lowfat)
white pepper and nutmeg, to taste

1) Place onion, potatoes, water, and salt in a large saucepan. Bring to a boil, cover, and simmer until the potatoes are tender. Remove from heat, add spinach and garlic cloves, and set aside.

2) Melt the butter over low heat in a small saucepan. Whisk in flour, and keep whisking over low heat 5 minutes. Drizzle in the milk. Continue to whisk and cook until smooth (about 5 to 8 minutes more).

3) Purée the vegetables in their cooking water; return the purée to the saucepan. Stir in the white sauce (or just the milk, if you're making the lowfat version). Adjust the salt, and add white pepper to taste. Serve hot, topped with a subtle sprinkling of nutmeg.

Gazpacho

20 to 30 minutes
to prepare,
plus time to chill.

Yield:
6 servings

4 cups tomato juice

½ cup finely minced onion

1 medium clove garlic, minced

1 medium bell pepper, minced

1 tsp. honey (optional)

1 medium cucumber,
    peeled, seeded, & minced

2 scallions, minced

juice of ½ lemon + 1 lime

2 Tbs. wine vinegar

1 tsp. each < tarragon
              basil

¼ to ½ tsp. cumin

¼ cup freshly minced parsley

2 to 3 Tbs. olive oil

salt, black pepper, and
    cayenne — to taste

2 cups freshly diced tomatoes

Combine all ingredients.

(Optional: purée all or some)

Chill until very cold.

Chilled Cucumber-Yogurt Soup

Preparation time:
less than 10 minutes,
plus time to chill.

4 cups peeled, seeded, &
      grated cucumber
2 cups water
2 cups yogurt (nonfat OK)
½ to 1 tsp. salt
1 small clove garlic, minced
1 tsp. dried dill (or 1 Tbs. fresh)
1 Tbs. honey (optional)
minced fresh mint and chives

Yield:
4 to 6
servings

Combine grated cucumber, water, yogurt,
salt, garlic, dill, and optional honey in a
medium-sized bowl. Stir until well blended,
and chill until very cold. Serve topped with
finely minced fresh herbs, if available.

~chilled, creamy
potato-onion soup

Vichyssoise

Butter: reduced
Cream: optional
Recipe: flexible

Preparation time:
45 minutes,
plus time
to chill

Yield:
about 6 servings

2 Tbs. butter
3 cups chopped onions
1 to 1½ tsp. salt
4 medium potatoes (about 2 lbs.),
  peeled and diced
4 cups water

2 cups milk (lowfat ok)
OPTIONAL: up to ½ pint heavy cream
white pepper, to taste
freshly minced chives for the top

1) Melt the butter in a kettle or Dutch oven. Add onions and salt, and sauté about 15 minutes, or until the onions are very soft and beginning to brown.

2) Add potatoes and water, and bring to a boil. Lower heat, cover, and simmer until the potatoes are tender (about 10 to 15 minutes).

3) Purée until very smooth in a blender or food processor, and transfer to a medium-large container. Stir in the milk and optional cream; add white pepper.

4) Chill until very cold. Serve topped with finely minced fresh chives.

Green
Variation

Make Vichyssoise exactly as described above. When stirring in the milk, also add some combination (the more, the better) of puréed:

    steamed spinach,
        steamed zucchini,
            steamed Boston (a.k.a. "butter") lettuce
            fresh watercress
                fresh herbs (basil, dill, parsley)

Top each serving with:

    peeled, seeded, and coarsely grated cucumber.

Cascadilla

1 small cucumber~ peeled,
  seeded, and minced
1 scallion, finely minced
1 small clove garlic, crushed
½ tsp. dill
4 cups tomato juice

1 cup yogurt (nonfat OK)
1 small bell pepper, minced
3 to 4 raw mushrooms,
  thinly sliced
salt and pepper, to taste
OPTIONAL { croutons (p.20)
{ minced watercress

Combine
everything,
and
chill well.

Top with
croutons

and
watercress.

Chilled Beet Borscht

Preparation time:
about 40 minutes,
plus time to chill.

Yield: about
6 servings

4 large (3-inch diameter) beets
3 cups water
1 tsp. salt
1 to 2 Tbs. lemon juice, to taste
2 to 3 Tbs. sugar or honey, to taste
black pepper
1 to 2 Tbs. freshly minced dill (or 2 tsp. dried)
1 medium cucumber, peeled, seeded, and grated
2 to 3 finely minced scallions (whites and greens)
OPTIONAL: 1 medium-sized dill pickle, finely minced
2 cups buttermilk

OPTIONAL GARNISHES {
a spoonful of sour cream or yogurt (nonfat OK)
slices of boiled potato
chopped hardboiled egg
}

1) Peel and trim the beets, and place them in a medium-sized saucepan with the water and salt. Bring to a boil, lower heat, partially cover, and simmer until the beets are tender (about 20 to 30 minutes). Remove the beets with a slotted spoon, and transfer the water to a medium-large bowl or container.

2) When the beets are cool enough to handle, grate them coarsely and return them to the water. Stir in remaining ingredients, except buttermilk and garnishes. Cover and chill until cold.

3) When the borscht is cold, stir in the buttermilk. Taste to adjust salt, pepper, lemon juice, sugar or honey. Serve topped with any combination of garnishes.

Chilled Berry Soup

Preparation time:
less than 15
minutes

Yield:
4 to 6
servings

Much more than just a soup, this refreshing tart-sweet preparation can be a summer beverage, a breakfast dish, or even a dessert.

Frozen berries work very well in here, so you don't need to wait for perfect fresh ones. Blue-, black-, rasp-, and strawberries can all be found in frozen, unsweetened form in the supermarket. You can also freeze your own during an abundant season. Frozen berries give off generous amounts of pure berry juice as they defrost, and you can include all of it in the soup. It creates an indescribably lovely color.

3 cups orange juice (preferably fresh-squeezed)
3 cups buttermilk or yogurt (nonfat OK)
1 to 2 Tbs. fresh lemon or lime juice
optional: 1 to 2 Tbs. sugar or honey
2 to 3 cups berries ~ any kind or any combination
   (Leave smaller berries whole. Larger ones
    should be sliced.)
optional: ― a dash of cinnamon and/or nutmeg
    a few sprigs of fresh mint, for garnish

1) Whisk together orange juice and buttermilk or yogurt. Add lemon or lime juice and optional sugar or honey (or not), to taste. Cover and chill until serving time.

2) When you're ready to serve, place about ½ cup berries in each bowl. Ladle the soup on top. If desired, dust very lightly with cinnamon and/or nutmeg, and garnish with a few small sprigs of mint.

SALADS

Salads can be the opening act of a larger meal, or the backbone of a smaller one—especially when teamed up with soup and bread. Leftover salads can double as great sandwich fillings (see Salad Sandwiches, p. 119) and are also perfect for those times when you need more than a snack but less than a meal.

As an alternative to an entrée, try serving an assortment of salads, lavishly garnished, for a festive occasion. This is a great menu-planning strategy that allows you to make everything ahead of time, and then relax and really enjoy the company.

TABLE OF CONTENTS: SALADS

a good method for assembling
GREEN LEAFY SALADS

Assembling a green salad is a highly personalized endeavor, and of course there is no absolutely correct method. But the truth is, some salads are much better than others. Here are a few guidelines to help your salads be among the better ones:

1) Use a large enough bowl, so you'll have plenty of room to toss the salad thoroughly. Make it your special salad bowl — it will acquire more depth and soul with each use, and this will enhance something nameless (I don't know what) about the experience.

2) The basis for a green leafy salad is leafy greens: lettuces, spinach, and other tender green leaves that can be eaten raw. Use only the freshest greens! They should be immaculate and absolutely dry (use a salad spinner plus paper towels). Store in a crisper or in dry plastic bags in the refrigerator.

3) The optional extras = delicate clippings, shavings, and gratings of other vegetables, plus cherry or plum tomatoes, olives, nuts, slices of fruit (anything from apple or pear slices to citrus sections to fresh figs), crumbled pungent cheese, grated hardboiled egg, or homemade croutons (see p. 20). Have whatever you choose to add ready to be mixed in gently or laid on top just before serving.

4) If you want to make the dressing right in the bowl as you toss the salad, place a few tablespoons of olive oil, nut oil, or a combination in the bottom of the bowl with a clove or two of crushed garlic. Add crisp, dry greens a handful at a time, and toss after each addition, making sure everything gets evenly coated. Add small amounts of additional oil, if needed, plus small amounts of salt and vinegar (red wine, herb-infused, balsamic, fruit-flavored — experiment!) right before serving, and add optional extras. Bring a pepper mill to the table.

RULE OF THUMB: Be a benefactor with the oil,

a miser with the vinegar,

a poet with the salt, and

a demon with the pepper!

Warm Salad

... featuring an assortment of ultranutritious leafy greens, lightly cooked and delicately marinated. This can be a main dish unto itself, or a prelude or accompaniment to a simple pasta supper. However you serve it, be sure to include some fresh crusty bread to mop up the juices.

NOTE: Other types of greens can be substituted for the escarole, chard, and mustard. Try kale, collard, or dandelion greens.

3 Tbs. olive oil
1 small bunch escarole, chopped
1 medium bunch red or green chard, chopped
about 8 large leaves Napa or savoy cabbage, chopped
2 cups (packed) chopped mustard greens

1 to 2 tsp. salt	1 stalk celery, sliced
2 large cloves garlic, minced	½ small cauliflower, chopped
2 medium leeks, chopped	3 Tbs. balsamic or wine vinegar
2 cups chopped red onion	6 Tbs. (or more) parmesan
¾ lb. mushrooms, sliced	lots of fresh black pepper

1) Heat 1 Tbs. olive oil in a large wok or deep skillet. Add the escarole, chard, cabbage, and mustard greens, a little at a time, salting lightly after each addition, and adding more greens as soon as the ones in the pot cook down enough to make room. Use a fairly intense level of heat under the pot, and stir as you cook. When all the greens are wilted and tender, stir in the garlic. Cook and stir just a minute or two more, then transfer to a platter.

2) Add the remaining oil to the wok or skillet, and when it is hot, add leeks, onion, mushrooms, celery, and cauliflower. Salt lightly, and stir-fry quickly over medium-high heat until just tender (about 5 to 8 minutes). Add to the platter, mix gently to incorporate the greens, and sprinkle with vinegar and parmesan while still hot. Grind black pepper over the top, and serve hot, warm, or at room temperature, with thick slices of toasted bread to mop up the juices. (Sourdough bread is especially good for this.)

RAW VEGETABLE SALAD
· · · · · · · · · · ·

Most vegetables can be eaten raw if cut properly. In this salad, everything is minced very small or grated, so chewing is light and delightful and not a cumbersome chore. Visually, Raw Vegetable Salad can be beautiful, like edible confetti. Serve in glass bowls to maximize the aesthetic impact.

Use whatever is in season, and in any proportion. Sprouts, tomatoes, and/or mushroom slices can be used as toppings. Try pairing this salad with the Very Green Dressing, which follows.

carrots
celery
broccoli
cauliflower
cabbage (green and red)
bell peppers (all colors)
zucchini or summer squash
spinach

beets
cucumber
green beans
sugar snap or snow peas
red onion
scallions
radishes
fresh herbs

Peel wherever necessary; mince or grate everything and mix well.

VERY GREEN DRESSING
· · · · · · · · · · · · · ·
Made with <u>no oil</u>!

a handful of parsley
a handful of fresh spinach
½ a small zucchini, cut in chunks
10 to 15 fresh basil leaves (2 tsp. dried)
1 medium clove garlic
1 cup buttermilk
¼ to ½ tsp. salt
1 tsp. lemon juice
OPTIONAL: a few pieces of ripe avocado;
    moderate amounts of other fresh
    herbs (chives, dill, cilantro)

whip it up in a blender or food processor. Makes a generous cup.

Special Salad Dressings

Basic Vinaigrette
~ the basic dressing for green salads. It keeps for weeks.

1 cup olive oil
4 to 5 Tbs. red wine vinegar
½ to 1 tsp. salt
1 to 2 medium cloves garlic, minced

Combine everything in a jar.
Cover tightly and shake well.

VINAIGRETTE VARIATIONS: (These are just a few suggestions. You can experiment even further with your own ideas.)
* add 3 to 4 Tbs. orange or apple juice, or
      2 Tbs. lemon juice plus a little grated lemon rind, plus
* very finely minced parsley and/or
* very finely minced other herbs (fresh or dried basil, dill, marjoram, chives, thyme)
* substitute some of the olive oil with a nut oil
* substitute different flavors of vinegar (fruit-infused, balsamic, champagne, etc.)
* add 1 to 2 tsp. good quality mustard
* for creamy vinaigrette: add 2 to 3 Tbs. mayonnaise, sour cream, or yogurt

Sweet & Tart Mustard Dressing
~ good on chilled cooked vegetables, especially Brussels sprouts, cauliflower, or broccoli

6 Tbs. olive oil
2 Tbs. Dijon mustard
4 Tbs. red wine vinegar
2 tsp. real maple syrup or honey
salt and pepper, to taste

Whisk everything together.
Cover and chill.

LOWFAT RANCH DRESSING

~ good on leafy salads made of sturdy greens, like romaine or spinach.

1 cup buttermilk
optional: 2 to 3 Tbs. sour cream or mayonnaise (see p.44) OR
         ¼ cup lowfat cottage cheese
2 to 3 Tbs. dried onion flakes
¼ to ½ tsp. salt (to taste)
1 tsp. lemon juice
lots of black pepper

~ whisk everything together. Keep in a tightly covered container in the refrigerator.

LOWFAT CREAMY ROQUEFORT DRESSING

~ Make Lowfat Ranch Dressing, and add ½ cup crumbled Roquefort.

LOWFAT CREAMY GARLIC DRESSING

~ Make Lowfat Ranch Dressing, and add 1 to 2 cloves crushed garlic.

NONFAT GAZPACHO DRESSING

Oil-free and nondairy!

1 cup tomato juice
1 cup diced cucumber (peeled and seeded)
1 minced scallion
1 medium clove garlic
a few leaves fresh basil (or ½ tsp. dried)
1 to 2 Tbs. fresh (or 1 to 2 tsp. dried) dill
a small handful of fresh parsley
1 to 2 tsp. lemon or lime juice
salt and pepper, to taste

Purée everything together in a blender or food processor. Cover tightly and chill.

❧❧❧ HOMEMADE MAYONNAISE: ❧❧❧

For an oil-free version, see Plain Fake Mayo, p. 91.

❧❧ REGULAR (REAL) MAYONNAISE:

> 1 large egg
> 3 Tbs. cider vinegar
> ½ tsp. salt
> ½ tsp. dry mustard
> 1¼ cups oil (vegetable, olive, canola
>   ~ or a combination)

1) Place the first 4 ingredients in a blender or food processor, along with 2 Tbs. of the oil. Process for a few seconds.

2) Keep the motor running as you drizzle in the remaining oil. As soon as all the oil is incorporated, turn off the machine. Scrape the mayonnaise into a container, cover, and refrigerate.

❧❧ TOFU (SOMEWHAT REAL) MAYONNAISE:

> 1 packed cup mashed tofu (firm or silken)
> 1 small clove garlic
> 1 tsp. good-quality prepared mustard
> 2 tsp. cider vinegar
> ¼ to ½ tsp. salt (to taste)
> ¼ cup olive or canola oil

1) Place everything except the oil in a blender or food processor. Process until very smooth.

2) Keep the machine running as you drizzle in the oil. When all the oil is incorporated, turn off the machine. Transfer to a container, cover, and refrigerate.

❧ VARIATIONS (use with either of the above):

❧ GREEN MAYO: Add a handful each of chopped parsley and chives to step 1.

❧ SESAME MAYO: Substitute a few tablespoons of the oil with Chinese sesame oil.

40 minutes to prepare, plus time to marinate.
TIME SAVER: Prepare other things while the eggplant cooks.

Macedonian Salad

Yield: 4 to 6 servings (possibly more, depending on the context)

...small cubes of roasted eggplant, marinated with fresh vegetables in a lemony, herby vinaigrette

1 large eggplant (about 9 inches long)-- or its approximate equivalent in medium or small eggplants-- peeled or not, and cut into 1-inch cubes, or even smaller

a little oil, for the baking tray

4 Tbs. olive oil
2 Tbs. red wine vinegar
1 medium clove garlic, minced
½ tsp. salt (more, to taste)
freshly ground black pepper
½ tsp. basil
¼ tsp. thyme
¼ tsp. marjoram or oregano
1 Tbs. fresh lemon juice

¼ cup (packed) finely minced parsley
2 small scallions, very finely minced
½ medium red bell pepper, minced
½ medium green bell pepper, minced
1 medium tomato, diced

OPTIONAL GARNISHES:
olives (Greek, oil-cured, or Niçoise)
yogurt
crumbled feta cheese

1) Preheat oven to 375°F. Spread the eggplant cubes onto a lightly oiled baking tray, and roast in the oven about 15 minutes, or until tender enough so a fork can slide in easily. Remove from oven.

2) Meanwhile, combine the olive oil, vinegar, garlic, salt, pepper, herbs, and lemon juice in a medium-sized bowl. Add the still-warm eggplant and stir. Cover, and let sit for at least 2 hours. (At this stage, it will keep in the refrigerator for several days.)

3) Add the remaining vegetables within an hour or two of serving. Serve garnished with olives and yogurt or crumbled feta cheese.

Tabouli

...the classic bulgur salad with garlic, parsley, lemon, mint, etc.

You can prepare Steps 1 and 2 as much as a day or two in advance. The flavors get deeper as it sits around. A food processor does a perfect job of mincing scallions, parsley, and mint into a fine feathery state, which makes the salad much prettier and easier to eat.

1 cup dry bulgur wheat
1½ cups boiling water
1 to 1½ tsp. salt
¼ cup fresh lemon juice
¼ cup olive oil
2 medium cloves garlic, crushed
black pepper, to taste

4 scallions, finely minced (whites & greens)
1 packed cup minced parsley
10 to 15 fresh mint leaves, minced
     (or 1 to 2 Tbs. dried mint)
2 medium-sized ripe tomatoes, diced
OPTIONAL: • ½ cup cooked chick peas
     • 1 medium bell pepper, diced
     • 1 small cucumber, seeded & minced

1) Combine bulgur and boiling water in a medium-large bowl. Cover and let stand until the bulgur is tender (20 to 30 minutes, minimum).

2) Add salt, lemon juice, olive oil, garlic, and black pepper, and mix thoroughly. Cover tightly and refrigerate until about 30 minutes before serving.

3) About 30 minutes before serving, stir in remaining ingredients (including optional additions) and mix well. Serve cold with warm wedges of lightly toasted pita bread. (For more serving ideas, see Mezza, p.100.)

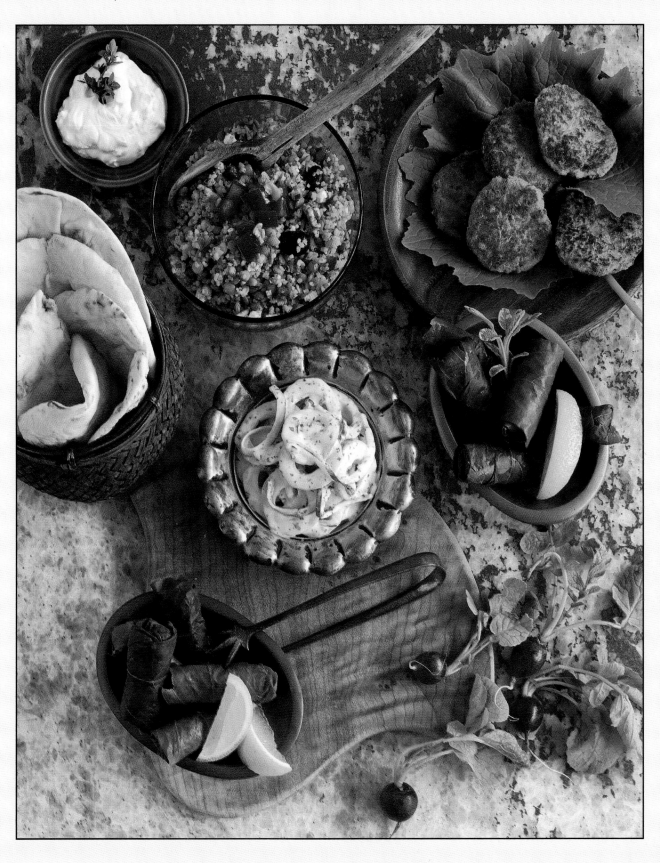

Mezza (clockwise from top left): Yogurt Cheese (page 102), Lentil-Bulgur Salad (page 47), Felafel (page 116), Stuffed Grape Leaves (page 149), Balkan Cucumber Salad (page 69), and Flatbreads (page 115)

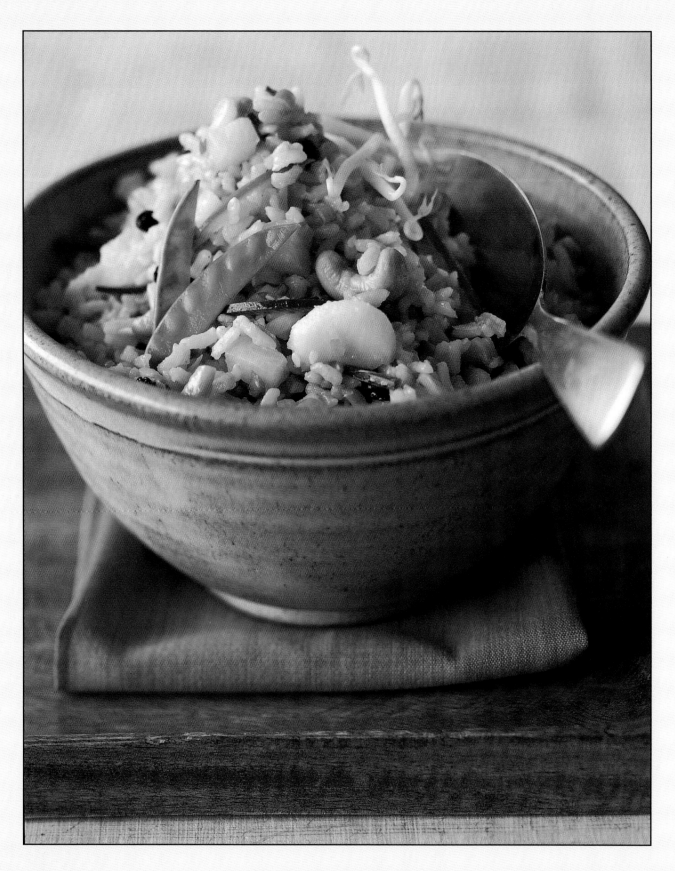

Sri Wasano's Indonesian Rice Salad (page 51)

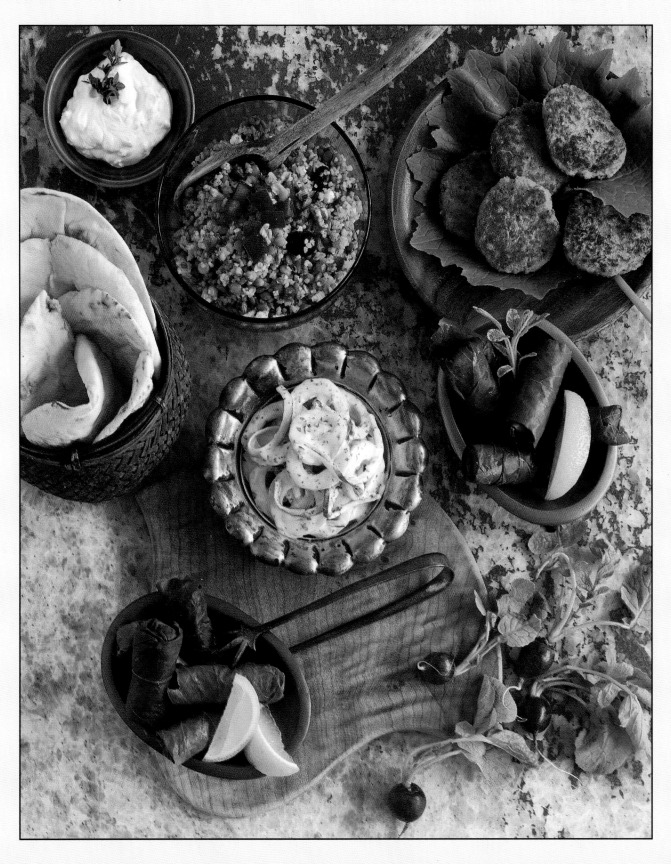

Mezza (clockwise from top left): Yogurt Cheese (page 102), Lentil-Bulgur Salad (page 47), Felafel (page 116), Stuffed Grape Leaves (page 149), Balkan Cucumber Salad (page 69), and Flatbreads (page 115)

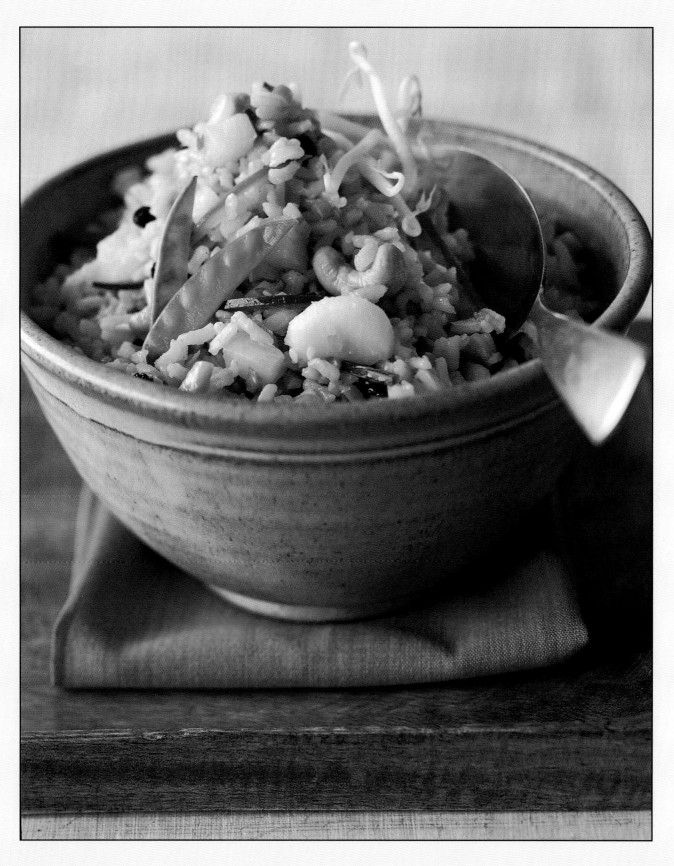

Sri Wasano's Indonesian Rice Salad (page 51)

Marinated Sweet Potatoes & Broccoli (page 71)

Maple-Walnut Pie (page 204)

Preparation time:
30 to 40 minutes

Lentil-Bulgur Salad

Yield: 6 servings
or more

Similar to Tabouli, but more complex (although no more difficult to prepare), this salad is a perfectly balanced protein dish that can be served as a main course ~ especially for lunch on a hot summer day. All you need to complete the meal is toasted pita bread and some ripe fresh fruit for dessert. This is also a good dish to bring to potluck parties. You can easily double the amounts.

{1 cup dry lentils
{2 cups water

{1 cup dry bulgur wheat
{1 cup boiling water

¼ cup olive oil
¼ cup lemon juice
2 medium cloves garlic, crushed
1 tsp. salt
½ tsp. oregano
2 Tbs. freshly minced mint
   (or 2 tsp. dried mint)

2 to 3 Tbs. freshly minced dill
   (or 2 to 3 tsp. dried dill)
fresh black pepper, to taste
¼ cup (packed) freshly minced parsley
⅓ cup finely minced red onion
1 small bell pepper (any color), diced
½ stalk celery, finely minced
½ cup crumbled feta cheese
½ cup Niçoise olives (a scant ¼ lb.)
1 medium-sized tomato, diced
½ cup chopped toasted walnuts
squeezable wedges of lemon,
   for garnish

1) Place the lentils in a medium-sized saucepan, cover with water, and bring just to the boiling point. Turn the heat way down, partially cover, and allow to simmer without agitation for 20 to 25 minutes ~ or until tender but not mushy. Drain well, then transfer to a large bowl.

2) While the lentils are cooking, place the bulgur in a small bowl. Add boiling water, cover with a plate, and let stand 10 to 15 minutes while getting the other ingredients ready.

3) Add everything to the lentils, except tomato chunks, walnuts, and lemon wedges. Mix gently but thoroughly. Cover tightly and refrigerate.

4) Just before serving, top with tomatoes and walnuts. Garnish with lemon wedges.

15 minutes to prepare

White Rabbit Salad

Yield: about 6 servings

3 cups cottage cheese (may be lowfat)

1 to 2 Tbs. honey (optional), to taste

2 to 3 Tbs. lemon juice, to taste

¼ cup (packed) raisins or currants

½ cup chopped, toasted nuts

1 Tbs. poppy seeds

2 medium-sized tart apples, diced

PLUS MANY OPTIONS:

fresh peach slices

fresh pear slices

seedless red or green grapes

orange sections

chunks of ripe honeydew or cantaloupe

Combine everything and chill.

March Hare

HUNKY DORY!

Invented in
March 1973

15 minutes
to prepare

6 to 8
servings

COMBINE AND CHILL:

3 cups cottage cheese (may be lowfat)

2 Tbs. toasted sesame seeds

¼ cup lightly toasted sunflower seeds

1 medium carrot, diced very small

1 medium-sized ripe tomato, diced

1 scallion (whites and greens included), minced

1 small bell pepper ~ any color, minced

1 stalk celery, diced

1 small cucumber ~ peeled, seeded, and minced

½ cup (packed) finely minced parsley

a handful or two of alfalfa sprouts

2 to 3 Tbs. fresh lemon juice ⎫
                              ⎬ to taste
salt (optional) & black pepper ⎭

1 to 2 hardboiled eggs, chopped (optional)

Thai Salad

Made entirely with ordinary and familiar supermarket items, this salad, with its tart-sweet-spicy-peanutty dressing, is surprisingly exotic. It's also very much fun to eat.

NOTE: Potatoes and eggs need to be cooked in advance. Ditto if you choose to fry the tofu. The dressing keeps for weeks, so make it any time.

THE DRESSING:

Place the peanut butter in a small bowl. Whisk in the water, and beat until well combined. Stir in remaining ingredients.

- 6 Tbs. good peanut butter
- 1 cup boiling water
- 4 Tbs. cider vinegar
- 1 Tbs. sugar or honey
- 1 to 1½ tsp. salt
- 3 to 4 medium cloves garlic, minced
- crushed red pepper or cayenne, to taste
- 2 tsp. lemon or lime juice

THE REST:

Pile up everything in a provocative yet compelling arrangement. Drizzle the dressing on top.

- 1 medium head crisp lettuce (Romaine is good.)
- 1 medium carrot, shredded or thinly sliced
- 1 small bell pepper, in thin strips
- 1 small cucumber ~ peeled, seeded, and sliced
- 2 medium-sized ripe tomatoes, in bite-sized chunks
- 2 medium (fist-sized) potatoes, boiled and sliced
- 4 to 6 hardboiled eggs, cut in wedges
- 3 cakes tofu ~ plain or fried, diced
- a small handful each (if available):
   minced fresh cilantro, mint, and basil
- optional: a handful or two of mung bean sprouts
- FUN OPTION: potato chips instead of, or in addition to, the boiled potato slices
- squeezable wedges of lemon or lime, for garnish

Sri Wasano's Infamous Indonesian Rice Salad ⊙

1) Place in a saucepan. Bring to a boil, lower heat, cover, and simmer until tender (35 to 45 minutes).

> 2 cups brown rice
> 3 cups water

2) While the rice cooks, combine in a large bowl:

⅓ cup peanut oil

3 Tbs. Chinese sesame oil

½ cup orange juice

1 to 2 medium cloves garlic, minced

1 tsp. salt

2 Tbs. soy sauce

½ tsp. crushed red pepper (to taste)

2 Tbs. rice or cider vinegar

1 cup chopped fresh pineapple (also ok to use canned-in-juice crushed pineapple)

3) Add the hot rice directly to the bowlful of dressing. Mix well. When it has cooled to room temperature, cover tightly and refrigerate until cold. Shortly before serving, stir in:

3 scallions, finely minced (whites and greens)

1 stalk celery, finely minced

1 medium-sized red or green bell pepper, thinly sliced

1 8-oz. can water chestnuts, drained & thinly sliced

½ lb. fresh mung bean sprouts

½ cup (packed) raisins or currants

1 cup coarsely chopped peanuts and/or cashews, lightly toasted

2 Tbs. sesame seeds

OPTIONAL: fresh snow peas, for garnish

Preparation time:
45 minutes to an hour
(depends on how
much stuff you
choose to put in)

Yield:
6 main dish portions
(more, if serving
with other things)

Kristina's Potato Salad

This is a kitchen-sink-type of potato salad, brimming with fresh vegetables, and texturally enhanced by the addition of toasted nuts and seeds. Make it as simple or as chock-full as you have time, ingredients, and desire for. You can keep the fat content very low if you use homemade Tofu Mayonnaise (p.44 & 91) and yogurt. Serve this salad as a main dish for a summer lunch, especially if paired with a chilled soup from the previous chapter.

Boil until tender; drain and cool.
{
6 medium potatoes (about 3 lbs.), scrubbed, and chopped into 1½-inch pieces (that's approximate, of course)
2 hardboiled eggs, chopped
1 medium bell pepper (any color), diced
3 to 4 finely minced scallions (whites and greens)
1 small cucumber (peel if waxed), seeded and minced
1 cup (packed) finely minced parsley
¼ cup (packed) minced fresh dill (about 1 Tbs. dried)
1 to 2 tsp. salt (to taste)
fresh black pepper
¼ to ⅓ cup cider vinegar (possibly more, to taste)
1 to 2 tsp. dry mustard
1 to 2 tsp. tarragon
1 to 2 Tbs. prepared horseradish
½ to 1 cup mayonnaise (see recipe for homemade, including Tofu Mayo, p.44 and Plain Fake Mayo, p.91)
½ to 1 cup yogurt or sour cream

OPTIONAL ADDITIONS:

a handful of alfalfa sprouts
1 medium carrot, diced
1 stalk celery, minced
thinly sliced radishes
fresh peas, raw or steamed

1 cup lightly toasted cashews
½ cup toasted sunflower seeds
2 to 3 Tbs. sesame seeds
fresh spinach leaves ⎫
cherry tomatoes ⎬ for garnish
olives ⎭

Combine well, season to taste, cover, and chill.

Preparation time: Soybeans and grains cook for 1¼ hours. Everything else takes about 15 minutes. (You can do the cooking up to several days in advance.)

Perfect Protein Salad

Yield: 6 to 8 servings

Crunchy cooked soybeans and chewy cooked wheat or rye berries are blended with minced fresh vegetables in a creamy lowfat dressing. A possibly interesting socio-historical note: I invented this recipe by default in 1973 while living in a house with about 10 other people. The ingredients of this salad— including a jar each of cooked soybeans and wheat berries—were the entire contents of our refrigerator. I just mixed them all together and behold, delicious!

The name was influenced by Frances Moore Lappe's first edition of Diet for a Small Planet, which I had just recently discovered at that time.

PRELIMINARILY: Soak the soybeans for at least 4 hours and the wheat or rye berries for at least 30 minutes. (Soaking them overnight is also fine.)

¾ cup dry soybeans, soaked
¾ cup dry wheat or rye berries, soaked
¼ to ⅓ cup cider vinegar (to taste)
1 tsp. salt
fresh black pepper, to taste
¼ cup minced fresh dill (or 2 tsp. dried)
¼ to ⅓ cup mayonnaise (see p. 44 and p. 91)

1 to 2 small cloves garlic, minced
½ cup finely minced parsley
1 cup cottage cheese or mashed tofu
3 scallions, finely minced
1 medium carrot, minced
1 small cucumber, peeled, seeded, & minced
a little bit of minced bell pepper

OPTIONAL: additional vegetables, such as minced red onion or celery, fresh alfalfa sprouts, sliced radish; fresh, ripe tomato slices, for garnish

1) Place the soaked soybeans in a medium-sized saucepan and cover with water. Place the soaked wheat or rye berries in another saucepan and add at least 2 cups of water. Bring each to a boil, partially cover, and simmer until tender. This will take between 1 and 1¼ hours. (You can also try just cooking them together in one large pot. Their cooking times are about the same.) When the soybeans are crunchy-but-tender, and the grains are chewy-but-tender, rinse them in a colander and drain well. Transfer to a medium-sized bowl.

2) Combine everything and mix well. Serve garnished with ripe tomato slices and behold, delicious!

How to Cut a Beautiful
♪ FRUIT SALAD ♪

If you just want to eat a piece of ripe, fresh fruit ~ or cut up a little assortment to serve to a few people ~ instructions are probably unnecessary. But the prospect of preparing a giant bowlful of freshly cut fruit (to serve to unpredictable numbers or just to have around for unlimited high-level snacking) can be daunting. Here, to undaunt you, are some tips which I hope will be encouraging and useful. Then you can regularly and confidently serve wonderful fruit medleys to volumes of appreciative friends, and everyone will want to come over to your house all the time.

ORANGES AND GRAPEFRUIT:

Use a sharp serrated knife. Cut the skin first from the polar ends, and then from the sides. (If you simply pull off the peel with your hands, citrus fruit will retain the inelegant white matter under the skin, which you probably don't want in your fruit salad.) Hold the peeled fruit over the bowl, and cut with a gentle sawing motion in and out along each membrane, releasing segments of fruit. You will end up holding a fanlike piece of juicy refuse. Squeeze all the juice from this unit into the bowl, and discard the remains. You will have before you a bowlful of captivating citrus sections.

PEACHES AND PLUMS; APPLES AND PEARS:

Make sure they are not over- or under-ripe. Cut in half first, take out the pit or seeds, and cut into slices or chunks just before serving. (If you want to cut them in advance, drizzle with lemon juice, and cover tightly.) Stir in gently as you serve.

PINEAPPLE:

You can tell if it's ripe by smelling it. Use a stainless steel knife to cut off the top and the bottom, then carve off the skin from the sides. Be sure to cut far enough into the pineapple to get off all the traces of prickly skin. It's preferable to lose a little of the goods than to accidentally get a thorn in the mouth. (People shouldn't have to examine each mouthful before eating it.) Cut the pineapple in half, then in quarters lengthwise. Cut the center core strip from each quarter, then chop the remaining fruit into 1-inch pieces.

WATERMELON:

The seeds of a watermelon grow in line patterns. Take your chunk of fruit salad-to-be and examine it to discover the pattern of seeds. Then take a teaspoon handle and pull it through the pattern to evict the seeds. When the seeds are mostly gone, chop the watermelon into 2- to 3-inch pieces. Don't make them too small, or they'll disintegrate.

MELONS OTHER THAN WATERMELON:

Use a stainless steel straight-bladed knife or a cleaver. Cut off the skin from each end, then stand the melon on one end, and carve off the skin from the sides. After the skin is off, cut in half and remove the seeds. Chop the remaining melon into 1-inch pieces.

CHERRIES AND BERRIES:

Halve and pit cherries, and mix them in, OR leave them whole and use to garnish the top. Cut larger berries in half; leave smaller ones whole. Mix in gently or lay decoratively on top.

BANANAS, PAPAYAS, MANGOS, KIWIS:

Make sure they are ripe, but not too, too soft. Peel, slice, and lay on top just before serving. (They will mush into oblivion if mixed in.) If you must cut these fruits ahead of time, sprinkle generously with lemon or lime juice.

DEAD-OF-WINTER FRUIT SALAD:

If you want to have a fruit salad in the off-season, and you'd like it to be more interesting than just apples and bananas, try using frozen unsweetened fruit. Plastic bags of various berries, pitted cherries, and sliced peaches can usually be found in the frozen foods section of larger supermarkets. Frozen berries give off delicious and deeply-hued juice as they defrost (empty the bag into a bowl while the fruit is still frozen), and the resulting fruit salad will be very juicy and a wonderful dark reddish-purple color.

In addition to defrosted frozen fruit, a winter fruit salad can also contain: citrus sections, pineapple (fresh or canned-in-juice), apples, pears, and bananas.

TOFU SALAD

15 minutes to prepare
plus time to marinate

Yield: 6 servings

Unadulterated tofu is cloudlike and bland. Sometimes it's comforting, but sometimes it cries out for a little more action. This recipe calls for adulterating your tofu by marinating it in deep, strong flavors, which it readily absorbs. The crunchy vegetables provide a refreshing contrast.

This delicious salad gets more and more flavorful the longer it sits around, so go ahead and make it up to several days in advance.

The Marinade

4 Tbs. Chinese sesame oil
5 Tbs. rice or cider vinegar
1 Tbs. sugar
3 Tbs. soy sauce
   optional: 1 to 2 Tbs. dry sherry or rice wine

2 to 3 medium cloves garlic, minced
½ tsp. salt (to taste)
crushed red pepper, to taste
optional: 1 tsp. minced fresh ginger

6 cakes (about 1 to 1½ lbs.) very firm tofu, well drained
8 to 10 medium-sized mushrooms
1 small carrot, shredded or cut into slender matchsticks
1 small bell pepper (preferably red), minced
optional: finely shredded cabbage
         1 to 2 minced scallions
         a handful or two of fresh mung bean sprouts
•optional toppings: • ½ cup coarsely chopped peanuts
                   • minced fresh cilantro
                   • diced fresh, ripe tomato
                   • a sprinkling of sesame seeds

1) Combine marinade ingredients in a large, shallow bowl or pan.
2) Cut the tofu into ½-inch cubes and add to the marinade, along with the vegetables. Stir gently.
3) Cover and let marinate at room temperature for at least 2 hours Serve cold or at room temperature, topped with all or some of the garnishes.

SERVING IDEAS: ☆ as a sandwich in Pita Bread (p.113) with shredded cabbage and chopped tomatoes ☆ on hot rice, with Duck Sauce (p.97) or Chinese Mustard (p.120) ☆ in lettuce cups, with Chinese Green Onion Pancakes (p.115) and either of the above-mentioned sauces.

Alsatian Salad

Preparation time: 15 minutes

Yield: 4 to 6 servings

    The original version of this dish was made with thinly cut cheese mixed with fresh vegetables in a creamy mustard dressing. Now that many people want to limit their cheese intake, I've added a Tofu Option, which is delicious! Use "savory baked" or "5-spice" tofu (a.k.a. "tofu kan"), both available in natural foods stores. Use either kind by itself, or in combination with very firm plain tofu.

    Made with tofu or cheese, this is a wonderful lunch entrée.

1) Toss together very gently in a medium-sized bowl:

3 cups cut cheese ~ in thin strips or in ½-inch cubes
    (Try a combination of cheddar and Swiss, or
    something smoked), OR:
3 cups firm tofu strips
1 small cucumber ~ peeled, seeded, and cut in thin strips
1 bell pepper (any color), in small, thin strips
1 minced scallion (include greens)
OPTIONAL: ½ cup finely minced red onion

2) Combine well and add to cheese or tofu mixture:

½ cup yogurt	¼ to ½ tsp. each:
3 Tbs. mayonnaise (see recipes, p.44 + p.91)	paprika
1 small clove garlic, minced	basil
2 tsp. Dijon mustard	tarragon
½ tsp. prepared horseradish	dill
salt and pepper, to taste	a handful of minced parsley

GARNISHES:
fresh greens (small and leafy, like spinach or arugula)
cherry tomatoes (in the summer, look for yellow pear-shaped ones)
raw or steamed vegetables
pickles
olives
crusty bread

Four Waldorf Variations

A cross between a fruit and a vegetable salad, Waldorf Salad can be a first or second course for dinner. It also makes a good lunch entrée. Serve it on a bed of crispy lettuce, with thick slices of whole wheat toast.

♫ MAYONNAISE NOTES: Two of these variations have mayonnaise in the dressings. You can find recipes for homemade (regular or tofu-based) on p. 44 and p. 91 (the latter recipe is oil-free!).

I. BLUE MOON

2 medium-sized tart apples, in chunks
2 perfectly ripe pears (any kind), sliced
1 stalk celery, minced
¼ cup (packed) raisins
2 to 3 Tbs. lemon juice
¾ cup chopped toasted walnuts

Dressing:
1 cup yogurt
3 to 4 Tbs. mayonnaise
⅓ cup crumbled blue cheese
1 Tbs. honey (optional, to taste)

Combine all salad ingredients. Stir together dressing ingredients in a separate bowl, then pour over salad and gently mix.

II. CALIFORNIA

3 medium-sized tart and/or sweet apples
2 navel oranges, sectioned
1 stalk celery, minced
¼ cup (packed) raisins or currants
1 cup sliced ripe mango or papaya
  (optional, if available)   } for the top
1 cup toasted cashew pieces

Dressing:
1 cup yogurt
½ tsp. lemon rind
2 to 3 Tbs. lemon juice
1 ripe avocado, mashed
1 to 2 Tbs. honey (to taste)

Combine apples, oranges, celery, and raisins or currants. Purée together all dressing ingredients in a blender or food processor. Combine apple mixture with dressing and mix well. Serve topped with slices of ripe mango or papaya (if you're lucky enough to have some) and toasted cashews.

III. WALDORF DELUXE

3 medium-sized tart apples, in chunks
2 to 3 Tbs. lemon juice
1 stalk celery, minced
1 to 2 cups seedless grapes, whole or halved
    (optional)
1 cup diced cheddar
1/4 cup (packed) minced dates
3/4 cup chopped toasted pecans

Dressing:
1 cup yogurt
1/4 cup mayonnaise
1/2 cup orange juice
1/2 tsp. grated orange rind

Combine salad ingredients. Whisk together dressing ingredients. Combine everything and mix well.

IV. FRUIT & VEGETABLE WALDORF

3 medium-sized tart apples, in chunks
1 cup freshly chopped pineapple
1 navel orange, sectioned
1 stalk celery, minced
1 small carrot, thinly sliced
1 red bell pepper, thinly sliced
1/4 cup (packed) raisins or currants
1/2 to 1 cup chopped toasted almonds

Dressing:
1 cup yogurt
1/2 cup pineapple or orange juice
    (or a combination)
1/4 tsp. cinnamon
a few dashes ground cardamom

Combine everything, and mix well.

Preparation time:
1½ hours (mostly
bean-cooking time),
plus time to chill

Just White Beans

Sometimes it's refreshing to have a bean salad that is a simple solo of lightly marinated beans, without a lot of little diced vegetables singing backup vocals. This is one such dish. It is delightful by itself, and down-right smashing when topped with a mound of Pickled Red Onions (see below).

This salad keeps well for days if tightly covered and refrigerated. The beans can be cooked without prior soaking.

1½ cups dry white pea beans
3 Tbs. olive oil
2 Tbs. red wine vinegar
¾ to 1 tsp. salt
1 to 2 medium cloves garlic, minced

freshly ground black pepper
½ tsp. basil
¼ cup finely minced parsley
2 Tbs. fresh (2 tsp. dried) dill
Pickled Red Onions (below)

1) Place the beans in a medium-sized saucepan and cover with water. Bring to a boil, reduce heat, and cook, partially covered until tender but not mushy (1 to 1¼ hours). Drain well, and transfer to a medium-sized bowl.
2) Add remaining ingredients, mix gently, and taste to correct seasonings. Cover tightly and chill until cold. Serve topped with Pickled Red Onions.

Pickled Red Onions

Try these with any bean salad, in or with sandwiches, in countless other salads, as an antipasto dish, or even on top of homemade pizza. Pickled Red Onions are ridiculously easy to make, and keep practically indefinitely.

1 cup cider vinegar
1 cup water
up to 3 Tbs. brown sugar

1 tsp. salt
1 tsp. whole peppercorns
4 medium red onions, very thinly sliced

PRELIMINARY: Fill a teakettle with water and put it up to boil.
1) Combine vinegar, 1 cup water, sugar, salt, and peppercorns in a medium-sized bowl and stir until the sugar is dissolved.
2) Place the onion slices in a colander in the sink, and slowly pour all the boiling water over them. They will wilt slightly. Drain well, and transfer to the bowlful of marinade.
3) Cover and allow to marinate, refrigerated or at room temperature, for at least several hours. Store in the refrigerator, and use as needed.

MULTI-BEAN SALAD

Presoaked beans need up to 1¼ hours to cook. (Get everything else ready during this time.) Allow at least a few hours to marinate.

Yield: 8 to 10 servings (possibly even more)

This festive and colorful salad is good with cornbread and any soup. Also, try serving it at room temperature over hot rice (you can melt some cheese into the rice) with steamed tortillas.

Try making this salad with a combination of 1 cup each: pinto, kidney, black, and garbanzo beans. Dry beans need to soak at least 4 hours – preferably overnight. Pinto, kidney, and black beans can be soaked, and then cooked, together. Garbanzos should be done separately.

4 cups dry beans, soaked
6 Tbs. olive oil
1 Tbs. minced garlic
3 to 4 Tbs. lemon juice
6 to 8 Tbs. red wine vinegar
1½ tsp. salt
lots of black pepper
¼ lb. fresh green beans

2 medium stalks celery, finely minced
⅓ cup very finely minced red onion
up to 1 cup (packed) finely minced parsley
1 small red or green bell pepper, minced
optional: a small amount of minced cucumber (peeled and seeded)
optional garnishes: cherry tomatoes sieved hardboiled eggs

1) Cook presoaked beans in plenty of gently simmering water, partially covered, until just done. Keep the agitation to a minimum during the cooking, so the beans don't explode. Begin checking the beans for doneness at the 45-minute mark, just in case they are getting done early. The goal is: perfectly tender, distinct little morsels.

2) Combine oil, garlic, lemon juice, vinegar, salt, and pepper in a large bowl.

3) Trim the tips of the green beans, and steam until tender (5 to 8 minutes, or to your preference). Refresh under cold running water and drain well.

4) Drain the cooked beans and add them, still hot, to the bowlful of dressing. Add remaining ingredients and mix well. Let marinate for at least 2 or 3 hours (even longer is better).

5) Serve cold or at room temperature, garnished with cherry tomatoes, and, if desired, sieved hardboiled eggs.

Bermuda Salad

Yield: 4 to 6 servings,
depending on what goes
with it

~ marinated fresh whole green beans
and onion slices
with a touch of cheese ~

6 Tbs. olive oil
3 to 4 Tbs. red wine vinegar
1¼ tsp. salt
2 medium cloves garlic, minced
fresh black pepper, to taste
1½ cups thinly sliced red onion
3 cups boiling water
1½ lbs. fresh green beans, ends trimmed
1 to 2 cups (packed) mild or medium cheddar, grated
optional: about ½ cup finely minced parsley

1) Combine oil, vinegar, salt, garlic, and black pepper in a medium-sized bowl.

2) Place the sliced onion in a colander over the sink, and slowly douse it with 3 cups boiling water. Drain thoroughly, and transfer to the marinade, mixing well.

3) Steam the green beans until just tender, then immediately transfer to a colander and refresh them under cold running water. Drain well, and add to the marinade, along with the grated cheese (sprinkle it in as you mix gently). You can also throw in some finely minced parsley.

4) Marinate for at least several hours, either refrigerated or at room temperature, stirring occasionally. Serve cold or at room temperature.

Marinated Vegetables

About 45 minutes to prepare.
NOTE: You can do steps 1 + 2 a day or two in advance.

Yield: approximately 6 to 8 servings

Delicately cooked vegetables, when marinated in a simple vinaigrette, make a festive and beautiful accompaniment to just about anything ~ or a light-but-filling main dish in their own right.

Steam the vegetables over water on the stove, or without water in the microwave. The following recipe is a sample method. Try substituting other vegetables ~ your favorites, or whatever is in season. Fresh or dry herbs can be used, depending on availability. Amounts are approximate and flexible.

1 medium cauliflower, in 1-inch pieces
1 medium bunch broccoli, cut in 2-inch stalks
2 medium carrots, sliced thin or in matchsticks
½ lb. mushrooms, sliced or quartered
1 small zucchini or yellow summer squash, in rounds
1 bell pepper (preferably red or yellow), thinly sliced
½ to ¾ cup olive oil
3 to 4 medium cloves garlic, minced
1 tsp. salt (maybe more later, to taste)
freshly ground black pepper
HERBS: (up to 1 tsp. if using dried; up to several Tbs. if using fresh):
    oregano or marjoram
    dill
    basil   } optional and flexible
    chives   ~ in other words, to taste
    thyme

OPTIONAL ADDITIONS: red onion slices (very thin), cooked beans, marinated artichoke hearts, minced scallions, raw sugar snap or snow peas, small cubes of mild white cheese or firm tofu
⅓ cup balsamic and/or red wine vinegar
GARNISHES: olives, hardboiled egg slices, cherry tomatoes, feta cheese

1) Steam the vegetables until just tender in the following groupings: cauliflower + broccoli + carrots; mushrooms + zucchini; bell pepper.
2) Meanwhile, combine oil, garlic, salt, pepper, and herbs in a large bowl. Add the steamed vegetables (OK if still hot) and whatever optional additions you may opt to add. Mix well.
3) Stir in vinegar within 30 minutes of serving. (Minimizing exposure to vinegar helps the vegetables retain their bright colors.)

ANTIPASTO

"Antipasto" is a broad term referring to the first of several courses served in a traditional Italian meal. This can mean a simple dish or two of sliced tomatoes or marinated beans or vegetables, or an elaborate platter of cold sliced meats and cheeses.

In this section, I've put together a variety of vegetable preparations, all of which are very simple, and when served all (or partially) together with fresh bread or breadsticks, olives, a small platter of fruit and cheese, and a bottle of red wine can make a complete and elegant light meal.

All of the following can be made up to several days in advance, and are good served either cold or at room temperature. Leftovers go beautifully as toppings or garnishes for green salads, or as accompaniments to simple pasta dinners. "Antipasto servings" translates to "modest-sized side-dish-type servings."

Gingery Marinated Chick Peas

Preparation time: Presoaked chick peas need about 1½ hrs. to cook; everything else takes only about 10 minutes.

Yield: about 5 cups

This tastes best when made several days ahead (it gets better and better). Keep a batch around to put on top of green salads, or to serve mixed with hot rice, or by itself as an antipasto.

NOTE: You can use canned chick peas if you're in a pinch (rinse and drain them very well). Use 5 cups.

3 cups dry chick peas (soaked at least
4 hours) cooked until tender (1¼ to 1½ hours)

5 to 6 Tbs. olive oil
3 to 4 Tbs. lemon juice
1 to 2 large cloves garlic, minced
1 to 2 Tbs. finely minced ginger

2 to 3 Tbs. red wine vinegar
1 tsp. salt
½ cup finely minced red onion
freshly ground black pepper

1) Rinse and thoroughly drain the cooked chick peas.

2) Combine everything, mix well, cover tightly, and let marinate practically indefinitely. Stir from the bottom periodically during marination.

marinated small Artichokes

15 minutes to prepare;
40 minutes to cook.

6 antipasto
servings

Sure, you could just open a jar, but these are a whole different animal, if you'll pardon the expression, and almost as easy. Really!

Use small artichokes (2-inch diameter or less). Unlike larger artichokes, in which the rough parts and the choke have had a chance to develop, little ones require only minimal trimming, and are otherwise completely edible.

1½ lbs. small artichokes	⅓ cup olive oil
3 cups water	1½ tsp. salt
juice from 1 medium-sized lemon	1 tsp. whole peppercorns
⅓ cup red wine vinegar	4 medium cloves garlic, peeled

1) Cut off the tips and stems of the artichokes. Shave off any extraneous outer leaves with scissors or a paring knife. You can leave the artichokes whole or cut them lengthwise into smaller chunks ~ whatever seems more appealing.

2) Combine everything in a saucepan. Bring to a boil, lower heat to medium, and gently boil, uncovered, until the liquid reduces to approximately 1 cup. This will take 30 to 40 minutes.

3) Remove from heat and cool to room temperature. This will keep for several weeks if stored in a tightly covered container in the refrigerator. Serve cold or at room temperature.

Bell Peppers

Preparation time:
15 minutes

Yield: about 6
antipasto servings

6 medium-sized bell peppers (try to get a mix of colors)	
2 Tbs. olive oil	fresh black pepper, to taste
½ tsp. salt	2 medium cloves garlic, minced
½ to 1 tsp. basil	
½ tsp. marjoram or oregano	1 to 2 Tbs. red wine vinegar

1) Stem and seed the peppers, then cut them into thin strips.

2) Heat olive oil in a heavy skillet. Add peppers, salt, herbs, and black pepper. Cook, stirring over medium heat for about 5 minutes. Then add garlic. Sauté another few minutes, or until the peppers are just tender.

3) Remove from heat, and immediately stir in the vinegar. Let marinate at room temperature for at least an hour. Store in the refrigerator, tightly covered. Serve at any temperature.

Cauliflower and Carrots

15 minutes to prepare

Yield: 6
antipasto servings

1 to 2 Tbs. olive oil
4 cups small (1-inch) cauliflowerets
3 medium carrots, in thin 1½-inch strips
½ tsp. salt (more, to taste)
2 large cloves garlic, minced

1 to 3 Tbs. balsamic vinegar
  (to taste)
fresh black pepper
OPTIONAL: a few leaves of
  fresh basil, cut in strips

1) Heat olive oil in a medium-sized skillet. Add cauliflower, carrots, and salt, and sauté over medium heat until tender (8 to 10 minutes). Stir in garlic during the last few minutes of cooking.

2) Transfer to a bowl; add vinegar, black pepper, and optional basil. Serve warm, cold, or at room temperature.

Preparation time:
20 minutes

Swiss Chard

Yield: 4 to 6
antipasto servings

The following instructions are for preparing the chard in two batches, as it is quite bulky until it cooks down. If you have a very large wok or skillet, you might be able to fit it all into one effort.

1½ lbs. Swiss chard (ruby and/or green)
2 to 3 Tbs. olive oil
6 medium cloves garlic, minced
salt and pepper, to taste
2 Tbs. balsamic or red wine vinegar

1) Coarsely chop the chard (include as much of the stems as feasible.)

2) Heat a wok or a large heavy skillet. Add 1 Tbs. olive oil and half the chard. Turn up the heat, and stir-fry for several minutes. When the chard begins to be limp, add half the garlic, and stir-fry for just a few minutes more.

3) Transfer to a platter or bowl. Sprinkle lightly with salt, heavily with pepper, and toss with 1 Tbs. vinegar.

4) Repeat with the remaining half of the ingredients. Taste to adjust seasonings. (You may wish to add a little more olive oil.) Serve hot, cold, or at room temperature.

Marinated Mushrooms

Preparation time:
25 minutes

Yield: 4 to 6
antipasto servings

```
1 lb. small mushrooms (1-inch diameter)
3 Tbs. olive oil
1 to 2 Tbs. lemon juice
½ tsp. salt
¼ to ½ tsp. thyme
1 medium clove garlic, minced
fresh black pepper
a handful of finely minced parsley
```

1) Clean the mushrooms thoroughly, slicing off and discarding the stems. Place the mushroom caps in a saucepan with no added water, cover, and cook them over medium heat 10 to 15 minutes.

2) Meanwhile, prepare the marinade by combining all the remaining ingredients in a medium-small bowl.

3) Drain the mushrooms. (For a great soup stock, reserve the liquid.) Place the mushrooms in the marinade, stir gently, and let marinate, either refrigerated or at room temperature, for at least several hours. Stir occasionally during marination. Serve cold or at room temperature.

Roasted Green Beans
with garlic & pine nuts

Preparation time:
30 to 40 minutes,
including roasting

Yield: 6
antipasto servings

```
2 Tbs. olive oil
1 lb. fresh whole green beans, trimmed
1 cup thinly sliced onion
10 to 12 medium cloves garlic, peeled
salt and pepper
1 to 2 Tbs. balsamic or red wine vinegar
1 cup lightly toasted pine nuts
```

1) Preheat oven to 400°F. Brush a large baking tray with 2 Tbs. olive oil.
2) Spread the green beans, onions, and garlic cloves on the tray and sprinkle lightly with salt and pepper.
3) Bake for 20 minutes, intermittently stirring or shaking the tray. Taste a green bean to see if it's as tender as you like it. If not, put it back in for another 5 or 10 minutes.
4) Remove from oven; transfer to a bowl. Drizzle with vinegar, and possibly grind in some additional black pepper. Serve at any temperature, topped with lightly toasted pine nuts.

Odessa Beets

Preparation time: The beets need 45 minutes to bake; after that, about 10 minutes

Yield: 6 or more servings

Except for its special guest ingredient, pineapple, this recipe is authentically Ukrainian. Traditional versions might have even more garlic and a little mayonnaise. You can try it that way if it sounds good to you. This version has no added oil.

Odessa Beets keep beautifully for at least a week. Serve them alongside just about anything, even as an accompaniment to other salads. Try using this recipe as a stuffing in baked acorn squash, or as a side dish with Solyanka (p.136). You can put it in a salad sandwich (p.119) or just eat it straight. Even if you think you hate beets, there's a good chance you will love this salad.

    5 to 6 medium beets (2- to 2½-inch diameter)
    2 to 3 Tbs. lemon juice
    8 to 10 prunes, pitted and thinly sliced
    2 to 3 medium cloves garlic, minced
    ½ tsp. salt
    black pepper, to taste
    ½ cup finely chopped walnuts
    1 cup finely chopped pineapple (fresh or
        canned-in-juice)

1) Preheat oven to 400°F. Wrap the beets in foil and bake until very tender (40 to 45 minutes). Rinse under cold running water as you rub off the skins. Trim the ends and coarsely grate. (A food processor fitted with the grating attachment does this in seconds.) Transfer to a medium-sized bowl.

2) Add all remaining ingredients and mix well. Chill until serving time.

Balkan Cucumber Salad

Preparation time:
10 to 15 minutes

a delicious, refreshing, very easy salad,
made without oil

Yield:
6 servings

½ cup very thinly sliced red onion
4 medium cucumbers (6 to 7 inches long)
1 tsp. salt
freshly ground black pepper
1½ cups yogurt
1 or 2 small cloves garlic, minced
1 to 2 tsp. honey (optional)
2 Tbs. freshly minced mint leaves (or 2 tsp. dried)
¼ cup (packed) finely minced parsley
2 scallions, finely minced (greens included)
1 to 2 Tbs. freshly minced dill (or 1 to 2 tsp. dried)
1 cup chopped walnuts, lightly toasted

1) Soak the onion in cold water for about 30 minutes while you get everything else ready. Drain thoroughly and pat dry before adding to the salad.

2) Peel (unless they're homegrown or unwaxed, in which case, don't) the cucumbers, seed them, and cut them into thin rounds. Place them in a medium-sized bowl.

3) Add remaining ingredients except walnuts, and mix well. Cover and refrigerate until serving time.

4) Sprinkle the walnuts on top just before serving.

Jicama, Orange, & Fennel Salad

20 to 30 minutes to prepare

Yield: 4 to 6 servings

❀ Jicama ("<u>hee</u>-ca-ma") is a Mexican tuber that looks like a light brown turnip. It is incomparably crisp and fresh-tasting as a snack, and goes beautifully with dips. If you can't find it, substitute sunchoke or radish.

❀ Serve this salad as a second course, in place of dessert. It is so satisfying and re-freshing, all yearnings for a sugary follow-up will instantly fade.

4 navel oranges
1 jicama (or a piece of one), about
   the size of a medium apple
1 small fennel bulb (2- to 3-inch diameter)
a few sprigs of arugula, if available
about 10 leaves of Belgian endive -OR-
   a handful of fresh spinach

DRESSING:
4 Tbs. olive oil
2 Tbs. orange juice
2 Tbs. balsamic or wine vinegar
2 tsp. raspberry vinegar (optional)
1 medium clove garlic, minced
½ tsp. salt
2 tsp. honey

optional garnish: Pickled Red Onions (p. 60)

1) Cut off the ends of the oranges with a sharp serrated knife, then slice the peel from the sides. With a gentle sawing motion, cut along each membrane to release the orange sections into a small bowl. Set aside.

2) Peel the jicama, and cut into very thin slices about 1½ inches long. Slice the fennel into very thin strips; include the feathery tops. Chop the arugula.

3) In a small bowl, whisk together the dressing ingredients until the honey is dissolved. Refrigerate everything until serving time.

4) Assemble the salad on a small platter shortly before serving. First, put down a layer of endive or spinach (a starburst pattern looks real nice), then a layer of jicama slices. Drizzle on some of the dressing, then sprinkle on fennel and arugula. Arrange orange sections on top, and spoon on a little more dressing. Garnish, if you are so inclined, with a few slices of Pickled Red Onion.

Marinated Sweet Potatoes & Broccoli

15 to 20 minutes to prepare;
at least 2 hours to marinate

Yield: about 6 servings

3 medium-sized sweet potatoes or yams (1½ to 2 lbs.)

MARINADE:
½ cup walnut oil (if unavailable, use olive oil)
1 large clove garlic, minced
3 Tbs. lemon juice
2 Tbs. raspberry vinegar (if unavailable, use red wine vinegar)
1 to 1½ tsp. salt
1 Tbs. dry mustard
1 Tbs. honey
freshly ground black pepper

1 large bunch broccoli (1 to 1½ lbs.), cut into small spears

OPTIONAL GARNISHES: thin slices of green apple
chopped, toasted pecans

1) Peel the sweet potatoes, cut them in halves or quarters, then into thin slices. Put them up to cook, either in or over boiling water (in a steamer). Meanwhile, prepare the marinade.

2) Combine the marinade ingredients in a medium-large bowl. As soon as the sweet potato slices are tender, add them, still hot, to the marinade. Mix gently.

3) Steam the broccoli until bright green and just tender. Rinse under cold running water and drain completely. Lay the broccoli spears carefully on top of the salad. Cover tightly and marinate for several hours.

4) Within 15 minutes of serving, mix in the broccoli from on top. Serve garnished with thin slices of green apple and chopped, toasted pecans.

Carrot-Yogurt Salad

Preparation Time:
10 minutes (w/ food processor); 20 minutes (by hand)

Yield: 4 to 5 main-dish servings for lunch. More, if serving as a side dish.

1 lb. carrots, peeled and coarsely grated
2 medium-sized tart apples, grated
1 to 2 Tbs. lemon juice
1 to 2 Tbs. honey (optional)
pinch of celery seed
salt and pepper to taste
1 cup firm yogurt

OPTIONAL ADDITIONS:
1 Tbs. poppy seeds or toasted sesame seeds
¼ cup minced almonds or cashews, lightly toasted
½ cup very finely minced celery
a handful of raisins or currants
¼ cup shredded unsweetened coconut, lightly toasted
½ to 1 cup finely chopped pineapple (or crushed canned-in-juice)

Combine all ingredients and mix well. Chill. (This preparation goes fast if you use a food processor with the grating attachment.)

COLESLAW VARIATION

Same as above, but with the following alterations:

1) Substitute 4 cups shredded cabbage plus 2 large carrots for the 1 lb. carrots.
2) Apples = optional.
3) Substitute cider vinegar for the lemon juice.
4) You can use half yogurt and half mayonnaise. (Recipes for homemade mayo are on p. 44 and p. 91)
5) Add ½ cup each: minced green pepper and red onion.
6) Same Optional Additions.

SAUCES
AND
DIPS

Even though they are often associated with complex and elusive cooking styles, sauces can actually be the key to simpler, not more complicated, menu planning. Those described in this chapter are accessible and nonmysterious, yet they have the impressive ability to transform plain cooked pasta, rice, beans, or vegetables into complete and interesting meals.

The sauce section begins with over a dozen ideas for pasta—some simpler, some a little more complex, and most showcasing vegetables and de-emphasizing oil or butter. Included are several variations on the theme of Italian Tomato Sauce, a traditional basil-and-oil pesto, plus two oil-free pesto ideas.

After the pasta sauces, you'll find a selection of ideas for dressing up plain cooked foods (vegetables, grains, etc.), including vegetable purées, which are the lightest of sauces, containing no fat or dairy. Also in the oil-free department is a series of tofu-based sauces, which are easy and delicious (and require no cooking). More traditional sauces are also included, plus sauces for stir-fried vegetables and a sample stir-fry recipe.

A few condiment recipes follow (including three versions of Salsa Fresca, two chutneys, and more), and then an assortment of dips, any of which could easily (and delightfully) be the focal point of a light meal. And if you love dips and appetizers so much that you would welcome an assortment of them—lavish or modest— as a complete meal, be sure to check out Mezza, p. 100.

TABLE OF CONTENTS: SAUCES AND DIPS

Pasta Sauces

This, plus the next 10 pages, contain ideas for pasta sauces, some traditional (Italian Tomato Sauce plus variations, Pesto, etc.), and some more unusual (Caramelized Onions, Stellar Mushroom Sauce, and more). I've tried to include some very easy and quick ideas, as well as a few more complex ones, so you can have a choice (and have lots of pasta in your life! There's nothing like a good plateful on a regular basis.)

These recipes assume you are using dried pasta. If you are using fresh, increase the amount of uncooked pasta by 50%. (So if the recipe calls for 1 lb. pasta, use 1½ lbs. fresh.) For a delicious and nutritious departure, try using cooked spaghetti squash sometimes, instead of pasta. Substitute 1 large (9- to 10-inch-long) squash, baked or boiled, for 1 lb. pasta.

TWO ULTRA-QUICK & EASY PASTA IDEAS

-For when you have no time to cook, and you need dinner Right Now.

1) <u>with Olive Oil, Garlic, Crushed Red Pepper, and Parmesan:</u>
  - Cook pasta.
  - Mince or crush some fresh garlic in the meantime.
  - Drain the pasta, drizzle it with olive oil, stir in the garlic and some crushed red pepper, to taste.
  - Sprinkle in some parmesan, and if you are slightly ambitious, top with a little minced parsley.

2) <u>with Marinated Artichoke Hearts from a Jar:</u>
  For every 2 people:
    ½ lb. pasta (smallish shells, ziti, fusilli, or penne = best)
    1 6-oz. jar marinated artichoke crowns or hearts
    parmesan
    black pepper
  - While the pasta cooks, drain the artichoke marinade into a serving bowl.
  - Cut the hearts or crowns into bite-sized pieces, and add to the bowl.
  - Add the drained pasta to the bowl, and toss. Serve immediately, passing the parmesan and a pepper mill.

Simplest Primavera

Pasta Primavera is a pasta-and-vegetable dish named in honor of the spring season. Ideally, it is full of the vegetable garden's earliest offerings. In keeping with that spirit, this simple version is made from the season's first greens: peas, scallions, herbs, and leafy greens.

....

1 lb. sugar snap or snow peas
5 or 6 scallions
4 Tbs. olive oil
OPTIONAL: 1 lb. leafy greens (kale, collard, or mustard),
      stemmed and coarsely chopped
½ tsp. salt
4 to 5 large cloves garlic, minced
a handful of fresh basil leaves, coarsely chopped (if
      unavailable, use parsley)
black pepper, to taste
½ lb. penne or fusilli (tube- or corkscrew-shaped pasta)
extra olive oil for the pasta
parmesan for the top

....

1) Trim the peas at both ends, remove the strings, and cut the pods in half across the middle (unless they're very small, in which case, leave them whole).
2) Cut the scallions in half lengthwise, then into 1½-inch pieces.
3) Put up the pasta water to boil. Cook the pasta while you sauté the vegetables.
4) Heat the olive oil in a large wok or skillet. If you are using the greens, add these first, along with the salt. Sauté for about 5 minutes over high heat, then turn heat down, and add peas, scallions, and garlic. Sauté for 5 minutes more. Stir in the basil (or parsley) and black pepper during the last minute or so. (If you are not using the greens, just begin the sauté with the peas, scallions, and garlic.)
5) When the pasta is done, drain it (or scoop it out of the hot water with a strainer or a slotted pasta scooper), and add it directly to the vegetables in the wok or skillet. Sauté the pasta with the vegetables for 2 or 3 minutes — until everything is fully mingled — and serve immediately. Pass a cruet of olive oil and some parmesan.

asparagus~mushroom sauce

Although designed for pasta, this sauce is also good in Crêpes (p. 142) or on rice or baked fish. If you have some left over, try filling an omelette with it. NOTE: The alcohol in the wine will evaporate during cooking.

1½ lbs. fresh asparagus — slender as possible, trimmed
    at the bottom and cut into 2-inch spears
2 Tbs. butter or margarine
1½ cups minced onion
1 tsp. salt
1 lb. mushrooms, sliced
½ tsp. tarragon
black pepper, to taste
1½ cups dry white wine
1 cup water
1 to 2 Tbs. flour (depending on how thick you like it)
6 to 8 cloves garlic, minced
½ to ¾ lb. pasta (any shape)
olive oil or extra butter for the pasta
parmesan for the top
minced fresh dill (optional)

1) Steam the asparagus until just tender. Transfer to a colander over a sink and refresh under cold running water. Drain well and set aside.

2) Melt the butter or margarine in a large skillet. Add onion and salt, and sauté for about 5 minutes. Add mushrooms, tarragon, and pepper. Cover and cook over medium heat for 15 minutes, stirring occasionally.

3) Add wine and water. Turn up heat until the liquid boils. Sprinkle in the flour, whisking constantly until it completely dissolves. Lower heat, cover, and simmer about 10 minutes, stirring frequently. Add garlic, and cook about 5 minutes more. Set aside until serving time.

4) Gently reheat the sauce while you cook the pasta. Stir the steamed asparagus into the sauce at the last minute. Toss the drained pasta with a little olive oil or butter, and serve topped with sauce, parmesan, and possibly a little freshly minced dill.

Caramelized Onion Sauce

Preparation time:
about 1 hour

Yield: enough for
4 to 5 pasta servings

The proportions of ingredients in this delicious recipe are somewhat flexible. You can play with the amounts of onions and greens, and you can substitute other leafy greens (collard, escarole, mustard, etc.) for the arugula or spinach. Other soft pungent cheeses can be substituted for the feta or blue cheese.

NOTE: The alcoholic content of the wine will dissipate with cooking.

½ cup olive oil
4 to 6 large onions (however many
   you have the patience to slice),
   thinly sliced (about 6 to 8 cups)
½ tsp. salt
½ to 1 cup dry white wine
1 medium bunch arugula or spinach,
   stemmed and minced

1 cup crumbled feta or blue cheese
¾ lb. pasta (a short, shapely
   variety, like penne or fusilli)

1 cup chopped, toasted walnuts
parmesan

1) Heat olive oil in a large skillet or sauté pan. Add onions, and sauté over medium heat for about 15 minutes. Add salt, lower heat, and continue to cook for at least another 10 minutes (and up to an hour for really deliciously well-done onions).

2) Add white wine, turn heat back up to medium, and simmer uncovered for about 15 minutes. At this point the sauce can be set aside until you are ready to cook the pasta.

3) Turn the heat back on under the sauce when you are ready to cook the pasta. When the onions are hot, add the chopped greens, stir, and cook for about 5 minutes. Stir in the crumbled cheese, and turn heat to low while cooking the pasta.

4) After the cooked pasta is drained, add it to the sauce, and stir briefly in the pan before serving. Sprinkle with walnuts and parmesan, and serve.

Stellar Mushroom Sauce

30 minutes to prepare

Yield: about 6 servings

2 oz. dried Chinese black mushrooms

2 Tbs. butter
1 lb. domestic mushrooms, chopped
3/4 lb. fresh shiitake, oyster, and/or chanterelle mushrooms, chopped
1 cup minced onion
1 tsp. salt

6 Tbs. dry sherry
3 Tbs. flour
1/2 to 3/4 lb. pasta (any shape)
1 large clove garlic, minced
black pepper, to taste
1/2 cup sour cream, at room temperature
parmesan for the top

1) PRELIMINARY: Place the dried mushrooms in a bowl. Add 2 cups boiling water, cover with a plate, and let stand 30 minutes. Drain the mushrooms in a cheesecloth-lined strainer over a bowl, squeezing out and saving all the liquid. Remove and discard the stems; coarsely chop the mushrooms. Measure out 2/3 cup of the liquid to use in this recipe. (Save any remaining liquid to use as a delicious soup stock.)

2) Put up some pasta water to boil. Melt butter in a deep skillet or Dutch oven. Add all mushrooms, the onions, and the salt. Cook uncovered over medium heat for 10 minutes. Stir in the sherry.

3) Turn heat to low, and have a whisk ready. Slowly sprinkle in the flour, whisking steadily. Keep whisking for a minute or two after all the flour is in. Meanwhile, begin cooking the pasta.

4) Add garlic and black pepper; continue cooking/stirring for 10 minutes.

5) Stir in the sour cream and the 2/3 cup reserved mushroom-soaking liquid from Step 1, mixing well until incorporated.

6) Drain the pasta, transfer to serving plates, and spoon a generous amount of sauce on top. Sprinkle with parmesan, and serve.

ITALIAN TOMATO SAUCE

The classic red sauce, without meat, and with 2 variations. Use any version of this in Lasagne (p. 132) or Eggplant Parmesan (p. 133), or on pasta of any size or shape.

Make a full batch even if you won't use it all in one meal. All of these variations keep well up to a week in the refrigerator, and much longer in the freezer.

2 to 3 Tbs. olive oil	1 1-lb., 13-oz. can tomatoes
2 cups chopped onion	1 6-oz. can tomato paste
1 medium-sized bell pepper, diced	1 Tbs. honey
2 tsp. basil	lots of black pepper
1 tsp. oregano	4 to 6 large cloves garlic, minced
1 tsp. thyme	
1½ tsp. salt	½ cup freshly minced parsley

1) Heat the olive oil in a Dutch oven or kettle. Add onion, bell pepper, herbs, and salt, and sauté over medium heat until the onion is very soft (8 to 10 minutes).

2) Add tomatoes, tomato paste, honey, and black pepper. Use a spoon to break up the tomatoes into bite-sized pieces. Bring to a boil, then lower heat and simmer, partially covered, for 20 to 30 minutes.

3) Add garlic, and cook about 10 minutes more. At this point, the sauce can sit for up to several hours, or be refrigerated for up to a week. Heat gently before serving, and add parsley at the last minute.

MARINARA VARIATION:

2 medium stalks celery, minced
1 lb. mushrooms, chopped
1 to 2 medium (6-inch) zucchini, diced
2 to 3 medium-sized ripe tomatoes, chopped
a handful of fresh basil leaves, chopped

} Add with step 1. Sauté until all vegetables are very tender.

CAVOLFIORE VARIATION:

1 large cauliflower, in 1-inch florets } Steam until tender. Add to Step 2.

🍅 SAUCE PUTTANESCA 🍅

🍅🍅🍅🍅🍅🍅🍅🍅🍅🍅🍅🍅

... intensely seasoned tomato sauce with a special guest star: the much-maligned but ever spunky anchovy. Of course, if you are a strict, not-even-fish vegetarian, this addition will be out of the question, and the sauce will still taste fine without it. But if you are a fish-eater, try the anchovies, even if you must overcome a degree of prejudice to do so. You will find that their flavor blends in surprisingly well.

This sauce is quick and easy — it doesn't require prolonged simmering—so you can whip it up after a busy day of work. Serve over any shape of pasta, accompanied by a green salad and some fresh crusty bread.

1 1-lb., 13-oz. can whole or crushed tomatoes
1 6-oz. can tomato paste
10 to 12 medium cloves garlic, thinly sliced
15 to 20 Kalamata (Greek) olives, carved off the pit and sliced
OPTIONAL: 3 to 4 anchovies, minced —OR— 1 to 2 Tbs.
anchovy paste (can be increased, to taste)
black pepper
crushed red pepper } to taste
3/4 to 1 lb. pasta (any shape)
olive oil for the pasta
parmesan
freshly minced parsley
for PASTA MEDITERRANÉE: 1 cup crumbled feta cheese

PRELIMINARY: Put up pasta water to boil.
1) For a smoother sauce, purée the tomatoes in their liquid in a blender or food processor. For a chunkier sauce, cut the tomatoes into chunks with a knife, saving the liquid. (Skip this step if using crushed tomatoes.)
2) Combine tomatoes, their liquid, tomato paste, garlic, olives, and anchovies in a medium-sized saucepan, and gradually heat to a boil. Reduce heat, season to taste with black and crushed red pepper, and simmer about 10 minutes. (You can cook the pasta during this time.)
3) Drain the pasta, and toss with a little olive oil. Add the sauce, and serve immediately, topped with parmesan and parsley (and feta cheese, if desired).

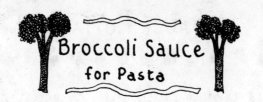

Broccoli Sauce
for Pasta

During the height of the produce season, you can make this lovely dish particularly colorful by pairing a yellow bell pepper with red cherry tomatoes — or a red bell pepper with yellow cherry tomatoes.

If you can't find Niçoise olives, use Kalamata (Greek) olives, carved off the pit and sliced. If using Niçoise olives, remind your guests to watch out for the pits.

3 Tbs. olive oil
2 cups chopped onion
1 1½-lb. bunch broccoli,
　in 1½-inch pieces
1 tsp. salt
1 red or yellow bell pepper,
　cut into 1½-inch strips
2 cups water or vegetable
　broth
2 Tbs. flour
2 cups cherry tomatoes, halved
½ cup Niçoise olives
6 large cloves garlic, minced

½ to ¾ lb. pasta (any shape)
Extra olive oil for the pasta
Parmesan ⎫
Black pepper ⎭ for the top

OPTIONAL ADDITIONS:
○ Sun-dried tomatoes, softened in
　hot water and chopped
○ A few dried mushrooms,
　softend in hot water and sliced
○ A handful of lightly toasted
　pine nuts

PRELIMINARY: Put up some pasta water to boil.

1) Heat the olive oil in a large, deep skillet or Dutch oven. Add the onion, and sauté over medium heat until very soft (10 to 15 minutes).
2) Add broccoli and salt, and sauté another 10 minutes or so — until the broccoli is just tender.
3) Add the bell pepper, stir, and sauté about 5 minutes longer.
4) Add water or broth, and turn up the heat until it boils. Lower heat to medium, and sprinkle in the flour, whisking until dissolved.
5) Stir in the tomatoes, olives, garlic, and optional sun-dried tomatoes and/or mushrooms. Keep the sauce warm while you cook the pasta.
6) Drain the pasta, toss it with a little extra olive oil, and transfer to a serving dish. Pour/spoon in the sauce, and sprinkle with parmesan, black pepper, and optional pine nuts. Serve hot.

Eggplant Scallopini Marsala } For Pasta

Preparation time: 45 minutes

Yield: about 4 to 5 servings

OPTIONAL PRELIMINARY: To peel and seed the tomatoes, heat a medium-sized potful of water, then lower heat to a simmer. Core the tomatoes, then drop them into the water for about 10 seconds. Retrieve them, pull off and discard the skins, then cut the tomatoes in half. Squeeze out the seeds, and chop the remaining pulp.

NOTE: The alcohol content of the wine will mostly dissipate during cooking.

- 2 to 3 Tbs. olive oil
- 2 cups chopped onion
- 2 bay leaves
- 6 cups diced eggplant (about 1 large eggplant) (peeling optional)
- 2 medium-sized bell peppers, any color, diced
- 1 lb. mushrooms, chopped
- 2 tsp. salt
- 2 tsp. dried basil (or 2 Tbs. minced fresh)
- 1 cup marsala or dry sherry
- 3 to 4 medium-sized ripe tomatoes, chopped (Peeling and seeding = optional. See "optional preliminary" above.)
- Black pepper, to taste
- 10 medium cloves garlic, minced
- ½ to ¾ lb. pasta (any shape)
- Additional olive oil for the pasta
- Parmesan } for the top
- Minced parsley

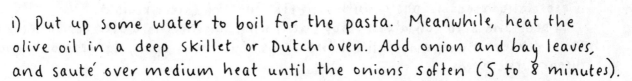

1) Put up some water to boil for the pasta. Meanwhile, heat the olive oil in a deep skillet or Dutch oven. Add onion and bay leaves, and sauté over medium heat until the onions soften (5 to 8 minutes).
2) Add eggplant, peppers, mushrooms, salt, and basil. Cover and cook until the eggplant is tender (10 to 15 minutes), stirring occasionally.
3) Add marsala or sherry, tomatoes, and black pepper. Simmer uncovered for 10 to 15 minutes. (The liquid will reduce.) Stir in the garlic during the last 5 minutes. Meanwhile, cook the pasta.
4) Drain the pasta and transfer to a serving dish. Drizzle and toss with a little extra olive oil, and spoon the eggplant mixture on top. Sprinkle with parmesan and parsley, and serve hot.

Pesto

This most-famous potent, green version of pesto features basil, garlic, and olive oil. When tossed with hot pasta (especially long, thin varieties, like spaghetti or linguine), it adheres to each available surface, coating the pasta with intense flavor. This pesto keeps for weeks, or even months, if stored in a tightly lidded sterile jar in the refrigerator.

3 cups (packed) fresh basil leaves
3 to 4 large cloves garlic
optional: 1/3 cup pine nuts or
   chopped walnuts, lightly
      toasted

1/3 cup olive oil
1/3 cup parmesan
optional: salt and pepper,
   to taste

1) Place the basil leaves and garlic in a blender or food processor and mince.
2) Add the nuts, if desired, and continue to blend until the nuts are ground.
3) Drizzle in the olive oil, as you keep the machine running. When you have a smooth paste, transfer to a bowl, and stir in the parmesan. Season to taste with salt and pepper. To serve, place room-temperature Pesto in a warmed serving bowl. Add hot pasta and toss thoroughly. Allow 2 to 3 Tbs. Pesto per serving.

MONDO BIZARRO SAUCE

Oil-free tomato-spinach pesto for pasta

You can choose to keep this fat-free or to add the optional nuts. This sauce is especially good on pasta with Ricotta Gnocchi (next recipe).

To peel and seed tomatoes: Drop them into simmering water for 10 seconds. Then retrieve them, and pull off the skins. Cut them open; squeeze out and discard the seeds.

4 or 5 large cloves garlic
1/3 cup fresh basil leaves
1/3 cup minced parsley
1 1-lb. bunch spinach, stemmed
2 to 3 medium-sized ripe tomatoes,
   peeled and seeded (see above)

1/2 cup parmesan, plus extra, for
   the top
1/2 tsp. salt
optional: 1/2 cup pine nuts or finely
   minced walnuts, lightly toasted
freshly ground black pepper
optional: olive oil for the pasta

Continued →

1) Place the garlic, basil, parsley, and spinach in a food processor or blender, and work into a uniform paste.

2) Add the tomatoes, and process just a few seconds more. Transfer to a bowl, and stir in parmesan, salt, and optional nuts (or save these for sprinkling on top).

3) Serve the room-temperature sauce with hot pasta (and possibly Ricotta Gnocchi) in a warmed serving bowl. Pass some extra parmesan, the pepper grinder, and if desired, a cruet of olive oil.

Ricotta Gnocchi

Preparation time:
30 minutes

Yield: about 2
dozen dumplings

Serve these savory cheese dumplings as an appetizer or with pasta. You can make and poach them ahead of time. Broil just before serving.

½ lb. mozzarella cheese	2 eggs	Black pepper, to taste
1 large handful parsley	½ tsp. salt	A little butter or olive
2 large cloves garlic	¼ cup parmesan	oil for the pan
1 lb. ricotta cheese	1¼ cups flour	Extra parmesan for the top

1) Fill a large kettle with water and put it up to boil.

2) Meanwhile, grate the mozzarella (the grating attachment of a food processor does this fast) and transfer to a medium-sized bowl.

3) Mince the parsley and garlic - either by hand or in the food processor - and stir this into the grated cheese.

4) Beat together the ricotta and eggs. (You can use the food processor.) Add this to the first mixture, with salt, parmesan, flour, and black pepper. Mix well.

5) When the water boils, reduce heat to a simmer, and drop in small blobs of batter (1 Tbs. each). Simmer for 15 minutes, then remove with a slotted spoon. The gnocchi will be soft. Refrigerate until 15 minutes before serving.

6) Shortly before serving, heat the broiler. Brush a baking dish with soft butter or olive oil, and arrange the gnocchi in the dish. Sprinkle with parmesan, and broil until golden. Serve hot.

VEGETABLE PURÉES

5 minutes to prepare
after vegetable is cooked.

Yield: about 1 cup each.
Easily multiplied.

These are the purest of sauces. Made almost entirely from a single cooked vegetable, each purée is full-flavored and a brilliant color. Use vegetable purées in any variety of ways. (Suggestions are included with each recipe.) You'll be amazed by how good such simplicity can be!

❀ RED PEPPER PURÉE ❀

2 large red bell peppers
1/4 tsp. salt
A pinch of sugar

1/2 tsp. fresh lemon juice
1 scant tsp. minced garlic
Black pepper, to taste

1) Core the peppers and cut them into large chunks.
2) Steam over boiling water for about 10 minutes, or until very soft.
3) Purée in a food processor or blender, and pass through a mesh strainer into a bowl. Stir in remaining ingredients, adjusting amounts to taste.

→ Spoon room-temperature sauce over Stuffed Eggplant (p. 151) or Zuccanoes (p. 154). OTHER USES: In or on omelettes; on fish, baked potatoes, or other cooked vegetables; as a garnish on soup — or just spread on toast.

NOTE: You can roast the peppers instead of steaming them. Just put them on an oiled tray in a 400°F oven, and roast until very tender (about 20 to 30 minutes). Transfer with tongs to a glass or ceramic bowl, cover it with a plate, and let sit for 30 minutes longer. Remove skins, stems, and seeds, and proceed with Step 3 above.

BEET PURÉE

2 beets (2 1/2-inch diameter)
1/2 cup apple or orange juice
2 Tbs. fresh lemon juice
1 Tbs. cider vinegar

2 tsp. honey
1/2 tsp. salt
Black pepper, to taste
Minced fresh tarragon or mint (optional)

1) Cook the beets until tender. (You can boil them, or roast them on an oiled tray in a 400°F oven.) Cool until comfortable to handle.
2) Rub off the skins, rough-chop the beets, and put them in a blender or food processor with the fruit juices and vinegar. Purée until smooth.

3) Transfer to a small bowl, and stir in honey, salt, pepper, and possibly the tarragon or mint. If necessary, thin to desired consistency with a little extra apple or orange juice.

→ Serve room-temperature sauce over hard boiled eggs, Kristina's Potato Salad (p. 52), Zuccanoes (p. 154), or Stuffed Squash (p. 152).

❀ CARROT PURÉE ❀

A little oil for the baking tray
{ 3 medium carrots, peeled and
   cut into 1-inch chunks   OR
(1 pound baby carrots

A scant ½ tsp. salt

¼ tsp. cumin (optional)
¼ tsp. minced garlic
1 tsp. minced fresh dill
3 Tbs. orange juice (maybe more)
½ tsp. fresh lemon juice
1 cup water

1) Preheat oven to 400°F. Lightly oil a baking tray, and spread out the carrots. Roast for 20 to 30 minutes, or until tender. Remove from oven, and allow the carrots to cool for about 15 minutes.

2) Put the cooked carrots in a food processor or blender with all the other ingredients, and purée until very smooth. (You may need to do this in batches.) For an even silkier result, pour the purée through a mesh strainer into a bowl.

3) Correct seasonings, if necessary. If you'd like, you could thin the purée a little by adding a small amount of extra orange juice.

→ Serve room-temperature purée on cooked aspargus or broccoli; as a garnish on soup; on Crêpes (p. 142), Zuccanoes (p. 154), baked or grilled fish, or on whatever else you can think of.

❀ SPINACH PURÉE ❀

1 lb. fresh spinach, stemmed and cleaned

¼ to ½ cup water
¼ to ½ tsp. salt

1 medium clove garlic, minced
black pepper, to taste

1) Cook the spinach without added water in a covered pot for just a few minutes — until tender and very bright green.

2) Transfer to a blender or food processor, and add ¼ cup water. Purée until very smooth, and place in a small bowl. Thin to desired consistency with a little more water (or leave it thick). Season to taste with salt, garlic, and black pepper. Serve on cold steamed vegetables, on hot baked potatoes, on baked fish, on cold pasta...etc.

Basic Stir-Fry Sauce

Designed to enhance Chinese-Style Stir-Fried Vegetables (recipe follows), this sauce is gingery, garlicky, and thickened just enough to give each vegetable a delicious, deeply flavored coating. You can also use this sauce (minus the cornstarch) for baked fish, or as a dipping sauce for Chinese Green Onion Pancakes (p. 115).

¼ cup soy sauce
1¼ cups water
1 Tbs. grated ginger
2 large cloves garlic, minced

1 tsp. sesame oil
1 Tbs. sugar
1 Tbs. plus 1 tsp. cider vinegar
2 Tbs. dry sherry or Chinese rice wine

3 Tbs. cornstarch

1) Combine all ingredients except cornstarch in a small bowl or a 2- to 4-cup liquid measuring cup.
2) Place the cornstarch in a separate small bowl, and whisk in the mixture from Step 1.

Chinese-Style Stir-Fried Vegetables

Preparation time:
20 minutes for chopping;
15 minutes to stir-fry

Yield: 4 to 6
servings

There is no one correct method for stir-frying vegetables, and many of us already have our own individual (if not idiosyncratic) style. But just in case you are new to this, here is a basic method. (If you would like a more detailed description, including methods for cutting various vegetables, there is an 8-page section on sautéed vegetable dinners in the sequel to this book, The Enchanted Broccoli Forest.)

NOTE: Cook the rice or noodles first. Begin the rice at least 30 minutes before you start the stir-fry. (For 6 servings: 2½ cups raw brown rice in 3¼ cups boiling water, covered, for about 40 minutes over lowest heat.) If you are using noodles, cook them just before you start the stir-fry. Use about ¾ lb. (raw measure) vermicelli or flat egg noodles. Drain the cooked noodles, drizzle with a little sesame oil, and, if desired, keep them warm in a 200°F. oven.

Here is a sample assortment of vegetables that will feed 4 to 6 people. Remember, the amounts are approximate, and the vegetables themselves are flexible. Use whatever is in season. Harder, firmer vegetables (carrots, broccoli, etc.) take longer to cook and should go into the wok earlier. Medium-soft vegetables (mushrooms, zucchini, etc.) go in midway through the cooking. Very soft vegetables (leafy greens, etc.) go in last.

Have the sauce prepared and all the vegetables cut and at hand before beginning. The stir-fry goes quickly, and you don't want to overcook anything.

2 to 3 Tbs. peanut oil
1 medium-sized (3-inch diameter)
   onion, chopped
½ tsp. salt
a 1½-lb. bunch broccoli, cut into
   3-inch spears
1 medium (7-inch diameter) head
   cauliflower, broken or chopped
     into 1-inch florets
1 large carrot, in thin slices
4 cups coarsely chopped cabbage

½ lb. mushrooms, sliced
1 medium (7-inch) zucchini,
   quartered lengthwise and cut
     into 1-inch pieces
a few handfuls fresh spinach
1 batch Basic Stir-Fry Sauce
   (preceding page) or a
   double batch of Orange-
   Ginger Sauce (next page)

cooked rice or noodles

1) Heat a large (12-inch diameter or more) wok or a deep skillet for about 1 minute over medium heat.
2) Add oil, onion, and salt. Stir-fry for about a minute.
3) Add broccoli, cauliflower, carrot, and cabbage, and turn up the heat. Stir-fry for about 3 or 4 minutes, or until the vegetables begin to get tender.
4) Add mushrooms and zucchini. Stir-fry another 4 or 5 minutes, or until the zucchini begins to get soft. Add spinach.
5) Whisk the sauce from the bottom to reincorporate the cornstarch, and pour all of it in. Stir from the bottom of the wok or skillet, and keep the heat constantly high. Within about 3 minutes the sauce will thicken and turn all the vegetables shiny.
6) Remove from heat, spoon over rice or noodles, and serve right away.

Orange-Ginger Sauce

–No oil; nondairy.

Serve on stir-fried vegetables (see preceding pages), on vegetable-filled Crêpes (p. 143), on plain cooked rice, on fish or chicken, or on Stuffed Squash (p. 152-3).

2 Tbs. cornstarch	salt, pepper, and cayenne, to taste
1 cup orange juice	OPTIONAL ADDITIONS:
2 to 3 medium cloves garlic, minced	½ tsp. grated orange rind
1 Tbs. minced fresh ginger	1 to 2 Tbs. honey
¼ cup soy sauce	1 to 2 Tbs. dry sherry
	1 scallion, finely minced

1) Place cornstarch in a small bowl (if you're using this for stir-fried vegetables) or in a small saucepan (if you're using this for anything else).
2) Add orange juice, and whisk until the cornstarch dissolves. Stir in all remaining ingredients (including optional additions).
3) If you are using the sauce for stir-fried vegetables, stir from the bottom, and add to the wok or skillet about midway through the cooking (see detailed instructions on the previous 2 pages). If you are using this for anything else, place the saucepan over medium heat, and gradually bring to a boil, whisking constantly. Lower heat to a simmer and cook, whisking frequently, until thick and glossy (3 to 5 minutes). Serve hot or warm.

Cashew-Ginger Sauce

–Nondairy.

Use this quick & easy sauce on plain cooked rice, steamed broccoli, or baked eggplant slices. It's also a good accompaniment to curries (p. 172-5) and Stuffed Cabbage (p. 155).

2 cups toasted cashews	1 Tbs. honey or sugar (white or brown)
1 cup water	2 Tbs. plus 1 tsp. cider vinegar
2 Tbs. minced fresh ginger	½ tsp. salt
1 Tbs. soy sauce	cayenne, to taste

Purée everything together in a food processor or blender. When it is as smooth as you like it, transfer to a tightly lidded container and refrigerate. Heat gently before serving.

TOFU-BASED SAUCES

♥ ♥

In my search for ways to make sauces without oil or dairy products, I was thrilled to discover something called silken tofu. It is the smoothest edible substance imaginable — and utterly neutral in flavor. Whether it is labeled "soft", "firm", or "extra firm", silken tofu has enough body to be whipped easily into a state resembling thick mayonnaise — and to hold this form, if stored properly, for days.

Here are 4 very simple sauces, made in less than 5 minutes each. They may put egg-and-oil-based mayonnaise out of a job in your home.

NOTE: Silken tofu comes in little vacuum-packed boxes, and is sold in most natural foods stores. Because of the ingenious way in which it is packaged, it has a long shelf life before it is opened.

♥ ♥

For each of the following, use <u>1 box (10 ½ oz.) silken tofu</u>, soft or firm. Place all ingredients in a blender, and whip until smooth. Store in a tightly covered container in the refrigerator. Serve cold or at room temperature. Each is good for sandwiches, baked potatoes, steamed vegetable topping, artichoke dipping, and anywhere you would use mayonnaise.

I. <u>Plain Fake Mayo</u>

1 small clove garlic, minced
2 to 3 tsp. cider vinegar
½ tsp. salt

▸ ▸ ▸ ▸

II. <u>Faux Aioli</u>

2 to 3 medium cloves garlic, minced
½ tsp. salt
½ tsp. dry mustard
½ tsp. cider vinegar
OPTIONAL: a small handful of freshly minced chives and/or parsley.

III. <u>Greek Lemon Sauce</u>

(NOTE: In earlier editions, this was made with an egg plus an extra yolk. No more!)
1 Tbs. fresh lemon juice
½ tsp. salt
a few dashes of white pepper

◂ ◂ ◂ ◂

IV. <u>Horseradish Sauce</u>

(Formerly, this contained sour cream and egg yolks. Unnecessary!)
2 tsp. fresh lemon juice
½ tsp. salt
2 tsp. prepared horseradish
white pepper, to taste
OPTIONAL: minced chives

♥ ♥ ♥ ♥ ♥ ♥ ♥ ♥ ♥ ♥ ♥ ♥

ZIPPY CHEESE SAUCE

Preparation time: 20 minutes

Yield: 4 to 5 servings

Here is your regular old-fashioned cheese sauce, spruced up a little. Whip this up whenever you need some comfort food in a hurry. Serve it in or over omelettes, over steamed vegetables (especially cauliflower, broccoli, or asparagus), or even over whole wheat toast with some sliced apples on top. And when you feel tugs of longing and nostalgia, you can mother yourself by mixing Zippy Cheese Sauce with cooked macaroni (use 3/4 lb. raw macaroni with a batch of this sauce for 3 to 4 servings) and some extra cheese. Bake it in a casserole with bread crumbs on top at 350°F. until heated through (about 30 minutes) for 1950s-style Macaroni and Cheese.

2 Tbs. butter
2 Tbs. flour
1 Tbs. dry mustard
2 cups warm milk (lowfat OK)
1 cup (packed) grated cheese (a medium-sharp
        cheddar works well)
salt and white pepper, to taste
OPTIONAL ADDITIONS:
        1 to 2 tsp. prepared horseradish
        a few shakes Tabasco Sauce
        1 small clove garlic, minced

1) Melt the butter over low heat in a small saucepan.

2) Whisk in the flour and dry mustard; keep whisking for about a minute after it dissolves.

3) Add the milk. Cook over medium heat, whisking frequently, for about 5 minutes, or until thickened.

4) Add the cheese, and stir until it melts.

5) Season to taste with salt, white pepper, and optional hot stuff.

Rarebit

... the old-fashioned Welsh cheese sauce, spiked with beer. Serve this over toast and/or steamed broccoli or asparagus. This also works beautifully as a sauce for baked or boiled potatoes.

NOTE: The alcohol content of the beer largely dissipates with cooking.

2 Tbs. butter or margarine
2 Tbs. flour
1 tsp. dry mustard
1½ cups beer or ale, at room temperature
   (ok if flat)
1 packed cup grated cheddar (about ½ lb.)
1 tsp. prepared horseradish
1 medium clove garlic, minced
salt, black pepper, and cayenne — to taste

UNDERNEATH THE SAUCE:
toast, and/or
steamed broccoli or asparagus, and/or
baked or boiled potatoes

NEXT TO, OR ON TOP OF, THE SAUCE:
chunks of ripe tomato
slices of tart apple
chopped, toasted walnuts

1) Melt the butter or margarine in a medium-sized saucepan. Sprinkle in the flour and dry mustard, whisking constantly.
2) Add the beer or ale, and keep whisking as you bring it to a boil. Lower the heat, and simmer for about 10 minutes, mixing frequently.
3) Add the remaining ingredients, and stir until the cheese melts. Serve hot over thick slices of toast (sourdough, rye, or pumpernickel are especially good) or over steamed vegetables and/or cooked potatoes. Garnish with tomatoes or apples, and if it appeals to you, a few toasted walnuts.

Nachos Sauce

Watch this sauce turn plain beans, rice, and tortillas into a special meal. Serve with a green salad topped with Guacamole (p. 108).

TO PEEL AND SEED THE TOMATOES: Cut out the cores, and immerse the tomatoes in simmering water for a slow count of 10. Retrieve the tomatoes, peel them, and cut them open. Squeeze out and discard the seeds; chop the remaining pulp.

2 Tbs. olive oil
1½ cups chopped onion
¾ tsp. salt
1 tsp. cumin
½ tsp. coriander
¼ tsp. cayenne
1 large bell pepper, diced
3 medium-sized ripe tomatoes, peeled, seeded, and chopped (see above)
2 Tbs. flour
12 oz. beer or ale (not too bitter)(OK if flat), at room temperature
3 medium cloves garlic, minced
1 to 2 tsp. sugar, if necessary (if the beer is still too bitter in spite of your best intentions)
2 cups (packed) mild white cheese (can be reduced or omitted)
optional: freshly minced cilantro, for the top

1) Heat olive oil in a medium-sized saucepan. Add onion and salt, and sauté for 5 minutes, or until the onion is soft.
2) Add cumin, coriander, cayenne, bell pepper, and tomatoes. Cover and cook over medium heat, stirring occasionally, for about 30 minutes. The peppers should be very tender.
3) Whisk in the flour, making sure all the lumps dissolve. Stir in the beer, bring to a boil, then lower heat to a simmer. Cook gently, uncovered for about 15 minutes. Stir in the garlic; cook 5 minutes more. Taste, and add sugar, if needed.
4) Add the cheese, stirring until it melts. Serve hot over beans and rice (or cooked vegetables or whatever) with freshly steamed tortillas. Sprinkle freshly minced cilantro over the top.

MEXICAN RED SAUCE

Preparation time:
about 30 minutes
mostly for simmering

Yield: enough for
6 servings of
Enchiladas (p. 167)
and 8 servings
of Tostadas (p.168)

2 tsp. olive oil

1 cup minced onion

½ tsp. salt

1½ tsp. cumin

2 tsp. chili powder

3 cups chopped tomatoes (4 to 6 medium-sized ones) – peeling
    and seeding optional (see instructions on opposite page)

1 cup water or tomato juice

black pepper and cayenne, to taste

4 to 6 medium cloves garlic, minced

optional: freshly minced cilantro, for the top

1) Heat olive oil in a medium-sized saucepan. Add onion and salt,
and sauté over medium heat for about 5 minutes, or until the
onion is translucent. Add cumin and chili powder, and sauté
about 5 minutes more.

2) Add chopped tomatoes and water or juice. Bring to a boil,
partially cover, and lower heat. Simmer at least 30 minutes
(or even longer). Add the black pepper, cayenne, and garlic at
any time during the cooking. (The later you add the garlic, the
more distinct its presence.) Add the cilantro when you are finished cooking the sauce.

3) The sauce can be left in chunky form, or you can purée all
or part of it in a blender or food processor.

HOT SAUCE VARIATION:

Follow the recipe for Mexican Red Sauce. When you sauté the
onion, add 1 Tbs. or more crushed red pepper or 1 to 2 tsp.
finely minced serrano or jalapeño chilies. (Be very careful to
wash your hands thoroughly after handling any part of the
chilies, or even after thinking about them.)

SALSA FRESCA

Great as a dip for chips, with any bean dish, next to omelettes, with plain rice, on top of Tostadas (p. 168-9), or in partnership with Zingy Bean Dip (p. 106) or Guacamole (p. 108). If you eat chicken or fish, try serving the Pineapple or Mango Salsa alongside — they make exquisite relishes.

Pineapple Salsa 🌱

2 cups minced fresh (or canned-in-juice) pineapple
2 medium cloves garlic, minced
2 to 3 Tbs. minced fresh mint
2 Tbs. fresh lime juice
¼ tsp. salt
¼ tsp. cumin
cayenne, to taste

15 minutes to prepare (w/ fresh pineapple) OR 5 minutes (w/ canned) — Yield: 2 cups

Combine everything, cover tightly, and refrigerate. This keeps a long time.
For an exotic taste sensation, try spooning a little of this onto a bowlful of Brazilian Black Bean Soup (p. 26).

Mango Salsa 🌿

2 Tbs. finely minced red onion
2 cups boiling water
1 average-sized (about 6 inches long) ripe mango (if you're lucky enough to find one)
  — about 1½ cups minced
2 Tbs. fresh lime juice
1 medium clove garlic, minced
½ tsp. salt
2 Tbs. minced fresh cilantro
optional: cayenne, to taste

10 minutes to prepare
Yield: 1½ cups

Place the minced onion in a small strainer over a bowl. Slowly pour the boiling water over the onion, then let it sit for 5 minutes. This will soften its bite, and turn it a striking shade of purple-pink.
Combine all ingredients and mix gently. Cover tightly and refrigerate.

Tomato Salsa 🌿

3 medium-sized ripe tomatoes
2 scallions, finely minced
2 medium cloves garlic, minced
a handful of parsley, finely minced
a handful of cilantro, finely minced
1 tsp. lightly toasted cumin seeds
¾ to 1 tsp. salt
1 Tbs. cider vinegar
1 Tbs. olive oil
1 Tbs. fresh lime juice
crushed red pepper, to taste

10 minutes to prepare
Yield: 1½ to 2 cups

Drop the tomatoes into a potful of simmering water for 10 seconds. Take them out, pull off the skins, and squeeze out the seeds. Dice the remaining pulp. Combine everything in a small bowl or container. Cover tightly and chill.

NOTE: To toast the cumin seeds, use a small skillet over a low flame or a toaster oven. With either method, watch them carefully so they won't scorch.

Preparation time: 10 minutes to assemble; 30 minutes to simmer

Yield: about 2 cups

You can buy duck or plum sauce in most Asian groceries, but homemade is easy – and distinctly better. Keep this around to use as a condiment for many different things. You can mix Eastern metaphors by serving this alongside Thai Salad (p. 50) or Indonesian Rice Salad (p. 51), or with Samosas (p. 170). Duck Sauce is also good with squash casseroles (p. 140) or Stuffed Squash (p. 152).

This keeps very well for weeks if stored in a sterile airtight container in the refrigerator.

    5 cups mixed peeled, chopped fruit (apples, pears, peaches,
      and/or plums
    1 cup water
    1/4 cup cider vinegar
    1/4 cup (packed) light brown sugar
    1/4 tsp. salt
    2 to 3 medium cloves garlic, minced
    1/2 tsp. dry mustard
    optional: up to 1/2 tsp. crushed red pepper

1) Combine everything in a medium-sized saucepan and bring to a boil.

2) Turn the heat down, and simmer uncovered until all the fruit is very soft (about 30 minutes).

3) Cool thoroughly, then chill.

CHUTNEY

Serve chutney with any Indian dish (see pages 170 through 175), and with whatever else you can think of: sandwiches (see p. 117, and pages 120-21), soups, stews, and if you are not a vegetarian, with fish or chicken.

These 2 chutneys are easy to make. Just combine everything in a saucepan, bring it to a boil, and let it simmer. It's hard to go wrong. <u>Preparation time for each</u>: a few minutes to assemble, plus 45 minutes to cook. Then cool and chill. <u>Yield</u>: about 1½ cups each. Chutney keeps very well in the refrigerator if kept in a sterile, tightly lidded jar — and it goes a long way.

APPLE CHUTNEY

1½ lbs. tart apples
1 medium clove garlic, minced
1 Tbs. minced fresh ginger
1 tsp. cinnamon
1 tsp. cloves or allspice
½ tsp. salt
½ cup (packed) brown sugar
⅓ cup cider vinegar
cayenne, to taste

1) Coarsely chop the apples (peeling is optional). Place them in a medium-sized saucepan with all remaining ingredients. Bring to a boil, then lower heat to a simmer.

2) Simmer uncovered for about 45 minutes, or until everything is very soft. Cool, then transfer to a sterile jar with a lid. Chill.

TOMATO CHUTNEY

2 lbs. unripe tomatoes (about 6 medium-sized ones, the greener, the better)
2 Tbs. minced fresh ginger
1 tsp. mustard seeds
1 tsp. cumin seeds
1 tsp. coriander (optional)
¾ tsp. salt
¼ cup cider vinegar
¼ cup (packed) brown sugar
¼ cup white sugar
cayenne, to taste
2 Tbs. minced garlic

1) Dice the tomatoes, and place them in a medium-sized saucepan with all remaining ingredients, except the garlic.

2) Bring to a boil, lower the heat, and simmer uncovered for 45 minutes or until everything is well mingled and very soft. Add the garlic during the last 5 or 10 minutes of cooking. Cool, then transfer to a sterile jar with a lid, and chill.

Preparation time:
just a few minutes

RAITA

Yield: 2 cups
(serves 6)

One of the many condiments served in a traditional Indian meal, Raita is a yogurt preparation with small amounts of seasoning and a hint of minced or grated fresh vegetables. It is designed to cool and relax the palate between bites of heavier, more intensely seasoned dishes. Serve Raita with any curry (see pages 172 through 175) or with Samosas (p.170) or with Gingered Carrot Soup (p.22) or Curried Squash and Mushroom Soup (p.15). This can be put together in just minutes.

NOTE: For a deeper flavor, the cumin and optional fennel seeds can be lightly toasted first. Cook them without oil in a small, heavy skillet over medium heat, stirring frequently, for about a minute — or until they give off a toasty aroma.

2 cups yogurt

1 tsp. cumin seeds

salt and cayenne, to taste

OPTIONAL ADDITIONS (add some or all):

1 small cucumber (about 5 inches long), peeled, seeded, and minced or grated

1 small ripe tomato, diced

¼ cup finely minced onion

½ cup finely minced bell pepper (any color)

½ tsp. fennel seeds

Combine everything in a small bowl and mix gently. Cover tightly, and refrigerate until serving time.

10 minutes to prepare
(after chick peas are
cooked)

HUMMUS

A tangy and delicious chick pea purée from the Middle East, Hummus is a perfect dip or sandwich spread, and an ideal component for a Mezza (see below). Preparation is super-quick if you use a food processor.

NOTE: This recipe calls for 3 cups cooked chick peas. You can soak and cook dry ones, but canned work just as well.

2 to 3 medium cloves garlic, sliced
a large handful of parsley
2 healthy scallions, in 1-inch pieces
3 cups cooked chick peas (2 15½-oz.
   cans, rinsed and well drained)

6 Tbs. tahini
6 Tbs. fresh lemon juice
¾ to 1 tsp. salt (to taste)
optional: cayenne and a little
   cumin, to taste

1) Place garlic, parsley, and scallions in a food processor or blender, and mince.
2) Add chick peas, tahini, lemon juice, and salt, and purée to a thick paste. (You can also do the mincing and mashing by hand. The Hummus will have a coarser texture, but that can be nice, too.)
3) Season to taste, if desired, with cayenne and cumin (and correct the salt, if necessary). Transfer to a tightly lidded container and chill.

MEZZA

In Middle Eastern and some Balkan cuisines, it is common to serve a variety of appetizers, dips, salads, and garnishes on a platter (or several platters) at the beginning of a festive meal — or as the meal itself. Here is a list of the dishes in this book that could be used in any combination to make a Mezza at home for your family and friends. Don't forget to garnish lavishly — make it beautiful! Serve with Pita Bread (p. 113) and/or sesame crackers.

Garnishes: ☆ small sprigs of fresh herbs (parsley, mint, thyme, marjoram, dill, cilantro) ☆ pepperoncini ☆ Kalamata olives ☆ radishes, plus small, artful cuts of other vegetables ☆ feta cheese ☆ cherry tomatoes ☆ beautiful red pomegranate seeds sprinkled over the top of everything

Two Exotic Walnut Pâtés

Feta-Walnut Dip

10 minutes to prepare
Yield: about 6 servings

1 cup chopped walnuts
a handful of fresh parsley
1 cup crumbled feta cheese
½ cup water or milk
optional: 1 small clove of garlic

1 tsp. paprika
cayenne, to taste
a little olive oil
a little oregano (dried, or even
   better: a few fresh sprigs)

1) Place the walnuts and parsley in a blender or food processor, and blend with a series of quick spurts.

2) When the nuts are ground, add remaining ingredients except olive oil and oregano, and purée until smooth.

3) Transfer to a small serving bowl, cover tightly, and chill. Just before serving, drizzle the top with a little olive oil, and garnish with small sprigs of fresh (or a light sprinkling of dried) oregano. Serve on sesame crackers or toasted pita wedges, or as a dip for raw vegetables.

Vegetable-Walnut Pâté

30 minutes to prepare
Yield: about 6 servings

It really does taste like chopped liver.

1 Tbs. vegetable oil
½ cup minced onion
½ tsp. salt
1½ cups chopped fresh green beans
2 hardboiled eggs (yolks may
      be omitted)

¼ cup chopped walnuts
1 to 2 Tbs. white wine — or
      2 tsp. fresh lemon juice
1 to 2 Tbs. Mayonnaise (p.44)
black pepper, to taste
a handful of parsley

1) Heat oil in a small skillet. Add onion and salt, and sauté over medium heat for about 10 minutes — until the onion begins to brown. Add the green beans, and sauté until they are tender (another 8 to 10 minutes).

2) Combine everything in a blender or food processor and grind into a uniform paste. (You can also chop or mash it by hand, à la countless grandmothers.) Serve as an appetizer with crackers and raw vegetables, or as a great sandwich spread.

❋ YOGURT CHEESE ❋

Yogurt can be made into a lovely soft cheese by simply pressing out much of its water. You can use lowfat or even nonfat yogurt, and still, the resulting cheese will be thick and rich tasting.

The procedure:

1) Start with double the amount you want to end up with. So, in order to get 1 cup of yogurt cheese, use 2 cups of yogurt. Place a colander in the sink, and line it with about 6 layers of cheesecloth, cut to about 10 inches.

2) Place the yogurt in the cheesecloth, wrap the cloth around it, and secure it tightly with a clip or a bag tie.

3) Place a 2- to 3-lb. bag of beans on top, and let it sit there for at least 6 to 8 hours. The water from the yogurt will slowly drip out the bottom, and the creamy solids will remain. (NOTE: The longer it sits, weighted and dripping, the thicker the cheese will be.)

4) Remove the cheesecloth, wrap the cheese well, and refrigerate. To serve, top with a drizzle of olive oil and small amounts of freshly minced herbs (marjoram, dill, parsley, chives), or just a little salt and some freshly ground pepper. Serve as an appetizer (see Mezza, p. 100) or keep on hand for sandwiches.

  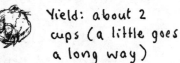

Preparation time: 20 minutes

Wicked Garlic Dip

Yield: about 2 cups (a little goes a long way)

3 medium (average fist-sized) potatoes, peeled and diced
3 medium cloves garlic, peeled
up to ⅓ cup mayonnaise (see p. 44 and p. 91)
½ tsp. salt

1) Boil the potatoes until very soft, and drain well. Transfer to a food processor fitted with the steel blade, or to a mixing bowl.

2) Without waiting for the potatoes to cool, add the remaining ingredients. Whip until very smooth, using either the food processor or an electric mixer.

3) Cover tightly and chill. Serve as an appetizer (see Mezza, p. 100) or by itself, garnished with raw vegetables, or as a spread (great on sesame crackers or toasted pita wedges).

Tahini-Lemon Sauce

10 minutes
to prepare

Yield:
1 to 2 cups

Make a batch of this on a regular basis — it's remarkably quick and easy. It can be thinned down to the consistency of a salad dressing (try it on romaine lettuce with chunks of ripe tomato and Kalamata olives) or left thick enough to be either a spread or a dip for raw vegetables and crackers. Find a consistency somewhere between thick and thin, and use it as a sauce for steamed greens, carrots, and cauliflower. Serve it with Felafel (p. 116), or drizzled over Hummus (p.100) in a pita bread (p. 113) sandwich. Tahini-Lemon Sauce is as indispensable as it is hard to categorize.   By the way, another attribute: it keeps for weeks if stored in the refrigerator in an airtight container.

NOTE: Earlier versions of this recipe contained yogurt or buttermilk. This one is dairy-free.

3/4 cup sesame tahini
5 Tbs. fresh lemon juice
1 small to medium clove garlic, minced
3/4 to 1½ cups water (depending on desired thickness)
½ to 1 tsp. salt, to taste (will vary with amount of water used)
a handful of very finely minced fresh parsley
optional: cayenne, to taste

1) Place tahini, lemon juice, and garlic in a food processor fitted with the steel blade. (You can also use a blender.) Begin to process.
2) Keeping the motor running, slowly drizzle in the water, checking every now and then to monitor the consistency. When it is as thick / thin as you want it, turn off the machine.
3) Transfer to a small bowl or container, and season to taste with salt, parsley, and, if desired, cayenne. Cover tightly and refrigerate until ready for use.

EGGPLANT DIPS

Baba Ganouj ("Ga-NOOSH")

The classic Middle Eastern eggplant appetizer, plus a few variations on the theme. The instructions call for baking the eggplant, but if you have the opportunity to grill it over hot coals or to roast it over a direct flame, the Baba Ganouj will taste even better.

40 minutes to prepare

a little oil, for the baking sheet
1 medium (7-inch) eggplant
2 medium cloves garlic, minced
¼ cup fresh lemon juice
¼ cup sesame tahini
½ tsp. salt
black pepper and cayenne, to taste
olive oil ⎫
freshly minced parsley ⎬ for the top

Yield: 4 to 6 servings

1) Preheat oven to 350°F. Lightly oil a baking sheet.
2) Slice the eggplant in half lengthwise, and place face-down on the baking sheet. Bake for 30 minutes or until very tender. Cool until it's comfortable to handle.
3) Scoop out the eggplant pulp, and discard the skin. Place the pulp in a food processor or blender, and add the garlic, lemon juice, tahini, and salt. Purée until smooth. (Another alternative is to mash by hand, leaving the eggplant a little chunky.)
4) Transfer to an attractive serving dish, cover tightly, and chill. Drizzle the top with a little olive oil and sprinkle with minced parsley just before serving. Serve with crackers. (Also, see Mezza, p. 100.)

VARIATIONS:

I. 1 Tbs. olive oil ⎫
    1 cup finely minced onion ⎪ Heat olive oil in a small skillet. Add every-
    ½ lb. mushrooms, minced ⎬ thing else and sauté 10 to 15 minutes,
    ½ tsp. salt ⎪ or until tender. Stir into puréed eggplant
    1 tsp. dill ⎭ mixture.

II. ½ cup firm yogurt or Greek Lemon Sauce (p. 91) ⎫ Add to purée;
    ½ tsp. cumin ⎬ mix well.

Spicy Eggplant Relish

Serve this as an accompaniment to any curry (p. 172-75), with Samosas (p. 170), Hummus (p. 100), Felafel (p. 116), or Tabouli (p. 46). It is also good on plain crackers or as a dip for raw vegetables.

2 Tbs. olive oil
1 cup minced onion
1 medium eggplant (7 to 8 inches long), diced
½ tsp. salt
½ tsp. cumin
1 medium-sized bell pepper, minced
1 medium clove garlic, minced
1 Tbs. lemon juice
cayenne, to taste

1) Heat olive oil in a medium-sized skillet. Add onion, eggplant, salt, and cumin, and sauté over medium heat for 15 to 20 minutes — until the eggplant is tender.

2) Add bell pepper, and sauté for about 10 minutes more.

3) Stir in garlic and lemon juice. Cook for about 5 more minutes. Add cayenne to taste, and adjust the salt, if necessary. You can leave it chunky, or mash a little bit by hand. Serve warm, at room temperature, or cold.

Zingy Bean Dip

Preparation time:
less than 10
minutes

Yield: about
2 cups

It's hard to find anything new to say in the Bean Dip Department, but this one gets a few words in.

Canned pinto beans work so well in here that I encourage you to use them. Be sure to rinse and drain them well. If you also use a food processor, this recipe will be very quick.

Serve it with chips, vegetables, crackers, or warmed flour tortillas. Pair it with any Salsa Fresca (p.96) for some serious appetizer activity.

To peel and seed a tomato: Drop it into a pan of boiling water for 10 seconds. Remove it, and peel off the skin. Cut the tomato open; squeeze out and discard the seeds. Chop the remaining pulp.

2 cups cooked pinto beans (1 15-oz. can),
    rinsed and well drained
2 Tbs. fresh lime juice
1 medium-sized tomato, peeled and seeded (see above)
1 to 2 medium cloves garlic, minced
a handful of parsley
a handful of cilantro
3/4 tsp. cumin
optional: 1 scallion, minced
1/4 to 1/2 tsp. salt
black pepper and cayenne, to taste

Whip it all up together in a food processor or a blender.

This sauce is verrrry intense! Try it as a dip for raw and/or lightly steamed vegetables, or as a dressing for cold cooked noodles (you can thin it with a little water for this). You can also use it for Eggplant and Peppers in Spicy Peanut Sauce (below), and serve it as an appetizer.

½ cup good peanut butter
½ cup water
2 Tbs. soy sauce
2 Tbs. sugar
3 medium cloves garlic, minced
1 tsp. cider vinegar
1 to 2 Tbs. minced fresh cilantro
cayenne, to taste
salt, to taste (if peanut butter is unsalted)

1) Place peanut butter in a small bowl. Add the hot water, and stir patiently with a spoon or a small whisk until uniformly mixed.
2) Stir in remaining ingredients and mix well. Cover tightly and refrigerate. Let come to room temperature before serving.

Eggplant & Peppers in Spicy Peanut Sauce

a little oil, for the baking tray
1 medium (7-inch) eggplant, unpeeled, and cut into
    inch-thick strips, then into 2-inch pieces
salt
1 large bell pepper ~ any color, cut into 1-inch pieces
1 recipe Chinese Peanut Sauce (above)

1) Preheat oven to 375°F. Lightly oil a baking tray.
2) Spread the eggplant pieces on the tray and salt lightly. Let stand 10 minutes.
3) Bake the eggplant until tender (about 15 minutes). (Prepare the sauce during this time.) During the last 5 minutes of baking, add the pepper pieces to the tray.
4) Cool the vegetables to room temperature, then transfer to a bowl or container. Add the Chinese Peanut Sauce and mix gently. Serve at room temperature or cold.

Guacamole

Preparation time:
about 10 minutes

Yield:
about 6 servings

For chips and raw vegetables
AND
For Tostadas (p. 168-9)
AND
For Sandwiches
AND
On top of Salads
AND
Wherever else you wish to invite it along

BASIC GUACAMOLE:
2 Tbs. fresh lemon or lime juice
2 medium-sized ripe avocadoes
1 to 2 medium cloves garlic, minced
½ tsp. salt (possibly more, to taste)

OPTIONAL AUGMENTATIONS:
½ tsp. cumin (possibly more, to taste)
½ tsp. chili powder
black pepper and cayenne, to taste
tiny amounts of: minced green or red bell pepper
            peeled, seeded, and finely minced cucumber
            diced ripe tomato
2 to 3 Tbs. mayonnaise (see p. 44 and p. 91)

1) Place the lemon or lime juice in a medium-sized shallow bowl.

2) Add the avocado (you can just cut it open and spoon it out of its skin), and mash with a fork to whatever consistency you like.

3) Stir in remaining ingredients. Cover tightly and chill. NOTE: To help the Guacamole retain its color, add the avocado pits. Remove them just before serving.

A FEW BAKED THINGS
AND
SANDWICHES

   Without expanding into a comprehensive thesis on bread baking (which can be found in the sequel to this book, <u>The Enchanted Broccoli Forest</u>), this chapter presents just a few choice recipes for simple breads. The popovers, corn breads, and flatbreads are all quick and unyeasted. Focaccia and Pita Bread are yeasted, but still quite easy and very rewarding.

   Except for Felafel, the sandwich fillings that follow the breads are more suggestions than actual recipes. Perhaps you just need a few ideas for fitting a decent little hand-held meal into the middle of your day — and perhaps these will help.

TABLE OF CONTENTS: BAKED THINGS AND SANDWICHES

CUSTARDY POPOVERS

Crisp and puffy, full of hot air and a layer of custard on the inside, Popovers are very easy to throw together on a moment's notice, and they can lend a festive spirit to even a simple bowl of soup. The custard quotient depends on how many eggs you use. This recipe is very flexible, and will work with 2, 3, or 4 eggs.

2 to 3 Tbs. melted butter or margarine, for the pan
2, 3, or 4 large eggs
1¼ cups milk (lowfat OK)
1¼ cups flour
½ tsp. salt

1) Preheat oven to 375°F. Brush the insides of 12 muffin cups with melted butter or margarine.
2) Beat together the eggs and milk in a medium-sized bowl. Add the flour and salt, and beat with a whisk until reasonably well blended. It's fine if the batter has a few lumps.
3) Fill each muffin cup about ½ to ⅔ full. Bake 25 minutes if using 2 eggs, 30 minutes for 3 eggs, and 35 minutes for 4 eggs. Try to refrain from opening the oven during baking.
4) Remove the popovers from the pan immediately, and prick each with a fork to let the steam escape. (This helps them hold their shape.) Serve as soon as possible, either plain or with butter and/or jam.

FOCACCIA

Preparation time:
about 2 hours
(mostly rising time)

Yield:
4 to 6
servings

~an easy olive oil- and- rosemary-flavored pizza bread. Great with soups, salads, pasta dishes, or chili.

> 1 cup wrist-temperature water
> 1½ tsp. (half a ¼-oz. packet) active dry yeast
> 1 tsp. sugar
> 1 tsp. salt
> approximately 3½ cups flour
> 2 to 3 Tbs. dried rosemary
> olive oil, for the bowl, dough, and baking tray
> extra flour, for handling the dough

1) Follow steps 1, 2, and 3 in the directions for Pita Bread (opposite), adding rosemary with the flour, and using olive oil to oil the dough and the bowl.

2) Punch down the dough, and transfer to a clean floured surface. Adding small amounts of extra flour as needed, to avoid stickiness, knead the dough for about 5 to 8 minutes—until it is smooth and elastic. Form the dough into a ball, and roll it into a 10- to 12-inch diameter circle. Let it rest for about 10 minutes. Meanwhile, preheat the oven to 400°F. Lightly oil a baking tray.

3) Transfer the circle of dough to the baking tray, and brush the top surface of the dough with a little more olive oil. Bake for 20 to 30 minutes, or until lightly browned. (Take it out sooner if you like it softer; later if you like it crisper.) Serve hot, warm, or at room temperature.

Pita Bread
(Arabic Pocket Bread)

Preparation time:
about 2 hours
(most of which
is rising time)

Yield: 6 larger
(or 12 smaller)
pocket breads

1 cup wrist-temperature water
1½ tsp. (half a ¼-oz. packet) active dry yeast
1 Tbs. sugar or honey
1 tsp. salt
about 3½ cups flour (1 cup of it can be whole wheat)
OPTIONAL: 1 Tbs. sesome seeds
a little oil for the dough
extra flour for rolling out
oil or cornmeal, for the baking tray

1) Place the water in a medium-sized bowl and sprinkle in the yeast. Let stand for 5 minutes — it will become foamy.

2) Add sugar or honey and salt. Stir until everything dissolves.

3) Add 3 cups of flour, one cup-at a time, mixing enthusiastically with a whisk. As the dough thickens, switch to a wooden spoon and, eventually, your hand. Knead the dough in the bowl for a few minutes, adding up to ½ cup more flour, as needed, to combat stickiness. When the dough is smooth, oil both the bowl and the top surface of the dough. Cover with a clean tea towel, and let rise in a warm place for about an hour, or until the dough has doubled in bulk.

4) Punch down the dough and transfer it to a clean, floured surface. Knead it for about 5 minutes, then divide it into either 6 or 12 equal pieces (depending on what size pitas you want). Knead each little unit for a few minutes, then use a rolling pin to flatten it into a very thin circle. (Make sure there is plenty of flour underneath!) The diameter of each circle is unimportant, as long as it is no thicker than ⅛ inch. Let the circles rest for 30 minutes.

5) Preheat oven to 500°F. Place a baking tray in the oven for a minute or two, to heat it. Then brush it with oil — or dust it with cornmeal. Place as many circles on the tray as will fit without touching, and bake for just 6 to 8 minutes, or until puffed up and very lightly browned.

6) Remove from the oven, and wrap the breads in a clean, slightly damp tea towel, then place in a brown paper bag, closed up, for 15 minutes. This will keep the breads supple. (If you'd prefer the pita bread to be crisp and cracker-like, bake 10 to 12 minutes and simply cool on a rack.)

Basic Corn Bread
plus two tasty variations

10 minutes to assemble;
20 minutes to bake

Yield:
1 8-inch square
panful

butter or margarine, for the pan
1 cup cornmeal
1 cup flour
2 tsp. baking powder
½ tsp. baking soda
½ tsp. salt
1 cup buttermilk or yogurt
1 egg
3 Tbs. sugar or honey
3 Tbs. melted butter or margarine

1) Preheat oven to 350°F. Grease an 8-inch square pan (or a 9- or 10-inch cast-iron skillet) with butter or margarine.
2) Combine the dry ingredients in a medium-sized bowl. Combine the wet ingredients (including sugar or honey) separately. Stir the wet mixture into the dry, mixing just enough to thoroughly combine. Spread into the prepared pan.
3) Bake for 20 minutes, or until the center is firm to the touch. Serve hot, warm, or at room temperature.

MEXICAN CORN & CHEESE BREAD

Make the batter as described above, with the following additions:
1 cup fresh or frozen/defrosted corn
½ cup (packed) grated mild white cheese } Stir into the
3 to 4 scallions, minced } batter.
OPTIONAL: replace the melted butter with olive oil

BLUEBERRY CORN BREAD

Make the batter as described above, increasing the sugar or honey to 1¼ cup. Add 1½ cups fresh blueberries, stirring them gently into the batter. (NOTE: You can also use frozen unsweetened blueberries. Defrost and drain before using.)

FLATBREADS:
FLOUR TORTILLAS, CHAPPATIS, & CHINESE GREEN ONION PANCAKES

Here are three variations on the theme of Flatbread — one Mexican, one Indian, and one Chinese. They are all basically the same — quick and easy, yet somehow exotic beyond the sum of their few simple ingredients.

FLOUR TORTILLAS
Serve with soups, salads, bean dishes, or rice.

1 cup flour   ½ cup water   a little oil, for cooking
½ tsp. salt   extra flour, for handling the dough

1) Place the flour and salt in a medium-sized bowl. Add the water, and stir until fairly well combined.

2) Transfer the dough to a clean, floured surface, and knead for a minute or two, adding extra flour, if necessary, to keep it from becoming sticky. Divide the dough into 6 equal balls, and roll each one into a very thin circle — no thicker than ⅛ inch. Use lots of flour, both on the rolling surface and the rolling pin.

3) You can either bake or pan-fry the tortillas. To bake, preheat the oven to 325°F. Place the tortillas on a lightly oiled tray, brush their top surfaces with a little more oil, and bake for 10 to 15 minutes, or until very lightly browned. (Bake them longer if you like them crisper, shorter if you like them softer.) To pan-fry, heat a heavy skillet or a griddle for a few minutes. Add a small amount of oil, and cook the tortillas for 3 to 5 minutes on each side. (Just as with baking, cooking them longer makes them crisper.)

4) Remove the tortillas from the oven, and serve hot or warm. If you need to reheat them, wrap tightly in foil, and place in a 300°F. oven for 10 to 15 minutes.

CHAPPATIS
Serve with any soup or with curries (p. 172-75).

Make Flour Tortillas as described above, but substitute ½ cup whole wheat flour for ½ cup of the white flour.

CHINESE GREEN ONION PANCAKES
Serve with any soup, with Tofu Salad (p. 56), or with Duck Sauce (p. 97) or Stir-Fry Sauce (p. 88) for an appetizer or snack.

Make Flour Tortillas as described above, adding to the flour mixture: 3 medium-sized scallions, very finely minced. After the pancakes are cooked, sprinkle on a little extra salt.

Felafel

Felafel are small, spicy chick pea patties. They are almost always topped with Tahini-Lemon Sauce (p. 103), and served either in a sandwich with Pita Bread (p. 113), or as an appetizer, either alone, or on a Mezza (p. 100). Traditionally, Felafel are deep-fried, but they are equally good — and satisfyingly crisp — if pan-fried in a very hot skillet with a small amount of oil.

4 cups cooked chick peas (OK to use canned. Two 15-oz. cans will provide the right amount.)

4 medium cloves garlic, minced	¼ cup (packed) minced parsley
2 tsp. cumin	¼ cup water
1 tsp. turmeric	1 Tbs. lemon juice
1 tsp. salt	a few dashes of cayenne
½ cup finely minced onion, or 6 scallions, minced	⅓ cup flour
	oil for frying

1) Rinse the chick peas, and drain them well.

2) Combine all ingredients except flour in a food processor or a medium-sized bowl and process — or mash — until you have a uniform batter.

3) Add flour, and stir until thoroughly combined. You can cook the Felafel right away, or store the batter in a tightly covered container in the refrigerator for several days.

4) Heat a heavy skillet and add about 3 Tbs. oil. When it is hot enough to sizzle a bread crumb on contact, drop tablespoonfuls of batter into the pan, flattening each slightly, like a small, thick pancake. Sauté for about 10 minutes on each side, until golden and crisp. Add small amounts of extra oil to the pan as needed throughout the cooking.

5) Place the cooked Felafel on a plate lined with paper towels, and, if necessary, keep warm in a 300°F. oven until serving time.

Celebratory Sandwich Fillings

If you pack a lunch for yourself or for members of your family, and you need some inspiration to get away from cheese, egg salad, and peanut butter and jelly, try some of these sandwich filling ideas. Remember that most of them keep for at least several days (and some for longer), so make a few fillings on a weekend, and you'll have inspiration and variety to get you through the week.

1) <u>Eggplant Dips</u> (p. 104 and 105) go perfectly in Pita Bread (p. 113) or on whole wheat bread.

2) <u>Walnut Pâtés</u> (p. 101) make a substantial sandwich with lettuce and tomato on sourdough or whole wheat bread.

3) Keep <u>Yogurt Cheese</u> (p. 102) on hand. It lasts a long time! You can use it wherever you would cream cheese. Some suggestions: ☆ with toasted cashews and minced candied ginger ☆ with minced fresh herbs (small amounts of parsley, chives, dill, marjoram, thyme, cilantro ~ in any combination) and a few slices of cucumber ☆ with pitted, chopped olives (your favorite kind), minced walnuts, and parsley

4) <u>Tahini-Lemon Sauce</u> (p. 103) – Make it thick; spread it on rye or pumpernickel, with tomato, red onion, cucumber, and possibly some minced bell pepper.

5) <u>Zingy Bean Dip</u> (p. 106) and <u>Hummus</u> (p. 100) make great sandwich fillings on any kind of bread (especially pita). Be sure to include a bag of tortilla chips with this lunch!

6) <u>Guacamole</u> (p. 108) can be a spread as well as a dip. It has a shorter shelf life than all of the above-suggested fillings, so make it no farther in advance than the day before.

7) Instead of peanut butter, try almond or cashew butter, just for variety. Instead of jam or jelly, try actual fresh fruit. The best: slices of tart apple, perfectly ripe peach, or banana. Try inserting some seedless grapes into your nut butter. You may forget you put them there, and at lunchtime you'll get a pleasant surprise.

BLUE CHEESE HEAVEN:
Two Simply Divine Blue Cheese Sandwiches

The ingredient amounts are open-ended in these two sandwich ideas, making them as much suggestions as recipes. This is for flexibility's sake, allowing you to accommodate the number of guests, plus your own tastes and refrigerator contents. ♩Note of encouragement: It's hard to go wrong.

I. SAUTÉED VEGETABLES WITH BLUE CHEESE ON TOAST:

minced garlic
sliced red onion
grated carrot
finely shredded cabbage
grated beets
OPTIONAL: minced broccoli
             minced bell pepper
             sliced mushrooms
a little oil
salt, pepper, and dill —to taste
crumbled blue cheese

Sauté the vegetables in a small amount of oil for about 8 to 10 minutes, or until tender.
Season to taste with salt, pepper, and dill. Stir the crumbled cheese into the hot vegetables.

Take some modest slices of whole wheat, rye, or pumpernickel bread, toast them lightly, and spread them with your choice of: mayonnaise (p.44), Horseradish Sauce (p.91), thick yogurt (or Yogurt Cheese—p.102), or mustard. Spoon the vegetable-cheese filling onto the bread, and serve it open-faced or closed.

II. OPEN-FACED BLUE CHEESE SANDWICH WITH PEARS:

softened cream cheese
cottage cheese
ricotta cheese

Use any of these, or a combination. Lowfat varieties work well.

crumbled blue cheese
finely minced toasted walnuts
whole wheat bread, lightly toasted
slices of fresh pear, sprinkled lightly
     with lemon juice or raspberry vinegar

1) Combine the cheeses and the walnuts. Mix well, and spread onto whole wheat toast.
2) Arrange slices of pear on top, and serve.

✿ Salad ✿
✿ Sandwiches ✿

Sometimes that leftover salad — not quite enough to serve again for lunch or even as a side dish for dinner — is really a sandwich filling waiting to happen. Just pile it onto some fresh or toasted bread, close it up, and lunch is ready.

Here are some good candidates for a salad sandwich:

- Warm Salad (p. 40) - Maybe it's room temperature or even cold by now, and it will go beautifully on thick slices of bread or toast.
- March Hare Salad (p. 49)
- Tofu Salad (p. 56) in Pita Bread (p. 113)
- Alsatian Salad (p. 57) — also perfect for Pita
- Marinated Vegetables (p. 63) — on toast, open-faced
- Various Antipasti: Bell Peppers (p. 65), Swiss Chard (p. 66), or Marinated Mushrooms (p. 67) — on toast, open-faced
- Odessa Beets (p. 68) - on rye or pumpernickel, with or without cream cheese

To construct a TOSSED SALAD SANDWICH:
 (seems obvious, but maybe you need permission to leave out the sliced meat or cheese)

- slices of great bread
- spread of choice (mayonnaise - p. 44; any dip - p. 100-108)
- clean, crisp fresh leafy greens (lettuces, spinach, arugula, herbs)
- sliced cucumber
- sliced tomato
- sliced mushrooms
- sliced red onion
- grated carrot
- slices of avocado
- salt and pepper

Broiled and Grilled Sandwiches

Here are some ideas for broiled or grilled sandwiches that can be served for lunch or dinner. You can adjust the amounts and proportions according to your taste, your guests, and what you have on hand. With the exception of Ideas for Cheese, these sandwiches are dairy-free.

IDEAS FOR CHEESE:

☆ Tomato Chutney (p.98) spread on rye, pumpernickel, or whole wheat toast. Place some cheese on top and broil.

☆ Coleslaw (p.72) and/or apple slices on rye, pumpernickel, or whole wheat, with cheese broiled on top.

☆ Chinese Mustard (see below) and/or Horseradish Sauce (p.91) with slices of tomato and Swiss cheese on any kind of bread. Leave open-faced and broil -OR- close up the sandwich and grill on a lightly oiled skillet.

GRILLED PEPPER, ONION, CHINESE MUSTARD & TOFU SANDWICH:

For 4 servings:

a little oil for sautéing
1 small red onion, thinly sliced
1 small bell pepper, in thin strips
salt and pepper, to taste
8 slices whole wheat bread
Chinese Mustard (recipe opposite)
1 cake firm tofu, thinly sliced
a little oil for grilling

CHINESE MUSTARD

2 Tbs. Dijon mustard
2 tsp. Chinese sesame oil
1 tsp. cider vinegar
1 tsp. honey or sugar
optional: a little bit of
  freshly minced cilantro

} Combine

1) Heat a little oil in a small skillet. Add the onion and bell pepper, sprinkle lightly with salt and pepper, and sauté over medium heat until the vegetables are tender (8 to 10 minutes).

2) Lightly toast the bread, and spread each slice with Chinese Mustard. Arrange the sautéed vegetables and slices of tofu on 4 of the slices, and place the remaining mustard-spread bread on top.

3) Grill on a lightly oiled skillet on each side until crisp and brown and heated through. Serve hot.

BROCCOLI & FRIENDS:

For 4 servings:

1 tsp. oil
1 cup thinly sliced onion
3 cups chopped broccoli
salt and pepper, to taste
6 to 8 slices of your favorite bread
Greek Lemon Sauce (p. 91)
freshly minced parsley

1) Heat the oil in a small skillet. Add the onion and broccoli, salt lightly, and sauté over medium heat until tender (8 to 10 minutes). Sprinkle generously with black pepper.

2) Toast the bread, and spread it with a little Greek Lemon Sauce. Spoon on some sautéed broccoli, and top with more sauce.

3) Broil for just a few minutes — until bubbly. Garnish with minced parsley, and serve.

BROILED EGGPLANT WITH FAUX AIOLI AND TOMATOES:

For 4 servings:

a little olive oil for the baking tray
1 small eggplant (about 6 inches long), sliced into ¼-inch-thick rounds
6 to 8 slices (depending on their size and shape) sourdough bread
    (or Italian bread)
Faux Aioli (p. 91)
a medium-sized ripe tomato (or 2), sliced
salt and pepper
freshly minced parsley

1) Heat the broiler. Lightly oil a baking tray, and add the eggplant slices. Broil about 10 minutes, or until tender. Remove the tray, but leave the broiler on.

2) Toast the bread, and spread it with Faux Aioli. Add some tomato slices. Layer the broiled eggplant on top, and add salt and pepper. Spoon a little extra Aioli on top, and return to the broiler for just a minute or two — until the sauce is bubbly. Garnish with parsley and serve hot.

Pepper & Onion Shortcake

~ Sautéed peppers and onions in a lightly seasoned yogurt sauce
over warm corn bread

Make a batch of Corn Bread (p. 114) ahead of time. You can warm
it in a 300°F. oven while preparing the topping, or toast corn bread
chunks or slices just before serving. This makes a perfect lunch on
a chilly day, especially when served with Spicy Tomato Soup (p. 4).

1 batch Corn Bread (p. 114)
2 Tbs. olive oil, butter, or margarine
2 cups thinly sliced onion
½ tsp. salt
3 medium-sized bell peppers (any color), in thin strips
½ tsp. cumin (optional)
black pepper } to taste
cayenne
3 medium cloves garlic, minced
½ cup yogurt (OPTIONAL: add 1 to 2 Tbs. sour cream)
   — at room temperature
freshly minced dill, if available
paprika

1) Heat oil (or melt butter or margarine) in a medium-large skillet.
2) Add onion and salt, and sauté over medium-low heat for 10 to 15
minutes, or until the onion is very soft and beginning to brown.
3) Add bell peppers, cumin, black pepper, and cayenne, and continue to
sauté until the peppers are tender (about 10 more minutes).
4) Add garlic, and cook just a minute or 2 more. Remove from heat
and stir in yogurt (and optional touch of sour cream).
5) Serve immediately, spooned over split chunks of warmed or toasted
corn bread and garnished with dill and paprika.

ENTRÉES

In this chapter you will find recipes for casseroles, chili, crêpes, stuffed vegetables, vegetable pies, strudels, Mexican dishes, Italian dishes, curries, stews, and more. (Pasta dishes and a stir-fry method can be found in the Sauce chapter, which begins on p. 73.) Most of the old standards from the original edition are still here, lightened up a bit in the butter, oil, cheese, and egg departments. In fact, of approximately 60 entrée recipes, only 15 now contain any eggs at all, and of these, many are egg- or yolk-optional. Where dairy products are used, lowfat alternatives are given, so you can trim these recipes even further.

TABLE OF CONTENTS : ENTRÉES

ᘓᘓᘓ Macaroni & Cheese Lite ᘔᘔᘔ

This is an adaptation of "Whole Wheat Macaroni ~ Russian-Style," which appeared in earlier editions. In this new version, there are more vegetables, the seasoning is intensified, and the sour cream has been replaced by lighter, zippier buttermilk. You can improvise further by increasing or varying the vegetables. Try modest amounts of chopped cauliflower, broccoli, and/or carrots (always colorful).

½ lb. (approximately 3 cups) dry pasta ~ a short, substantial shape, like fusilli, penne, macaroni, 1-inch shells, etc.

2 Tbs. butter or margarine

2 cups chopped onion

2 medium cloves garlic, minced

½ lb. mushrooms, sliced

4 cups shredded cabbage (about ½ an average head)

1 tsp. salt

1 tsp. caraway seeds

1 bunch fresh spinach ~ stemmed and coarsely chopped

1 lb. (2 cups) cottage cheese (can be lowfat)

½ cup buttermilk or yogurt

2 Tbs. fresh (or 2 tsp. dried) dill, finely minced

fresh black pepper, to taste

2 cups (packed) grated cheddar

a handful of sunflower seeds (optional)

1) Preheat oven to 350°F. Lightly grease a 9 x 13-inch baking pan.

2) Cook the pasta until just barely tender. Drain thoroughly, and transfer to a large bowl.

3) Melt the butter in a large, deep skillet, and add the onions. After sautéing for about 5 minutes, add garlic, mushrooms, cabbage, salt, and caraway. Stir, cover, and cook until the cabbage is just tender (10 minutes). Stir in spinach, and remove from heat. Add to the pasta.

4) Stir in cottage cheese, buttermilk, dill, black pepper, and half the cheddar. Taste to adjust seasonings, and spread into the prepared pan. Sprinkle with the remaining cheddar and a few sunflower seeds, and bake uncovered for 20 to 30 minutes, or until heated through.

Broccoli Mushroom Noodle Casserole

30 minutes to prepare; 45 minutes to bake.

Yield: about 6 servings

1 1-lb. (or 12-oz.) package wide flat egg noodles
2 Tbs. butter or margarine
2 cups chopped onion
3 medium cloves garlic, minced
1 large bunch fresh broccoli, chopped
1 lb. mushrooms, sliced or chopped
½ tsp. salt (more, to taste)
lots of fresh black pepper
optional: ¼ cup dry white wine
optional: 3 eggs, beaten
3 cups (1½ lbs.) cottage cheese (may be lowfat)
1 cup sour cream (may be lowfat) or buttermilk
1½ cups fine bread crumbs and/or wheat germ
optional: 1 cup (packed) grated medium or sharp cheddar

1) Preheat oven to 350°F. Butter or oil a 9 x 13-inch baking pan.

2) Cook the noodles in plenty of boiling water until about half-done. Drain and rinse under cold water. Drain again and set aside.

3) Melt the butter or margarine in a large skillet, and add onions and garlic. Sauté for about 5 minutes over medium heat, then add broccoli, mushrooms, salt, and pepper. Continue to cook, stirring frequently, until the broccoli is bright green and just tender. Remove from heat and possibly add optional white wine.

4) In a large bowl, beat together optional eggs (or not) with cottage cheese and sour cream or buttermilk. Add noodles, sautéed vegetables, and 1 cup of the bread crumbs. Mix well.

5) Spread into the prepared pan, and top with remaining bread crumbs and, if desired, grated cheese. Bake covered for 30 minutes; uncovered for 15 minutes more.

noodle kugel

About 1 hour to prepare

Yield: about 8 servings

You can make this recipe richer or lighter. Options for both persuasions are listed below.

1 1-lb. (or 12-oz.) package wide egg noodles
2 to 3 Tbs. butter or margarine (optional)
3 eggs (yolks can be omitted)
2 cups (1 lb.) cottage cheese (lowfat OK)
¾ cup sour cream or yogurt
8 oz. cream cheese (lowfat OK) - optional
1 tsp. vanilla extract
1 to 2 tsp. cinnamon
¼ to ½ cup sugar (to taste)
½ to 1 tsp. salt (to taste)
OPTIONAL ADDITIONS: 1 to 2 Tbs. lemon juice (to taste)
                     ½ cup (packed) raisins
                     1 tart apple, peeled and sliced
                     2 ripe peaches, peeled and sliced
TOPPING (ALSO OPTIONAL): 1 cup bread crumbs and/or wheat germ
                          1½ tsp. cinnamon
                          ¼ cup (packed) brown sugar

1) Preheat oven to 375°F. Lightly grease a 9 x 13-inch baking pan.

2) Cook the noodles until about half-done. Drain, and toss with butter or margarine (or simply rinse in cold water and drain again). Transfer to a large bowl.

3) Combine eggs, cottage cheese, sour cream or yogurt, cream cheese, cinnamon, sugar, and salt in a blender or food processor and whip until smooth. (Do this in several batches, if necessary.) Stir this into the noodles, along with whatever optional additions you choose. Transfer to the baking pan.

4) Combine the topping ingredients and sprinkle them over the top. Bake uncovered for about 40 minutes. Serve hot, warm, or at room temperature.

Cauliflower Marranca

1 hour to prepare,
including baking.
(Sauté vegetables
while millet cooks.)

Yield:
4 to 6
servings

~a simple cauliflower-mushroom-millet casserole~

oil for the pan
1½ cups raw millet
2½ cups water
1 Tbs. butter or oil
2 cups chopped onion
1 lb. mushrooms, sliced
black pepper, to taste

1½ tsp. salt
1 tsp. basil
1 large cauliflower, in 1-inch pieces (or smaller)
3 medium cloves garlic, minced
2 to 3 Tbs. lemon juice
OPTIONAL: 1 to 2 cups grated cheese (your choice)
paprika, for the top

PRELIMINARY: Preheat oven to 350°F. Oil a 9×13-inch pan.

1) Place the millet and water in a small saucepan. Bring to a boil, cover, and simmer until tender (15 to 20 minutes). Transfer to a large bowl, and fluff with a fork to let steam escape.

2) Melt butter or heat oil in a large skillet. Add onion, mushrooms, pepper, salt, and basil, and sauté about 5 minutes - until the onions soften. Add cauliflower and garlic, and sauté about 10 minutes more - until the cauliflower is tender. Add lemon juice.

3) Stir the sautéed vegetables into the millet, along with the optional cheese, and mix well. Spread into the prepared pan, dust with paprika, and bake for 30 minutes.

Mushroom Moussaka

This is a meatless and eggless version of the famous Greek eggplant casserole, with two deceptively rich-tasting sauces. One is tomato-based and loaded with mushrooms; the other is a traditional Béchamel.

The mushroom sauce can be prepared well ahead of time. You can make the Béchamel while the eggplant slices bake, then assemble the casserole, using the same hot oven for the final baking.

3 medium eggplants (about 7 inches long), peeled or not, depending
      on your preference and the condition of the eggplants
salt

Mushroom-Tomato Sauce

2 Tbs. olive oil
2 cups chopped onion
1 ¼ tsp. salt
1 ½ lbs. (or even 2 lbs.) mushrooms, coarsely chopped
5 medium cloves garlic, sliced or minced
1 14½-oz. can tomatoes, including all the liquid
1 6-oz. can tomato paste
1 tsp. cinnamon
lots of black pepper
1 tsp. each: oregano and basil
1 packed cup freshly minced parsley
½ cup fine bread crumbs, plus extra for the top
½ cup grated parmesan cheese

Béchamel Sauce

3 Tbs. butter or margarine
6 Tbs. flour
2 ½ cups hot milk (lowfat works fine!)
½ cup grated parmesan cheese, plus extra for the top
nutmeg

1) Slice the eggplants into quarter-inch-thick rounds. Salt the slices lightly on both sides, then layer them gently in a colander, and place over a sink or bowl. Let stand for 20 to 30 minutes. This will allow them to sweat out their bitter juices. (Meanwhile, you can work on the mushroom sauce.)

2) Lightly oil a baking sheet, and preheat oven to 375°F. Retrieve the eggplant slices from their spa, and pat them dry with a clean towel. Spread the slices on the tray (it's ok if they pile up a little) and bake until tender (20 to 25 minutes). Meanwhile, prepare the Béchamel sauce.

. . . . .

MUSHROOM-TOMATO SAUCE:

1) Heat the olive oil in a large, deep skillet or a Dutch oven. Add onions and salt, and cook over medium heat, stirring, for 8 to 10 minutes, or until the onions become translucent. Add mushrooms and garlic, stir, and cover. Cook over medium heat another 8 to 10 minutes.

2) Add tomatoes, tomato paste, cinnamon, pepper, oregano, and basil. (Use a spoon or a dinner knife to break the tomatoes into bite-sized pieces.) Bring to a boil, then lower heat, and simmer, uncovered, another 12 to 15 minutes. Remove from heat, and stir in parsley, bread crumbs, and parmesan. Set aside.

. . . . .

BÉCHAMEL SAUCE:

1) In a medium-sized saucepan, melt the butter or margarine over low heat. Whisk in 4 Tbs. of the flour, keeping up a steady motion with the whisk even after the flour is added. Cook for several minutes, whisking still.

2) Slowly pour in the hot milk, whisking even yet. Cook and stir over low heat another 5 to 8 minutes, or until the sauce is very smooth and thickened slightly. Sift in the remaining 2 Tbs. flour, whisking yet some more, to prevent lumps. After another 5 to 8 minutes of cooking with occasional stirring, add the parmesan and a few shakes of nutmeg. Remove from heat. The sauce should be smooth and quite thick.

. . . . .

ASSEMBLY: Preheat oven to 375°F. Oil a very large casserole or a deep oblong baking pan with dimensions of at least 9 x 13 inches. Place a double layer of eggplant on the bottom, and add the entire batch of mushroom sauce. Lay the remaining eggplant slices over the mushroom sauce, and spread the Béchamel over the top. Dust lightly with fine bread crumbs and a small handful or two of parmesan. Bake uncovered for 35 to 40 minutes, or until bubbly on the bottom and ever so lightly browned on top. Serve hot.

Lasagne

Preparation time:
1½ hours

Yield:
6 to 8 servings

Have ready:
1) 1 batch Italian Tomato Sauce ~ any variation (p. 80)
2) 12 lasagne noodles, half-cooked or even uncooked (it will work!)
3) 1½ to 2 cups ricotta or cottage cheese (lowfat OK)
4) 1 lb. grated or thinly sliced mozzarella cheese
5) at least ½ cup grated parmesan, romano, or asiago cheese
6) a 9 x 13-inch pan

Proceedings:
1) Preheat oven to 375°F.
2) Spread a little sauce over the bottom of the pan.
3) Cover with a single layer of noodles (⅓ of them. Break as necessary, to fit.)
4) Place mounds of ricotta/cottage cheese here and there. Use half.
5) Add ⅓ the sauce, followed by
6) ½ the mozzarella, randomly scattered, then
7) another ⅓ the noodles, and
8) the remaining ricotta (cottage), followed by
9) another ⅓ the sauce, which gets covered by
10) the remaining mozzarella.
11) Add every last noodle, and
12) the final sauce.
13) Sprinkle the parmesan (romano/asiago) over the top.

Bake for 45 minutes. Cover loosely with foil toward the end of the baking, if it is getting too brown. Let stand 10 minutes before serving.

Eggplant Parmesan

1¼ hours to prepare (most of which is baking time). This assumes the tomato sauce is already made.

Yield:
at least
8 servings

Eggplant is highly absorbent, and when fried, it soaks up oil like a sponge. Because it is usually fried for Eggplant Parmesan, this dish ends up being much heavier than it needs to be. Here is a way to prepare crispy eggplant without frying ~ I suppose you could call it the shake-and-bake method. It is easier and much neater than frying, in addition to being lighter and better for you ~ and all those things you are possibly tired of hearing about. But people seem not to get tired of things tasting good, and this does taste really good.

2 medium eggplants (about 7 inches long)
¾ cup milk (more, as needed)
2 cups fine bread crumbs or wheat germ (or a combination)
1 tsp. basil
½ tsp. each: oregano and thyme
1 batch Italian Tomato Sauce (p.80)
1 lb. mozzarella cheese, thinly sliced or grated
parmesan cheese ~ about ½ cup (amount = flexible)

1) Preheat oven to 375°F. Lightly oil a baking tray and a 9 x 13-inch pan.

2) Cut the eggplants into ⊚'s ½ inch thick. Place the milk in a shallow bowl; combine bread crumbs (wheat germ) with herbs on a plate. Dip each eggplant slice in the milk, moistening both sides, then coat it thoroughly with the crumb mixture. Spread the prepared slices on the baking tray and the pan, and bake until tender (about 20 to 30 minutes). Remove from oven, and pile them gently on the baking tray.

3) Without cleaning the 9 x 13-inch pan, ladle some tomato sauce into the bottom. Add a layer of eggplant slices, and cover with more sauce. Arrange some mozzarella over the sauce, then repeat the layering until you run out of something or you run out of room, whichever comes first. Generously sprinkle the top with parmesan.

4) Bake uncovered at 375°F. for about 40 minutes, or until heated through and bubbly around the edges. Remove from oven and let sit about 10 minutes before serving. Serve hot or warm.

Tart & Tangy Baked Beans

Preparation time:
Presoaked beans need
up to 1½ hours to cook.
Get everything else
ready during
this time.

Yield:
6 to 8
Servings

A version of this recipe appeared in earlier editions as "Cheese-Beans." This one is more deeply seasoned, but basically the same. Cheese is optional.

Serve this with rice, corn bread (p. 114), or warmed tortillas (p. 115).

NOTE: The beans need to soak for at least 4 hours ahead of time.

3 cups dry pinto beans, soaked
4 cups chopped onions
2 Tbs. olive oil
1½ to 2 tsp. salt
1 Tbs. chili powder
2 tsp. cumin
1½ tsp. dry mustard
6 to 8 medium cloves garlic, minced
6 Tbs. dry white wine (optional)

6 to 8 Tbs. cider vinegar (to taste)
3 to 4 Tbs. molasses (to taste)
2 cups grated mild cheese (optional)
lots of black pepper
crushed red pepper, to taste
3 medium-sized tart apples, cut
   into medium-sized chunks
4 medium-sized ripe tomatoes,
   chopped

1) Place the presoaked beans in a kettle and cover them with plenty of water. Bring to a boil, lower to a simmer, partially cover, and cook slowly until tender (1¼ to 1½ hours), checking the water level during cooking. Drain off any excess when the beans are done. (This can be saved for soup stock.)

2) Begin cooking the onions in olive oil in a medium-sized skillet. Add salt, chili powder, cumin, and mustard, and sauté over medium heat for about 8 to 10 minutes. Add garlic, and sauté for another 5 minutes or so. Add this sauté to the cooked beans, along with all remaining ingredients.

3) Preheat oven to 350°F. Mix the beans well and transfer to a deep casserole or a 9 x 13-inch baking pan. Cover tightly with foil, and bake 1 hour.

Spinach-Rice Casserole

The original version contained 4 eggs. This one has only 2, and they're optional. Also, you can experiment by replacing some or all of the spinach with other greens: mustard, kale, collard, etc.

2 cups uncooked brown rice (long- or short-grain)
1 Tbs. butter or margarine — or olive oil
2 cups minced onion
2 lbs. fresh spinach, stemmed and finely chopped
1 tsp. salt
4 to 5 medium cloves garlic, minced
1/4 tsp. nutmeg
1/4 tsp. cayenne
black pepper, to taste
optional: 1 to 2 tsp. prepared mustard
1/2 cup sunflower seeds
2 beaten eggs (optional)
1 cup lowfat milk (optional)
1 1/2 cups (packed) grated cheddar (optional)
paprika

1) Place the rice in a medium-sized saucepan with 3 cups water. Cover, bring to a boil, then lower to the slowest possible simmer. Cook, covered and undisturbed, for 35 to 40 minutes. Remove from heat, transfer to a medium-sized bowl, and fluff with a fork.

2) Preheat oven to 350°F. Oil a 9 X 13-inch baking pan.

3) Heat the butter, margarine, or oil in a deep skillet. Add onion, and sauté 5 to 8 minutes ~ until soft. Add spinach, salt, and garlic, and cook about 5 minutes more over medium heat, stirring frequently. Add this to the rice, along with the seasonings and half the sunflower seeds. Mix well.

4) PURELY OPTIONAL: Beat together eggs and milk, and stir this into the spinach-rice mixture, along with the grated cheese.

5) Spread into the prepared pan, sprinkle with the remaining sunflower seeds and dust with paprika. Bake uncovered for 35 to 40 minutes ~ until heated through and lightly browned on top.

Solyanka

1¼ hours to prepare
(including baking)

Serves about 6

Very simple ingredients comprise this tasty casserole. Serve it with Beet Borscht (p. 35) or Odessa Beets (p. 68) and Balkan Cucumber Salad (p. 69).

4 medium potatoes (about 2 lbs.)
1½ cups cottage cheese (lowfat ok)
1 cup firm yogurt
1 Tbs. butter or margarine
2 cups chopped onion
¾ to 1 tsp. salt
1 tsp. caraway seeds
1 small head green cabbage, shredded (about 6 cups)

2 medium carrots, shredded
4 to 5 medium cloves garlic, minced
1 Tbs. dill (3 Tbs., if using fresh)
lots of black pepper, to taste
3 Tbs. cider vinegar
½ cup sunflower seeds } toppings
paprika

1) Preheat oven to 350°F. Lightly grease a 2-quart casserole or its equivalent.
2) Scrub the potatoes, cut them into small pieces, and boil until mashable. (You can do Steps 4 and 5 while the potatoes boil.) Drain and transfer to a large bowl.
3) Mash the potatoes while still hot, adding cottage cheese and yogurt.
4) Melt the butter or margarine in a large, deep skillet. Add onions and salt, and sauté about 5 minutes. Add caraway and cabbage, and sauté about 10 more minutes, stirring occasionally and covering in between.
5) When the cabbage is tender, add carrots, garlic, and dill. Cook about 5 more minutes, and remove from heat.
6) Add the sautéed vegetables and all remaining ingredients -except toppings- to the mashed potatoes. Mix well and spread into the prepared pan. Sprinkle the sunflower seeds and paprika on top.
7) Bake uncovered 35 to 45 minutes, or until heated through and lightly browned on top. Serve hot.

MEXICAN PEPPER CASSEROLE

The original version of this recipe contained butter in addition to the oil, plus more oil, 4 eggs, sour cream, and ½ lb. cheese. This trimmed-down version deletes the butter, reduces the oil and eggs, replaces sour cream with yogurt (if desired), and makes the cheese optional. The seasonings are intensified.

If you want to serve this with beans and rice, don't forget to get them ready beforehand.

1 Tbs. olive oil

2 cups sliced onion

6 to 8 medium-sized bell peppers (a mix of colors, if available), thinly sliced

4 to 5 medium cloves garlic, minced

1 tsp. salt

1½ tsp. cumin

optional: 1 tsp. dried coriander

1 tsp. dry mustard

black pepper, to taste

cayenne, to taste

2 Tbs. flour

2 to 3 eggs

2 cups yogurt and/or sour cream

optional: a handful of freshly minced cilantro

2 cups sliced jack or cheddar cheese (optional)

paprika, for the top

1) Lightly grease a 10-inch square pan or its equivalent. Preheat oven to 375°F.

2) Heat the olive oil in a deep skillet or Dutch oven. Add onions and sauté about 5 to 8 minutes over medium heat, until the onions begin to soften.

3) Add peppers, salt, cumin, dried coriander, mustard, black pepper, and cayenne. Sauté another 8 to 10 minutes, then sprinkle in the flour. Cook and stir another 5 minutes, or until the peppers are very tender. Transfer to the baking pan.

4) Beat together the eggs and yogurt or sour cream. Stir in the minced fresh cilantro. Pour this custard over the peppers. Top with slices of cheese, if desired, and dust with paprika.

5) Bake uncovered for 40 to 45 minutes until firm in the center and bubbly around the edges. Serve hot with rice and beans and/or warmed tortillas.

BULGARIAN PEPPER CASSEROLE

❋ ❋ ❋

Preparation time: about
1½ hours, including baking

Yield: enough
to feed at least
6 to 8

Garlicky herbed sautéed peppers and onions are blended with feta cheese, dilled lemon rice, and whipped cottage or ricotta cheese, then topped with tomatoes, olives, and more garlic, and baked until bubbly hot.

The peppers can be sautéed and the rice prepared several days in advance. Assemble and bake the casserole just before serving.

NOTE: In earlier editions, a version of this casserole was called Bulgarian Pepper and Cheese Delight. It had bulgur instead of rice, contained 4 eggs, and was far less intensely seasoned than this one, which is eggless.

❋ ❋ ❋ ❋ ❋ ❋ ❋ ❋ ❋ ❋ ❋ ❋ ❋ ❋ ❋

1½ cups uncooked brown rice
2¾ cups water
1 Tbs. lemon juice
2 to 3 Tbs. freshly minced dill (or 2 tsp. dried dill)
1½ Tbs. olive oil
2 cups minced onion
4 to 5 medium green and/or red bell peppers, chopped into ½-inch pieces
¾ tsp. salt (more, to taste)
fresh black pepper
½ tsp. oregano
2 tsp. basil
8 medium cloves garlic, half of them minced, half of them sliced
    (keep minced and sliced garlic separate)
1 cup crumbled feta cheese
1½ cups cottage or ricotta cheese (may be lowfat)
2 medium-sized fresh, ripe tomatoes
1 cup whole Niçoise olives (or sliced, pitted Kalamata olives)
    (possibly more, to taste)

... continued on next page →

1) Place rice and water in a saucepan. Cover and bring to a boil. Turn the heat down as low as possible, and simmer without interruption for about 40 minutes, or until the rice is tender. Remove from heat, fluff with a fork, and stir in lemon juice and dill. Set aside.

2) Meanwhile, heat the olive oil in a large skillet. Add onions, and sauté over medium heat 5 to 8 minutes, or until the onions become soft. Add peppers, salt, pepper, and herbs, and continue to cook, stirring occasionally, for about 10 more minutes, or until the peppers are tender. Stir in the minced garlic (save the sliced garlic for later) and cook for just a minute more. Remove from heat, and stir in the feta cheese.

3) When you are ready to assemble the casserole, preheat the oven to 375°F. Lightly oil a 9 x 13-inch baking pan.

4) Place the cottage or ricotta cheese in a blender or food processor fitted with the steel blade, and whip until smooth.

5) Combine rice, pepper sauté, and whipped cheese in a large bowl, and mix until very well combined. Transfer to the prepared pan, and spread into place. Top with tomato slices, then scatter olives and slices of garlic in a liberated, random fashion over the tomatoes.

6) Bake uncovered at 375°F. until bubbly ~ about 30 to 40 minutes. Serve hot or warm.

Arabian Squash Casserole

Preparation time: about 1 hour, after the squash is cooked and puréed

Good served with Tabouli Salad (p.46), or with warmed pita bread and a spinach salad with ripe tomatoes.

Yield 4 to 5 servings

4 cups cooked squash or pumpkin, mashed or puréed
1 Tbs. olive oil
1½ cups chopped onion
1 tsp. salt
2 small bell peppers (one red and one green, if possible), minced
4 or 5 medium cloves garlic, minced
black pepper and cayenne, to taste
½ cup firm yogurt
1 cup crumbled feta cheese
OPTIONAL: sunflower seeds and/or minced walnuts, for the top

PRELIMINARY: Preheat oven to 375°F.

1) Place the mashed or puréed squash in a large bowl.

2) Heat the olive oil in a medium-sized skillet. Add onion, and sauté over medium heat for about 5 minutes. Add salt and bell peppers. Sauté about 5 more minutes, or until the peppers begin to get soft.

3) Add garlic, black pepper, and cayenne, and sauté a few more minutes.

4) Add the sauté, along with yogurt and feta, to the squash, and mix well. Spread into an ungreased 9-inch square baking pan; sprinkle the top lightly with sunflower seeds and/or minced walnuts.

5) Bake uncovered for 25 to 30 minutes, or until bubbly.

Chilean Squash (a variation)

Delete: yogurt, feta, sunflower seeds, walnuts.

Add to step 2: 1 tsp. cumin, ½ tsp. dried coriander (optional), 1 tsp. chili powder, 2 cups corn (frozen/defrosted = OK)

Top with: 1 cup grated cheddar

Preparation time:
1¼ hours after
soybeans are soaked

SCHEHERAZADE CASSEROLE

This is one of my favorite recipes, and I strongly recommend it: ground soybeans baked with bulgur, vegetables, garlic, tomatoes, feta cheese. The texture is deeply satisfying, and the seasonings are bold. It tastes great!

Few changes have been made from the original, other than to intensify the seasonings. It was – and remains – eggless.

You can assemble the casserole a day or 2 in advance of baking it. Also, it can be frozen before or after baking. It doesn't mind being reheated.

PRELIMINARY: The soybeans need at least 4 hours to soak beforehand.

1 cup raw bulgur	black pepper and cayenne, to taste
1 cup boiling water	1 large bell pepper, diced
1 Tbs. olive oil	¾ cup dry soybeans, soaked
2 cups minced onion	1 14½-oz. can tomatoes, drained
3 large cloves garlic, minced	3 Tbs. (half a small can) tomato paste
½ tsp. salt	½ cup (packed) finely minced parsley
2 tsp. cumin	1½ to 2 cups crumbled feta cheese
1½ tsp. basil	

1) Preheat oven to 375°F. Lightly oil a 9 x 13-inch baking pan.

2) Place the bulgur in a small bowl. Add boiling water, cover with a plate, and let stand at least 15 minutes.

3) Meanwhile, heat the olive oil in a large skillet. Add onion, garlic, salt, and seasonings. Stir occasionally as you sauté over medium heat for 5 to 8 minutes. Add bell pepper and sauté about 5 minutes more.

4) Drain the soybeans, if necessary, and place them in a blender or food processor with 1 cup fresh water. Grind until the soybeans resemble a coarse batter. Transfer to a large bowl.

5) Add the soaked bulgur and sautéed vegetables to the soybeans. Stir in the tomatoes, breaking them up into bite-sized pieces. Add tomato paste, parsley, and 1 cup of the feta. Mix well.

6) Spread into the baking pan and sprinkle the remaining feta on top. Cover and bake for 30 minutes at 375°F, then uncover and bake 15 minutes more with the oven turned down to 350°F. Serve hot.

Crêpes

Preparation time:
The batter takes
a few minutes.
Cooking the crêpes
takes about 15
minutes.

Elegant, but not extravagant, these thin pancakes are at the same time sturdy and delicate. You can make them just to have around. Keep them stacked on a plate, tightly covered and refrigerated. They will last at least a week — just fill and heat as desired. Wrap crêpes around many varieties of foods (a great way to use leftovers!) for different occasions, different times of day. They can quickly transform otherwise ordinary food into something special.

1 large egg
1 ¼ cups milk (can be lowfat)
1 cup flour
¼ tsp. salt
a few drops of oil for the pan

NOTE: You will need a 6-or 7-inch crêpe or omelette pan — ideally a heavy one with a nonstick surface.

1) Place egg, milk, flour, and salt in a blender or food processor, and whip until smooth.

2) Heat a crêpe or omelette pan. After a few minutes, lightly brush its entire inside surface with oil. When the pan is hot enough to sizzle a drop of water instantly on contact, pour in approximately ¼ cup batter. Slowly tilt the pan in all directions until the batter thoroughly coats the bottom. Pour off any excess batter (the pancake should be thin). Cook on one side over medium heat until set (about 20 seconds), then turn over and cook for just another second or two on the other side.

3) Turn the crêpe out onto a clean, dry dinner plate, and repeat the procedure until you have used up all the batter. (If you keep the pan hot, you won't have to add any additional oil.) You can pile the finished crêpes on the plate — they won't stick together.

4) Cover the plate tightly with plastic wrap, and refrigerate until use. The crêpes will keep well for at least several days.

5) To fill, simply place a small amount of whatever filling at one end of the crêpe and fold over sides and end to make a neat little packet. Filled crêpes can be heated gently — covered, in a 325° oven — or sautéed in a little butter just before serving.

SUGGESTED FILLINGS

FOR DESSERT:
- Sauté in butter, fold in quarters, and sprinkle with powdered sugar.
- Lightly sauté some slices of tart apple; drizzle with lemon juice, cinnamon, and a little maple syrup or honey. Fill the crêpes and serve warm — plain, or with ice cream or whipped cream.
- Heat crêpes gently and serve with room-temperature Berry Sauce (p.207) — with or without ice cream.

VEGETABLES:
- Steamed whole green beans with almonds
- Steamed asparagus or broccoli spears with Zippy Cheese Sauce (p. 92), Rarebit (p.93), or a Vegetable Purée (p.86)
- Steamed carrot sticks with Cashew-Ginger Sauce (p.90)

LEFTOVERS:
- White Rabbit Salad (p.48) — inside room-temperature crêpes
- Ratatouille (p.179) or Vegetable Stew (p.177)
- Stellar Mushroom Sauce (p.78)
- Asparagus-Mushroom Sauce (p.77) — delete water
- Caramelized Onion Sauce (p.78)
- Etc. (whatever ideas you come up with are probably just brilliant)

Zucchini-Feta Pancakes

...Light and very satisfying (also quite attractive, with lovely flecks of green). A food processor will grate the zucchini in seconds flat.

NOTE: This recipe calls for 4 eggs. Some or all of the yolks can be deleted.

4 eggs, separated (yolks optional)
4 packed cups coarsely grated zucchini (about 4 7-inchers)
1 cup finely crumbled feta cheese
½ cup finely minced scallions
1 tsp. dried mint (or 1 Tbs. fresh, finely minced)
a little salt (optional, to taste)
lots of black pepper
⅓ cup flour
oil for frying
sour cream or yogurt for topping

1) Beat the egg whites until stiff.

2) In a medium-sized bowl, combine zucchini, egg yolks (or not), feta, scallions, seasonings, and flour. Mix well.

3) Fold the egg whites into the zucchini mixture.

4) Heat a little oil in a heavy skillet. When it is very hot, add spoonfuls of batter, and fry on both sides until golden and crisp.

5) Serve immediately, topped with sour cream or yogurt.

Cottage Cheese & Apple Pancakes

Preparation time:
30 minutes

Yield: serves
about 4

Great for brunch!

The batter keeps well for days, so you can have it on hand for breakfast cheer on an otherwise depressing weekday. (And these pancakes are equally uplifting for dinner.)

        4 eggs, separated (yolks optional—use all, some, or none)
        1 cup cottage cheese (lowfat ok)
        1 cup (packed) grated tart apple
        ¾ cup flour
        1 to 2 tsp. lemon juice
        optional: 1 Tbs. honey
        ½ tsp. cinnamon
        ½ tsp. salt
        optional: 2 to 3 Tbs. finely minced walnuts or almonds
        oil or butter for frying
        real maple syrup   ⎫
        sour cream or yogurt   ⎬ optional toppings
        Berry Sauce (p. 207)   ⎭

1) Beat the egg whites until stiff.
2) Combine all other ingredients (except toppings and frying oil) in a medium-sized bowl and mix well. Fold in the egg whites.
3) Heat oil or melt butter in a skillet. When it is hot enough to sizzle a drop of batter on contact, add spoonfuls of batter. Fry on both sides until firm and lightly browned. Serve right away, topped with syrup, sour cream or yogurt, and/or Berry Sauce.

Sweet Potato Pancakes

30 minutes to prepare   Yield: 4 to 6 servings

These can be for breakfast, brunch, lunch, or supper, depending on what you serve them with (and, of course, what time of day or night it is).

The sweet potatoes and onion can be grated by hand or in a food processor fitted with the grating attachment. Peeling the sweet potatoes is optional. If you choose not to peel, scrub.

NOTE: The batter stores well for several days if kept in a tightly covered container in the refrigerator.

4 cups (packed) coarsely grated sweet potatoes or yams
    (approximately 1 large or 2 medium)
½ cup grated onion
3 to 4 Tbs lemon juice
1 tsp. salt
black pepper, to taste
4 beaten eggs (yolks optional)
⅓ cup flour
optional: ¼ cup minced parsley
oil for frying
TOPPINGS: sour cream or yogurt
          applesauce

1) Combine all ingredients and mix well.

2) Heat a small amount of oil in a skillet until it is very hot. (It should sizzle a fleck of batter upon contact.)

3) Use a non-slotted spoon to form thin pancakes, patting the batter down. Fry on both sides until brown, adding small amounts of additional oil, if/as needed.

4) Serve hot, with toppings.

35 minutes to prepare;
1 hour to chill;
15 minutes to cook

Yield:
4 to 6
servings

Lentil-Walnut Burgers

These are delicious fried or broiled, with or without some cheese melted on top. Try serving Lentil-Walnut Burgers with thickly sliced, very ripe homegrown tomatoes and Faux Aioli (p. 91).

NOTES: ☆ You can sauté the vegetables while the lentils cook. ☆ The burgers can be made up to several days in advance and stored in the refrigerator until just before cooking. ☆ Uncooked burgers can be individually wrapped and frozen. Defrost before cooking.

¾ cup dry lentils
1½ cups water
2 Tbs. cider vinegar
1 Tbs. peanut or olive oil
1 cup finely minced onion
4 to 5 large cloves garlic, minced
about 10 large mushrooms, minced
½ cup very finely minced walnuts
1 tsp. salt
OPTIONAL: ½ lb. fresh spinach, finely minced
1 tsp. dry mustard
fresh black pepper, to taste
½ cup fine bread crumbs or wheat germ

1) Place lentils and water in a small saucepan and bring to a boil. Lower the heat and simmer, partially covered, for about 30 minutes, or until the lentils are soft and the liquid is gone. Transfer to a medium-sized bowl, add vinegar, and mash well.

2) Heat oil in a medium-sized skillet. Add onions and sauté over medium heat for about 5 minutes. Add all remaining ingredients except wheat germ or bread crumbs, and sauté 5 to 10 minutes, or until all the vegetables are tender. Add the sauté and crumbs to the lentils and mix well. Chill for about 1 hour before forming patties.

3) Form 4-inch-diameter burgers. Fry in a small amount of hot oil on both sides until heated through and crispy on the outside, or broil for 5 to 8 minutes on each side.

Greek Pilaf

45 minutes
to prepare

Yield:
about 6
servings

Greek Pilaf is a simple rice preparation that can be used as a filling for grape leaves or artichokes (following page), or for eggplant (p.151). It is also delicious all by itself.

1½ cups raw brown rice (long- or short- grain)
2¼ cups water
1 to 2 Tbs. olive oil
1½ cups minced onion
1 small stalk celery, minced
½ tsp. salt
½ cup lightly toasted sunflower seeds or pine nuts
black pepper, to taste
4 to 5 medium cloves garlic, minced
2 Tbs. lemon juice
¼ cup freshly minced parsley
1 Tbs. dried mint (or 3 Tbs. fresh, minced)

1) Place rice and water in a small saucepan. Bring to a boil, cover, and simmer until tender (about 40 minutes).
2) Meanwhile, heat the olive oil in a small skillet. Add onion, celery, and salt, and sauté until the vegetables are tender (5 to 8 minutes). Add sunflower seeds or pine nuts, black pepper, and garlic. Sauté for 5 minutes.
3) Stir the sautéed mixture into the cooked rice along with the lemon juice and herbs. Mix well.

Stuffed Grape Leaves

These can be served with an assortment of other dishes to make an appetizer sampler that is really main-course material (see Mezza, p. 100). You can also serve Stuffed Grape Leaves as a light entrée with any soup, especially Lentil Soup (p. 25).

If you have grapevines in your yard, pick leaves for stuffing early in the season, when they are large enough to stuff, but still tender. You can also buy preserved leaves in specialty shops or in the imported foods section of a good grocery store.

1 recipe Greek Pilaf (preceding page)
about 24 grape leaves (3 to 4 inches across)
1 batch Greek Lemon Sauce (p. 91)

1) Preheat oven to 325°F. Lightly oil a baking tray.
2) Place each leaf down flat on a clean surface. Add a heaping tablespoon of filling near the stem end. Roll tightly, folding in the sides.
3) Arrange the stuffed leaves on the prepared tray. Bake about 20 minutes or until heated through. You can also skip this step and just serve them cold, with the sauce on top or on the side. Serves 4 to 6.

to Stuff an Artichoke

1 recipe Greek Pilaf (preceding page)
6 medium artichokes
1 batch Greek Lemon Sauce (p. 91) or
   Horseradish Sauce (also on p. 91)

1) Trim and cook the artichokes as you normally would. Drain and cool until handleable.
2) Pull off the centermost leaf cluster. Use a teaspoon to scoop out the fibrous choke, being careful not to scoop out the tender heart beneath it. Fill the cavity with pilaf. Serve at room temperature, with sauce for dipping. Serves 6.

150 ENTRÉES

STUFFED EGGPLANT

I. 1970s ALTERNATIVE LIFESTYLE-STYLE — still good!

3 medium eggplants
(about 7 inches long)

2 Tbs. olive oil

2 cups minced onion

½ lb. mushrooms, chopped

1 tsp. salt (or more, to taste)

2 tsp. basil

a dash of thyme

1 tsp. oregano

fresh black pepper, to taste

5 to 6 medium cloves garlic, minced

2 cups cooked brown rice

1½ cups cottage cheese (lowfat ok)

1 cup grated cheddar

½ cup (packed) freshly minced parsley

Tabasco and soy sauce, to taste

a handful of sunflower seeds

a handful of sesame seeds

paprika

Red Pepper Purée (p.86) - optional

1) Cut the eggplants in half lengthwise. Use a spoon to scoop out the insides, leaving a ½-inch shell. Mince the eggplant scoopings.

2) Heat the olive oil in a large skillet. Add onion, mushrooms, salt, herbs, and pepper. Sauté over medium heat for about 5 minutes, then add the minced eggplant. Cook until the eggplant is tender (about 15 minutes), stirring occasionally. Add garlic, and sauté for about 5 more minutes. Transfer to a large bowl.

3) Add rice, cheeses, parsley, Tabasco, and soy sauce, and mix well. Taste to correct seasonings.

4) Preheat oven to 375°F. Fill the eggplant shells, and top with seeds and a fine dusting of paprika. Bake for 30 to 40 minutes — until heated through. Serve hot, with room-temperature Red Pepper Purée drizzled on top, for a lovely effect.

II. MEDITERRANEAN STYLE

3 medium eggplants (about 7 inches long)

a double recipe Greek Pilaf (p. 148)

1 cup crumbled feta cheese

3 medium-sized ripe tomatoes

1) Preheat oven to 375°F. Slice eggplants in half lengthwise, and bake face-down until tender (20 to 30 minutes). Scoop out and mince the insides.

2) Combine chopped eggplant with Greek Pilaf. Stir in the feta. Stuff the eggplant shells and top with slices of tomato.

3) Turn oven down to 350°, and bake until heated through (about 30 minutes).

1 hour to prepare   Yield: at least 4 servings

Each of these filling recipes makes plenty for 4 servings of Stuffed Squash — half a medium-sized squash apiece. Any winter squash will work; the most common are acorn and butternut.

The 2 squash need to be prebaked. Preheat the oven to 350°F. Split the squash lengthwise down the middle and remove the seeds. Bake face-down on an oiled tray for about 30 minutes or until very soft (a fork should slide in easily). Make your choice of fillings while the squash bake.

I. SAVORY FRUIT-STUFFED SQUASH

2 medium-sized winter squash, halved lengthwise and prebaked
1 cup raw brown rice (long- or short-grain) + 1¾ cups water

1 Tbs. butter	1 tsp. salt
1½ cups minced onion	1 to 2 Tbs. honey or brown sugar
2 medium cloves garlic, minced	1 cup chopped almonds and/or pecans
2 medium-sized tart apples, diced	TOPPINGS:
3 large navel oranges, sectioned	Orange- Ginger Sauce (p.90)
½ tsp. cinnamon	yogurt
½ tsp. allspice or cloves	

1) Place rice and water in a small saucepan. Bring to a boil, cover, and let simmer undisturbed for 30 to 40 minutes — until tender. Transfer to a medium-sized bowl.

2) Meanwhile, melt butter in a medium skillet. Add onion and sauté for about 5 minutes, or until translucent.

3) Add garlic, apples, oranges, and spices, and sauté over medium heat about 5 minutes more. The orange sections may fall apart, but that's OK.

4) Add the sauté to the rice and mix well. Season to taste with salt and honey or brown sugar.

5) Preheat oven to 350°F. Fill the prebaked squash halves, and top with chopped nuts. Bake uncovered until heated through — about 20 to 30 minutes (depending on how warm the ingredients were to begin with).

II. COMPREHENSIVELY STUFFED SQUASH

Perfect for a holiday meal, especially Thanksgiving. For a colorful accompaniment, choose Odessa Beets (p.68) or Vegetable Purées (Beet or Red Pepper - p.86) to go alongside or on top.

2 medium-sized winter squash, halved and prebaked
2 Tbs. butter
1 cup minced onion
½ lb. mushrooms, minced
1 large clove garlic, minced
1 stalk celery, minced
½ tsp. salt
lots of black pepper
½ tsp. sage
½ tsp. thyme
2 Tbs. lemon juice
¼ cup minced walnuts
¼ cup sunflower seeds
¼ cup raisins (optional)
2 cups good bread crumbs (from good bread)
6 to 8 dried apricots
1 cup (packed) grated cheddar (entirely optional)

1) Melt the butter in a large skillet. Add onion, and sauté over medium heat for about 5 minutes, or until the onion is translucent.

2) Add mushrooms, garlic, celery, and seasonings, and sauté about 10 minutes — until everything is tender and well mingled.

3) Stir in remaining ingredients and mix well. Taste to correct seasonings.

4) Preheat oven to 350°F. Fill the prebaked squash and bake, covered, until heated through (20 to 30 minutes).

⌒Zuccanoes⌒
(Stuffed Zucchini)

PRELIMINARY: You'll need 1½ cups cooked rice.

4 medium-sized zucchini (about 2 lbs.)
1 to 2 Tbs. olive oil
1½ cups minced onion
1 tsp. salt
½ lb. mushrooms, minced
6 medium cloves garlic, minced
1½ cups cooked rice (any kind)
1½ cups minced almonds or pecans, lightly toasted
3 Tbs. fresh lemon juice
black pepper and cayenne, to taste
a few pinches of freshly minced – or dried – herbs:
  ~ any combination of parsley, basil, dill, thyme, or marjoram
1 cup (packed) grated Swiss or cheddar cheese
1 batch Vegetable Purée (pages 86 & 87) – OPTIONAL

1) Cut the zucchini lengthwise down the middle. Use a smallish spoon to scoop out the insides, leaving a canoe with a ¼-inch shell. Mince the insides, and set everything aside.

2) Heat the olive oil in a medium-sized skillet. Add the onion and salt, and sauté over medium heat until the onion is soft (5 to 8 minutes).

3) Add the minced zucchini innards and the mushrooms. Turn up the heat and cook for about 8 minutes, stirring, letting the liquid evaporate. Stir in the garlic and remove from heat.

4) Stir in the rice and nuts, along with the lemon juice, and season to taste with black pepper, cayenne, and the herbs of your choice.

5) Preheat oven to 350°F. Fill the zucchini shells, top with cheese, and bake for 30 to 40 minutes, or until heated through. Serve hot, sauced with a lovely Vegetable Purée, if desired.

Stuffed Cabbage

Preparation time:
1½ hours
(This includes time
for making the sauce.)

Yield:
6 servings
(2 rolls apiece)

Serve over rice.

1 large head green cabbage
1 Tbs. butter
1 cup minced onion
1 small clove garlic, minced
1 stalk celery, minced
1 small carrot, diced
¾ cup minced cashews (optional)
¼ cup sunflower seeds

salt and black pepper, to taste
2 cups (1 lb.) ricotta cheese
1 small tart apple, finely chopped
¼ cup raisins or currants
3 to 4 Tbs. lemon juice
1 to 2 Tbs. soy sauce
1 Tbs. honey (optional)
1 batch Cashew-Ginger Sauce (p.90)

1) Heat a large kettleful of water to boiling. Core the head of cabbage, and carefully lower it into the water. Turn the heat down to a simmer, and leave the cabbage in there for about 10 to 15 minutes, or until the outer leaves can be removed easily. Retrieve the cabbage from the water, and pull off the 12 outermost leaves. Make sure the cabbage is cooked well enough so the leaves will not break when rolled, but not so well done that they disintegrate. Set aside the 12 leaves, and save the rest of the cabbage to use for another dish. (It's great for soup!)

2) Melt the butter in a medium-sized skillet and add the onion, garlic, celery, and carrot. Sauté over medium heat for about 10 minutes, then add nuts, seeds, salt, and pepper. When the vegetables are tender, remove from heat.

3) Place the ricotta in a medium-large bowl. Add the sauté, plus the apple, raisins, lemon juice, soy sauce, and optional honey. Mix well, and taste to adjust seasonings. Meanwhile, preheat oven to 325°F.

4) Place 3 to 4 Tbs. filling near the base of each cabbage leaf. Roll firmly, folding in the sides. Arrange the cabbage rolls in an oblong baking pan, pour Cashew-Ginger Sauce over the top and bake, covered, until heated through — about 30 minutes.

✦✦✦ Spinach-Ricotta Pie ✦✦✦

40 minutes to prepare;
40 to 45 more to bake

Yield:
4 to 6 servings

The Crust: 6 Tbs. butter or margarine, cut into small pieces
1½ cups flour
about 4 Tbs. cold water, milk, or buttermilk

The Filling: 1 tsp. butter or margarine
1 cup minced onion
1 lb. spinach, stemmed and finely chopped
½ tsp. salt
freshly ground pepper, to taste
1 tsp. basil
1 lb. ricotta cheese
2 or 3 beaten eggs
3 Tbs. flour
½ cup (packed) grated sharp cheese of your choice
a dash of nutmeg (optional)

Optional topping: 1 cup sour cream (may be lowfat), lightly beaten
paprika

CRUST

1) Use a pastry cutter, two forks, or a food processor to cut together the butter and flour until the mixture is uniformly blended and resembles coarse corn-meal. (The food processor will do this in just a few spurts.)

2) Add just enough liquid (water, milk, or buttermilk) to hold the dough to-gether. Roll out the dough and form a crust in a 9- or 10-inch pie pan. Set aside.

3) Preheat oven to 375°F. Melt the butter or margarine in a medium-sized skillet, add the onion, and sauté for 5 minutes over medium heat. Add spinach, salt, pepper, and basil, and cook, stirring, over medium-high heat until the spinach is wilted. Remove from heat.

4) Combine all filling ingredients in a large bowl, and mix well. Spread into the unbaked pie shell. For an extra rich pie, top with sour cream, spread to the edges of the crust. Dust generously with paprika.

5) Bake 40 to 45 minutes, or until firm to the touch at the center. Serve hot, warm, or at room temperature.

Swiss Cheese & Mushroom Quiche

Preparation time:
about 1¼ hours,
including baking

Yield:
1 10-inch pie
(4 to 6 servings)

1 10-inch pie crust (recipe on preceding page), pressed into either
  a pie pan or a springform tart pan
1 tsp. butter or margarine
1½ cups chopped onion
¼ lb. mushrooms, sliced or minced
½ tsp. salt
black pepper
a pinch of thyme
½ tsp. dry mustard
4 large eggs (or 2 whole eggs plus 2 egg whites)
1½ cups milk (can be lowfat)
2 Tbs. flour
1½ cups (packed) grated Swiss cheese
paprika

OPTIONAL VARIATIONS : ★ substitute other delicious cheeses for the Swiss
  ★ add fresh tomato slices (no need to sauté first)
  ★ minced fresh herbs (chives, parsley, chervil,
    marjoram, basil, dill, etc.)
  ★ a hint of Hot: 1 tsp. prepared horseradish
    and/or cayenne or Tabasco

1) Preheat oven to 375°F.
2) Melt the butter in a small pan. Add onions, and sauté over
   medium heat for a few minutes. When they begin to soften, add
   mushrooms, salt, pepper, thyme, and mustard. Sauté about 5 minutes
   more and remove from heat.
3) Combine eggs, milk, and flour in a blender or food processor, and beat
   well.
4) Spread the grated cheese over the bottom of the unbaked crust, and
   spread the onion-mushroom mixture on top. Pour in the custard, and
   sprinkle the top with paprika.
5) Bake for 35 to 45 minutes, or until solid in the center. Serve hot,
   warm, or at room temperature.

Old Country Pie

1 unbaked 9- or 10-inch pie crust (see 2 pages back)

1 Tbs. butter, margarine, or oil

1½ cups minced onion

1 tsp. caraway seeds

1 tsp. salt

½ lb. mushrooms, chopped or sliced

1½ cups shredded cabbage

1 medium stalk broccoli, chopped

1 medium carrot, thinly sliced

2 tsp. dill

lots of black pepper

3 medium cloves garlic, minced

2 Tbs. flour

½ cup cottage cheese (lowfat OK)

2 eggs (one or both yolks can be omitted)

2 medium scallions, finely minced

OPTIONAL: ¾ cup sour cream and/or yogurt; paprika

1) Prepare pie crust. Preheat oven to 350°F.

2) Melt butter (or heat oil) in a medium-sized skillet. Add onion, caraway, and salt, and sauté over medium heat until the onions begin to brown (10 to 15 minutes).

3) Add mushrooms, cabbage, broccoli, carrot, and dill, and sauté until everything is just tender – about 8 more minutes.

4) Stir in black pepper, garlic, and flour, and cook, stirring, for just a few minutes more. Remove from heat.

5) Beat together cottage cheese and eggs. Add this to the sauté along with the scallions and mix well.

6) Spread into the unbaked crust and, if desired, top with a layer of sour cream and/or yogurt. Sprinkle with paprika, and bake for 40 minutes or until set. Serve hot, warm, or at room temperature.

Cauliflower-Cheese Pie
with Grated Potato Crust

CONVENIENCE TIPS: ☆ Use food processor with grating attachment to grate cheese, potato, and onion in that order. (No need to clean in between.)
☆ Prepare the filling while the crust bakes.

CRUST:

2 cups (packed) grated raw potato
¼ cup grated onion
½ tsp. salt

1 egg white, lightly beaten
flour for your fingers
a little oil

FILLING:

1 Tbs. olive oil or butter
1 cup chopped onion
2 medium cloves garlic, minced
½ tsp. salt
black pepper, to taste
½ tsp. basil

¼ tsp. thyme
1 medium cauliflower, in small pieces
2 eggs (or 1 whole egg plus 1 egg white)
¼ cup milk (lowfat OK)
1 cup (packed) grated cheddar
paprika

1) Preheat oven to 400°F. Oil a 9-inch pie pan.

2) Combine grated potato and onion, salt, and egg white in a small bowl and mix well. Transfer to the pie pan and pat into place with lightly floured fingers, building up the sides into a handsome edge.

3) Bake for 30 minutes, then brush the crust with a little oil and bake it 10 more minutes. Remove from oven, and turn the temperature down to 375°.

4) Heat the olive oil or butter in a large skillet. Add onion, garlic, salt, pepper, and herbs, and sauté over medium heat for about 5 minutes. Add cauliflower, stir, and cover. Cook until tender, stirring occasionally (about 8 to 10 minutes).

5) Spread half the cheese onto the baked crust (OK if it's still hot). Spoon the sautéed vegetables on top, then sprinkle on the remaining cheese. Beat the eggs and milk together, and pour this over the top. Dust lightly with paprika.

6) Bake 35 to 40 minutes, or until set. Serve hot or warm.

CALZONE

A calzone is a savory Italian pastry resembling a large overstuffed turnover made with pizza dough. Traditionally, the filling is a mixture of cheeses, contrasting perfectly with the crispy crust.

I've included a cheese filling, plus a few ideas for nondairy ones as well.

One calzone per person plus a green salad make a very satisfying dinner.

Preparation time:
about 2 hours

Yield:
6 servings

- Make the filling while the dough rises, to save time.
- The dough can be made in advance and refrigerated or even frozen until use. Let come to room temperature before assembling, then knead for a few minutes to warm it up.

THE DOUGH:
1 cup wrist-temperature water
1½ tsp. active dry yeast
1 Tbs. honey or sugar
1½ tsp. salt
2½ to 3 cups flour
olive oil

1) Place the water in a medium-sized bowl. Sprinkle in the yeast, and stir in the honey or sugar until everything dissolves.

2) Use a whisk to stir in the salt and flour. When it gets too thick to whisk, mix with one floured hand. Knead in the bowl for about 5 minutes.

3) Brush a little olive oil over the dough, cover the bowl, and let rise in a warm place until doubled in bulk (about 1 hour). In the meantime, you can get the filling ready.

SPINACH-CHEESE FILLING:

1 Tbs. olive oil
1 cup minced onion
1 lb. spinach, stemmed and minced
about 1/2 tsp. salt
lots of black pepper

4 or 5 medium cloves garlic, minced
1 Tbs. dried (or 3 Tbs. minced fresh) basil
1 lb. ricotta or cottage cheese
2 cups (packed) grated mozzarella
about 1/4 cup grated parmesan

1) Heat the olive oil in a medium-sized skillet. Add onion, and sauté over medium heat until translucent — about 5 minutes.

2) Add spinach, salt, and pepper. Cook, stirring, over high heat for several minutes — until the spinach wilts. Stir in the garlic and basil and cook for about 2 more minutes.

3) Place the cheeses in a medium-sized bowl. Add the spinach sauté and mix very well. Taste to correct seasonings.

TO ASSEMBLE:

1) Preheat oven to 450°F. Oil a baking tray.

2) Punch down the risen dough. Divide it into 6 equal sections, and roll out on a floured surface into circles 1/4 inch thick.

3) Place 1/2 to 3/4 cup filling on one half of the circle, leaving a 1/2-inch rim. Use your fingers or a brush to moisten the rim with a little water. Fold over the empty side and crimp the edges with your favorite fork. Use that same fork to prick little holes here and there on the top surface.

4) Arrange the completed calzones on the oiled tray, and bake for 15 to 20 minutes, or until crisp and lightly browned. OPTIONAL: You can brush each pastry with a little melted butter or some olive oil during the last 5 minutes of baking.   Serve hot.

ALTERNATIVE FILLINGS:

- 1 batch Eggplant Scallopini Marsala (p.83) — it's nondairy.
- 1 batch Asparagus-Mushroom Sauce (p.77). Replace the butter with olive oil; reduce wine to 1/2 cup; delete water. (Also nondairy.)
- Thick slices of fresh tomato — with mozzarella and Pesto (p.84). [If you don't have pesto made, just add a few cloves of sliced garlic, some freshly minced basil, and a drizzle of olive oil.]

SAVORY FILO PASTRIES

Once you get past the mystique of filo pastry, you will see how easy it is to make delicious, mouthwateringly crisp, savory vegetable strudels. Buy the pastry (sometimes called "Fillo Leaves" or "Greek Phyllo") in a long rectangular package in the frozen foods section of most good grocery stores. Let it thaw out thoroughly while still wrapped (this will take an hour or two). Unwrap just before using, take out a pile of however many sheets you will need, and rewrap (airtight!) and refrigerate the rest until next time. Cover the sheets you are about to use with a slightly damp tea towel — they dry out quickly!

When I first learned to make strudels, I always brushed melted butter between the pastry layers. In recent years, however, I discovered I like using olive oil much better. You don't have to mess around with melting it; it goes further, so you can use much less of it; and it is lighter, has a great flavor, and is cholesterol-free. But if you just love butter so much that it would break your heart to substitute olive oil, try adding some melted butter to the oil, to flavor it. You can also use oil spray.

Broccoli Strudel

- Try making your own bread crumbs by grating some good bread in the food processor. The better-tasting the bread, the better.
- Each of these strudels uses about 10 sheets of filo pastry, which is approximately half a 1-lb. package.

(A little oil, butter, or
oil spray for the baking tray)
1 Tbs. butter or olive oil
1 cup minced onion
1 large bunch broccoli, finely chopped
½ tsp. salt
lots of black pepper
2 medium cloves garlic, minced

2 cups good bread crumbs
2 cups grated cheddar
2 Tbs. lemon juice (more, to taste)

10 sheets of filo pastry
3 to 4 Tbs. olive oil — OR 6 Tbs.
 melted butter — OR oil spray,
 for the filo

1) Preheat oven to 375°F. Oil a baking tray.

2) Melt butter or heat 1 Tbs. olive oil in a large skillet. Add onion, and sauté for about 5 minutes over medium heat.

3) Add broccoli, salt, and pepper, and cook, stirring, for about 5 more minutes. Add garlic, and sauté until the broccoli is just tender (about 5 more minutes). Remove from heat.

4) Stir in bread crumbs, cheese, and lemon juice. Taste to adjust seasonings.

5) TO ASSEMBLE: Place one sheet of filo on a clean, dry countertop. Brush the top lightly with oil, then add another sheet. Brush with oil, then add another. Continue until you have a pile of 5 leaves. Add half the filling (as illustrated), fold in the sides, and gently roll until you have a neat little log. Brush the top with more oil, then carefully lift the pastry, and place it on the oiled baking sheet. Repeat this procedure to make a second roll, and place it next to the first one on the tray.

filling

6) Bake 25 to 30 minutes, until golden and exquisitely crisp. Cut with a serrated knife, using a gentle sawing motion. Serve hot or at room temperature.

ℜ ℜ ℜ ℜ ℜ ℜ ℜ ℜ ℜ ℜ

Mushroom Strudel

1 lb. mushrooms, chopped
1 cup (8 oz.) cream cheese or
   cottage cheese (lowfat OK)
1 cup sour cream and/or yogurt
1 tsp. salt
lots of black pepper
1 tsp. dill
1 cup good bread crumbs

2 scallions, finely minced (whites & greens)
¼ cup (packed) minced parsley
3 Tbs. lemon juice
   . . . . .
10 sheets of filo pastry
3 to 4 Tbs. olive oil, for the filo
optional: poppy seeds, for the top

1) Preheat oven to 375°F. Oil a baking tray.

2) Place the mushrooms in a saucepan, and cook them all by themselves over medium heat for about 10 minutes. Drain them, squeezing out all the excess liquid, and transfer the mushrooms to a medium-sized bowl. (You can save the discarded liquid for a great soup stock.)

3) Add cream cheese, cut into small pieces, or cottage cheese to the hot mushrooms. Mix well. Stir in remaining filling ingredients.

4) Follow directions in steps 5 and 6 above. A very nice optional touch: sprinkle some poppy seeds on top before baking.

Spanakopita

Heavenly Greek Spinach Pastry

1½ hours
to prepare
and bake

Yield:
about 8
servings

2 Notes ♫: ‘Stores well (unbaked) for up to several days. Cover tightly and refrigerate.
‘Detailed information about filo pastry on p. 162.

(A little oil, butter, or
oil spray for the pan)

2 Tbs. olive oil

2 cups minced onion

½ tsp. salt

1 Tbs. dried basil

1 tsp. dried oregano

2½ lbs. fresh spinach, stemmed and finely chopped

5 medium cloves garlic, minced

3 Tbs. flour

2 to 3 cups (packed) crumbled feta cheese (about 1 lb.)

1 cup cottage or pot cheese

black pepper, to taste

⅓ cup olive oil — OR ½ cup melted butter — OR oil spray
1 lb. filo pastry (16 to 20 leaves), thoroughly defrosted

1) Preheat oven to 375°F. Lightly grease a 9 x 13-inch baking pan.

2) Heat the oil in a Dutch oven or deep skillet. Add onion, salt, and herbs, and sauté for about 5 minutes, or until the onion softens. Add the spinach, turn up the heat, and cook, stirring, until the spinach wilts (5 to 8 minutes). Stir in the garlic.

3) Sprinkle in the flour, stir, and cook over medium heat 2 to 3 more minutes. Remove from heat.

4) Mix in the cheeses, then correct the seasonings, adding black pepper to taste along the way.

5) Place a sheet of filo in the prepared pan, letting the pastry edges climb up the sides. Brush it all over with olive oil or melted butter, or spray it with oil spray, then add another sheet. Keep going until you have a stack of 10 oiled or buttered sheets.

6) Add the filling, spreading it evenly to the edges. Continue layering and oiling or buttering the remaining filo on top of the filling. Oil or butter the top layer.

7) Gently (with a serrated knife in a sawing motion) cut the unbaked Spanakopita into squares. Bake uncovered for about 45 minutes, or until golden and crispy. Serve hot or warm.

POLENTA PIE

Easy deep-dish pizza
with a thick and crunchy
cornmeal crust

1¼ hours to prepare
(most of which is
crust-baking time)

Yield:
1 10-inch pie
(serves 4)

FILLING:

CRUST:

1 Tbs. olive oil

1½ cups coarse cornmeal

1 small onion, thinly sliced

1 tsp. salt

½ cup thinly sliced bell pepper

1½ cups cold water

about 10 mushrooms, sliced

2 cups boiling water

1 small zucchini, thinly sliced

a little olive oil

5 to 6 medium cloves garlic, sliced

2 tsp. dried basil (or 2 Tbs. minced fresh basil)

½ tsp. oregano

fresh black pepper

¼ lb. mozzarella cheese, grated

2 small — or 1 medium — ripe tomato(es), sliced

1) Combine cornmeal, salt, and cold water in a small bowl. Have the boiling water on the stove in a saucepan, and add the cornmeal mixture, whisking. Cook about 10 minutes over low heat, stirring frequently. It will get very thick. Remove from heat, and let cool until handleable.

2) Preheat oven to 375°F. Oil a 10-inch pie pan. Add the polenta, and use a spatula and wet hands to form it into a smooth, thick crust over the bottom and sides of the pan. Brush the surface with olive oil, and bake uncovered for 45 minutes.

3) While the crust bakes, heat 1 Tbs. olive oil in a medium-sized skillet. Add the onion, and sauté for 5 to 8 minutes, or until it begins to soften. Add bell pepper, mushrooms, and zucchini, and sauté until everything is tender. Stir in the garlic and herbs, and sauté just a few minutes more.

4) Turn up the oven to broiling temperature. Sprinkle half the cheese onto the bottom of the baked crust, then add the tomato slices. Spread the sautéed mixture over the tomatoes, and sprinkle the remaining cheese on top. Broil until brown (about 5 minutes), and serve hot.

Zucchini-Crusted Pizza

~ a normal pizza on top, with a beautiful, substantial-yet-tender crust: golden, with flecks of green and a slight crunch.

~ If possible, use a food processor with the grating attachment for the zucchini and mozzarella.

~ You can make the crust up to several days in advance.

olive oil and flour for the pan
2 cups (packed) grated zucchini (about 2 7-inchers)
2 eggs, beaten (OK to delete one or both yolks)
¼ cup flour
½ cup grated mozzarella
½ cup grated parmesan
OPTIONAL: pinches of basil, marjoram, and/or rosemary
2 Tbs. olive oil

TOPPING SUGGESTIONS:

extra olive oil
1 large ripe tomato, sliced
extra mozzarella, sliced or grated
2 to 3 large cloves garlic, thinly sliced
sautéed mushrooms
thinly sliced bell peppers
sliced olives

1) Preheat oven to 400°F. Generously oil a 10-inch pie pan and coat lightly with flour. (You can also use a jelly roll pan.)
2) Combine zucchini, eggs, flour, mozzarella, parmesan, herbs, and 1 Tbs. olive oil in a bowl and mix well.
3) Spread into the prepared pan and bake for 35 to 40 minutes, or until golden brown. About halfway through the baking, brush with the remaining tablespoon of olive oil (optional). Remove from oven. When it has cooled for about 10 minutes, use a spatula to loosen the crust from the pan, so it won't break later.
4) Top with your favorite pizza items and bake at 400°F. until heated through.

Eggplant-Almond Enchiladas

... slightly different enchiladas, with deep flavor and wonderful textural contrasts

Serve with rice and plain beans or Refritos (following page). You'll need a batch of Mexican Red Sauce (p.95) made in advance.

1 Tbs. olive oil
1 cup minced onion
6 cups diced eggplant (approximately 1 large or 2 small)
1 tsp. salt (possibly more, to taste)
lots of black pepper
4 medium cloves garlic, minced
1 medium green bell pepper, minced
1 cup lightly toasted almonds, minced
1 packed cup grated jack cheese (or a similar mild white cheese)
12 corn tortillas
1 batch Mexican Red Sauce (p.95)

1) Heat olive oil in a deep skillet or Dutch oven. Add onion, and sauté for about 5 minutes over medium heat.

2) Add eggplant, salt, and pepper, and mix well. Cover and cook for about 10 minutes over medium heat, stirring occasionally, until the eggplant is soft.

3) Add garlic and bell pepper. Stir and cook 5 to 8 more minutes, or until the pepper is just tender. Taste to correct salt.

4) Remove from heat; stir in almonds and cheese.

5) Preheat oven to 350°F. Moisten each tortilla briefly in water, then place approximately ¼ cup of filling on one side and roll up. Gently situate the filled enchiladas in a baking pan. Pour a batch of sauce over the top. Bake uncovered for about 30 minutes.

REFRITOS
(REFRIED BEANS)

The beans need to soak for at least 4 hours; then to cook for about 1¼ hrs. Do other preparations while the beans cook.

𝔻𝔻𝔻𝔻𝔻𝔻𝔻

Yield: 6 to 8 servings

Serve Refritos in Tostadas (see below) or stuffed into bell peppers and baked, then served over rice with Nachos Sauce (p. 94). Or, for a plain and inexpensive dinner, serve with rice, green salad, and warm tortillas.

    2 cups dry pinto beans, soaked
    2 to 3 Tbs. olive oil
    2 cups minced onion
    5 to 6 (or even more) medium cloves garlic, minced
    2 tsp. cumin
    1½ tsp. salt
    black pepper
    optional: 1 small bell pepper, minced

1) Cook the presoaked beans in plenty of boiling water until very soft. Drain and set aside.

2) Heat the olive oil in a large skillet. Add onion, half the garlic, cumin, and salt. Sauté over medium heat about 10 minutes, or until the onions are soft. Add (or don't add) the optional bell pepper, and sauté another 5 minutes. Add remaining garlic; season with black pepper.

3) Turn heat to low, add beans, and mix well. Mash with a fork or a potato masher, and cook for just a few minutes more. Serve right away, or store in refrigerator or freezer until time to reheat. (Refritos reheat beautifully.)

ᏻᏻᏻᏻᏻᏻᏻᏻᏻ   TOSTADAS   𝔻𝔻𝔻𝔻𝔻𝔻𝔻𝔻𝔻

A tostada is a kind of open-faced Mexican sandwich, with many contrasting layers of food piled onto a crispy corn tortilla. Invite your friends over for a tostada-building party. Spread a large table with dishes of tostada components, and do it buffet-style. (Continued →)

Tostada Components:

1) DEEP-FRIED TORTILLAS: Fry corn tortillas in hot oil until crisp. Drain well on paper towels, and serve in a basket.

2) REFRITOS (preceding page)

3) ACCESSORIES: (use all or some ~ or add your own inspired ideas)
   shredded lettuce   minced olives   chopped hardboiled egg
   finely shredded cabbage   grated cheese   minced mild chilies
   Guacamole (p.108)   chopped tomatoes   sour cream

4) HOT SAUCE (p.95) or NACHOS SAUCE (p.94) or SALSA FRESCA (p.96).

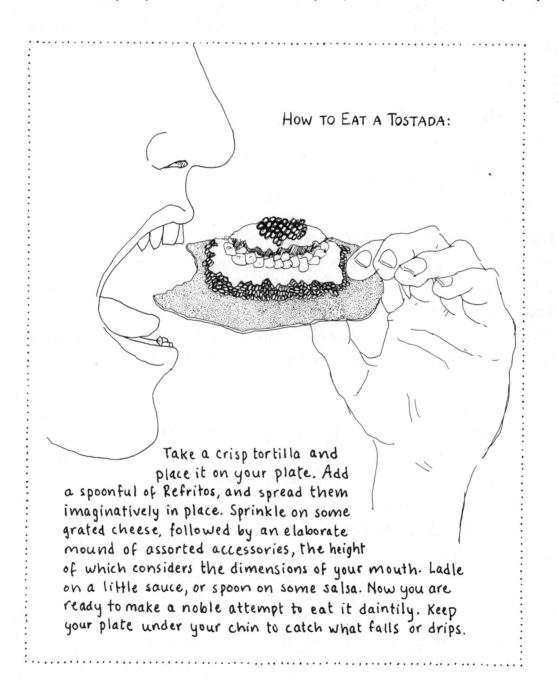

HOW TO EAT A TOSTADA:

Take a crisp tortilla and place it on your plate. Add a spoonful of Refritos, and spread them imaginatively in place. Sprinkle on some grated cheese, followed by an elaborate mound of assorted accessories, the height of which considers the dimensions of your mouth. Ladle on a little sauce, or spoon on some salsa. Now you are ready to make a noble attempt to eat it daintily. Keep your plate under your chin to catch what falls or drips.

SAMOSAS

1½ hours to prepare;
25 minutes to bake

Yield: 15 or 16 medium-sized, very satisfying pastries (enough to feed 6 to 8 people, at least)

Samosas are flaky pastries filled with spicy potatoes and peas. In traditional Indian cuisine, they are deep-fried (and that is still an option). But baking them works very well, and is easier and more healthful.

All components can be made well ahead of time. Finished Samosas can be stored for days in the refrigerator or freezer. Make the Dipping Sauce while the Samosas bake.

Serve Samosas with any curry, or as a simple supper with Gingered Carrot Soup (p.22) and Raita (p.99).

THE DOUGH:

2½ cups flour
½ tsp. salt
1 cup buttermilk or yogurt
extra flour, as needed

1) Place the flour in a medium-sized bowl. Mix in the salt.
2) Make a well in the center, and add the buttermilk or yogurt. Mix first with a spoon and then with your hand, to make a smooth dough.
3) Add extra flour, as needed, to keep the dough from being sticky. The dough will be quite soft. Knead in the bowl for about 5 minutes. Cover tightly and refrigerate until you are ready to assemble the pastries.

THE FILLING:

2 large potatoes (the size of a large person's fist)
1 Tbs. butter
1 cup finely minced onion
2 medium cloves garlic, minced
1 Tbs. freshly grated ginger

1 tsp. mustard seeds
1 tsp. dried coriander (if available)
¾ tsp. salt
1½ cups uncooked green peas (frozen, thawed = fine)
2 Tbs. lemon juice
cayenne, to taste

1) Peel the potatoes and chop them into 1-inch pieces. Place in a saucepan, cover with water, and boil until very soft. Drain and transfer to a medium-sized bowl. Mash and set aside. (continued on next page...)

2) Melt the butter in a heavy skillet. Add onion, garlic, ginger, mustard seeds, coriander, and salt. Sauté over medium heat about 8 to 10 minutes, or until the onions are quite soft. Add this to the mashed potatoes, along with the remaining ingredients. Mix well, but try not to smash the peas. Cool for at least 15 minutes before filling the pastries.

THE DIPPING SAUCE:

½ cup cider vinegar
½ cup water
3 Tbs. brown sugar
1 small clove garlic, minced
1 tsp. salt

1) Place all ingredients in a small saucepan. Stir until the sugar dissolves.
2) Heat to boiling, then let simmer uncovered for about 10 minutes. It will reduce slightly.
3) Serve warm or at room temperature with hot Samosas.

TO ASSEMBLE AND BAKE:

1) Preheat the oven to 425°F. Generously oil a baking sheet.
2) Keep a small container of flour, a fork, a small bowl of water, and a pastry brush close at hand. Flour a clean surface, and, one by one, roll 1-inch balls of dough into 5-inch circles, using a rolling pin.
3) Place approximately 1½ Tbs. filling in the center of each circle, and fold over, just like a turnover. Brush the inside edges of each circle with a little water, and fold the edges together to make a small hem. Crimp the edges firmly with the fork.
   NOTE: If you are storing the Samosas to bake later on, place them on a heavily floured plate or tray, dust the tops with more flour, and cover tightly. Store in the refrigerator or freezer until baking time.
4) To bake: Place the Samosas on the oiled baking sheet. Brush the tops with oil. Bake 15 minutes at 425°F., then reduce heat to 375°F. and bake for 10 minutes more. For maximum crispiness, turn the Samosas over when you turn the oven down.
5) Serve within 15 minutes of baking, with Dipping sauce. A nice way to serve the sauce is in individual saucers or tiny bowls, so each person can hold both Samosa and sauce directly under his or her face while eating, and the sauce bowl can catch the drips. (It does drip, but that's one of the charms of this ritual.)

EGGPLANT CURRY

Preparation time: 45 minutes
(Put up rice when you begin.)

Yield: 6 to 8 servings

2 to 3 Tbs. butter and/or peanut oil
1 Tbs. mustard seeds
2 Tbs. sesame seeds
2 tsp. cumin seeds
1½ cups chopped onion
1½ to 2 tsp. salt
2 tsp. turmeric
¼ tsp. cayenne (possibly more, depending on your tolerance/preference)
2 medium eggplants (7 to 8 inches long; 4-inch diameter at roundest
    point), cut into 1-inch cubes
water, as needed
2 cups frozen or fresh green peas
optional: 1 small bunch fresh cilantro, minced

1) Heat butter or oil over medium heat in a very large, deep skillet or
   Dutch oven. Add seeds, and sauté until they begin to pop (5 minutes).

2) Add onion, salt, turmeric, and cayenne. Cook, stirring occasionally,
   for 8 to 10 minutes, or until the onion is translucent.

3) Add eggplant and salt. Cook, stirring from the bottom regularly,
   for 15 to 20 minutes—until the eggplant is soft. You might need
   to add a little water if the mixture is too dry. Cover the pan between stirrings.

4) Steam the peas until they are just tender and bright green. Serve
   the curry over rice, topped with peas and freshly minced cilantro.

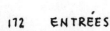

సత్యమ్మ ప్రసిద్ధి గోపి పువ్వు కూర

(Satyamma's Famous Cauliflower Curry)

30 to 40 minutes
to prepare

Yield:
about 6 servings

ON THE SIDE

Begin cooking some rice at around the same time you start preparing the curry.

2 cups brown rice in 3 cups water will be the right amount.

2 medium-small (3-inch diameter) potatoes, cut into small chunks
½ cup shredded unsweetened coconut
1 Tbs. mustard seeds
3 medium cloves garlic, peeled
1½ Tbs. minced fresh ginger
½ cup lightly toasted peanuts
1 tsp. turmeric
½ tsp. ground cloves or allspice
2 Tbs. toasted cumin seeds
1 to 2 Tbs. toasted sesame seeds
¼ tsp. cayenne
½ cup water (more, as needed)
1 to 2 Tbs. peanut oil
1½ cups chopped onion
1 tsp. salt
1 large cauliflower, cut in 1-inch pieces
1 medium carrot, thinly sliced
optional: 1 cup cooked chick peas
3 to 4 Tbs. lemon juice

ON THE SIDE

Your choice of condiments:

Raita (p. 99)
Lemon Slices
Orange slices
Toasted Nuts
Toasted Coconut
Raisins
Sliced Cucumbers
Sliced Tomatoes
Thin Strips of Bell Pepper (assorted colors)

1) Boil the potatoes until just tender. Drain and set aside.

2) Place the next 11 ingredients in a blender and purée until fairly homogenous. Add extra water, as needed, to form a soft, workable paste.

3) Heat the oil in a large, deep skillet or Dutch oven, and add onion and salt. Sauté for 5 minutes over medium heat, then add cauliflower and carrot and mix well. Cover and cook about 10 minutes, then add the paste. Mix well. Cook, covered, over low heat until the cauliflower is tender, stirring every few minutes. Add more water, if necessary, to prevent sticking.

4) Add the cooked potatoes, chick peas, and lemon juice, and cook a few more minutes. Taste to adjust salt, and serve hot, with rice and condiments.

✴ Mushroom Curry ✴

50 minutes to prepare
(put up rice when you
begin)

Yield:
4 to 6
servings

There are a few surprises in this tart-savory-sweet curry. Try sautéing chopped almonds in a little butter or margarine for the topping.

The tomatoes work best if peeled and seeded ahead of time. It's easy: just core them and plunge them into boiling water for 10 seconds. Pull off the peel, then cut them open and squeeze out the seeds. Chop the remaining pulp.

2 Tbs. butter or margarine

2 cups chopped onion

3 medium cloves garlic, minced

1 tsp. cumin

1 tsp. cinnamon

1 tsp. turmeric

1 tsp. powdered ginger

1 tsp. mustard seeds

½ tsp. cloves or allspice

1½ tsp. salt (possibly more, to taste)

1 cup chopped celery

1½ lbs. mushrooms, coarsely chopped

3 medium-sized tomatoes, chopped

2 medium-sized tart apples, chopped

½ cup shredded unsweetened coconut

1 Tbs. honey (optional, to taste)

3 to 4 Tbs. lemon juice

cayenne, to taste

optional toppings { yogurt / sautéed or toasted almonds

1) Melt the butter in a large, deep skillet or a Dutch oven. Add onions and garlic, and sauté over medium heat. After a few minutes add spices and salt. Sauté another 5 to 8 minutes ~ until onions are soft.

2) Add celery and mushrooms. Mix well, cover, and simmer another 8 to 10 minutes, stirring occasionally. You can add up to ½ cup water during this time, to prevent sticking. (It makes a nice broth.)

3) When the celery is slightly tender, add tomatoes, apples, coconut, honey, and lemon juice. Cover, and continue to cook until everything is tender, but not mushy. (Additional water may be needed. Use small amounts at a time.) Add cayenne to taste, cover, and let sit for about 10 minutes before serving. Serve over rice.

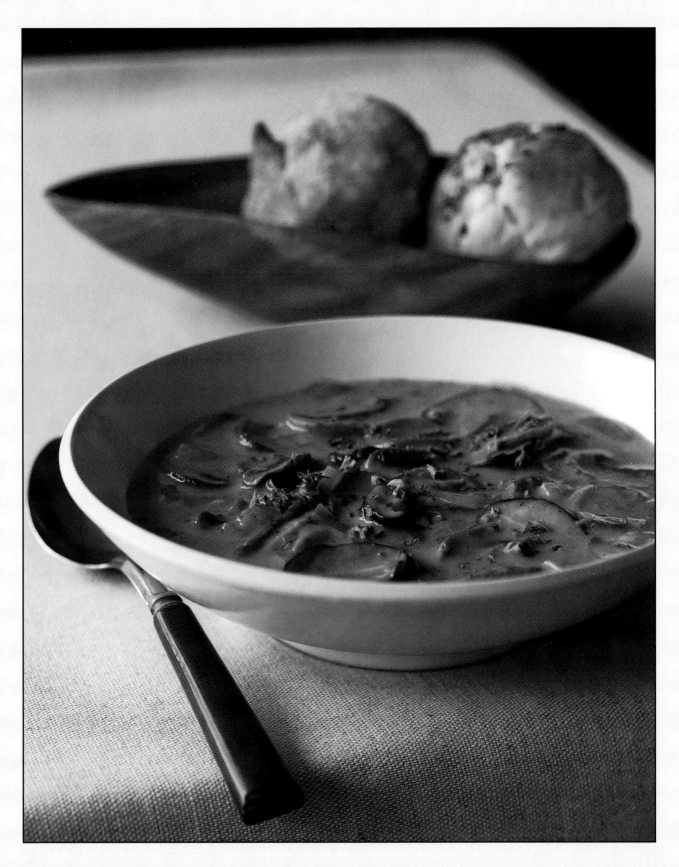

Hungarian Mushroom Soup (page 18)

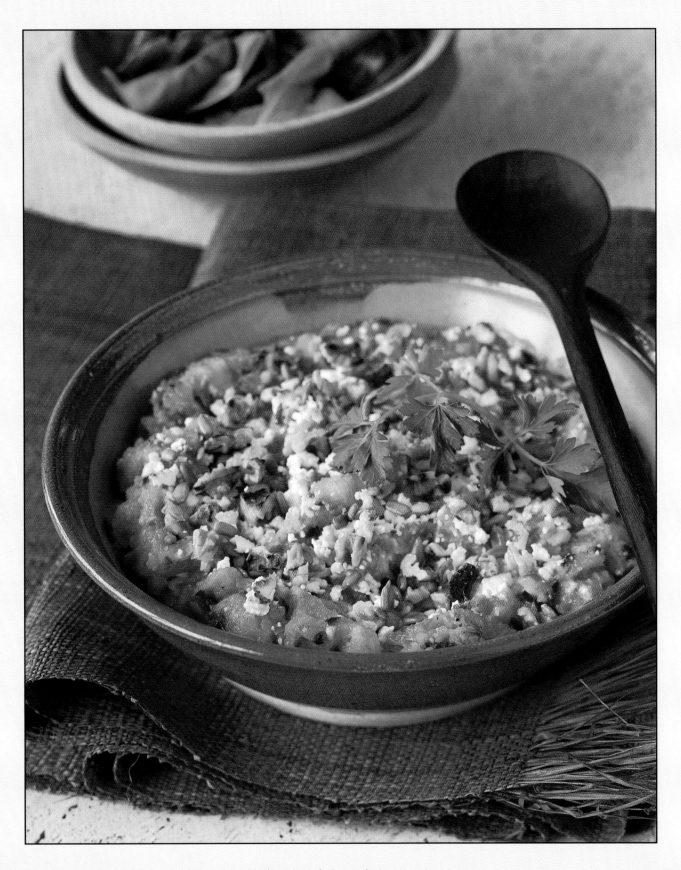

Arabian Squash Casserole (page 140)

Antipasto Platter (clockwise from top right): Just White Beans (page 60), Roasted Green Beans (page 67), Bell Peppers (page 65), Marinated Small Artichokes (page 65), Pickled Red Onions (page 60), and Cauliflower & Carrots (page 66)

Gado Gado (page 180)

Yield:
4 or 5
servings

TOMATO CURRY

... delicious on rice, with chutney (p.98) and Raita (p.99) or plain yogurt. Good, also, as an accompaniment to other curries. The eggs go well with the tomatoes, or you can use tofu, which is very similar to the Indian cheese, panir.

PRELIMINARY: Peel and seed the tomatoes beforehand. First, core the tomatoes, and drop them into a saucepanful of boiling water for 10 seconds. Then hold them over a sink and pull off the skins. (They will come right off.) Cut the tomatoes open; squeeze out and discard the seeds. Coarsely chop the remaining pulp.

1 Tbs. butter or oil

1½ cups chopped onion

1 tsp. salt

1 small bell pepper, minced

6 medium-sized ripe tomatoes, peeled and seeded (see above)

2 cups tomato purée

½ tsp. cinnamon

2 tsp. cumin

optional: ½ tsp. ground fenugreek
          ½ tsp. dried coriander

¼ tsp. cayenne (more, to taste)

optional: 3 hardboiled eggs, peeled and cut into wedges
          ½ lb. very firm tofu, cut into small cubes
          fresh cilantro, minced

2 tsp. mustard seeds

2 tsp grated ginger

3 to 4 medium cloves garlic, minced

1) Melt butter (or heat oil) in a Dutch oven. Add onion, salt, and mustard seeds. Sauté over medium heat for 8 to 10 minutes, or until the onions soften and the seeds begin to pop.

2) Add ginger, garlic, and minced bell pepper, and cook another 5 minutes, or until the pepper begins to be tender.

3) Add remaining ingredients, mix well, and heat just to boiling, stirring frequently. Turn the heat down to a simmer, cover, and cook for 15 to 20 minutes.

4) Serve hot, over rice, with wedges of egg or cubes of tofu artfully arranged on top, and a final sprinkling of minced cilantro.

Preparation time:
about 1¾ hours
after beans are soaked

Vegetarian Chili

A traditional chili, except with bulgur and without ground meat. Although the concept of "meat substitutes" is hardly compelling, the bulgur really does give a ground-beef-like texture. It also enhances the protein content.

Soak the beans for at least 4 hours (preferably overnight) before cooking. Prepare all other ingredients while the beans are cooking, to save time.

2 ½ cups dry kidney beans, soaked
1 cup tomato juice
1 cup uncooked bulgur wheat
2 Tbs. olive oil
2 cups chopped onion
6 to 8 large cloves garlic, minced
1 medium carrot, diced
1 medium stalk celery, diced
2 tsp. cumin

2 tsp. basil
2 tsp. chili powder (more, to taste)
1½ tsp. salt (more, to taste)
black pepper and cayenne, to taste
1 medium bell pepper, chopped
1 14½-oz. can tomatoes
3 Tbs. tomato paste (half a small can)
finely minced parsley ⎫
grated cheese ⎭ optional toppings

1) Place the soaked beans in a Dutch oven or kettle, cover with water, and bring to a boil. Partially cover, turn heat down to a simmer, and cook until tender (about 1¼ hours). Watch the water level during cooking, adding more if necessary. Drain off any excess water when the beans are done.

2) Heat the tomato juice to boiling. Add it to the bulgur in a small bowl, cover, and let stand 15 minutes. Add this to the cooked beans.

3) Heat the olive oil in a medium-sized skillet. Add onion, half the garlic, carrot, celery, and seasonings. Sauté over medium heat about 5 minutes, add bell pepper, and sauté until all the vegetables are tender.

4) Add the sautéed vegetables, tomatoes (au jus), and tomato paste to the beans. Simmer over lowest possible heat, stirring occasionally, for 20 to 30 minutes or longer. After about 15 minutes, add remaining garlic. Taste to adjust seasonings, and serve hot, topped with parsley and/or cheese.

VEGETABLE STEW

Preparation time:
about 50 minutes

Yield:
about 6 servings

2 Tbs. olive oil and/or butter
3 cups minced onion
3 medium cloves garlic, minced
2 medium potatoes, diced
1 medium (7-inch or so) eggplant, diced
1 tsp. salt (more, to taste)
fresh black pepper, to taste
2 medium stalks celery, chopped
1 healthy stalk broccoli, chopped small
2 to 3 medium carrots, sliced or diced
½ cup dry red wine (optional)
2 small (6-inch) zucchini, diced
3 Tbs. (half a small can) tomato paste
½ lb. mushrooms, coarsely chopped
3 Tbs. molasses
2 tsp. dill
sour cream or yogurt } optional
finely minced parsley } toppings

1) Heat oil (or melt butter) in a Dutch oven. Add onion, garlic, potatoes, eggplant, salt, and pepper. Cover and cook over medium heat, stirring often, until the potatoes are tender. Add small amounts of water, as needed, to prevent sticking.

2) Add celery, broccoli, and carrots, along with optional red wine. Continue to cook over medium heat, covered but occasionally stirring, until all the vegetables begin to be tender (8 to 10 minutes).

3) Add remaining ingredients (except toppings) and stir. Cover and simmer very quietly about 15 minutes more, stirring every once in a while. Taste to correct seasonings.

Serve piping hot, topped
with sour cream or yogurt
and minced parsley.

Polenta

Cornmeal mush with Class

For a super-easy, super-fast meal, serve Polenta in a bowl topped with a little olive oil or butter and some cheese. Or top it with Pesto (p. 84), Gorgonzola (or any blue cheese), chopped fresh tomatoes, and a generous amount of coarsely ground black pepper. You can also serve Polenta under or next to Ratatouille or its Spicy Variation (see following page) or paired with any kind of chili or bean dish (see pages 176 and 134).

> 5 cups water
> 1½ cups coarse cornmeal
> ½ tsp. salt
>
> OPTIONAL TOPPINGS : See above

1) Place 4 cups of water in a medium-sized saucepan and bring to a boil.

2) Combine the cornmeal with the remaining cup of water in a small bowl, and mix until uniform.

3) Spoon the cornmeal mixture into the boiling water, add salt, and whisk until smooth.

4) Turn the heat down to a simmer, and cook, stirring often, for about 10 minutes, or until very thick.

Ratatouille

Mediterranean vegetable stew

3 Tbs. olive oil
4 medium cloves garlic
2 cups chopped onion
1 bay leaf
1 medium eggplant (7 to 8 inches long; 4 to 5-inch diameter), cubed
1½ tsp. salt
1½ tsp. basil
1 tsp. marjoram or oregano
½ tsp. rosemary
½ tsp. thyme
1 medium (6-to 7-inch) zucchini, cubed

2 medium bell peppers, in strips
fresh black pepper
1 14½-oz. can tomatoes
freshly minced parsley} optional
minced olives

FOR SPICY VARIATION:
- omit bay leaf, marjoram, rosemary,
- add in their place:
    1½ tsp. cumin
    2 tsp. chili powder
    cayenne, to taste
- (optional): add 1 cup pitted, sliced oil-cured olives

1) Heat olive oil in a deep skillet or Dutch oven. Add garlic, onion, and bay leaf, and sauté over medium heat for about 5 minutes.

2) Add eggplant, salt, and herbs, and stir. Cover and cook over medium heat, stirring occasionally, for 15 to 20 minutes, or until the eggplant is soft.

3) Add zucchini, bell peppers, black pepper, and tomatoes. (Break the tomatoes into smaller pieces with a spoon.) Cover and simmer for about 10 more minutes, or until the zucchini and bell peppers are tender.

4) Serve hot, warm, or at room temperature — plain, or topped with parsley and/or olives.

Gado Gado

Preparation time: about 1 hour
(Much of this can be made
in advance.)

Yield: approximately
6 servings

An Indonesian extravaganza: Yellow rice on a bed of spinach, covered with vegetables, tofu, and hardboiled eggs. A gingery peanut sauce gets drizzled over the top, and crunchy, flavorful "final toppings" add a delightful finishing touch. AND IT'S ALL QUITE EASY - EVEN FOR BEGINNERS! HAVE FUN WITH THIS!

NOTE: All the ingredients can be prepared in advance and served warm or at room temperature.

GADO-GADO:

NOTE: You can vary the vegetables and their amounts. Also, they can be cooked or raw — or some of each. Arrange everything on a platter or on individual plates.

1) A bed of <u>fresh spinach</u> goes on the bottom.

2) <u>Yellow rice</u> goes on the spinach. (To make yellow rice, cook 2 cups rice in 3 cups simmering water with 1/2 tsp. turmeric. Add a little extra water toward the end of the cooking, if needed.) until tender.

3) <u>An assortment of vegetables</u> goes on the rice. Such as:
   ∼ A small bunch of broccoli, cut into small spears and steamed
   ∼ Fresh green beans, lightly steamed
   ∼ Red and green cabbage, very finely shredded
   ∼ Thin slices of carrot, lightly steamed or raw
   ∼ Mung bean sprouts

4) <u>Tofu and hardboiled eggs</u> (sliced or chopped) go on the vegetables.

PEANUT SAUCE:

1 cup creamy peanut butter
1 heaping Tbs. grated ginger
1 heaping Tbs. minced garlic
3 Tbs. brown sugar
1½ cups hot water

4 Tbs. cider vinegar
2 Tbs. soy sauce
1 tsp. salt (possibly more, if peanut butter is unsalted)
Crushed red pepper, to taste

1) Put everything in a blender and purée until smooth. If it's too thick, add a little extra water.

2) Transfer to a serving bowl and adjust seasonings to taste. Serve at any temperature, drizzled over Gado Gado. (This makes about 2 cups sauce.)

FINAL TOPPINGS:

3 Tbs. peanut or canola oil
2 Tbs. sliced fresh ginger (<u>very</u> thin slices, done with your sharpest paring knife)
1 cup finely minced onion
12 medium cloves garlic, peeled and thinly sliced

OPTIONAL {
Shredded, unsweetened coconut, lightly toasted
Crushed red pepper
Slices of fruit:
    lemons, limes, oranges, apples, pineapple
}

1) Heat 1 Tbs. oil in a small skillet. Add ginger, and sauté over medium heat for a minute or so, then transfer to a small bowl.

2) Repeat with the onion and garlic, sautéing each separately in 1 Tbs. oil for 8 to 10 minutes (onion) and about 20 seconds (garlic). Place each in a small bowl.

3) Place some or all of these toppings on the table with the Gado Gado, so each person can liberally garnish his or her own portion.

Vegetable Kebabs

Preparation time = 30 minutes, plus at least 2 hours to marinate. Actual cooking time is about 10 to 15 minutes.

Serves 6
(2 skewers apiece)

MARINADE: (can be doubled, if you like lots of extra for basting)

2/3 cup olive oil

1/4 cup red wine vinegar

5 medium cloves garlic, minced

1/2 tsp. salt

lots of freshly ground black pepper

1/2 tsp. marjoram or oregano

1/2 tsp. thyme

1/2 tsp. basil

a pinch or two of rosemary

1 medium (6-to 7-inch long) eggplant, cut into 1½-inch cubes

about a dozen cherry tomatoes

about a dozen medium-sized mushrooms

1 or 2 bell peppers (any color), cut into 2-inch strips

1 medium onion, cut into 1½-inch wedges

1½ lbs. very firm tofu, cut into 1½-inch cubes

OPTIONAL ADDITIONS:

1-inch slices of corn-on-the-cob, parboiled 5 minutes

1½-inch chunks of potato or sweet potato, parboiled about 8 minutes (until just tender)

1-inch chunks of zucchini or any summer squash

1) Prepare marinade in a long, shallow baking pan.

2) Add all other ingredients and stir gently. Let marinate, stirring occasionally, for at least 2 hours, and as long as overnight. (You don't have to get up and stir in the middle of the night.)

3) Arrange the marinated tidbits on 9- or 10-inch skewers in an imaginative sequence. Grill over hot coals or broil, basting frequently with the marinade and turning every few minutes. The cooking time is not exact, so watch them carefully, and remove from the heat as soon as they seem done (tender, browned, perfect). Baste one more time, and serve hot to your delighted guests, not forgetting to mention that the skewers, if metal, might be hot. Serve with rice or pasta.

Szechwan Eggplant & Tofu

Yield: 4 servings

Most of the preparation for this deeply seasoned stir-fry can be done well ahead of time. In addition, put up some rice to cook about 30 to 40 minutes before beginning the stir-fry.

3 Tbs. soy sauce
¼ cup dry sherry or Chinese rice wine
1 Tbs. white or brown sugar
1 Tbs. cider vinegar
3 Tbs. cornstarch

2 Tbs. peanut oil
1 medium onion, thinly sliced
1 large eggplant, cut into strips
   (thin slices lengthwise, then
   cut across. This should make
   about 7 to 8 cups of strips.)

¾ tsp. salt
2 Tbs. minced garlic
1 Tbs. minced fresh ginger
¼ tsp. black pepper

cayenne pepper, to taste
3 cakes (about ¾ lb.) firm tofu, cut into strips
8 scallions: greens minced, whites in strips (keep separate)
1 medium bunch fresh cilantro, minced (optional)

1) Combine soy sauce, sherry, sugar, and vinegar in a liquid-measuring cup. Add enough water to make 1 cup. Place cornstarch in a small bowl, pour in the liquid, and whisk until dissolved. Set aside, keeping the whisk handy.

2) Heat a large wok over a high flame. Add oil and onion, and stir-fry for about a minute. Add eggplant and salt, and stir-fry for 8 to 10 minutes, until the eggplant is soft. Add garlic, ginger, black pepper, and cayenne. Cook a few minutes more.

3) Add tofu and scallion bottoms. Stir the bowl of liquid (step 1) from the bottom, using the whisk, and add to the wok. Mix well, and stir-fry another few minutes, until the sauce is thick.

4) Remove from heat, and serve over rice, topped with minced scallion greens and fresh cilantro.

Carrot-Mushroom Loaf

30 minutes to assemble;
45 minutes to bake

Yield: 6 to 8 servings

I don't know why this is called a loaf, since it is baked in a 9 x 13-inch pan. But it's been called a loaf for so long, I hate to tamper with tradition. The original version had 4 Tbs. butter and 5 eggs. Now it's been pared down to 1 Tbs. butter and 2 eggs. Also, the amount of vegetables has been increased, keeping the yield at a good 6 to 8 servings — although it's a hard dish to stop eating, especially if it comes out of the oven when everyone is hungry.

A food processor fitted with the grating attachment makes short work of this casserole. Use it first to make the bread crumbs, then to grate both the carrots and the cheese — without cleaning it in between.

You can use store-bought bread crumbs, but homemade ones will make this dish taste exceptional. To make superb bread crumbs, the trick is to use superb bread.

NOTE: Once baked, this casserole can be frozen. It reheats beautifully.

2 cups minced onion
1 Tbs. butter
1 lb. mushrooms, chopped
1½ tsp. salt
1 tsp. basil
1 tsp. thyme
1 tsp. dill

3 to 4 medium cloves garlic, minced
1½ lbs. carrots, grated (about 6 cups)
2 cups superb bread crumbs
1 cup (packed) grated cheddar
2 eggs, beaten
black pepper, to taste
OPTIONAL TOPPINGS: extra dill, cheese, bread crumbs; a sprinkling of sesame seeds } any, some, or all (ALL = GREAT!)

1) Lightly oil a 9 x 13-inch baking pan. Preheat the oven to 350°F.

2) In a large skillet, sauté onions in butter over medium heat for about 5 minutes. Add mushrooms, salt, herbs, and garlic, and continue to sauté for about 10 more minutes.

3) In a large bowl, combine carrots, bread crumbs, cheese, eggs, and pepper. Add the sautéed mixture and mix well. Spread into the prepared pan and sprinkle with your choice of toppings. Cover the pan with foil.

4) Bake for 30 minutes covered, then uncover and bake 15 minutes more. Serve hot or warm.

DESSERTS

I've tried to include something for just about everyone in this fun collection of desserts: a variety of cakes and pies, some simple fruit desserts, baked puddings, a selection of cheesecakes, and, of course, the old stand-bys—Moosewood Fudge Brownies, Carrot Cake, and No-Fault Pumpkin Pie. There are also some new treats here: Caribbean Dream Pie, Lemon or Chocolate Meringues, Danish Cherries, Bittersweet Chocolate Custard, and more! I hope you find many things here to love.

TABLE OF CONTENTS: DESSERTS

Date-Nut Cake

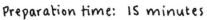

Preparation time: 15 minutes
Baking time: 40 to 50 minutes

Yield: about 6 servings

butter and flour for the pan
3 eggs, separated and
  at room temperature
1/4 cup sugar
1/2 tsp. vanilla extract

1/3 cup flour
1/4 tsp. salt
3/4 cup very finely chopped
  nuts (walnuts, almonds, or pecans)
1 cup chopped dates

TOPPING
1/2 pint heavy cream or 1 cup ricotta cheese
1/2 tsp. vanilla extract
2 to 3 Tbs. powdered sugar (or, to taste)

1) Preheat oven to 350°F. Generously butter and flour a 9-inch round pan.

2) In a medium-sized bowl, beat the egg whites with an electric mixer at high speed until stiff but not dry.

3) In a second medium-sized bowl, beat the egg yolks with sugar and vanilla for several minutes — until smooth and thick.

4) Stir the flour, salt, nuts, and dates into the yolk mixture and blend well. Gently fold in the beaten egg whites.

5) Transfer to the prepared pan and bake for 40 minutes, or until the surface of the cake springs back when touched lightly. Remove from the oven and allow to cool in the pan. Invert onto a serving plate.

6) Combine the cream or ricotta with vanilla and powdered sugar, and whip to your favorite consistency. Spread over the top of the cake, and chill. Serve cold.

Orange Cake

Preparation time: 30 minutes
Baking time: 50 to 60 minutes
-Allow time to cool and glaze.

Yield: 1 large cake,
serves 12 to 16

butter for the pan
1½ cups (3 sticks) butter, softened
1¾ cups sugar
4 eggs

1 tsp. grated orange rind
1 tsp. vanilla extract
3 cups flour
1 Tbs. baking soda

½ tsp. salt
1 cup sour cream or yogurt } whisked together
½ cup orange juice

ORANGE GLAZE:
½ cup orange juice
1 to 2 Tbs. sugar
1 Tbs. lemon juice
optional: 2 to 3 Tbs. dry sherry or orange liqueur

1) Preheat oven to 350°F. Butter a 10-inch tube or bundt pan.
2) In a large bowl, beat together the butter and sugar until light and fluffy.
3) Add the eggs, one at a time, beating well after each.
4) Stir in the orange rind and vanilla. Set aside.
5) Sift together the dry ingredients in a separate bowl. Add this to the butter mixture alternately with the combined sour cream (or yogurt) and orange juice, beginning and ending with the dry ingredients. Mix by hand after each addition—just enough to combine well.
6) Turn into the prepared pan. Bake 50 to 60 minutes, or until a knife inserted all the way down comes out clean. Cool for about 15 minutes, then invert onto a plate. Allow to cool completely.
7) Combine the glaze ingredients in a small saucepan and bring to a boil. Lower heat and simmer uncovered for about 3 minutes. Pour the hot glaze onto the cooled cake. Let stand at least 10 minutes before slicing.

Ukrainian Poppy Seed Cake

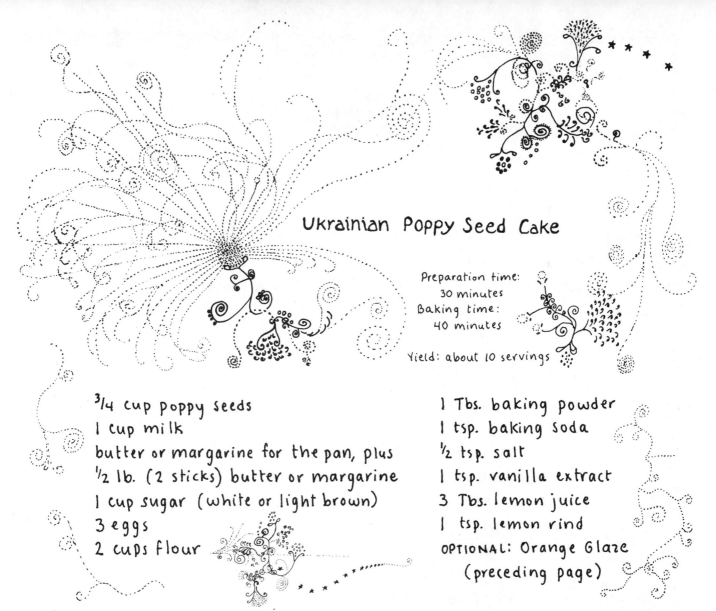

Preparation time:
30 minutes
Baking time:
40 minutes

Yield: about 10 servings

¾ cup poppy seeds
1 cup milk
butter or margarine for the pan, plus
½ lb. (2 sticks) butter or margarine
1 cup sugar (white or light brown)
3 eggs
2 cups flour

1 Tbs. baking powder
1 tsp. baking soda
½ tsp. salt
1 tsp. vanilla extract
3 Tbs. lemon juice
1 tsp. lemon rind
OPTIONAL: Orange Glaze
   (preceding page)

1) Place poppy seeds and milk in a small saucepan. Heat just to the boiling point, but remove from heat before it actually boils. (This is called scalding.) Set aside and allow to cool for at least 15 minutes.

2) Preheat oven to 350°F. Butter a 10-inch tube or bundt pan.

3) Cream the butter and sugar in a large mixing bowl. Add eggs, one at a time, beating well after each.

4) Sift together the dry ingredients in a separate bowl. Add this to the butter mixture alternately with the poppy seed-milk, beginning and ending with the dry mixture. Stir just enough to blend thoroughly, adding the vanilla, lemon juice, and lemon rind at the end.

5) Spread the batter into the prepared pan, and bake for about 40 minutes, or until a cake tester comes out clean. Cool for 10 minutes, then invert onto a plate. Allow to cool completely before adding the Orange Glaze (same method as on preceding page) and/or slicing.

Pound Cake

Preparation time:
15 minutes

Baking time: 50
to 60 minutes

Yield:
12 to 16
servings

The most basic cake - and the most buttery. Try it plain for dessert, or topped with fresh Fruit Salad (p. 54) for a serious snack. You can also slice it thinly and toast it for tea or brunch. A few variations appear on the opposite page, and you can explore even further with your own ideas.

butter and flour for the pans
1 lb. (4 sticks) butter, softened
3 cups sugar
6 eggs
4 cups flour
1 Tbs. baking powder
1/2 tsp. salt
1 cup milk
2 tsp. vanilla extract

1) Preheat oven to 350°F. Butter and flour the bottom and sides of a 10-inch tube or bundt pan.

2) In a large bowl, cream together butter and sugar with an electric mixer at high speed until light and fluffy.

3) Add eggs, one at a time, beating well after each. Set aside.

4) Sift together the dry ingredients in a separate bowl. Mix together the milk and vanilla. Add dry and wet alternately to butter mixture, beginning and ending with dry. Mix by hand — just enough to blend thoroughly without excess beating.

5) Spread the batter into the prepared pan. Bake 50 to 60 minutes, or until a sharp knife inserted all the way down comes out clean. Allow to cool for 10 minutes in the pan, then turn out onto a plate. Cool completely before slicing.

Pound Cake Variations

Here are some delightful adulterations you can perform in your own kitchen. For each of these variations, follow the pound cake recipe on the opposite page, with the following changes:

Lemon Pound Cake

1) Replace vanilla with lemon extract.

2) Add ¼ cup fresh lemon juice.

3) Add 1 tsp. freshly grated lemon rind.

Blueberry Pound Cake

~ Same changes as for Lemon Pound Cake, plus:
2 cups fresh blueberries, folded in gently with the last addition of dry ingredients

Mocha-Swirl Pound Cake

1) Replace the milk with 1 cup strong black coffee.

2) After the batter is all assembled, transfer about ⅓ of it to a small bowl, and add 1 oz. (1 square) melted unsweetened chocolate. Mix thoroughly.

3) Spread the plain batter into the prepared pan and spoon clumps of chocolate batter on top. Using a humble dinner knife, cut through to the bottom of the pan and swirl the dark and light together to create a marbled effect. Bake as directed.

Carrot Cake

20 minutes to prepare;
35 to 50 minutes
to bake

Yield: about 12
to 16 servings

butter, margarine, or oil for the pan(s)
optional: about ¼ cup poppy seeds

1½ cups (3 sticks) butter or margarine, softened
1¾ cups (packed) brown sugar
4 eggs
3 tsp. vanilla extract
1 tsp. grated lemon rind
4 cups flour
1 tsp. salt
½ tsp. baking soda
1 Tbs. baking powder
1 tsp. allspice
2 tsp. cinnamon
2½ cups (packed) finely shredded carrot } combined
¼ cup lemon juice

OPTIONAL ADDITIONS: ¾ cup raisins or currants
¾ cup chopped pecans or walnuts
½ cup shredded unsweetened coconut

1) Preheat oven to 350°F. Generously grease 2 standard-sized loaf pans
or 1 oblong pan (9 x 13, or 10 x 14). Sprinkle in the poppy seeds; tilt
and shake the pan(s) to distribute the seeds. They will stick nicely.
2) Beat together butter or margarine and sugar in a large bowl. Add
eggs, one at a time, beating well after each. When the mixture is fluffy,
stir in the vanilla and lemon rind.
3) Sift together the dry ingredients. Add this to the butter mixture alternately with the carrots, beginning and ending with the dry mixture. Mix
just enough after each addition to combine — don't overmix. Stir in the
optional items (or not) with the last flour addition.
4) Spread the batter evenly in the pan(s), and bake 40 to 50 minutes
(loaf pans) or 35 minutes (oblong pan) — or until a probe inserted into
the center comes out clean. For loaf pans: cool 10 minutes in the pan,
then rap the pan sharply, and dislodge and remove the cake. Transfer to
a rack, and let it cool at least 1 hour before slicing.

Banana Bread

Banana Bread is basically the same recipe as Carrot Cake (opposite page), but with the following changes:

1) Replace the poppy seeds with sesame seeds.

2) Use 2½ tsp. vanilla extract and ½ tsp. almond extract.

3) Use orange rind, instead of lemon.

4) Substitute ½ tsp. nutmeg for the allspice.

5) Replace the carrot with 2 cups puréed ripe banana soaked in 1 cup strong black coffee (can be decaf).

6) Omit the raisin/currant and coconut options.

Apricot-Almond Bread

40 minutes to prepare;
about 1½ hours to bake

Yield: 1 large loaf

Moist and tart with apricots and crunchy with almonds, this bread is ideal for brunches and teas. It's also good as a mid-evening semi-dessert, when you want <u>Something</u> — sweet, but not too — and you don't know exactly what. Try this bread at such times.

butter for the pan
1½ cups thinly sliced
   dried apricots
1½ cups water
2½ cups flour
1 tsp. baking soda
2 tsp. baking powder

1 tsp. salt
2 Tbs. softened butter
½ cup honey or real maple syrup
1 egg, beaten
1 tsp. vanilla extract
½ to 1 tsp. orange rind
1 cup finely chopped almonds

1) Preheat oven to 350°F. Butter a large loaf pan.

2) Place apricots and water in a medium-sized saucepan and bring to a boil. Lower the heat, cover, and simmer for 10 minutes. Transfer to a medium-sized bowl, and allow to cool for about 15 minutes.

3) Sift together dry ingredients (except almonds) in a separate bowl.

4) Stir the butter plus honey or syrup into the cooled apricot mixture. Beat in the egg and vanilla.

5) Add the dry ingredients, orange rind, and almonds. Mix minimally but well.

6) Spread into the prepared pan, and bake about 1½ hours, or until a probe inserted all the way down comes out clean. Let cool for 10 minutes in the pan, then rap the pan firmly a few times on its sides and bottom. The bread should slip right out. Cool at least 15 minutes more before attempting to slice.

Cardamom Coffee Cake

Very rich ~ very delicious

1¾ hours to prepare and bake

16 servings

oil or butter for the pan
1 lb. (4 sticks) butter or margarine (or a combination), softened
2 cups (packed) light brown sugar
4 eggs
2 tsp. vanilla extract
4 cups flour
2 tsp. baking powder
2½ tsp. baking soda

½ tsp. salt
1 Tbs. powdered cardamom
2 cups sour cream, yogurt, or buttermilk

NUT MIXTURE:
¼ cup (packed) light brown sugar
1 Tbs. cinnamon
½ cup finely chopped walnuts

1) Preheat oven to 350°F. Butter or oil a 10-inch tube or bundt pan.

2) In a large mixing bowl, beat butter or margarine with sugar until light and fluffy. Add eggs, one at a time, beating well after each. Stir in the vanilla.

3) Sift together the dry ingredients (not including nut mixture ingredients) in a separate bowl.

4) Add the flour mixture, ⅓ of it at a time, to the butter mixture, alternating with the sour cream (or yogurt or buttermilk). Stir just enough to blend after each addition. Don't beat or otherwise over mix.

5) Combine the nut mixture ingredients in a separate small bowl.

6) Spoon approximately ⅓ the batter into the prepared pan. Sprinkle with half the nut mixture, then add another third of the batter. Cover with remaining nut mixture, then top with remaining batter. Lightly spread into place.

7) Bake approximately 1¼ hours or until a knife inserted all the way in comes out clean. Allow to cool in the pan for 20 minutes, then invert onto a plate. Cool at least 30 minutes more before wildly devouring.

🍎 APPLE STRUDEL 🍎

This delicious and straightforward Apple Strudel can be made several days in advance and stored, unbaked, in the refrigerator (tightly wrapped). Baked strudel also keeps very well in the refrigerator or freezer if wrapped airtight. If you freeze it, defrost it completely before reheating it, uncovered, in a 350°F oven for about 20 minutes—or until crispened.

NOTE: To make fine bread crumbs, cut several thick slices of whole wheat or white bread, and let them dry out for a few hours. Then toast the slices lightly, and grind them to a fine meal in a blender or a food processor.

6 Tbs. vegetable oil—OR ½ cup melted butter—OR oil spray

1½ lbs. tart apples (about 8 medium ones), peeled and chopped

¼ cup sugar

A pinch of salt

1 tsp. cinnamon

3 Tbs. fresh lemon juice

1 Tbs. grated lemon rind

½ cup minced walnuts, lightly toasted

½ cup fine bread crumbs

¼ cup raisins (optional)

1 cup grated cheddar (optional)

A 1-lb. package filo pastry

1) Preheat oven to 375°F. Brush a baking tray with a little of the oil or melted butter, or spray it with oil spray. (Save most of the oil or butter for the filo.)

2) Place all the ingredients except the filo in a large bowl, and toss gently until everything is evenly distributed.

3) Place a sheet of filo on a clean, dry surface, and brush it lightly all over with oil or melted butter—or spray it with oil spray. Lay another sheet on top, oil or butter it all over, and continue until you have a pile of 6. Distribute ⅓ of the apple mixture here, fold over the sides, and roll up this way.

4) Oil or butter the top of the roll, then transfer it to the prepared tray. Repeat with the remaining ingredients to make 2 more rolls.

5) Bake for about 35 minutes, or until lightly browned and exquisitely crisp. Serve warm or at room temperature.

⚜ MERINGUES ⚜

Meringues have the great ability to satisfy all longings for a rich dessert, yet they contain no butter, oil, egg yolks, or flour.

These two versions provide a contrast of textures: an ethereal crunch on the first bite, followed by full-bodied chewiness. The baking process is slow and gradual — almost more of a drying-out than an actual baking.

<u>TO BAKE MERINGUES</u>: Preheat oven to 250°F. Lightly grease a baking tray - OR line it with parchment or waxed paper. Bake the meringues for 2½ to 3 hours without opening the oven. Then turn off the oven, and leave them in there for at least 15 minutes. (You can also leave them in for up to an hour or two. This part is flexible!) Cool completely before removing them from the tray.

Meringues will turn out softer or firmer, depending on the humidity in your kitchen. Store them in an airtight bin lined with waxed paper.

ONE MORE THING: Separate the eggs while they're cold, then let the whites come to room temperature. See the opposite page for a few ideas for the unused yolks.

---

10 minutes to prepare
3 hours to bake

⚜ CHOCOLATE MERINGUES ⚜

Yield: 1½ dozen
(easily doubled)

	OPTIONAL:	4 egg whites
1 cup powdered sugar	¼ cup hazelnuts,	½ tsp. vanilla
2 Tbs. cocoa	pecans, or almonds	optional: ½ cup chocolate chips
a pinch of salt		

1) Sift together powdered sugar, cocoa, and salt. If you're adding nuts, place them in a blender or food processor with the sugar mixture, and grind in a series of spurts until the nuts and sugar form a fine powder.
2) Beat together the egg whites and vanilla at high speed until they form stiff peaks. Fold in the sugar-nut mixture (or just the cocoa-sugar) and the chocolate chips.
3) Drop by rounded tablespoonfuls onto the prepared tray. Bake as described above.

---

15 minutes to prepare;
3 hours to bake

⚜ LEMON MERINGUES ⚜

Yield: 1 dozen
(easily doubled)

	¼ cup fresh lemon juice	
2 Tbs. cornstarch	¼ cup water	3 egg whites
½ cup powdered sugar	½ tsp. grated lemon rind	1 Tbs. granulated sugar

1) Place cornstarch and powdered sugar in a small saucepan.
2) Combine the lemon juice and water, and whisk this into the cornstarch-sugar. Stir in the lemon rind.
3) Heat to boiling, whisking frequently. Lower heat to a simmer; cook and whisk until very thick. (This will only take about a minute.) Cool for 15 minutes.
4) Beat the egg whites at medium speed until they get foamy. Add the granulated sugar, then beat at high speed until the egg whites form stiff peaks.
5) Add the lemon mixture, and fold until fairly well mixed. (It won't be uniform.) Drop by rounded tablespoons onto the prepared tray. Bake as described above.

STOVETOP RICE PUDDING

~ Eggless, and possibly even dairy-free!

Eggs are not going to be missed in this good rice pudding – it's as rich-tasting as one could desire. Use lowfat or even nonfat milk – or make a dairy-free version with rice milk (plain or vanilla) or soy milk. Both of these are available in most natural foods stores.

To make this recipe with leftover cooked rice: place 2 cups cooked rice in a saucepan with 1 cup milk. Heat to boiling, lower heat to a simmer, and cook, covered, for 20 to 30 minutes, or until the milk is mostly absorbed. Add remaining ingredients and mix well.

1 cup short-grain brown rice
3 to 3½ cups milk (low-or nonfat, rice, or soy)
½ to ¾ tsp. salt
3 to 5 Tbs. sugar, honey, or real maple syrup
½ tsp. vanilla extract

½ tsp. cinnamon
a dash of nutmeg
a handful of raisins ⎱
2 to 3 tsp. lemon juice ⎰ OPTIONAL
extra cinnamon or
   nutmeg

possible toppings: yogurt
chopped fresh or dried fruit
chopped nuts

1) Rinse the rice in a strainer. Drain well, and place in a saucepan with 3 cups milk. Bring to a boil, cover, and lower heat as much as possible. Simmer until the rice is very tender. This will take up to 1½ hours.

2) About 1 hour into the cooking, stir in salt, sweetening, vanilla, spices, and optional raisins. (When adding the sweetening, start with about 3 Tbs. This dish is naturally sweet, and it's easy to overdo it.)

3) Optional Step: If you want an extra-thick and creamy rice pudding, purée about 1 cup of the rice in a blender with ½ cup additional milk. Return the purée to the rest of the rice; mix well.

4) Stir in lemon juice to taste, if desired, and adjust sweetening. Optional: sprinkle a little extra cinnamon and/or nutmeg on top (go easy!) for a finishing touch. Serve at room temperature or cold, possibly topped with yogurt, fresh or dried fruit, and/or nuts.

old-fashioned
BREAD PUDDING

Humble and easy, yet very rewarding. And transcendent served warm, with ice cream!

This is one of the few instances where ordinary white bread is actually preferable to whole grain.

3 to 4 packed cups cubed bread
(OK if stale or frozen)
3 eggs
3 cups milk (lowfat OK)
1/3 cup sugar (more or less, to taste)
1/2 tsp. salt
2 tsp. vanilla extract

OPTIONAL TOPPINGS:
{
ice cream
Berry Sauce (p. 207)
sliced fresh peaches and/or strawberries
}

1) Preheat oven to 350°F. Have ready a 9 x 13-inch baking pan.
2) Spread the bread in the pan.
3) Beat together remaining ingredients. Pour this custard over the bread.
4) Bake about 35 minutes, or until firm but not dry. Serve warm or at room temperature.

VARIATIONS

POOR PERSON'S TRIFLE

add to custard
{
1/4 cup rum
1 1/2 cups crushed pineapple au jus (canned-in-juice = fine)
1 1/2 cups berries or pitted cherries (frozen unsweetened = fine. No need to defrost.)
}
OPTIONAL: 1 cup chopped walnuts

BREAD & CHOCOLATE PUDDING   Add to the bread: 1 1/2 cups semisweet chocolate chips

BANANA BREAD PUDDING   Add to the bread: 1 or 2 ripe bananas, sliced.
OPTIONAL: a few dashes of cinnamon and nutmeg.

◯ Baked Custard ◯
(Bittersweet Chocolate; Maple; Maple-Peach)

Easy super-comfort food

Yield: 6
custard cups

BITTERSWEET CHOCOLATE CUSTARD:

Preparation time:
20 minutes
(45 minutes to bake)

2½ cups milk (lowfat works just fine)
¾ to 1 cup semisweet chocolate chips (depending
   on how deeply chocophilic you are)
4 eggs
½ tsp. salt
1 tsp. vanilla extract

1) Preheat oven to 350°F. Have ready six ovenproof custard cups and a
   9 x 13-inch baking pan.
2) Place the milk and chocolate chips in a small saucepan. Heat gently,
   stirring occasionally, until all the chips are melted. Remove from heat
   and stir until blended. Allow to cool for about 15 minutes.
3) Place remaining ingredients in a blender or food processor. Add the milk
   mixture, scraping in all the wayward clumps of chocolate, and whip
   until frothy.
4) Divide the batter among the custard cups. Place them in the baking
   pan, and half-fill it with water. Bake 40 to 45 minutes, or until the
   custards are solid in the center when shaken.
5) Carefully remove the cups from the baking pan. Cool to room temperature,
   then cover each one tightly with plastic wrap and chill.

MAPLE CUSTARD

Preparation time:
10 minutes

omit chocolate chips
add ⅓ cup real maple syrup
optional: a dash each of cinnamon and nutmeg

~ Skip Step 2. Blend all ingredients together in Step 3. Bake as directed.

MAPLE-PEACH CUSTARD

Preparation time:
15 minutes

1½ to 2 cups sliced fresh peaches

~ Make Maple Custard batter. Divide the peaches among the custard cups,
pour the custard over the peaches, and bake as directed.

STRAWBERRY·RHUBARB CRISP

Preparation time: 15 minutes   Baking time: 35 to 40 minutes   Yield: about 6 servings

...An easy cobbler with a very crunchy top. Use the smaller amount of sugar if you like it tart. It would be a good idea to have some vanilla ice cream on hand, since you might decide that you can't bear not to have this dessert à la mode.

2 lbs. fresh rhubarb,
   cut into 1-inch chunks
3 to 4 cups sliced strawberries
1/3 to 1/2 cup white sugar

1 1/4 cups rolled oats
1 cup flour
1/4 cup brown sugar
3/4 tsp. cinnamon
a dash or two of both
   allspice and nutmeg
1/2 tsp. salt
1/2 cup (1 stick) melted butter

1) Preheat oven to 375°F.
2) Combine the rhubarb and strawberries in a 9-inch square pan. Sprinkle with white sugar.
3) Mix together the remaining ingredients in a medium-sized bowl. Distribute over the top of the fruit and pat firmly into place.
4) Bake uncovered for 35 to 40 minutes, or until the top is crisp and lightly browned and the fruit is bubbling around the edges. Serve hot, warm, or at room temperature, plain or à la mode.

variations using other fruits:
APPLE CRISP
- Use 6 to 8 cups peeled and sliced tart apples
- 2 to 3 Tbs. lemon juice
- 1/4 cup white sugar
- increase cinnamon (use up to 1 tsp.)
- optional: add 1/2 cup finely chopped walnuts to the topping

PEACH (or APRICOT)·CHERRY CRISP
- Use about 4 cups peeled and sliced peaches or apricots, plus
  2 cups pitted, halved dark cherries (OK to use frozen unsweetened)
- Same adjustments as in Apple Crisp. In addition, you can increase the nutmeg to 1/4 tsp. and use almonds instead of walnuts in the topping.

Apple
Custard
Pie

Preparation time: 25 minutes

Baking time: 45 minutes

Yield: 4 to 6 servings

2 cups peeled and thinly sliced tart apples

1 unbaked 9-inch pie crust (see p. 156)

4 eggs (ok to omit 2 of the yolks)

¼ to ⅓ cup brown sugar or honey

1 cup yogurt

1 tsp. vanilla extract

½ tsp. cinnamon

¼ tsp. salt

OPTIONAL VARIATIONS:
- Replace the sugar or honey with real maple syrup.
- Replace the apples with sliced peaches or pitted, halved dark cherries.
- Sprinkle a small handful of chopped nuts on top.

1) Preheat oven to 375°F.

2) Spread the apple slices evenly over the unbaked pie crust.

3) Combine all remaining ingredients in a food processor or blender and whip until frothy. Pour this custard over the apples.

4) Bake for 45 minutes, or until solid in the center. Cool for at least 1 hour before slicing. This pie tastes best at room temperature or cold.

20 minutes to prepare
(including crust);
50 minutes to bake

No-Fault Pumpkin Pie

FILLING:

2 cups cooked, puréed pumpkin or squash
   (Canned pumpkin is fine)
1/4 cup white sugar
1/4 cup brown sugar
2 Tbs. molasses
1/2 tsp. ground cloves or allspice
2 tsp. cinnamon
2 tsp. powdered ginger
3/4 tsp. salt
2 beaten eggs
1 cup evaporated milk (lowfat OK)
1 unbaked 9-inch pie crust (recipe on p. 156)

OPTIONAL TOPPINGS:
whipped cream with a little sugar and rum
whipped cream with a little sugar and vanilla extract
vanilla ice cream

1) Preheat oven to 375°F.
2) Place pumpkin or squash purée in a medium-sized bowl, and add
   all other filling ingredients. Beat until smooth.
3) Spread into the pie crust and bake at 375° for 10 minutes. Turn
   the oven down to 350°, and bake another 40 minutes, or until
   the pie is firm in the center when shaken lightly.
4) Cool at least to room temperature before serving. This pie tastes
   very good chilled, with rum- or vanilla-spiked whipped cream, or
   some high-quality vanilla   ice cream.

Maple-Walnut Pie

Delicious — and very easy!

Preparation time:
20 minutes

Baking time:
30 minutes

Yield:
about 6
servings

4 large eggs
3/4 cup real maple syrup
2 Tbs. lemon juice
1/4 to 1/2 tsp. cinnamon (to taste)
1 1/2 tsp. vanilla extract
1/4 tsp. salt
2 cups chopped walnuts
1 unbaked 9-inch pie crust (p.156)
OPTIONAL: whipped cream, for the top

1) Preheat oven to 375°F.

2) Beat together all ingredients, except walnuts and pie crust, until light and frothy.

3) Spread the walnuts into the unbaked crust. Pour in the batter.

4) Bake for 30 minutes or until solid in the center. Remove from oven and allow to cool for at least 30 minutes before serving.

5) Serve warm, at room temperature, or cold, with or without whipped cream.

Crunchy-Top Peach Pie

Preparation time: about 40 minutes

Baking time: about another 40 minutes

Yield: 6 servings

Make this at the height of peach season, with the finest, ripest peaches available. Or, you can freeze some of those same fine, ripe peaches (peel and slice them first; spread on a tray and freeze, then transfer to a plastic bag, seal, and store in the freezer), and surprise everyone with this delightful pie in November.

If you have access to some equally fine and ripe apricots, they will work equally well.

6 cups sliced ripe peaches

¼ to ⅓ cup sugar

3 Tbs. fresh lemon juice

3 Tbs. flour

1 tsp. cinnamon

a few dashes of nutmeg

1 unbaked 9-inch pie crust (p. 156)

TOPPING:

2 cups rolled oats

¼ cup flour

½ tsp. salt

½ tsp. cinnamon

½ cup minced almonds

3 Tbs. brown sugar

5 Tbs. melted butter

POSSIBLE ACCOMPANIMENTS:

ice cream (recommended: vanilla, almond, or amaretto)

whipped cream

nothing at all

1) Preheat oven to 400°F.

2) Place peaches in a medium-sized bowl and sprinkle with sugar and lemon juice.

3) Combine 3 Tbs. flour and spices, and sprinkle this into the peaches. Mix gently but thoroughly. Spread this filling into the unbaked crust.

4) Combine topping ingredients in the same bowl (no need to wash it first), and mix well. Apply the topping evenly over the top, patting it firmly into place.

5) Bake for 10 minutes at 400°F, then turn the oven down to 375° and bake for about 30 minutes more. Serve warm or cold, with ice cream or whipped cream, or just plain.

REAL BLUEBERRY PIE

About 1¼ hours
to prepare
(including baking)

Yield:
4 to 6
servings

1 <u>double</u> recipe pie crust (p. 156)
extra flour for handling the dough

6 cups blueberries (fresh or frozen/defrosted)
2 tsp. grated lemon rind
2 Tbs. fresh lemon juice
¾ cup sugar
6 Tbs. flour

1) Preheat oven to 375°F.

2) Make a double recipe of pie crust dough, and divide it into
   2 pieces, one slightly larger than the other. Lightly sprinkle a
   clean work surface with flour, and roll out the larger piece
   until it becomes a circle large enough to fit a 9-inch pie pan.
   Fit it into the pan, building it up slightly at the edges.

3) Now roll out the smaller piece of dough to a thin circle. Cut
   it into narrow strips (about ¼ inch wide), and gently set them aside.

4) Place the berries in a medium-sized bowl, and sprinkle them
   with all the remaining ingredients. Toss very gently until the
   berries are evenly coated.

5) Pour the berry mixture into the crust, and decorate the top
   with the strips of dough in a criss-cross pattern.

6) Place the pie pan on a tray, and bake in the bottom half of
   the oven for 45 minutes, or until the filling is bubbly around
   the edges and the crust is lightly browned. Cool for at least
   15 minutes before serving.

Samosas (page 170) and Eggplant Curry (page 172)

Zuccanoes (page 154) with Vegetable Pureés (pages 86–87)

Vegetable Kebabs (page 182)

Blueberry Pound Cake (pages 190–191)

Berry Sauce

Preparation time:
5 minutes

Yield: about ¾ cup
(easily multiplied)

Lovely, light, and easy, this sauce consists purely of berries, lightly sweetened and sieved to smoothness. Serve it as an elegant complement to many other desserts. It is incredibly good on vanilla ice cream with pieces of bittersweet chocolate on top.

This sauce can also be made with frozen unsweetened berries. Look for them in the supermarket. They usually come in sealed plastic bags.

1 cup fresh (or frozen, defrosted) berries
(rasp-, black-, or straw-)
1 to 2 Tbs. sugar
a few drops of fresh lemon or lime juice

1) Place all ingredients in a blender or food processor, and purée.
2) Strain through a fine sieve to separate out and discard the seeds. Taste to adjust sugar and lemon juice.
3) Transfer to a container, cover tightly, and refrigerate. This sauce keeps very well for a week or longer.

Berry Sorbet or Ice

~ a wonderful nonfat dessert! Try pairing Berry Sorbet or Ice with Meringues (p.197), to make an even more wonderful, equally nonfat treat.

1) Make Berry Sauce as described above.
2) Place the sauce in an ice cream maker, and follow the instructions for your particular machine.

If you are not the proud owner of an ice cream maker (I've never owned one myself), you can make Berry Ice:

Make Berry Sauce, place it in a tightly covered container; put it in the freezer for 30 minutes. Take it out and stir, then return it to the freezer for another 30 minutes. This would be an ideal time to serve it, but if you must wait longer, keep it frozen until about 20 minutes before serving time. Let it sit at room temperature for those 20 minutes, and stir before serving.

Ricotta Cake
~Italian-style cheesecake~

15 minutes to prepare;
50 minutes to bake

Yield: about 8 servings

Simple and plain, but full of soul.

A little soft butter for the pan
A little flour for the pan
2 lbs. (or 2 15-oz. containers) ricotta cheese
2 or 3 large eggs
²/₃ cup sugar
¹/₃ cup flour
1 Tbs. vanilla extract
½ tsp. almond extract
½ tsp. salt
1 Tbs. grated lemon rind
3 Tbs. fresh lemon juice
OPTIONAL TOPPINGS: Fresh berries
Berry Sauce (p. 207)

1) Preheat oven to 350°F. Butter the bottom of a 9-inch springform pan, and dust it lightly with flour.

2) Place the ricotta, eggs, sugar, flour, vanilla and almond extracts, salt, lemon rind, and lemon juice in a food processor, and whip everything together until smooth. (Or put everything in a large bowl and beat with an electric mixer until smooth.)

3) Pour the batter into the prepared pan, and spread it into place.

4) Bake in the center of the oven for 50 minutes, or until solid in the center. Cool completely before serving, then chill until cold. Serve with fresh berries or Berry Sauce.

Montana's Mom's Dynamite Cheesecake

"Loved by millions from coast to coast" — Montana

Preparation time: 15 minutes

Baking time: 25 minutes, then
  a cooling period, then
  8 minutes more

Yield: enough
for 8 to 10

Basic cheesecake: unadorned and unabashed.

Make it a day ahead, so it will have plenty of time to set.

NOTE: Use a food processor or blender to make the graham cracker crumbs.

CRUST:
2 cups graham cracker crumbs
½ stick butter or margarine, melted

~Combine, and press firmly into the bottom of a 10-inch springform pan.

FILLING:
16 oz. (2 packages) cream cheese, softened   1½ tsp. vanilla extract
⅓ cup sugar   3 Tbs. lemon juice
4 eggs   ½ tsp. lemon rind

1) Preheat oven to 375°F.
2) Beat all filling ingredients together until smooth.
3) Pour onto crust and bake for 25 minutes, or until set. Remove from oven and cool to room temperature. You will need the oven again, so you can either leave it on, or reheat it.

TOPPING:
1½ cups sour cream
3 Tbs. sugar
½ tsp. vanilla extract

1) Reheat oven to 375°F.
2) Blend topping ingredients well, and pour on top of cooled cake.
3) Bake for 8 minutes. Remove from oven and cool to room temperature, then cover tightly (still in the pan) and chill at least 12 hours.

YOGURT PIE

The earlier version of this pie, called Yogurt-Cream Cheese Pie, had aspirations of being a purely yogurt pie, but needed a large proportion of cream cheese to hold it together. I have since discovered how to thicken nonfat yogurt, not by adding anything, but by slowly squeezing out much of the water. The result is a luxuriously rich-textured yogurt cheese, which can hold this pie together all by its nonfat self.

This is how you do it:

1) Place 6 layers of cheesecloth about 16 inches long in a large (12-inch diameter) colander. (If you haven't one that large, you can use 2 smaller colanders, and cut slightly shorter pieces of cheesecloth.) Place the colander(s) over a bowl or in the sink.

2) Add 2½ quarts nonfat yogurt, and wrap the cheesecloth around it tightly, securing the cloth with a clip or a bagtie.

3) Place a 3- or 4-lb. bag of beans on top, and let it sit there for 6 to 8 hours. The yogurt will solidify as its water content slowly drips out the bottom. When you unwrap it, you will find about 5 cups of thick, creamy yogurt cheese.

> 1 Sweet Crumb Crust (see opposite page)
> approximately 5 cups yogurt cheese (see above)
> 5 Tbs. sugar (or more, to taste)
> 1¼ tsp. vanilla extract
> OPTIONAL TOPPINGS :
> fresh fruit (berries, pitted cherries, sliced peaches)
> Berry Pudding (p. 206)
> Berry Sauce (p. 207)

1) Make the crust as directed. Bake and cool.

2) Place the yogurt cheese in a medium-sized bowl with the sugar and vanilla, and beat lightly with a whisk until completely blended.

3) Turn into the prepared crust. Optional: top with leftover crust mixture. Cover tightly and chill. Serve plain or with a topping.

Caribbean Dream Pie

About 40 minutes
to prepare- plus
time to chill

Yield: 1
rich
9-inch pie

SWEET CRUMB CRUST:

2 cups crushed graham crackers or ginger snaps (easily
    done in a food processor)
½ cup shredded unsweetened coconut (optional. If you prefer,
    you can substitute another ½ cup crushed
    graham crackers or ginger snaps.)
¼ cup finely minced pecans
6 Tbs. butter, melted

1) Preheat oven to 350°F.
2) Combine all ingredients and mix well. Press the mixture firmly
into the bottom and sides of a 9-inch pie pan, building a handsome
½-inch ridge around the edge. You will have more than enough to
fill the pie pan — sprinkle the rest in another pan. Place both in the
oven, and bake for 10 minutes. Remove from the oven and cool
completely.

FILLING:

1 14- or 15-oz. can sweetened condensed milk
1 Tbs. grated lime rind
½ cup plus 1 Tbs. fresh lime juice
2 bananas, peeled and sliced
½ a ripe mango, peeled and sliced (or chopped)

1) Pour the milk into a medium-sized bowl.

2) Add the grated rind and juice, and whisk for a few minutes
until the milk thickens.

3) Layer the banana and mango slices in the baked, cooled crust.
Pour the thickened milk mixture over the fruit, spreading it
into place. Sprinkle the top with extra crumb mixture, and chill
until cold. Serve cold.

Ginger-Brandy Cheesecake

Preparation time: 20 minutes

Baking time: 40 minutes

Yield: 8 to 10 servings

I. CRUST: 2 cups ginger snap crumbs (make them in a food processor or a blender. Or the old-fashioned way, with a rolling pin)

5 Tbs. melted butter

Mix together well. Press firmly into the bottom of a 10-inch springform pan.

II. FILLING: 12 oz. (1½ packages) cream cheese, softened (lowfat OK)

1½ cups sour cream or yogurt (or a combination)

4 eggs (some or all yolks can be omitted)

¼ cup honey or sugar (or, to taste)

¼ cup brandy

2 Tbs. finely grated fresh ginger

a dash of salt

Wild Ginger

1) Preheat oven to 350°F.

2) Whip everything together until very smooth. Taste to adjust sweetening.

3) Pour onto the crust in the springform pan. Bake for 40 minutes, or until the center is firm to the touch and the edges are slightly brown. Cool completely before removing the rim of the pan and glazing.

III. GLAZE: 2 Tbs. cornstarch

¾ cup orange juice

2 Tbs. honey or sugar

1 Tbs. brandy

½ tsp. orange rind

optional: candied ginger, cut into thin strips

1) Place cornstarch in a small saucepan. Whisk in the orange juice.

2) Cook over medium heat, whisking constantly, until smooth and glossy (about 5 minutes).

3) Remove from heat, and whisk in the remaining ingredients, except the candied ginger. Pour the hot glaze onto the cooled cheesecake, spreading it evenly. If desired, decorate in an expansive pattern with strips of candied ginger. Chill thoroughly before serving.

On a brownie-intensity scale of 1 to 10, these are about an 11; in other words, not for the faint-hearted. You should probably have some good vanilla or coffee ice cream on hand, or you'll find yourself running out to the store to get some as soon as you take a bite, and this will rudely interrupt your dessert hour.

> butter for the pan
> 5 oz. (5 squares) unsweetened chocolate
> ½ lb. (2 sticks) butter or margarine, softened
> 1¾ cups (packed) light brown sugar (white sugar also OK)
> 5 eggs
> 1½ tsp. vanilla extract
> 1 cup flour (use ¾ cup for fudgier brownies)
> MANY OPTIONAL EMBELLISHMENTS:
> 1 cup chopped walnuts or pecans
> 1 tsp. freshly grated orange rind
> ½ tsp. cinnamon
> a small ripe banana, mashed
> 2 to 4 Tbs. strong black coffee
> 1 cup semisweet chocolate chips
> OR anything else you might think of
> OR, for purists, none of the above

1) Butter a 9 x 13-inch baking pan. Preheat oven to 350°F.

2) Gently melt the chocolate. Let it cool for about 10 minutes.

3) Cream the butter and sugar in a medium-sized bowl until light and fluffy.

4) Add the eggs, one at a time, beating well after each. Stir in the vanilla.

5) Stir constantly as you drizzle in the melted chocolate. After all the chocolate is in, beat well for a minute or two.

6) Stir in flour and possible embellishments. Mix just enough to blend thoroughly.

7) Spread the batter into the prepared pan. Bake 20 to 25 minutes, or until a knife inserted into the center comes out clean. Cut into squares while still hot, then allow to cool for at least 10 minutes, if you can wait that long.

Iced Carob Brownies

If you think of carob as itself and not as a chocolate substitute, you'll appreciate these lovely brownies even more than you would anyway.

butter or margarine for the pan
½ cup (1 stick) melted butter or margarine
¼ cup carob powder
2 eggs
½ cup (packed) light brown sugar
1 tsp. vanilla extract
¼ cup water
1 cup flour
1 tsp. baking powder
¼ tsp. salt
½ cup raisins or currants
½ cup finely chopped walnuts
optional: a dash or two of cinnamon and/or allspice

1) Preheat oven to 350°F. Butter an 8-inch square pan.

2) Beat together butter, carob, eggs, sugar, and vanilla in a medium-sized bowl. Stir in the water.

3) Sift together flour, baking powder, and salt. Stir this into the first mixture along with raisins, nuts, and optional spices. Mix just enough to blend thoroughly.

4) Spread into the prepared pan, and bake 20 to 25 minutes, or until a probe comes out clean. Cool completely before icing.

• • • • • • • • • • •

ICING: ¼ cup carob powder
           8 oz. (1 package) cream cheese, softened
           ¼ cup powdered sugar
           ½ tsp. vanilla

Beat everything together until very smooth. Spread on top of the cooled brownies.

LEMON MOUSSE

Ethereal, yet it packs a tangy punch. Serve Lemon Mousse by itself or topped with Berry Sauce (p. 207). It also goes beautifully served in tandem with many different cakes, especially Ukrainian Poppy Seed Cake (p. 189).

Lemon Mousse will keep well for several days if tightly covered and refrigerated.

¼ cup cornstarch
½ cup sugar
½ cup freshly squeezed lemon juice
½ cup water
1 tsp. grated lemon rind
2 egg whites, at room temperature
½ pint heavy cream
OPTIONAL VARIATIONS:
1 cup berries or sliced peaches
orange rind, instead of lemon

1) Place cornstarch and sugar in a small saucepan. Add lemon juice and water and whisk until smooth.

2) Cook, whisking constantly, over medium heat until thick (5 to 8 minutes). Remove from heat, transfer to a medium-sized bowl, and stir in the lemon rind. Let cool to room temperature.

3) Place the egg whites in a medium-sized mixing bowl and beat at high speed with an electric mixer until stiff but not dry. Fold this into the lemon mixture, cover tightly, and chill at least 1 hour (longer = also ok).

4) Without cleaning the beaters, whip the cream until it is firm but still fluffy. Fold this into the mousse (add optional berries or peaches at this point), cover tightly again, and chill until serving time.

♪ DANISH CHERRIES

Make this delicious, beautiful, and very simple stovetop dessert well in advance OR right before serving. You can get fine results from frozen cherries (they come pitted and unsweetened in sealed plastic bags), if fresh are unavailable. No need to defrost before using.

NOTES: ♪ To blanch almonds, place them in a colander over a sink. Pour boiling water over them, and rub off the skins. Cut vertically with a sharp knife to sliver them.

♪ To whip ricotta, beat it vigorously with a whisk, or at high speed with an electric mixer.

4 cups pitted cherries
1½ Tbs. cornstarch
3 to 4 Tbs. sugar
¼ cup lemon juice
½ tsp. grated lemon rind
¾ tsp. almond extract
OPTIONAL: ½ cup blanched, slivered almonds
TOPPINGS: whipped cream
        or
    whipped ricotta cheese   } with a few blanched,
        or   slivered almonds
    plain yogurt   folded in

1) Place cherries in a heavy medium-sized saucepan, and cook over medium heat, covered, for 10 minutes.

2) Meanwhile, combine cornstarch and sugar in a small bowl. Add lemon juice and whisk until smooth. Stir this into the hot cherries, and cook over medium heat, stirring frequently, until thick (5 to 8 minutes).

3) Remove from heat and stir in lemon rind, almond extract, and slivered almonds. Serve hot, warm, room temperature, or cold, topped with whipped cream, whipped ricotta, or yogurt.

Fruited Yogurt Desserts

Almost any combination of fruit and yogurt will taste delicious - and make a filling lowfat dessert. Here are a few suggestions. Combine as close to serving time as possible.

I.

3 cups plain yogurt
1 cup fresh blueberries
1 cup seedless grapes
1 cup pitted, halved cherries
sugar, maple syrup, or honey
~ to taste

Combine and chill.

II.

3 cups plain yogurt
1 cup fresh strawberries, halved
1 to 2 medium-sized ripe
    peaches, sliced
1 perfectly ripe banana, sliced
sugar, honey, or maple syrup
    ~ to taste

Combine and chill.

III.

3 cups plain yogurt
1 to 2 medium-sized apples,
    grated
1/2 cup lightly toasted minced
    almonds
a dash of cinnamon
sugar, maple syrup, or honey
    ~ to taste

Combine and chill.

APPENDIX

Lowfat Soups

(less than 3 tablespoons oil or butter per 5 or more servings)

Brazilian Black Bean, 26
Cream of Asparagus, 3
Cream of Spinach, 30
Curried Squash and Mushroom, 15
Gingered Carrot, 22
Herbed Carrot (also has nonfat option), 23
Light Cream of Celery, 6
Mushroom-Barley, 28
Mushroom Bisque, 19
Potato-Fennel, 29
Russian Cabbage Borscht, 27
Succotash Chowder, 11
Vegetable Chowder, 12

Nonfat Soups

Cascadilla, 34
Chilled Beet Borscht, 35
Chilled Berry, 36
Chilled Cucumber-Yogurt, 32
Chinese Vegetable Chowder, 13
Hot and Sour, 8
Lentil, 25
Miso, 9
Split Pea, 17
Summer Vegetable, 10

Oil-Free Salads and Dressings

Balkan Cucumber Salad, 69
California Waldorf, 58
Carrot-Yogurt Salad, 72
Fruit and Vegetable Waldorf, 59
Fruit Salad, 54
Lowfat Creamy Garlic Dressing, 43
Lowfat Creamy Roquefort Dressing, 43
Lowfat Ranch Dressing, 43
March Hare, 49
Nonfat Gazpacho Dressing, 43
Odessa Beets, 68
Pickled Red Onions, 60
Very Green Dressing, 41
White Rabbit Salad, 48

Oil-Free Sauces and Dips

Apple Chutney, 98
Beet Purée, 86
Carrot Purée, 87
Chinese Duck Sauce, 97
Faux Aioli, 91
Greek Lemon Sauce, 91
Guacamole (no added oil), 108
Horseradish Sauce, 91
Mango Salsa, 96
Mondo Bizarro Sauce, 84
Orange-Ginger Sauce, 90
Pasta Mediterranée, 81
Pineapple Salsa, 96
Plain Fake Mayo, 91
Raita, 99
Red Pepper Purée, 86
Sauce Puttanesca, 81
Spinach Purée, 87
Tomato Chutney, 98
Yogurt Cheese, 102
Zingy Bean Dip, 106

Nondairy Sauces and Dips

(or optionally nondairy)

Apple Chutney, 98
Basic Stir-Fry Sauce, 88
Beet Purée, 86
Carrot Purée, 87
Cashew-Ginger Sauce, 90
Chinese Duck Sauce, 97
Chinese Peanut Sauce, 107
Eggplant Dips, 104–5
Faux Aioli, 91
Greek Lemon Sauce, 91
Guacamole, 108
Horseradish Sauce, 91
Hummus, 100
Mango Salsa, 96
Mexican Red Sauce, 95
Orange-Ginger Sauce, 90
Pineapple Salsa, 96
Plain Fake Mayo, 91
Red Pepper Purée, 86
Spinach Purée, 87
Tahini-Lemon Sauce, 103
Tomato Chutney, 98
Tomato Salsa, 96

INDEX

MOLLIE KATZEN

JOHN BRAIN

With close to 4 million books in print, Mollie Katzen enjoys a coveted position on the *New York Times* list of the ten best-selling cookbook authors of all time. Selected by *Health* magazine as one of the "Five Women Who Changed the Way We Eat," Mollie is widely credited with moving healthful cooking from the fringe of American society squarely onto mainstream dinner tables.

Born in Rochester, New York, Mollie studied at the Eastman School of Music, Cornell University, and the San Francisco Art Institute, where she received a BFA in painting. Her classic *Moosewood Cookbook*, first published in 1977, was followed by *The Enchanted Broccoli Forest* (1982), *Still Life with Menu* (1988), and *Mollie Katzen's Vegetable Heaven* (Hyperion 1997). All of Mollie's books are vibrantly illustrated with her original artwork.

To inspire young cooks to explore the wonders of the kitchen, Mollie illustrated and authored the award-winning children's cookbooks, *Pretend Soup* (1994) and *Honest Pretzels* (1999). Mollie is now a featured writer and illustrator for Children's Television Workshop On-Line, and for *Sesame Street Parents' Magazine*.

Since its debut in 1995, the acclaimed *Mollie Katzen's Cooking Show* has been appearing on public television stations nationwide. The new editions of *Moosewood* and *The Enchanted Broccoli Forest* are companion volumes to Mollie's third television series.

You can keep up with all of Mollie's projects by tuning in to
www.molliekatzen.com.

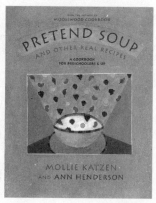

Surviving in an
ANGRY WORLD

Finding Your Way to Personal Peace

CHARLES F. STANLEY

HOWARD BOOKS
A DIVISION OF SIMON & SCHUSTER, INC.
New York · Nashville · London · Toronto · Sydney

Howard Books
A Division of Simon & Schuster, Inc.
1230 Avenue of the Americas
New York, NY 10020

Copyright © 2010 by Charles Stanley

First Howard Books hardcover edition October 2010

HOWARD and colophon are trademarks of Simon & Schuster, Inc.

For information about discounts and bulk purchases, please contact Simon & Schuster Special Sales at 1-866-506-1949 or business@simonandschuster.com.

The Simon & Schuster Speakers Bureau can bring authors to your live event. For more information or to book an event, contact the Simon & Schuster Speakers Bureau at 1-866-248-3049 or visit our website at www.simonspeakers.com.

Manufactured in the United States of America

10 9 8 7 6 5 4 3 2 1

Library of Congress Cataloging-in-Publication Data is available

ISBN 978-1-4391-8356-4
ISBN 978-1-4391-8999-3 (ebook)

CONTENTS

Surviving in an

ANGRY WORLD

OUR ANGRY WORLD

P eople are so angry today. They're mad at what happened yesterday and bitter about things that occurred years ago. Perhaps you are angry with your spouse, a coworker, or a friend. The truth is, we all get mad at one time or another. The question we need to ask ourselves is, *How should we deal with anger in ourselves and respond to it in others?*

Many people are angry and don't even realize it. They just know something's not right on the inside. What they need is to be set free from the bondage of bitterness and resentment.

Then there are those who know they're angry and just don't care. These people nurture their anger. They cultivate and feed it, keeping hostility and hatred simmering for years.

Countless people have lost their marriages because of anger. They've lost their children, their jobs, and their health—all because they let this one emotion get out of control and take over their entire lives.

We live in an angry world. Like a windswept wildfire, anger leaves scorched lives and devastating loss in its wake. This emotion reaches into our families, our neighborhoods, our communities, across our nation, and around the world.

If we're honest, many of us will admit to feeling a degree of anger deep inside that is greater these days than we have felt before. It's not a question of *if* we've ever been angry—all of us have been angry at one time or another. And there's no way to guarantee we'll never get angry again. But the Bible gives us very clear instruction regarding how we should handle this powerful and potentially damaging emotion.

Anger in itself is not necessarily evil or destructive. There's good anger and there's bad anger. The problem is that most people have more experience with bad anger than with good anger.

So let me ask you a question: Are you angry?

And if you are, do you know why?

As we are about to discover, anger can be a very dangerous thing.

CHAPTER 1

DEFINITIONS

Anger: The Good, the Bad, and the Destructive

Though most people don't see themselves as angry, they do feel deeply frustrated and upset about past wrongs and hurts. Sometimes, without even realizing it, they become filled with hateful, bitter thoughts that churn deep inside.

So how can we recognize anger in ourselves and others? Consider the following:

- Angry people are quick-tempered, often lashing out in word or deed before they're even aware of it. Their anger triggers instantly, and their anger ignites.

- Angry people hold on to their anger; they feel as angry today as when the anger-causing event happened. Perhaps you know just what I'm talking about. Are your tears just as quick to flow now as then? Does the pain in your heart sting just as much? Does the memory of an event still cause your hands and jaw to clench? If so, you too have been affected by our angry world.

- Angry people justify their anger, so they have no problem holding a grudge. They make excuses for their anger and try to get others to agree that they have a "right" to be angry.

If any of the above applies to you, own up to the fact that more than likely you are an angry person.

God's Word instructs us to be patient when we are wronged and long-suffering when we are hurt (1 Corinthians 13:4–5). Any other response to life's painful moments is contrary to what the Lord desires for His children.

"But," someone may say, "I'm not angry; I'd rather think of myself as just a little irritated or a little frustrated."

That may be true, because anger doesn't feel the same to everyone. In fact, its definition may change depending on whom you ask.

ANGER DEFINED

I define anger as a strong, intense feeling of displeasure, hostility, or indignation resulting from a real or imagined threat, insult, injustice, or frustration to you or others who are important to you.

Let's break down that definition phrase by phrase.

Anger Is Intense

Countless things in life can cause you to feel upset or frustrated. You discover your favorite shirt or blouse is missing a button. You break a glass as you hurry to fix breakfast. You sleep through your alarm clock ringing. Feelings of being "just a little mad" can set in. In the vast majority of cases, the irritation from these minor incidents disappears rather quickly. Real feelings of anger tend to remain until the cause is addressed, defeated, and eliminated. The intensity of that anger extends beyond the moment; it rules the day.

Anger Is a Feeling

It is a strong emotion that is often intertwined with other emotions. We need to be honest about our emotions. They are our frontline response to life. As much as a person may desire or strive to act and live in a rational, objective, and dignified manner, acting that way all the time is *not* realistic. We respond to life events first out of our emotions and with a very basic two-option determination—"I like this" or "I don't like this." We decide whether something is good or evil, right or wrong, helpful or harmful almost instantly. Most people make up their minds before they have the time or the opportunity to gather objective data and determine the best decision to make.

God, who created every aspect of our being *for our good*, made us feel and express emotions. He created us with a capacity to feel love, joy, and peace. The Lord also allows us to experience frustration, hate, and fear. He gave us specific emotions to help us intuitively, instinctively, and immediately recognize danger, injustice, and evil intent.

If a person says to me, "I'm not emotional" or "I don't want to be emotional," I know something is not right. God intends for us to experience, express, and use our emotions to direct right behavior. They are intended to be triggers that prompt us to action, and our action is to be guided toward good and godly ends.

That is a major concept that I cannot overemphasize.

You have been given emotions so that *by an act of your human will*, you might be directed toward right behavior.

Your emotions are never to rule over you. You are to be the master of your responses and reactions. The person who allows himself to be ruled by emotions is on a continual roller coaster. He fails to resolve the issues that trigger an emotional response and is always pulled from one high to the next low. Such a person is easily swayed by others and very often "acts out" in inappropriate, unproductive, or ungodly ways.

We are to subject our emotions to our human will, which is also a gift that our Creator freely gives to each person for the purpose of making choices and decisions. The moment you feel an intense emotion, the first thing you need to do is ask, *How should I respond?*

Behavior always has an element of free will. We make willful, deliberate choices about what we do and don't do, what we say and don't say, and what attitudes and beliefs we hold on to.

Emotions can be random and unstable.

Behavior is nearly always directed and measurable.

This is not to say, of course, that all behavior is rational or predictable. The truth is that almost all emotional responses eventually end up coming out in words and deeds. The deeper we feel an emotion, the more compelled we feel to express it in a way that is observable to the outside world.

Ideally, our emotions are filtered through a will that is bent toward God's purposes and commandments. However, if the filter has been damaged or has never been put in place, emotions will usually give rise to behavior that is unchecked. Emotions that are not subject to godly thinking tend to run amok and cause great damage.

"But I like to be spontaneous," a person may say.

"I want to live free!" declares someone else.

"I am a person of intense passion, and I can't help but express it," still another might say.

People often make those statements when they see themselves as especially creative, artistic, entrepreneurial, innovative, or free-thinking. In truth, the person who is always ruled by emotions is far more likely to produce a creative mess, an entrepreneurial mistake, or an innovative disaster than something that is truly beautiful, wise, or beneficial.

Understanding that our emotions are a gift from God, and that we base behavior on filtered or unfiltered emotions, we must also realize that a lot of what you and I are going to feel will be negative. No one has a 100 percent positive emotional response to life all the time and in all circumstances. We *should* have a negative response about some things:

When you come across a homeless person curled up on a sidewalk as the snow begins to fall . . .

When you see a child whose face is drawn and belly swollen from malnutrition . . .

When you hear the story of a battered wife and mother of small children forced to seek protection in a women's shelter . . .

There *should* be an emotional response that shouts from the depths of your soul: *This is wrong! This is bad!*

And out of that response should come a desire to *change* the situation.

Anger Encompasses Other Feelings

Emotions linked to anger are usually ones of displeasure, hostility, or indignation. All these are negative feelings, though that doesn't necessarily mean they are wrong. They are legitimate emotions, but they don't need to be expressed in negative behavior.

For example, you can dislike a situation yet not have strong feelings that the situation needs to change. You can dislike someone and not demand that the person be removed from your presence. You can be offended by something that's said without feeling the need to speak up and set the record straight. On the other hand, you can dislike a situation and feel motivated to change it. You can respond to hostility with kindness and defuse it. You can confront critical comments and seek to establish truth and a sense of balance.

Anger is the intense feeling that compels a person to act—to remove or resolve whatever is causing the intense displeasure, hostility, or indignation. It is the feeling that compels a person to flee or fight a real or imagined threat.

Anger Comes in Response to a Threat—
Real or Imagined

Each of us has a built-in fight-or-flight response mechanism. This is a gift from God to us for our human survival. If you awaken while on a camping trip and see the shadow of a grizzly bear on your tent, you are likely to feel immediate fear and a compelling desire to run for your life. If you are on a high mountain trail and see something coiled on the path ahead, your response is likely to be "Snake!" not "Oh, a garden hose."

Your reaction is going to be immediate and emotional. Again, you will make an almost instinctive response to either fight or take flight.

Anger Can Follow a Threat of Loss

You can become angry over a threat aimed at you personally or at someone important to you. Ask any mother how she felt after learning that her child was threatened with unfair criticism or bullying, and she's likely to say, "Angry!"

We don't even need to know people personally to feel anger toward a situation they are experiencing. We can become angry when we witness a group being treated unfairly as the result of prejudice or bigotry.

We may feel threatened by an emergency weather report that tells us a tornado or hurricane is headed in our direction. Or we may feel threatened when a large number of people at our school, workplace, or community are falling ill to a dreaded disease. However, we rarely respond to those types of threats with anger. An angry response is most likely generated when the threat comes from an identifiable person or group of people.

Several years ago a woman told me about an incident in the early years of her marriage. Her husband attended church, but it was more out of social obligation than genuine faith. He resented very deeply the growing faith of his wife.

One day he noticed her Bible, which she had left open. He could clearly see how she had written notes in the margins and underlined or highlighted certain passages of Scripture. The man picked up his wife's Bible and threw it across the room. In anger, he shouted to her, "There will be no Bible study in this house!"

The woman was hurt. Her husband was angry. And at the core of it all, he felt threatened. He felt threatened out of a fear that the "religious crowd" would influence his wife. He also was afraid that through her, his life might change in ways he didn't want. He was threatened in particular by the impact a few preachers were having on his wife through their sermons at church and on television.

The good news is that this man eventually came to have a desire for more of God. He began to read his own Bible and grew in his faith.

When this woman shared her story, I felt anger welling up in me!

How could a husband say and do those things? How could he so blatantly and willfully hurt his wife's feelings? I felt anger on her behalf. I wanted to go to him and say, "How dare you do this!" My anger was focused on him because he had threatened someone who was sincerely and innocently seeking more of God.

Now, this man had died a number of years before his wife told me her story—and I knew this when she began telling me her story. But it still made me angry.

You may be thinking, *But you had no right to be angry.*

Yes, I did. My right to be angry wasn't born of a relationship with this man or woman. But I had a right born of principle and of my beliefs and awareness of what God has declared is good and acceptable.

You do not need to know an abused child to be angry at the problem of child abuse.

You do not need to know a battered woman to be angry at spousal abuse.

You do not need to know someone who has been the victim of a crime in order to be angry with criminals who are becoming more and more bold in threatening people.

Not long ago, I had a conversation with a man who has more than forty years of marketing experience. He said, "One of the things I learned early on in my career of helping people through charitable giving is that you need to put a face to an injustice. You need a photo of a starving child, an impoverished family, or a homeless person by the side of the road. You need a forceful image that makes people not only feel sad about the situation or feel sorry for the victim, but makes them angry that somebody or some group allowed this to happen. And if you can identify the 'somebody' and put a face on the person who has created the bad situation, then the only thing left to do is point out what a person's contribution can do to change the situation or remove the source of the problem. That is really a winning combination."

Unfortunately, many times it's not just one person who creates the injustice. And sadly, there are countless situations in which many people are responsible for bad decisions and choices that lead to desperate needs and horrible circumstances. Even so, we should recognize this truth: When we are faced with a threat, we are wise to understand who is making it and why.

We are wise to ask:

Is the threat real or imagined?

Is it temporary or ongoing?

Is it coming from an identifiable person or group?

The force behind a threat is the "enemy." We need to know the enemy and make sure we are not it.

ANGER

Threat (Real or Imagined)	Against Self or Someone Important to You	Creates Feelings of Indignation, Displeasure, or Hostility	Focused as ANGER	Ideally Filtered Through Godly Human Will	Producing BEHAVIOR that Resolves, Reconciles, or Removes the Threat

THREE CORE TRUTHS ABOUT ANGER

In addition to a solid definition, we need to understand three core truths about anger and how it is manifested in our angry world.

The Universality of Anger

Anger is a universal emotion. It affects every person, regardless of race, sex, nationality, or age—from a screaming toddler to an elderly person red in the face with rage; from the wealthy businessman to the impoverished housewife; from the cold of the Arctic to the heat of the Sahara; from a war zone to a tropical paradise—anger is an emotion known to all people. Regardless of how peaceful or passive a person might seem or desire to be, everyone gets angry at some time in his or her life.

But the fact that everyone gets angry is not a justification for it. The universality of anger is not an excuse for getting angry, nor is it an excuse for failing to deal with it or failing to direct it toward godly goals.

The Persistence of Anger

Anger will not go away on its own. It doesn't die out. It must be rooted out. Dealing with anger, especially deep-seated anger, requires intentionality.

Episodic Anger Versus Pervasive Anger

We are wise to differentiate between angry episodes and a pervasively angry nature.

Is there evidence that you are a chronically angry person? Are you angry about something nearly all the time, even if you wear a smile on your face and speak in a soft, calm voice?

There is a big difference between the person who feels anger as a response to a specific situation or circumstance, and the one whose anger doesn't go away. If you are angry at the first step of a journey and are still angry a thousand miles later, you likely live with pervasive anger.

IS ANGER A SIN?

The apostle Paul wrote to the Ephesians, "Be angry, and yet do not sin" (Ephesians 4:26). He openly and directly admitted that anger exists, that it is part of everyone's emotional makeup—even the most mature and spiritually minded person's—and that we *all* get angry from time to time.

Paul is also presenting the truth that anger, in and of itself, is not a sin. How we handle it and what we *do* with it is the key. So anger as an emotion is not necessarily sinful. Some situations and circumstances in life warrant our anger.

And you *can* be angry without sinning.

Rather than describing a person who is perpetually or pervasively angry as a sinner, the Bible describes him or her as

- *A foolish person.* Proverbs 14:17 tells us, "A quick-tempered man acts foolishly."

- *A person likely to cause arguments and dissension.* Proverbs 15:18 says, "A hot-tempered man stirs up strife, but the slow to anger calms a dispute."

- *A person who should be avoided.* We read in Proverbs 22:24, "Do not associate with a man given to anger, or go with a hot-tempered man, or you will learn his ways and find a snare for yourself." The angry person is usually someone with a short fuse. Scripture is clear that a quick or hot temper is to be avoided.

- "He who is slow to anger is better than the mighty, and he who rules his spirit, than he who captures a city" (Proverbs 16:32).

- "Do not be eager in your heart to be angry, for anger resides in the bosom of fools" (Ecclesiastes 7:9).

Three principles are reflected in the verses above and in other parts of the Bible:

Principle 1: Avoid Associating with Angry People

As stated above, Proverbs warns us, "Do not associate with a man given to anger" (22:24). I have quoted this verse to many people through the years—especially men and women as they prepare to marry and those who come to me for advice about business partners.

One of the great descriptions of godly character is found in Galatians 5:22–23. Here Paul tells us, "The fruit of the Spirit is love, joy, peace, patience, kindness, goodness, faithfulness, gentleness, [and] self-control." If you are considering a long-term relationship with a person—in marriage, friendship, business, and so forth—I strongly encourage you to evaluate your relationship with that person on the basis of this fruit.

A few verses earlier, the apostle Paul warns everyone to avoid "deeds of the flesh." His list includes behaviors that are either variations of anger or somehow associated with it. They are "immorality, impurity, sensuality, idolatry, sorcery, enmities, strife, jealousy, outbursts of anger, disputes, dissensions, factions, envying, drunkenness, carousing and things like these" (Galatians 5:19–21).

If you are considering entering into a relationship with someone, I strongly encourage you to subject your character and the other person's to Paul's template of behavioral traits.

There simply is nothing good to be gained from linking yourself with an angry person. Choose instead someone who bears the characteristics of spiritual maturity.

A young woman once said to me in a marriage-counseling session many years ago, "I like the fact that Herb is so passionate about what he believes. I see his anger as a strength. He stands up to people who are sinning or mistreating other people."

I replied, "You won't see this as a strength when he begins to believe that something *you* are doing is wrong or inappropriate."

The more she described some of Herb's "passionate" outbursts in defense of his own opinions, the more I saw trouble ahead for this young woman. So I advised her to postpone her marriage until Herb could get counseling to help him deal with the root of his anger.

She did not take my advice but admitted five years later that she wished she had. Herb had become increasingly angry and vocal in just about every area of his life—at work, in church meetings, in their home, at political rallies, and in their relationships with their neighbors.

One of the things I noticed when this woman admitted feeling caught in a trap was that *she* seemed angry herself.

I told her, "Don't let your husband's anger infect your sweet personality."

She said, with a tone of sadness in her voice, "Oh, Dr. Stanley, I think it already has. I am very angry with Herb. Some weeks it seems I'm mostly angry with him and not very loving. His anger has worn me out and is infecting our two-year-old daughter. I feel upset every waking hour."

Again, I recommended counseling to her. And this time, she and Herb did seek out a godly counselor. They began to address the deep problems underlying Herb's anger, as well as to explore how she could address and overcome her developing feelings of anger.

The truth is, in the majority of cases, it is far more likely for a hot-tempered person to influence a peaceful, nurturing individual than the other way around. It is difficult for the peaceful person to change the basic nature of one who is quick-tempered.

As a person once said to me, "It is a lot easier to get riled up than to get calmed down."

Principle 2: Anger Is Linked to Foolishness

The Bible associates anger with foolish behavior. Why? Because the hot-tempered or quick-tempered person rarely has the discipline or takes the time to make wise, informed, rational decisions. The angry person is impetuous and acts instinctively. And, generally speaking, that kind of behavior has a far greater chance of being problematic and harmful than purposeful and helpful.

Our language is filled with phrases that depict quick-tempered behavior:

- Fly off the handle

- Knee-jerk reaction

- Blow your top

- Let off steam

All these indicate that the angry person tends to act before he has a chance to think. His behavior is faster than his brain. A person who is caught up in any emotion, especially anger, doesn't take the time to weigh all his options or consider all the consequences. The end result is often foolishness, which by its very definition means a lack in judgment and a ridiculous appearance.

Principle 3: An Unruly Spirit Rules Poorly

Let me give you a little insight into the verse that says, "He who is slow to anger is better than the mighty, and he who rules his spirit, than he who captures a city" (Proverbs 16:32).

Many powerful warriors and political rulers in the ancient world were men prone to anger. They tended to "look for a fight" to prove themselves as leaders. Anger was perceived as almost a given trait for those who became "mighty."

God's Word says that the person who is *slow* to anger should be in authority. The individual who can rule his own spirit can be trusted to take a disciplined, measured approach in ruling others. Furthermore, while a pompous, power-hungry, anger-driven person may capture a people or a city, he rarely has the wisdom and demeanor to successfully manage or maintain control. He is unable to lead and empower his people to be productive and prosperous.

Angry leaders tend to zap the resources of those they govern. An appetite for power often devours everything in its wake. The slow-to-anger person is the one who has a much better opportunity for nurturing growth and stability. This is true in family, church, business, and political settings, as well as almost any other setting you can imagine.

ANGER SURFACES AS BEHAVIOR

Although it's an emotion, anger almost always surfaces as *behavior*. It is seldom contained within the person who is angry. Anger usually finds a way to display itself.

In the fourth chapter of Ephesians, the apostle Paul urges believers to avoid sinning in their anger and to deal with it before the sun goes down. Then he wrote this: "Do not give the devil an opportunity" (verse 27).

To what "opportunity" is Paul referring? It is the opportunity for the devil to influence the way you express your anger and the way you justify its cause and the behavior that follows.

Let me assure you that the devil will tempt you to display your anger in the meanest, vilest, and most vindictive way possible. Satan wants you to get away with being angry. He wants you to have your say and win the day, so to speak. He wants you to inflict as much pain as possible on the person to whom you are speaking or lashing out. He wants the consequences to be as severe as possible. And the Enemy's lie is that if you treat the other person in the worst possible way, he or she will never seek to injure or criticize you in the future.

The devil is quick to help scheme or devise ways to display anger so you can appear very witty in your use of sarcastic language, or so you may appear extremely cool, calm, and collected in your demeanor. Satan wants you to look good while being as damaging as possible to another person's heart and mind.

Let me also warn you—the devil will present all sorts of arguments for you to justify why you lashed out in anger. They include telling you that the other person "deserved" your angry tirade and that the other person would not have been punished for her hurtful behavior by anyone else if you hadn't reacted and taken action.

It's a pack of lies. But the person who holds on to his or her anger is often incapable of discerning lie from truth.

I once had a conversation with a person who seemed to be taking great pride in telling me all he had said to someone he said was persecuting him. He was almost bragging about his angry, hateful behavior as he said, "I really put him in his place."

I asked, "Did he stay there?"

The man was startled. He paused for a moment and then said, "No, not for very long."

ANGRY WORDS ARE ANGRY DEEDS

Angry behavior is not limited to violent deeds, flying fists, or thrown objects. Angry words *are* a form of angry deed.

When we speak angry words without any concern for the consequences associated with them, we are reflecting immaturity and a callous nature. It demonstrates a lack of love and caring for others.

We live in a time, of course, when many people do not want to talk about consequences. They would rather not be responsible for anything negative that results from something they do or say. They prefer to say whatever they want and let the hearer deal with it.

The truth is that all words have an impact of some kind and to some degree. What we say matters. Words have meaning, and what we say sends a message that hits both the head and the heart. Our words trigger both ideas and emotions in all who hear—and overhear.

Who you are today, right this moment, is a consequence of what happened yesterday—and all the yesterdays before it. Your very nature and character are composites of all that you have said and done in the past and all that others have said and done to you in the past.

Where you will be tomorrow will be a consequence of what you say and do today as well as how you internalize what others around you say and do.

None of us is immune to the impact of others' words and actions. Much of what happens to you and me is directly linked to our use of words and the choices and decisions we have conveyed through what we say.

A woman once told me that she felt entirely justified after blasting her supervisor with an angry tirade of critical comments and accusations. "If I hadn't said it, nobody would have, and she would have continued in her hurtful and prejudicial behavior without any consequences."

"Where is that woman today?" I asked.

"I don't know," she said. "I no longer work there."

"Why not?" I asked.

"Because nothing happened to my supervisor. She didn't change, and nobody in upper management cared."

The energy expended in a negative outburst rarely produces a positive result. I found myself asking later, "What *might* have happened if this woman had put the same amount of energy into praying for her supervisor and getting to know the woman a little better?" That may have opened the door for a positive conversation with her supervisor.

Angry words rarely have long-lasting influence. In this woman's case, her anger led to resentment, disillusionment, and the loss of a job. It had no apparent impact on the person who needed to make changes but likely rejected the entire outburst.

You may think you are settling a score when you erupt at another person. In nearly all cases, you are still going to lose the game.

"But I feel so much better when I get things off my chest," a man said to me.

"Do you really?"

"Oh, yes! I feel great."

"How long does that good feeling last?"

He paused and then said, "Right up until bedtime, when I realize that I'm sleeping on the couch."

Anger expressed in words always has consequences, and they are usually just as severe as anger expressed physically.

Monitor all that you say. I vividly remember the first time I felt anger in my heart. I was about four years old. Certainly I may have manifested anger before that, but I didn't *know* I was angry then. This time, I *knew* I was burning hot on the inside as I insisted on having my way.

The incident was not particularly earth-shaking. My mother was getting ready to walk into town, and she told me to stay at home and wait for her to return. But I wanted to go with her, not wait for her.

I made a major fuss. And although I'm sure my vocabulary wasn't developed enough at that point to fully express all that I was feeling inside, I am also sure I knew enough words to let my mother know with full force that I did not like her decision, did not agree with her decision, and did not intend to obey her decision. I wanted to go with my mother!

I also remember vividly what happened. My mother turned to me, looked me directly in the eyes, and said, "A gentle answer turns away wrath, but a harsh word stirs up anger."

I didn't know my mother was quoting Proverbs 15:1, and I'm not sure if she knew either. But in that moment, I did know—and fully understood—that she was speaking truth to me. Her gentle voice matched her message and defused my anger on the spot.

Even though I was only four years old, I immediately felt ashamed and sat down to quietly await my mother's return.

As I have reflected upon that incident throughout my life, I remain absolutely convinced that it is not only *what* we say that matters but *how* we say it. Words spoken with gentleness can quiet an angry heart. Words spoken with harshness—or with a stern, prideful, cynical, or critical edge—stir up anger.

You may think your harsh words anger only the person to whom you are speaking. But your harsh words stir up anger in *you* as well. It's as if your opinions about the other person become solidified in your own heart as you speak harshly. The net result is that a negative attitude takes firmer root in you. Once you have spoken harshly to a person, it becomes much easier to speak harshly to him or her in the future. You're also more likely to talk that way to others who irritate or frustrate you.

But not all our harsh words are spoken to the people around us. Most of the time, we save the worst criticism for ourselves.

Just about everyone I know talks to himself or herself throughout the day. Sometimes our self-talk is a form of self-instruction. We remind ourselves how to perform a specific task or not to forget something important. We may be encouraging ourselves to control our own attitudes and behavior. But many times, self-talk takes on the form of self-criticism.

Do you speak to yourself in gentle tones—encouraging yourself to do better and to live according to the highest and most noble standard?

Or do you put yourself down and speak words of criticism and judgment over yourself?

Very often, the harshness of a person's own words becomes the fuel that keeps the embers of anger burning.

Before you marry someone, be sure to meet his or her family. Pay attention to the dynamics of their communication with one another. Do tempers flare? Are arguments frequent and heated? Do disputes and debates erupt at every mealtime? Be sure that none of the negative traits you witness have taken hold in the person you're dating. If they have, walk away.

THE PATH TO PEACE

Why is it so important that we recognize and deal with anger? Because until we do, we will never find the peace that we all so desperately seek.

Only when we *admit* and *deal with* anger can we truly live in peace with ourselves and others.

Through the years, I have discussed the issue of anger with many, many people and have drawn these two conclusions:

- Some people admit to feeling deep-seated anger, but their response is "I don't want to deal with it." That means they don't want to explore the causes or extent of their anger in order to be set free from it. If they have any concern at all, it is about how to control or "manage" their anger. They have virtually no interest in exploring ways to rid themselves of the displeasure, hostility, and indignation that have taken root deep within. They are *suppressing* anger.

- Other people refuse to admit they are angry, even though a variety of observable indicators suggests otherwise. Their family members see them as being angry. Their coworkers consider them to be angry. Pastors and fellow church members think they are angry. But remarkably, these angry people refuse to see the anger in themselves. They are in denial. They are *repressing* anger.

The most destructive anger is that which is resident but not recognized or addressed. Anger does not just lie dormant in a person. If it is present, it is active. It is fermenting and fomenting, and eventually, it will find expression.

There are no advantages to suppressing or repressing anger.

ADMIT IT—DEAL WITH IT

Consider each question below. You might find it helpful to use a journal to answer these and the ones at the end of each chapter.

1. Are you currently angry with a person? If so, can you identify who that person is?

2. Is the anger rooted in a justifiable cause—one that is consistent with God's commandments and His purposes here on earth?

3. Is your anger seeking vengeance? In other words, are you seeking to get even with the person?

4. Is the anger cherished?

5. Is the anger associated with an unforgiving spirit?

If your heart answered "yes" to most of these questions, your anger has the potential to destroy you. Choose to admit your anger and deal with it *now*.

CHAPTER 2

EXPRESSIONS

\|\|\|\|\|\|\|\|\|\|\|\|\|\|\|\|\|\|\|\|\|\|\|\|\|\|\|\|\|\|\|\|\|\|\|\|\|\|\|\|\|\|\|\|\|\|\|\|\|\|\|\|\|\|\|\|\|\|\|\|\|\|\|\|\|\|\|\|\|\|\|\|

The Three Ways Anger Is Manifested

Most people display or release their anger in a way that is unique to them.

A man said to me one day, "Have you noticed the wide variety of victory dances that football players have when they score a touchdown?"

"Sure," I said.

"Well," he continued, "my wife has a little anger dance. The minute I see that dance, I batten down the hatches. I know she's hopping mad and I'm going to hear about it."

What is your anger dance?

Anger is generally expressed in one of three ways: rage, resentment, or righteous indignation.

ANGER EXPRESSED AS RAGE

\|\|\|\|\|\|\|\|\|\|\|\|\|\|\|\|\|\|\|\|\|\|\|\|\|\|\|\|\|\|\|\|\|\|\|\|\|\|\|\|\|\|\|\|\|\|\|\|\|\|\|\|\|\|\|\|\|\|\|\|\|\|\|\|\|\|

Rage is anger that erupts. I call it "powder-keg" anger. It wells up and explodes with little or no warning. It lashes out at anybody close enough to be in the path of the explosion. It is the behavior we sometimes associate with a person who has a violent temper.

I thought I detected anger in a person one day and asked, as innocently as I knew how, "Are you angry?"

The person exploded at me, "No, I am not angry! And don't ask me again!"

Well, I had my answer—and it was not his words that revealed the truth. The person's attitude and tone confessed his anger.

Rage is responsible for most violent crime and is at the root of virtually all forms of domestic abuse.

Walking on Eggshells

When we encounter a person filled with rage, or who expresses his anger in powder-keg fashion, we tend to walk on eggshells around him. If you wonder whether you have powder-keg anger, ask yourself, "Do people tiptoe around me at times? Are they reluctant to talk to me? Do they avoid me?"

I heard about a man who was considered a very hard worker. But his anger was so destructive that his coworkers were afraid of him. His employer said to me, "I really don't have any choice but to let him go. He's a stick of dynamite just waiting to be lit."

I asked, "Did you know he was angry when you hired him?"

"No," he said. "At least I didn't pick up on it. I didn't sense any anger directed toward me or his last employer." Then, after thinking for a moment, he added, "Maybe I should have asked more questions about why he had held so many different positions in the past two years. I probably should have asked him point-blank, 'Did you like the people you worked with? Were they good to you? Did they treat you fairly?'"

I agreed that those might have been insightful questions to ask. I also made a mental note to suggest to other people that they ask those same kinds of questions—not only employers but people who wonder whether they should marry a particular person. It would provide helpful information in most relationships.

"You are in a difficult circumstance," I finally said, agreeing that this situation was one that needed to be addressed quickly.

We prayed that the situation might be resolved in the best way possible. And at the close of our prayer, the employer said to me, "Please don't stop praying for me. I know that only God can give me the right words for this man and the right discernment not to hire anyone who has similar pent-up anger."

No Excuse for a Short Fuse

Perhaps because rage is the most visible and public expression of anger, people use all sorts of excuses to justify it. The three most common ones seem to be:

- "This is just the way I am." This person is content to see himself as an angry person, and he shows no desire to control his anger or to refrain from venting it.

- "God made me this way." The person who says this is blaming his Creator, rather than taking responsibility for himself.

- "Everyone in my family has a short fuse." This person blames his parents and other external factors, seeing it almost as a genetic factor. This person also refuses to take responsibility for his own anger.

If you have a short fuse, my recommendation is that you do whatever it takes to develop a longer one.

ANGER EXPRESSED AS RESENTMENT

A second major expression of anger is resentment, which also can be labeled "hostility." Resentment is seething anger that sets up residence within a person. This "Crock-Pot" anger is closely related to bitterness and hatred. You know what a Crock-Pot is. You fill it up, turn the heat on, and it slowly boils and stews and simmers and churns its contents. It just goes on and on and on. A lot of people live with that kind of anger on the inside. They think it's okay and is not going to hurt them.

Yes, it is.

Resentment is a dangerous form of anger. It appears to be nonviolent because it is internal. In truth, resentment is anger that generates tremendous pain, ill health, and suffering within the person who bears it. It is like an emotional malignancy, spreading slowly throughout a person's life to destroy his sense of peace, fulfillment, and well-being. Resentment can be difficult to detect from the outside because it often does not manifest itself in immediate, overt behaviors. Eventually, however, it surfaces. Resentment does not dissipate or diminish over time. Rather, it festers until it can no longer be contained. When that happens, the explosions are ugly and highly damaging.

I recently read an article about a man whose wife deeply resented him for more than two decades. She was angry about the hours he spent at work and jealous of the relationships he developed with his colleagues. She resented the rewards and praise he received from his superiors.

Her resentment was rooted in her own deeply held belief that her life as a homemaker and mother to their four children rendered her as less in the eyes of the world. She saw herself as less accomplished, less desirable, less worthy of recognition. The resentment built over time, regardless of the appreciation she received from her husband and children.

One day, she wrote a letter to her family members, telling each one in explicit detail how he or she had destroyed her life. Then, tragically, she took her own life.

Not only did this woman allow her resentment to destroy her from the inside out, but her actions devastated her husband and their four children. The effects of her desperate decision echoed in that family for decades—even affecting her children's marriages, as well as her grandchildren's.

What a waste of emotional energy! And what a vivid example of how resentment works to undermine and ultimately destroy a person's life.

Is there any situation that justifies holding on to our anger? Is it ever acceptable to nurture and nurse resentment or hostility?

No.

Every type of anger—no matter what type or what caused it—can be resolved if a person will choose to address it and deal with it.

THE LOSS THAT RESULTS FROM BAD ANGER

Both rage (powder keg) and resentment (Crock-Pot) are expressions of bad anger. They always result in loss to some degree over a period of time.

An outburst related to a specific situation may be fairly minor in its intensity, last for just a few seconds, and impact only the person who explodes. Consider the man who slams the hammer down on his finger rather than on the nail. Or the woman who finds a pot of soup boiling over on the stove. A sense of urgency, intensity, frustration, or pain shouts, "This is *not* what I had in mind!" The result is a loss of personal peace, even in the briefest expression of anger.

On the other hand, an angry outburst can be intense, affect many people, and continue for years. I recently read an article about Cambodia's killing fields. That country's former leader, Pol Pot, made one decision in anger that led to the death of millions in his nation over a period of twenty years. Many of his victims were forced to dig their own graves before being buried alive in them.

Bad anger has many names: animosity, revenge, hostility, lashing out, retaliation, payback, dissension, antagonism, and hatred—to name a few. Nothing good comes from anger expressed in these forms. As I stated previously, anger can destroy your marriage, your children, your job, and even your health.

CAN ANGER EVER BE GOOD?

Most people think of anger only in negative terms because we are much more aware of the harm anger causes. We've not seen enough examples of anger affecting our lives and our world in positive ways.

Can anger ever be *good*?

Yes!

Good anger can be described as righteous indignation, and it has the potential to produce lasting, positive results.

Righteous indignation (good anger) stands in sharp contrast to rage and resentment (bad anger), which is undisciplined, unfocused, and unyielding. Good anger is

- *Disciplined*—It does not rage like an out-of-control wildfire. For anger to have positive results, it must have boundaries and be reined in. It must be subjected to discipline.

- *Focused*—Good anger is not pervasive or generalized. It is focused toward the resolution of a particular problem or the meeting of a particular need. It is directed toward a singular purpose.

- *Short-lived*—It produces good results, and it ends when positive goals have been achieved.

- *Within the boundaries of God's commandments and His justice*—Good anger, or righteous indignation, must always be rooted in what God calls justice. It stands up for our "unalienable rights" because they have been given to us by our Creator.

At the outset of the United States of America, we had a revolution. On what premise? That taxation without representation was unacceptable.

The fight for our freedom from tyranny began with demonstrations—not with muskets and bayonets. But on a misty April morning in 1775, a brave minuteman's "shot heard round the world" in Lexington, Massachusetts, set off a series of events that changed history. Within fifteen months, leaders from America's thirteen colonies gathered to sign perhaps the most important document ever written: the Declaration of Independence. It begins by stating that "all men" are "endowed by their Creator with certain unalienable Rights, that among these are Life, Liberty and the pursuit of Happiness." The Declaration of Independence was a statement in words, not gunpowder. If England had seriously negotiated the demands of these independence-minded colonists, further bloodshed might very well have been avoided. Instead, a new nation was born through the blood and sweat of patriots. God rewarded their good anger and righteous indignation.

It is not a sin to stand for what is right, to speak for justice, or to defend the powerless. It is not a sin to advocate for those who have no voice, or to stand beside those unable to protect themselves.

Sin comes into play only when a person steps beyond the boundaries of God's law—either to seek outcomes that He does not honor or desire or to use methods that He condemns.

EVIDENCE FOR GOOD ANGER

How do I know there is such a thing as good anger?

First, the Bible says, "Be angry, and yet do not sin; do not let the sun go down on your anger, and do not give the devil an opportunity" (Ephesians 4:26–27).

This phrase, *be angry*, is one that many people do not expect to find in the Bible. The apostle Paul, who wrote these words to the Ephesians, knew that anger is an inevitable part of life. But he is not merely acknowledging the inevitable. Paul is stating that it is entirely acceptable—perhaps even desirable—for a person to feel anger. But it must be aimed at godly goals. The apostle clearly recognized that not all anger is related to negative or sinful expression and that some anger can be good.

Second, the Bible has nearly 500 references to anger. In 350 of those instances, the one who is angry is God.

If our heavenly Father gets angry, then there must be good anger, because God does not sin.

So what did the Lord get angry about?

Repeatedly, He told His people that they were not to worship idols. God made it very clear to the Hebrews that they were His chosen people. He expressed His love for them repeatedly and was jealous of their sole affection and worship. The Lord had protected and provided for His people, and He longed for their willful obedience so that He might bless them even more. The truth is that God neither winks at nor overlooks sin. The Father sees our sin, and because He is holy and righteous, He cannot reward or bless those who are sinful. He knows that sin puts people in bondage and leads to suffering and death. God longs to free His people from that bondage and put them on a path to life at its very best.

For these reasons, the Lord was strong in His commands to the people regarding their fidelity and loyalty to Him. Some of the angriest words from God are against those who disobey His command against idolatry.

Throughout the Bible, our heavenly Father is most angry not at specific individuals but at situations and behaviors that affect His kingdom on earth and His plan for the redemption of mankind. God was, is, and always will be angry at sin. But He loves each of us individually and longs to free His children from the bondage of sin. We see this clearly in the life and ministry of Jesus.

The Righteous Anger of Jesus

In the gospel of Mark, we read about Christ's encounter with a man who had a withered hand. The incident took place in the local synagogue on the Sabbath. The religious leaders watched Jesus closely to see if He would heal the man and violate the holy day's command to rest. The Lord said to the man, "Get up and come forward!" And then to the Pharisees and Sadducees who hoped to ensnare him for breaking the Sabbath, Jesus said, "Is it lawful to do good or to do harm on the Sabbath, to save a life or to kill?" All remained silent, knowing that whatever they said would be wrong.

The Bible then tells us that Christ looked around at them "with anger, grieved at their hardness of heart" (Mark 3:5). Jesus said to the man, "Stretch out your hand." When the man stretched it out, his hand was restored.

The Son of Man was angry at two things: their lack of compassion and their misinterpretation of the Law. The Law of Moses states, "Remember the Sabbath day, to keep it holy" (Exodus 20:8). To remember is to regard, to honor, to steadfastly commemorate. To "keep it holy" means to set it apart from all other days and, specifically, to set it apart to worship God.

Then the Law goes on to say, "The seventh day is a Sabbath of the LORD your God; in it you shall not do any work, you or your son or your daughter, your male or your female servant or your cattle or your sojourner who stays with you" (Exodus 20:10).

"Work" refers to anything one does to support oneself—food growing, buying and selling, business ventures, cooking and clean-ing, and anything else that is related to providing for and protecting one's family.

The religious leaders through the centuries had become particular in defining how much work a person could or could not do. For example, only a certain number of steps could be walked on the Sabbath.

In this instance, they had confused "ministry" work with work re-lated to a person's livelihood. If God had intended no effort whatso-ever be expended on the Sabbath, a person would have to stay in bed all day and avoid talking, eating, or any other activity. Every priest and levite who served in the temple would have been in violation.

The Pharisees and Sadducees believed that the Law allowed for a man to rescue his ox if it fell into a ditch on the Sabbath, but not to speak a command of healing to a person with a withered hand. It made no sense. They were misinterpreting God's loving command. Jesus knew it and did what was right before the Father.

Let me assure you that when people misinterpret God's Word and stand on the letter of the Law instead of the intent, it still angers the Lord.

God hates sin for what it does to His children. And misinterpreting His Word leads people off the path of righteousness and away from Him. God wants us to acknowledge our sin, ask His forgiveness, and move forward with a spirit of repentance and change.

Jesus said on more than one occasion that He came to fulfill the Law, not to do away with it. He came to show us how to live out the Law in the frailty of our human flesh. The Son of God wants us to be in right standing with the Father so we can experience the freedom, forgiveness, and confidence that come from a close relationship with Him.

Righteous Indignation Intended to Warn

In chapter 23 of the gospel of Matthew, Jesus delivered one of the angriest speeches I have ever heard. He's speaking to the Pharisees and Sadducees, calling them hypocrites, fools, and blind guides. Was Jesus angry? Yes, He was. Why was the Lord angry? Because their interpretation was so legalizing the law that it was preventing people from trusting Him and obeying Him.

In this chapter, Jesus used the word *woe* eight times as a strong warning to those who, through legalism, were keeping people out of heaven. *Woe* is not a gentle word. It means "warning and destruction to you." Christ used it as a strong challenge to the religious leaders who

- "Shut off the kingdom of heaven" (verse 13).

- "Devour widows' houses" by taking money from them in exchange for prayers (verse 14).

- Make the gold of the temple more important than the temple itself (verses 16–22).

- Require all kinds of giving but neglect "justice and mercy and faithfulness" (verse 23).

- Are "full of robbery and self-indulgence" (verse 25).

- Have become "full of hypocrisy and lawlessness" by focusing on outward appearance (verses 27–28).

- "Build the tombs of the prophets and adorn the monuments of the righteous" while being the "sons of those who murdered the prophets" (verses 29–31).

Their legalism and man-made requirements escalated to the point where the "scribes and Pharisees" had no compassion for—and provided no hope to—those who truly wanted to be in right relationship with God. Was Jesus right to be so angry with them? Absolutely. Did He sin in His anger? Absolutely not.

Righteous Indignation That Cleanses and Restores

Perhaps the best-known example of Jesus' anger is an incident known as the cleansing of the temple (see Matthew 21:12–13). The temple was the center for all Jewish worship. Everything about Jewish faith that was considered holy, beautiful, and meaningful had the temple as its focal point. At the heart of their worship was the sacrifice of animals and birds. These rituals were a sign of the Jews' total dependency upon God and their total surrender to Him.

People who came to the temple seeking to keep the Law and make a sacrifice had to purchase a lamb or dove with temple currency. They had to exchange regular currency for temple coins. But greedy high priests could set the exchange rate and price of the animals very high.

In Matthew 21, Jesus went to the temple to teach, heal, and worship. But what the Lord found there made him so angry that He "drove out all those who were buying and selling in the temple, and overturned the tables of the money changers and the seats of those who were selling doves" (Matthew 21:12).

The high priests had made it impossible for the poor to enter the temple and worship God through sacrifice.

So Jesus drove them from the temple, saying, "It is written, MY HOUSE SHALL BE CALLED A HOUSE OF PRAYER; but you are making it a ROBBERS' DEN" (Matthew 21:13).

The Lord's anger was motivated by the extortion in the temple and the damage it was doing. His righteous indignation was in opposition to the greedy, manipulative behavior of the religious authorities who were mistreating Israel's poor.

What makes an angry expression or behavior justified? Justified anger is purposeful and beneficial to someone who is being mistreated, hurt, or taken advantage of. Let me restate a point made earlier: Justified anger always seeks to bring a situation or circumstance in line with God's commandments and to further His kingdom here on earth.

Unjustified anger is self-motivated and vengeful. It seeks to get even or destroy. It is ultimately of no benefit to any person, although the angry person may *think* he is reaping a temporary victory. Most anger these days is bad or unjustified because it's centered only on the individual and what he or she wants.

Was Jesus' anger justified in cleansing the temple? Absolutely. People were abusing the house of the Lord God. The chief priests and scribes were stealing, lying, and misusing their positions and privileges. They were preventing a host of people from coming and worshipping at the temple because the poor couldn't afford the price of a dove or a lamb.

Any time the Bible reveals Jesus or God the Father being angry, there is a common, consistent reason for it. They are angry at injustice and at things that hurt God's people—those who are His followers and believers. When the Lord gets angry, it's always with a reason and purpose.

Righteous Indignation in Nehemiah's Day

One of the best examples of good anger in the Bible is found in Nehemiah. After the Jews returned from decades of exile in Babylon, Nehemiah was the leader who organized the people to rebuild the walls and gates of Jerusalem. The Jews who did the work were under constant threat and ridicule from their enemies. Nehemiah had a major challenge in keeping the Jews motivated and hopeful because the fear surrounding their work was intense. In the end, the wall was completed in fifty-two days—an amazing feat.

During those two months of intense struggle and effort, we do not see Nehemiah getting angry with either the enemies of the Jews or the ones working on the wall around the clock. We do read, however, that Nehemiah becomes very angry when he hears that Jews are being treated in an unjust manner.

They were being charged a high interest rate on money they borrowed to pay taxes to the king of Persia. Some Jews who couldn't pay saw their sons and daughters forced into slavery. Nehemiah's response to the situation was justified: "I was very angry when I had heard their outcry and these words" (Nehemiah 5:7).

Then we read that Nehemiah "consulted with myself." In other words, he thought long and hard about the situation until he decided in his mind and heart what should be done. Later in that same verse, it says Nehemiah "contended with the nobles and the rulers," which means he confronted them about this injustice against the Jews. And third, he "held a great assembly against them."

Nehemiah made his arguments before the people as a whole. In the end, the moneylenders agreed that they would return what they had taken—including fields, vineyards, olive groves, houses, money, grain, new wine, and oil (verse 12).

Then Nehemiah stood before the people and shook out the front of his garment and said, "Thus may God shake out every man from his house and from his possessions who does not fulfill this promise; even thus may he be shaken out and emptied." All the people gathered said "Amen!" They praised the Lord and acted in accordance with their promise (verse 13).

Was Nehemiah angry? Yes, indeed.

Did he channel his anger in the right ways? Yes.

Nehemiah rationally and calmly came to right decisions before saying a word. He sought out the offenders and addressed them. He gathered public support for his position. Nehemiah spoke to all involved and appealed to their sense of fairness and decency because they too had been freed from slavery. He called them to a well-reasoned, well-stated course of action and took an oath from them that they would do the right thing.

This is good anger at work!

THE CHALLENGE OF EXPRESSING ANGER AS RIGHTEOUS INDIGNATION

Feelings of righteous indignation can and should be expressed. But even good anger can create inner turmoil if these feelings do not find godly expression aimed at resolving ungodly situations. Righteous indignation does not brew inside a person the way resentment and bitterness do. But, if unexpressed, it can produce a spirit of confusion, doubt, and frustration. When you feel righteous indignation, and something can be done, take action.

Stand Up

Our good anger should cause us to stand up for what's right. You could join a group that's fighting against a negative situation or injustice. If you cannot find one, you may need to form such a group yourself.

Work within the law. Work peacefully. Find ways of protesting and problem solving that are effective. It is important not only that you pursue godly goals but also that you act in godly ways.

Get involved in ministry efforts to change, correct, and end things that are contrary to God's desires: abuse, ignorance, poverty, slavery, pornography, abortion, and anything else that you know is in clear violation of His commandments.

Speak Up

Righteous indignation also should cause us to speak up. When you or I recognize that something is being taught or preached that is contrary to God's Word, we have an obligation to say something.

Not long ago, a friend of mine told me that her pastor had preached a sermon on two ways for a person to be saved. He stated that one way to experience God's forgiveness and receive the promise of eternal life was through faith in Jesus Christ. The second way was through "being good to other people."

I said, "You need to confront this pastor. The Bible does not have a two-path system. God's Word says that a person comes to the Father only through His Son, Jesus Christ."

She said, "My going to him wouldn't make any difference. He said as part of his sermon that anyone who disagreed with him was hard-hearted and ignorant."

"Then you need to get out of that church," I said.

She replied, "I've been considering that, but all my friends go there."

If she stays in that church, my friend will live with ongoing inner turmoil. She feels righteous indignation at what was preached. Her anger is good. Now she needs the courage to follow her convictions.

Don't let anything stop you from speaking up when you hear lies, false doctrine, and wrong teaching.

Find the right time and use the right method to speak the truth. The right time may be at the next meeting of church members, the city council, the board of education, or the PTA at your child's school. Get on the agenda. Prepare yourself in advance.

The right method may be writing a letter, taking out a newspaper ad, or even writing and publishing a blog on the Internet. Ask God to show you the best way to speak up.

Pray Up

It is always appropriate to express righteous indignation in a prayer request voiced to God. If you see someone hurting or taking advantage of another person, your first response should be to pray. When you fight your battles on your knees, you win every time.

Our righteous indignation kicks in when we see people being mistreated. We want to be able to correct it. The best way to do that is to fully commit the situation or circumstance to the Lord through prayer—and then watch Him work.

WORKING AND BELIEVING FOR GOD'S BEST

Righteous indignation is intended to produce God's best in your life and in the lives of others. Expressions of good anger require two things: hard work and right believing.

We can feel righteous indignation and have very little opportunity to remedy the situation that generated our anger. I found that out a number of years ago. My mother was telling me about my father and, more specifically, about the illness that took his life. In describing his final hours on earth, my mother said, "Your father was very weak, and the realization finally came that he was dying. I asked him, 'What will I do without you?'

"He said, 'You will just have to do the best you can.'"

The moment my mother spoke those words, I felt anger welling up in me. His words sounded so cold and heartless. I had never felt any anger toward my father, but in that moment, my anger was full-blown. How could my father say such a thing? Why didn't he have a better answer? Couldn't he have said something a little more encouraging or comforting?

But as I have reflected on my father's words and had discussions with my aunts over the years, I have come to understand more fully the situation my parents were in. First, the kidney disease that took my father's life came upon him suddenly. With today's medicine, his condition would not have been fatal. At the time, however, there was little understanding about his condition and no effective treatment for it. The result? There really wasn't much my father could have done to plan any type of ongoing support for my mother and me. And given their economic situation at the time, there was very little money to set aside, invest, or spend on life insurance.

Second, one of the things I heard repeatedly from my mother during my growing-up years was the very thing my father had said to her: "Do your best." The underlying belief in our family was that doing your best was really all you *could* do. My father may well have been trying to reassure my mother that nobody could ever expect more than her best effort. He may have been giving her his vote of confidence that she was not a woman who was going to fold in tough times. Rather, she would continue to do her best at work, pray her best prayers, and give her best mother's love and care to their only son.

Finally, I have made peace with this statement of my father in one additional way: Part of "doing one's best" is believing in God to the best of one's ability. When we truly trust the Lord to the best of our faith ability, we are in the best position to receive His best protection and provision.

You may be asking, "Aren't you just trying to put the best possible spin on this?"

Yes, I am. But I make no apology for that. When you find yourself filled with anger, one of the wisest things you can do is believe that the other person is acting with the best motives, best intentions, and best character. You have nothing to lose by believing the best.

In addition, choosing to believe the best will motivate you to come up with the best solution or response possible—even if you are reeling inside from a strong blow of rejection or emotional pain.

The truth is that, more than forty years after my father's death, I could do nothing to change what happened or make his words more comforting to my mother. The best response I could give at that moment was to encourage her that she had done her best. I also told her that I was forever grateful for all she had given me and for the way she loved me.

There may be injustices in your family history or from your own childhood that you cannot fix at this stage in your life. But you can pray for those who have been hurt and still may feel wounded today. Speak words of comfort and appreciation to them. Let them know that you are aware of what they went through and are sorry for what they had to endure. Tell them you admire their perseverance of faith and that you highly value their lives and their example.

I recently heard the story of a young woman who was put into foster care when she was six or seven years old. The man her mother was living with had molested the girl's siblings. Thankfully, she was removed from the home before she was harmed. Eventually, the girl was placed with a family that adopted her. But this woman's teen years were not happy ones. Her adoptive father ended up sending her to reform school, and it was there that she came to know about Jesus. She accepted the forgiveness God makes possible through Christ, and she forgave herself for the inappropriate ways in which she had behaved.

Today this young woman is working in a church-sponsored orphanage and home for displaced girls—as she once was. As house parents, this woman and her husband care for several little girls. They show these precious souls the love of the Lord and parent them in very special ways.

She said to a friend of mine not long ago, "I was an angry teenager, upset with both God and other people for the ways I felt neglected and abandoned. But none of my anger produced anything positive. Today I'm still angry that some little girls must be taken from their parents to be safe and receive the care they need. But I'm putting that anger into positive action to help heal their broken hearts and build stronger futures for them."

What a wonderful example of the way God can turn bad anger into good anger.

ADMIT IT—DEAL WITH IT

1. Have you experienced anger as rage, either in yourself or in someone else?

2. What was the physical, emotional, and spiritual fallout on you or on your relationship with the other person?

3. Have you ever held anger in and allowed it to fester as resentment and bitterness? What can you do to release that bitterness?

4. How can you focus righteous indignation into positive goals and action?

CHAPTER 3

CONSEQUENCES

|||||||||||||||||||||||||||||||||||||||||||||||||||||||||||||||||||||||||||||||||||

Anger's Impact on Us, Others, and God

A nger affects our lives physically, psychologically, emotionally, and spiritually. It also influences our performance in completing tasks or fulfilling our work responsibilities. Anger is never entirely self-contained. It always has consequences that touch those around us. More important, anger has an impact on God.

THE IMPACT OF ANGER ON YOU PERSONALLY

||||||||||||||||||||||||||||||||||||||||||||||||||||||||||||||||||||||||

Anger affects you personally in a number of ways, five of which we will explore in this chapter.

Anger Affects Your Health

More and more, scientific and medical researchers are finding that a significant number of serious diseases—including some of the most deadly—are chronic in nature, related to our lifestyle choices, and linked to the way we think or process our emotions. Anger certainly is one of the negative emotions that has been linked to a wide variety of ailments.

God did not create the human body to accommodate long-term anger. The medical profession currently puts high cholesterol, smoking, and anger on equal footing when it comes to their destructive influence. Anger has both immediate and lasting effects.

When a person becomes angry, her heart beats faster, her blood pressure rises, and her hands sweat. These natural responses occur immediately and require no thought or intention. The stomach tenses, and digestion is hindered. The face turns red, the muscles tense, and the person tends to speak in a louder than normal voice. All these are outcomes that God created as part of our flight-or-fight response to danger or a threat.

In addition, the body produces a surge of adrenaline to deal with crisis. This allows the person to have greater strength to fight or run away as fast as possible. But adrenaline can be both friend and foe.

When anger is suppressed, the body continues to produce adrenaline in small quantities to address the perceived danger that the mind and heart indicate is present. Over time, this drip-drip-drip of adrenaline and other hormones within the human body is extremely detrimental. It produces a state of internal stress—a little like trying to drive with one foot on the gas pedal and the other on the brake. The long-term effects include ulcers, heart ailments, strokes, arthritis, and depression. Every system and organ in the body is affected in a negative way.

Rather than own up to anger, people tend to attribute negative physical symptoms to stress. They are either not aware or refuse to acknowledge that anger is to blame. A doctor once said to me, "It seems a third of my patients are on stomach meds, a third are on pain meds, and the rest are on tranquilizers. And most of them wouldn't need any of them if they'd deal with the emotional issues in their lives."

A few months ago, a man came forward at the end of a church service. He was bent over and used a cane. He had heard me talk about the negative physical effects of anger and said, "Dr. Stanley, the doctors have told me that my stroke was caused by anger. I'm in the shape I am today because of anger. Tell people that anger can do to them what it did to me."

No issue and no amount of anger is worth holding on to if it destroys your health.

Anger Influences Your Attitude and Behavior

You cannot hide anger. It doesn't take long for a sensitive, astute person to recognize it in another person. There's something in the flashing of the eyes, the clenching of the jaw, or the edgy tone in the voice. As much as a person attempts to hide it, anger will reveal itself. At times, the words an angry person speaks—even if dripping with kindness—give the person away.

Those who study human behavior have noted a number of characteristics in angry people:

- *Tardiness*—Very often in an attempt to control a situation or draw attention to himself so he can express anger.

- *Obstructive behavior in groups*—A lack of cooperation to the point that the person is truly disagreeable. She objects to every idea suggested with an air of disdain. I have been in countless meetings where one person objects to *anything* that is proposed or offered as a solution. I have come to recognize the obstructive person as someone who is almost always angry.

- *Cynicism*—Finding fault in every person or situation.

- *Jabbing jokes*—Telling embarrassing stories with the intent of hurting the subject of the joke.

- *Disrupting conversations*—The angry person often feels a deep need to interject his or her opinion, even if it's off the topic.

- *Sloppy job performance*—The angry person is often resentful to the point that he no longer cares about doing a good job. He is not motivated to give his best effort.

- *Loss of enthusiasm*—The angry person does not want to be happy. This very often translates into a down-in-the-mouth attitude. The angry person may withdraw from social settings or turn down invitations to public events. The angry person would rather brood than laugh.

- *Depression*—What begins as a self-imposed lack of enthusiasm can end up as full-blown depression. Angry people often slide into periods of deep discouragement and despair, in part because they hate the fact that nobody seems to take their anger as seriously as they do.

- *Procrastination*—The angry person has little desire to start new things that require focus or creativity.

- *Eating disorders*—Angry people can overeat, undereat, or overexercise. They frequently find themselves facing obesity or anorexia or bulimia.

- *Sexual dysfunction*—Many people have problems in their sexual lives because they're angry. When a person is angry and wants sex, what that person is doing is expressing anger to someone else through an act. Sex without love is an act. Animals do that. And angry people don't realize that a loving and sensitive husband or wife knows there's no love in what he or she is doing. It's damaging and can destroy a life and a marriage. That's how powerful and deceptive anger is. But when genuine, godly, wonderful, intimate, true love is present, it's a whole different story.

Anger Disturbs Your Sleep

Angry people generally are incapable of experiencing deep inner peace. Even if their anger is aimed at just one person or situation, it will spill over into other areas. It cannot be compartmentalized. Anger will taint every aspect of one's life.

This is clearly evident when it comes to getting proper rest. Your body rejuvenates itself during sleep—old cells are replaced by new ones, hormone levels are rebalanced, and tissues are cleansed of toxins. The mind is also renewed. Sleep has benefits too numerous to mention here.

But anger can disrupt sleep patterns and can keep people from getting the full night's rest they need. Is someone keeping you awake at night because of his or her insulting remarks or critical comments? Are you facing a situation that has you so frustrated you can't seem to let it go? Do you find yourself tossing and turning over what someone did or said?

A person once said to me, "I've been arguing with my husband, Dan, for ten years. Sometimes the arguments are intense. They can last half a night."

"That's a very long time to be arguing with someone," I replied.

She said, "Yes, it is—especially since we've been divorced for eleven years."

This woman was still having "conversations" with her former husband long after he had left their bedroom. Dan could not hear her complaints, her reasoning, or her sobbing. She felt such anger toward him that it kept her awake for hours at a time. She would express her frustration and anger out loud as if he could hear, would care, or it would make a difference.

The deception is that when you finally do get to sleep after an angry conversation with a person who is or isn't there, you may think that your anger has been fully vented and is, therefore, gone. But that isn't the case. Your anger hasn't disappeared. It has simply moved into your subconscious, where it will simmer and brew. Your anger will surface again, in some way at some time. And it's not a matter of *if*. It's a matter of *when*.

The Bible tells us clearly: "Do not let the sun go down on your anger" (Ephesians 4:26). In other words, don't go to bed angry. Get rid of your anger before you fall asleep.

The importance of getting a good night's rest cannot be overemphasized. And one of the keys to making sure you get the best sleep possible is guarding your heart and mind from potentially harmful or distracting messages that your brain will process through the night.

The portions of the brain that govern your body's involuntary muscles and systems continue working to keep your lungs breathing and your heart beating while you sleep. Your brain keeps the body functioning, coordinates the replenishment, repair, and nourishment of cells and tissues, utilizes the nutrients you have consumed during the day, and infuses you with energy and strength to face the day ahead.

A similar thing happens in your cognitive and emotional realms. What you feed your mind is processed all night long in a way that either contributes to or detracts from your well-being.

If you fall asleep with your last thoughts being ones of joy and thanksgiving, peace in your relationship with God, and enthusiasm for what the coming day holds, then you are likely to sleep well through the night and awaken refreshed, energetic, and ready to take on the challenges ahead. You may well awaken with creative ideas that you didn't have yesterday. They could include answers and solutions to questions and problems that were confusing or puzzling to you the day before.

On the other hand, if your last thoughts before falling asleep are ones marked by bitterness, revenge, hatred, and anger, you are most likely going to have a fitful night's sleep. You can count on waking up feeling worn out, lethargic, and with little motivating energy to do your work or contribute your best to the responsibilities that lie ahead.

For years I have encouraged people to pray and read the Bible—especially the Psalms and other books that are comforting and encouraging—as the last two things they do before going to bed at night. Reading the Scriptures and talking to God are the two best sleep aids I know.

Reading the Bible fills us with positive and eternal truth. It makes us aware of the fact that God is, has been, and always will be in control of every aspect of our lives. When that knowledge becomes part of our thinking night after night, it creates a deep sense of confidence. Life's minor problems don't have much impact, and the major ones can be taken in stride. We will see every challenge and opportunity in the context of God's eternal will, plan, and purpose for our lives—and each situation and circumstance can be seen in the context of the heavenly Father's abiding love and awesome grace.

Having a conversation with God just before going to sleep fills your heart and mind with the awareness and assurance that you have a personal relationship with the One who is all-wise, all-powerful, and all-loving. In those final moments of the day, I encourage you to get on your knees and thank Him for what He enabled you to accomplish. Ask God to guide your thinking and your work tomorrow, and thank Him for His constant presence in your life. Ask the Lord to forgive any sin in your life and to help you forgive the sin of others. Pray for Him to make any necessary changes in your life so you can become the person He intends and created you to be. Such a conversation will leave you feeling cleansed, renewed, and at peace with God. In the Bible, every day was thought to begin at sundown. When the sun set on Monday night, it was actually the start of Tuesday. In Genesis, we learn from the creation story that "There was evening and there was morning, one day" (Genesis 1:5, 8, 13, 19, 23, 31).

Adam and Eve walked with God "in the cool of the evening"—which is the time just after the sun sets and before the sky is completely dark. They began their next day with God by discussing the previous day with Him. Each of Adam and Eve's days began with rest, accomplishment, and peace between them and God.

For thousands of years, Jewish men have gathered together between sundown and bedtime to read and study the Torah and the Talmud. They allowed their minds to be filled with the Word of God, so that all night the Lord could work to sink His truth into their minds, renew their desire to obey His commands, and apply His law to their lives.

Compare that to how many people in our modern world spend their late-evening hours. In the last few hours before they go to bed, most men and women eat some kind of junk food or sugary snack that sends their digestive and nervous systems into overdrive. They watch a news program that often presents images of war or criminal activity. Or they turn on a television program filled with violence, sexual innuendo, or inappropriate language. Some read a novel filled with those same things. Then they turn off the lights and wonder why they can't seem to relax.

Their bodies are trying to digest and absorb what they have eaten, while their minds are reeling in an attempt to make sense of all the negative images they have seen and heard. Any peace they hope to have gives way to agitation, frustration, and worry—all of which intensify the longer they stay awake. It is a vicious cycle and, too often, a nightly ritual.

I can guarantee you this: If you go to bed angry, you will wake up angry.

If you go to bed angry with someone, you will still feel anger toward that person the next day—and your anger is likely to be greater and more intense.

If you go to bed angry with yourself, you will wake up angry at yourself—and feel like a victim to your own emotions. You are likely to develop a sense of personal failure and low self-worth. You will have less optimism, less enthusiasm, and less of a desire to pursue good goals.

If you go to bed angry with God, you will awaken feeling a loss of hope, joy, and peace. You will not have the faith to conquer what lies ahead.

Anger Influences Your Perspective

Angry people often put up a shield against the person who hurt or upset them. They may go out of their way to avoid that man or woman. Most of us are reluctant to accept invitations or receive affection from people who have made us angry.

Do any of those actions describe how you deal with people you're angry with? Even if you don't think you're hurting yourself by doing one or more of those things, you are. If you put up a shield against one person, it's likely to go up against everybody. Those who are intensely angry at another person who has hurt or rejected them often make strong statements such as: "I will never trust anyone again in that area of my life" or "I'm going to protect myself and not get close to another person as long as I live." Anger has an isolating effect and will interfere with your ability to form close, lasting, and intimate friendships.

Few people enjoy associating with angry people. The vast majority of us will choose a peaceful, joyful person over a dark, brooding one. This holds true for nearly all relationships, whether they are personal or professional, intimate or casual. As a result, angry people are increasingly alone and not included, invited, or involved. This isolating effect makes many angry people even angrier! They resent being rejected and seek to justify or express their anger all the more. The net result is an empty life. Over time, the angry person finds himself or herself intensely lonely.

Anger Affects Your Thought Processes

Long-lasting anger changes the way a person thinks. It invariably becomes part of one's thought processes. We've all seen it happen or experienced it personally. When you're angry with someone, you very often find it difficult to stay focused on your work. You struggle to come up with creative ideas, or you may find yourself unable to maintain a high level of output. Angry people often find their thoughts wandering off task to what they could have or should have said or done to the subject of their anger.

An ancient Jewish proverb reads: "Anger deprives a sage of his wisdom, a prophet of his vision." I have no doubt as to the truth of that statement. Anger produces a double mind. A person's concentration can linger on her anger and the incidents that gave rise to it, even as she attempts to focus on the work and responsibilities of any given day. Very little mental energy is left for creativity, for innovation, or for processing information in the light of God's Word. Anger weakens our ability to have a clear, inspired vision and make new plans.

THE IMPACT OF ANGER ON YOUR RELATIONSHIPS

Anger always affects your relationships, especially those that matter most to you. The greater your anger, the greater the potential for long-lasting negative impact. It simply is not possible to work in harmony with another person, set goals, or accomplish anything if one or both people in a relationship harbor anger. A marriage will suffer greatly if it is present. Anger disrupts family life and interferes with parent-child relationships. A work group will not be as productive or creative if one or more members is angry. A church will not minister effectively if it is filled with angry people.

A man argued with me one day, saying, "My anger doesn't hurt anybody. If they get hurt, it's because they choose to be hurt. If they don't want to hear my angry words, they can walk away."

That isn't really a valid argument. No one can totally tune out another person's tirade. You may choose not to take to heart the other person's anger. But you cannot avoid having to deal with it in some way. Often, innocent people are victims of anger from a person they don't even know.

That was the case at an Orioles baseball game in 1894. The players began to argue with members of the opposing team, and then the fans got involved. A full-scale riot ensued, and for reasons that aren't fully clear, the wooden stands of the stadium caught fire. Before the fire was extinguished, 107 buildings in Baltimore were burned beyond restoration.

Outbursts of anger cause everyone within range to feel some degree of emotional pain, whether it's intended or not. That's one reason people seek to distance themselves from an angry person. And we often see anger as a sign that someone is distancing himself or herself from a group or individual. Feelings of isolation, alienation, and rejection are common in angry people.

A salesman admitted to erupting in anger frequently. "But never in public," he declared. Yet he saw absolutely no connection between the anger he vented at home and the fact that his wife had been admitted to a mental hospital. Her psychiatrists saw the situation in a different light and suggested that the angry husband seek counseling. "What for?" the man asked. "I'm not the one with depression." A nurse standing nearby muttered to herself, "But you are the depressor."

Anger not only rises from criticism and accusations, it also generates criticism and accusations. Anger in any environment creates unrest, tension, and frustration. All aspects of productivity, quality, and morale are affected negatively.

The sad truth is that this environment exists even if the angry person didn't intend to create it.

A few months ago I heard about a woman who had spent more than twenty years married to a very angry man. He wasn't angry with his wife but, rather, with the people at work. He maintained a pleasant outward demeanor toward his supervisors and fellow employees. But once he arrived at home, he vented all his anger in profane tirades that sometimes lasted two to three hours.

His wife shriveled on the inside at his outbursts. She knew he wasn't angry with her. But still, his words and tone deeply disturbed her inner peace. She wondered what might happen if she ever disappointed him the way his coworkers seemed to. She began to seek ways of escaping emotionally and closing off parts of her heart from him so that she would not feel wounded.

So when the time came for them to go to bed at night, the last thing this woman wanted was for her husband to be intimate with her. She pulled away from him both emotionally and physically.

Her pulling away, of course, *did* make him angry over time. Although this man never struck his wife or shouted at her, he created a state of constant turmoil through his inability to control his anger or maintain a loving atmosphere in his relationship with her. He turned to alcohol to help him calm his anger, and before long he wasn't just angry—he was an angry alcoholic. This spiral downward picked up speed over the years, and their marriage eventually ended in a bitter, ugly divorce.

In most cases, anger is cyclical. Let me assure you that time—on its own—does not heal it. If not dealt with properly, anger grows ever greater and does not diminish on its own.

Children and parents can become angry with one another. And that too can be a cycle that escalates over time. More and more instances of neglect, hurt, abuse, criticism, or dishonesty become folded in to the decaying relationship, and the result is a growing pool of anger. If that anger results in estrangement or tragedy of some type, the anger doesn't dissipate—it takes new forms associated with guilt, blame, recrimination, vengeance, and further criticism and pain.

Not long ago, a lady told me what happened after her mother died. All the children and grandchildren started wrangling over the dead woman's estate. Money was the primary issue and seemed to be the only thing that mattered. They were all angry at one another and fighting over who was going to get this and who was going to have that. But one of the things they were most angry about was who would get the woman's Bible!

Now, I understand that perhaps the notes this devoted Christian woman had made in the margins of her Bible may have been the greatest legacy she left her children. But to fight over a copy of God's Word is totally unacceptable.

THE IMPACT OF ANGER ON GOD

Can a person's anger affect God? Most definitely.

Through the years, I have become increasingly amazed at how many people believe that God has no emotions and that their behavior does not prompt an emotional response in Him. The truth is that what we say and do causes God to rejoice or to grieve. And bad anger does not please our heavenly Father. So the Bible warns us, "Do not grieve the Holy Spirit of God" (Ephesians 4:30).

Anger hinders the work He has called us to do. It is a roadblock to experiencing God's love, faith, hope, joy, and peace in our lives. The witness of a constantly angry person who identifies Jesus Christ as Savior tends to fall on deaf ears. Any message of the Father's loving-kindness tends to be viewed with suspicion. And our anger can hinder the work that God desires to do in the life of another person.

Finally, anger will hinder God's blessings in our lives. Sin separates us from the Father and prevents us from receiving His best. Anger can upset us to the point where we fail to perceive God's blessings and, in consequence, fail to receive them.

DO NOT DISMISS THE IMPACT OF YOUR ANGER

Your anger is no laughing matter. Refuse to make light of it. Do not allow others to laugh about their short fuse. Take anger seriously.

Resist any attempts to dismiss or trivialize the impact of anger. The effects of anger can be devastating in terms of physical, emotional, and spiritual pain and suffering.

Health, happiness, prosperity, and purpose are all negatively affected by anger. If you want a better future, you must deal with it.

ADMIT IT—DEAL WITH IT

1. Make a list of what you believe are consequences of anger. Reflect on what you wrote.

2. How have the consequences helped resolve the root issue that leads to anger?

3. How have these consequences hindered the resolution of the issue? Discuss your thoughts with one or two persons you trust and ask for honest feedback.

4. Now write down precisely what you can and will do to address your anger.

CHAPTER 4

ROOTS

|||||||||||||||||||||||||||||||||||||||||||||||||||||||||||||||||||||||||||||||||

Exploring the Causes of Anger

The roots of a person's anger can run very deep. Anger's history can reveal a lifelong struggle to overcome resentment, bitterness, and hostility. And the reasons for a person's anger may or may not be justified. Here are seven roots of anger that I invite you to explore and submit to deep consideration and prayer.

SEVEN ROOTS OF ANGER

|||||||||||||||||||||||||||||||||||||||||||||||||||||||||||||||||||||||||||||||||

1. Blame and Shame

Who was the first person in the Bible to get angry?

When I ask that question, most people reply, "Cain!"

Without a doubt, he was a very angry man. But I don't believe Cain is the first person in the Bible who got angry.

Consider carefully what happened in the Garden of Eden. Adam found himself married to the most beautiful woman imaginable. His life was paradise. He had a close relationship with God, ruled over creation, and enjoyed constant renewal of life. And then one day, he took a bite of the forbidden fruit and his entire world came crashing down around him. He was cast out of the garden and became destined to work by the sweat of his brow until the day he died.

Now, isn't it possible that Adam was more than a little angry with Eve? Absolutely. How do I know that? Because he blamed her for what happened to them. When God confronted him in the garden, Adam responded, "The woman whom You gave to be with me, she gave me from the tree, and I ate" (Genesis 3:12).

The blame game finds its roots in anger. Ashamed and not wanting to take responsibility for what he had done, Adam lashed out and placed the blame on Eve. It's a pattern that has continued for thousands of years and still happens hundreds of times a day all around us.

For Eve's part, she was also angry. When God confronted her about what she did, Eve played the blame game too: "The serpent deceived me, and I ate" (Genesis 3:13).

Blame is easy.

Taking responsibility is hard.

Anger is easy.

Self-control is hard.

Externally, we may become angry with others who tempt or entice us to do something morally wrong and against our better judgment. And we might get angry when someone lies or preys upon our vulnerability or weakness.

Internally, we may become very angry with ourselves for being gullible, buying in to a lie, or participating in a sinful act—even though we knew it was wrong.

Very close to blame is shame—feeling disgraced, dishonored, unworthy, or embarrassed. We usually experience shame when someone else points out our bad behavior. And shame is especially powerful when someone points out our bad behavior in front of a group of people. Many people react to shaming with anger.

I want to be quick to point out that not all shame is warranted. Some people feel it after being forced to participate in a sinful act against their will. For example, children who are the victims of sexual abuse often struggle with guilt and shame long into their adult years. But those feelings of guilt and shame are unwarranted because what happened to them was entirely beyond their control.

2. Pride

Most people are born with a desire to be number one. It has been part of our human nature since Adam and Eve rebelled against God in the Garden of Eden and introduced sin into the world.

Babies cry as a demand to be fed in their first hours of life. As children grow, they tend to learn that crying "works." It's a way to have their desires met. And if a child is not disciplined and trained "in the way that he should go," crying can turn into a full-blown tantrum.

Several months ago, I was holding a little boy who was as sweet as he could be. So I was telling his mother how much I love him, and she immediately responded, "Oh, he has another side to him."

Children will start throwing tantrums when they are just a few months old. And the sad truth is that some people are still throwing tantrums even when they are twenty, forty, sixty, eighty, or a hundred. Why? Because they want their own way. They want *what* they want *when* they want it, regardless of another person's needs or feelings. Pride is their driving force.

Pride was also at the root of Cain's sin.

We should not be all that surprised that the first two people to feel anger would have a son who was angry and resorted to blame.

Abel was a keeper of flocks—likely cattle, goats, and sheep. Cain was a tiller of the ground—a farmer who sowed and reaped.

Both brought sacrificial offerings as a way of acknowledging or worshipping God. Abel brought an offering from his flocks, which acknowledged the blood sacrifice that the Father required. Cain brought a sacrifice from the earth, which God had cursed. It was a sacrifice that involved hard labor—part of the curse to Adam and his descendants—but no blood.

The Bible tells us that God accepted Abel's offering but had "no regard for Cain's offering." As a result, Cain became "angry and his countenance fell" (see Genesis 4:15).

God saw Cain's anger and asked him, "Why are you angry?" And then the Lord gave Cain an opportunity to amend his offering and have his second sacrifice accepted. God's offer came with a set of consequences: "If you do well, will not your countenance be lifted up? And if you do not do well, sin is crouching at the door; and its desire is for you, but you must master it" (Genesis 4:7).

Cain sought out his brother. We don't know exactly what transpired between them. But the Bible does tell us that as they were in the field together, Cain rose up against Abel and killed him. The first murder occurred in the first family as the result of unbridled anger rooted in pride. Cain wanted things his way more than he wanted to do things God's way.

If you look closely at Cain's words and actions, you will see how perverted his disappointment had become. It is entirely likely that Cain killed his brother not out of jealousy but out of an angry, get-even-with-God attitude. It was as if Cain was saying in his heart, *You want blood? Then I'll give it to You!*

Any time a person does not get what he deeply desires, anger is likely. It may be a matter of

- *Jealousy*—desiring a relationship that another person rightfully has.

- *Envy*—feeling that you didn't receive or win something because someone else received or won it.

- *Greed*—a desire to have more than you presently have or need.

- *Self-devaluing*—anger over having something taken away that is closely linked to your identity.

- *Fear of loss or damage*—feeling denied something you truly
   believe you need for its emotional or psychological value.

Nobody can have his or her way at all times and in all situations. Many people become angry when they do not have control over a desired situation or individual. Their anger can spin out of control when they realize they cannot and will not have control over God.

On the flip side of the pride coin is a human desire for fame and adoration. Many people become angry when they do not get the attention or recognition they feel they deserve. This aspect of pride spins out of control when a person wants the fame and adoration that are owed to God.

The truth is that our heavenly Father will always be the One who alone is worthy of our highest praise and obedience.

Examples of pride-related anger are found throughout the Bible. Moses is a major Old Testament figure who showed his anger on many occasions. The first time we see him angry is when he kills an Egyptian soldier who was beating a Hebrew slave (Exodus 2:11–12). Moses ended up fleeing for his life and remained on the back side of the desert for decades—until God called him to return to Pharaoh's court and deliver the children of Israel out of bondage and into the Promised Land.

Moses was angry again when the Israelites rebelled under his leadership as they wandered through the desert. In anger, Moses destroyed the tablets on which God had written the Ten Commandments. He struck the rock at Meribah in anger. And at times Moses was angry with God for requiring him to be the leader of a people who continually reverted to rebellion and idolatry. Moses could not control God's people the way he wanted to.

Saul, the first king of Israel, frequently displayed anger, especially toward David. Even though Saul intuitively recognized David as the anointed and chosen servant of God to lead the Hebrew people, the king was angry when the people praised the younger man for his victory over Goliath. Saul even tried to kill David by throwing a javelin at him, twice. On one occasion, Saul ordered David murdered in his bed, and later, he pursued the future king relentlessly into some of the most remote regions of Israel. All this was done in a jealous rage rooted in King Saul's perception that David was trying to seize control of his kingdom.

The prophet Jonah became angry when God spared the Ninevites, who had been severely persecuting the Jews. He became angrier when a plant that had given him shade was attacked by a worm and withered. Why was Jonah angry? Because he did not have the control he desired. Jonah wanted things done his way, not God's (see Jonah 4).

In the New Testament, Peter cut off the ear of a temple guard in the Garden of Gethsemane. The apostle was angry that Jesus was being arrested, but the Lord immediately said to him, "All those who take up the sword shall perish by the sword" (Matthew 26:52). Time and again, God's Word reveals that His people displayed anger in ways that did not produce good results. In fact, their bitterness, hostility, and rage resulted in rebuke or negative consequences for them and sometimes the people around them. Most of these examples are related directly to pride and their desire to have things done their way.

3. Insecurity

The more insecure people are, the easier it is for them to feel anger. Why? Because insecurity is often related to feelings of low self-worth that come from

- Rejection

- Fears, especially fear of loss

- Disappointment

- Feelings of inadequacy

Not everyone who has these feelings becomes angry, but many people do. They blame themselves. They blame others. They feel shame. A deep inner frustration develops that takes the form of anger. And, as stated previously, when the person begins to act out based on his or her emotions, the results are almost always negative.

Insecurity in most people results from not experiencing the love that was needed and desired when they were children. If you are a parent, let me strongly encourage you to love your children. Let your sons and daughters know that you value, cherish, and desire to be with them. Tell your children that you are proud of them and consider them to be gifts from God. The child who is deeply loved is not likely to manifest great anger. The child who does not know he is loved, or fears that he may not be loved, could become an angry child.

4. Dreams Deferred or Denied

I once knew a man who dreamed of becoming a medical doctor. He studied hard all the way through elementary school and high school. He made excellent grades, but when the time came for him to go to college, his father refused to help. Instead, he was forced to stay on the family farm and work. Times were tough, money was in short supply, and this young man felt he had to obey his father's demands.

At the age of twenty-three, this man had taken all he could of farm life. He packed his belongings, loaded his car, and drove away. Along with his clothes and a few books, he took with him a heart filled with bitterness and resentment toward his father. For the rest of his life, he held on to that anger and blamed his father for the loss of his life's dream.

As the years passed, this young man allowed few people to get close to him. The bitterness he held inside spilled out on every relationship he developed, so he was constantly coping with feelings of rejection and isolation. He moved from job to job, unable to settle down or to succeed in his work.

Finally he met a woman who genuinely cared for him, and after a short engagement, they married. Three weeks into the marriage, an unexpected explosion of anger nearly ended all affection his bride felt toward him. She did not leave him, but she cringed at his violent temper and vile language. Most of her friends refused to come to their home—they simply could not tolerate being in the presence of a person so filled with anger and bitterness.

This man held on to his rage until the last days of his life. Even when he was nearly blind, senile, and unable to care for himself, the poisons of resentment and bitterness continued to eat away at him. The longer he held on to his anger, the hotter it burned inside him.

I would love to be able to tell you that this man had an amazing spiritual healing and became a person filled with joy and peace. But that was not the case. He died a bitter, angry person.

I do not know all the reasons why this man's father would not let him leave the farm. He may have been threatened by his son's intellect or educational goals. He may have been selfish, not wanting to lose a farmhand. He may have had the best interests of his son at heart. What I do know with certainty is that none of the reasons relating to the father's decision was justified in the son's mind. As a young man, he no doubt felt justified in his anger. But let me ask you, "Who suffered the most through those years?" It certainly wasn't the father. It was the son.

Anger and bitterness poisoned his entire life.

5. Lies and Cover-ups

Sometimes a kernel of a lie is at the core of anger. That lie may have been expressed as a rumor, words of slander, or criticism. It may have been a lie that represented a cover-up of the truth, sidestepping the truth, or a partial truth.

Have you ever been angry about something you heard another was saying about you—perhaps a rumor that was being spread to attack your character or tarnish your good name? Did the rumor have any truth to it? If not, how did you feel? How much time and energy did you spend being angry with someone or over something that was never true in the first place?

If what was said was true, how much time and energy did you waste railing against the rumor rather than addressing the truth and making the changes necessary to live a godly life?

A woman told me not long ago that she had watched a particular soap opera for about five years. In her terms, she watched it with "one eye and two ears" during an hour in which she did household chores. I asked her what benefit had come from this, suspecting that no real benefit could have been possible. She said, "I have a new understanding of what has a lot of marriages in our nation in turmoil. The show presents a constant stream of vengeance and sexual misconduct."

She went on to say, "I also have a new understanding of what issues mainstream Americans find of interest. Some of them are very good issues to address, such as the impact of drunk driving, the need for organ transplants, and the problems of teens running away from home. And I have a new understanding that at the core of most of the 'drama' on this show, you will nearly always find an example of miscommunication. It may be in the form of rumor, failing to ask the right questions, neglecting to give all the necessary information, or an act of out-and-out lying."

"And what have you concluded?" I asked.

"You can have good issues and good intents. But if you have bad communication and immoral behavior, the things you value most end up in a heap of suffering and ruin." I would add, a heap of anger.

Not long ago, I heard about a man who was accused of bad behavior in his dealings with various staff members and contractors who worked at the country club where he was a member. This man was on the club's board of directors, and he took it upon himself to make certain that some jobs were done solely because *he* thought they needed to be done. And it was "his way or the highway."

When his bullying behavior came to light and the results were calculated in terms of money wasted, this man was asked to resign from his position on the board. The entire intent was for the matter to be dealt with privately. The club's leadership decided that the members did not need to hear any of the details or become wounded in their personal friendships with this man and his family.

His wife saw only that her husband was away from home a great deal and was doing "good work for the club." She felt that her husband had been treated unfairly when the board asked him to resign. She jumped to his defense, and before long, the entire club knew what had happened. Sides began to be drawn about who was right and who was wrong. The wife openly, and in detail, described all the ways she thought her husband had been wronged.

The man and his wife further decided, in their mutual anger, that they would sell their club membership. Now their hasty and noisy departure from the club meant their children would no longer have use of the club's facilities or be included in the activities of the other young people who had become their friends. It also meant that the couple would no longer have the same kind of access to or contact with their friends. The couple left a number of unanswered questions and hurt feelings in their wake.

This happened in a fairly small city. So one of the most disappointing aspects of this story is that many of their friends at the club were also their friends at church. Feeling they could no longer associate with the club or its members, the couple uprooted their family and left the only church their children ever attended. And when this man tried to join another club, his application was denied after the membership committee reviewed the reasons behind his departure from the previous club. Behavior rooted in anger led this family down a steep decline.

Over the months that followed, the wife who had stood by her husband in denial and anger was forced to face the truth about his control and anger issues.

The very things she had believed could not be true were true. Behaviors she once considered unthinkable were not only present but pervasive. She had spent years in denial. When the truth finally came to light, this woman and her children were emotionally devastated—and without the support of their closest friends.

What is the lesson here?

Anger based on rumors, partial truth, or a full-blown lie can take you down a long, dark road of disappointment, frustration, and heartache. Confronting the truth may be painful, but the alternative is far worse.

6. Brain Dysfunction

A root of anger that is more common than many people realize is brain dysfunction or mental illness.

Brain dysfunction may be the result of a degenerative disease or an accident. Or the brain may function improperly due to a chemical imbalance present from birth that may manifest itself as mental illness. Or it might be self-inflicted through alcohol and drug use.

We are wise to recognize that some people have lost the ability to control their anger as a result of an accident, injury, disease, or addiction. Any one of those things can destroy brain cells or compromise brain function.

For example, many war veterans who were wounded physically or traumatized emotionally have angry outbursts that are far more automatic than intentional. Dealing with anger as a result of brain dysfunction or mental illness is extremely difficult in marriage, friendship, and work relationships.

I heard not long ago about a woman whose husband was in a terrible automobile accident while on his way home from working the night shift. He fell asleep at the wheel, ran off the road, hit a tree head-on, and was in a coma for two months. His wife said, "The man who emerged from that accident was not the sweet, peaceful, loving man I had married. He came home from the hospital angry and violent. I had to learn how to relate to him on completely different terms."

Of course, not all brain-injured or mentally ill people are constantly angry. But, sadly, some are.

Certain types of dementia also bring about negative personality changes and increased anger. Again, this is not true in every case, but it is for some.

Hope in these situations lies in the peace and healing power of God. The person can do very little for himself. Those who care for and love him need tremendous support from family members and friends. At all times, we must understand that God is at work and is healing the person in ways that may not be visible to us but are nonetheless real.

While my heart aches for those who are in these situations, I choose to believe for their healing as long as they are alive. The truth is that God can heal any disease or condition, and ultimately, He is in control. God may not heal the person this side of heaven, but healing will come. Of that I am certain. And until the healing occurs, I choose to continue believing for God's best, not only in the life of the individual who has suffered injury or disease but also of those who surround that person.

Very often it is the caregivers of the person—perhaps a spouse or adult child—who experience the great miracle of healing and personal growth. Caregivers may find God resolving certain issues in their lives and bringing important changes in their attitudes and behaviors. We must never underestimate or devalue the Lord's faithfulness to fulfill His will, plan, and purpose for everyone involved in a brain-injury or brain-disease situation.

If the brain dysfunction is the result of something a person did to himself—whether accidentally or intentionally—there may be a need to forgive. This can be very difficult, especially if the person's actions left him brain damaged and filled with anger. Whatever the cause, forgiveness is vital for two reasons. First, it frees caregivers and family members from their feelings of anger or resentment. And second, it creates an attitude in which care is given with patience, peace, and perseverance.

Ask God to help you forgive, to give you a loving heart for the person, and to bless you with the daily strength and patience you will need to provide whatever level of care you can or must provide.

7. Chemical Addiction

Even as we consider brain dysfunction, we are wise to recognize that certain chemicals are poison to the brain. Alcohol is one of them. A number of other drugs and medications are toxic to the brain when used in great quantity or over great lengths of time.

Most people are familiar with the term *mean drunk*. Some individuals become increasingly angry the more alcohol they consume. If you are the victim of an angry outburst from a person who has consumed too much alcohol or used drugs, the best thing you can do is walk away. Don't try to argue or reason with the person. You will not be successful, and in the end you may be injured physically or psychologically if you remain in the person's presence.

The Bible tells the story of a man named Nabal who was very rich, with three thousand sheep and one thousand goats. It was customary in his day to reward self-employed and self-appointed vigilantes or mercenaries who protected flocks from thieves. Before he became king, David led such a band of men. The owners of the livestock usually compensated those who had protected their investment at the time the sheep were sheared. David sent some of his young men to Nabal to collect what was owed them, but the rich man refused to give them anything. When the future king heard this, he was furious and set off with four hundred armed men to destroy Nabal and all that he owned.

But Nabal's wife, Abigail, intervened. Without her husband's knowing it, she packed up a large amount of food and other provisions for David and his men. Abigail also went to David humbly to ask him to refrain from shedding blood. She called on David to remember his position before the Lord and begged him not to do anything that might damage his reputation or ability to rule in the future. Abigail was a brave, wise woman. David received her gifts and responded to her plea, "Go up to your house in peace. See, I have listened to you and granted your request" (1 Samuel 25:35).

Abigail returned home and found Nabal hosting a lavish feast. The Bible tells us he was "very drunk." We learn more about Abigail's wisdom when Scripture explains: "She did not tell him anything at all until the morning light" (1 Samuel 25:36). Abigail waited until "the wine had gone out of Nabal" (verse 37), and then she told him what David had intended and what she had done to avoid bloodshed.

I heartily recommend Abigail's approach if you must deal with someone who is drunk, an alcoholic, or a person high on drugs. Alcohol and drugs do not make anyone more mellow or more pleasant to be around. Most of the time, people who use these substances are rude, crude, and annoying. Their lifestyle frequently leads to increased agitation and frustration. They have problems or issues that led to their alcohol or drug use, and if addiction sets in, there's the added stress of overcoming that as well.

Even if a person does not become an addict, small amounts of alcohol or drugs will

- *Cloud a person's perceptions*, leading to poor judgment.

- *Reduce a person's response time*, which can be very dangerous if a vehicle or machinery is being operated.

- *Diminish a person's fine-motor and large-muscle skills*, leading to falls and other physical injury.

- *Diminish a person's ability to reason and to speak clearly.*

- *Tend to increase a person's negative emotions*, including anger, frustration, hatred, bitterness, and resentment.

There is absolutely nothing to be gained from alcohol or drug use. But there is so much to lose.

If you are constantly angry, evaluate your alcohol and drug use. Depending on your situation and circumstance, you may want to consider seeking professional help to ensure that those substances are not preventing you from receiving God's best in your life.

If you know someone who is an alcoholic or drug addict, do whatever you can to get him or her into treatment. Ask a psychiatrist, medical doctor, pastor, or pharmacist how to get your friend or loved one the help he or she needs. Don't wait. The life you save may be your spouse's, friend's, or coworker's. It may even be your life or the life of your child.

ANGER'S LINK TO OTHER EMOTIONS

Anger has a way of linking itself to many other emotions—with the end result almost always negative. Consider these combinations:

Anger + Hatred = Rage

Anger + Bitterness = Revenge

Anger + Worry = A divided mind

Anger + Confusion = Turmoil/indecision

Anger + Insecurity = Manipulation/control tactics

Anger + Stress = Physical, mental, or emotional breakdown/burnout

Anger + Resentment = Retribution

Anger + Fear = Irrational response

Anger + Sorrow = Disorientation/inability to function

Certainly these aren't all the combinations possible between anger and other emotions. And these are not the only results that occur from the combinations. Anger is unpredictable.

Even so, consider the implications of combining two or more toxic emotions. Just as certain chemicals explode or react when combined, anger is very often a catalyst for intensely negative behavior.

ANGER'S LINK TO OTHER FACTORS

Anger also tends to take on different forms depending on time, space, and situation. Consider these combinations:

Anger + Urgency = Panic

Anger + Confinement = Explosive behavior

Anger + Constraint = Tantrum

Anger + Grief = Cloudy thinking

Anger + Too many options = Poor decision making

Why should we be concerned with other factors associated with anger? Because of its volatility. What makes a person angry usually is not consistent over time. Nor does anger in a relationship always stem from the same set of circumstances or follow the same behavioral patterns.

If you are able to identify another factor associated with anger, very often you can deal with a situation in a way that diffuses or lessens it. For example, if you realize that your anger is caused by stress, addressing that specific issue either personally or professionally will make a big difference. People who are continually stressed out are wise to learn time-management skills and anger-management techniques. In today's world, it's easy to take on too many obligations in too short a time frame and with too high a level of expectation.

Recognize that the causes and effects of anger are not always straightforward. In your attempts to get to the primary cause of an anger problem, you may find yourself dealing with a number of issues. But that's okay. Address each of them as they come up, and don't stop dealing with them.

ADMIT IT—DEAL WITH IT

1. Which of these root causes of anger seem applicable to you or someone you love?

Blame or shame

Pride

Insecurity

Dreams deferred or denied

Lies and cover-ups

Brain dysfunction or mental illness

Addiction

2. How does knowing the root cause of your or another's anger better enable you to address it and deal with it?

3. What can you do to help the angry person in your life release his or her anger?

4. What will you do to let go of your own anger?

CHAPTER 5

RELEASE

Letting Go of Anger

I have always been amazed at the lengths to which people will go to hold on to their anger instead of releasing it, since the benefits of releasing our anger far outweigh any perceived "right" or "benefit" to keeping it locked up inside. But how can we release anger and find freedom and peace?

SIX PREREQUISITES FOR RELEASING ANGER

Consider the following six prerequisites that serve as the foundation for releasing anger.

1. Shed the Excuses

People give a number of excuses to justify their anger. The top five excuses I hear are

1. Everyone gets angry. I'm no different from anybody else.

2. I've always had a short temper.

3. I have a very good reason for being angry.

4. I've been hurt so deeply that I can't help but feel anger.

5. If I don't stay angry, I'll be hurt even more than I already have been.

These excuses aren't good enough to justify hanging on to anger that can destroy your life. Give up your excuses and get on with releasing your anger.

2. Be Willing to Change Your Attitude

I can recall being told as a child to "change my attitude." I found that troublesome. It seemed as if there must be some button I could push that would instantly change something inside my head. But I never could find that button.

Letting go of anger nearly always involves a serious attitude adjustment. There's no magic button involved. An attitude change occurs when new information produces in us a sense of compassion rather than rage.

I heard the story of a little boy who lived with his mother and grandfather. Though not elderly, the grandfather was confined to a wheelchair and had little use of his arms. His face was badly scarred, and he had a difficult time swallowing food. On most days, he needed someone to assist him with eating. This task fell to the little boy at lunchtime. He did his job faithfully but not joyously. It was quite difficult and messy to feed Grandfather.

As the boy got older, he grew weary of his responsibility. One day he stormed into the kitchen and said in anger, "Mom, from now on, you can feed Grandfather!"

The mother turned from her chores, motioned for her son to sit down, and said, "You are a young man now. It's time you know the whole truth about your grandfather." She continued, "Your grandfather has not always been confined to a wheelchair. In fact, he used to be quite an athlete. But when you were a baby, there was an accident."

The son leaned forward in his chair. He had not heard this before.

The mother said, "There was a fire. Your father was working in the basement, and he thought you were upstairs with me. I thought you were downstairs with him. We both rushed out of the house and left you alone in your room upstairs. Your grandfather was visiting us at the time, and he was the first to realize what had happened. Without a word, he went back into the house, found you, wrapped you in a wet blanket, and made a mad dash through the flames. He brought you safely to your father and me.

"The scars on your grandfather's face and the scarred tissue in his mouth and esophagus that keeps him from eating normally are a result of the burns he received that day."

Without a word, the young man picked up his grandfather's lunch tray. With tears filling his eyes, he went to tend to his grandfather and never complained about feeding him again.

Attitudes change when we get all the facts or when we see the big picture. Ask God to reveal exactly what you need to know in order to address your anger. Also ask Him to give you a glimpse of what life might be like when you are fully able to let go of your anger.

3. Choose Not to Worry

Anger often flows out of a person's worries about the future.

You cannot control all the difficulties that come your way. But you can do a great deal to control the anxiety level you experience in the face of adversity. The apostle Paul wrote, "Be anxious for nothing" (Philippians 4:6).

"But how?" you may ask.

In that same verse, Paul went on to say: "In everything by prayer and supplication with thanksgiving let your requests be made known to God." In other words, talk to the Lord about the situation. Turn the problem over to Him, thank Him for hearing your prayer, dealing with the problem, and providing the solution you need.

Thanksgiving produces wonderful fruit in a person's soul. As you thank God for all that He has done and is doing on your behalf, you will gain renewed confidence that He cares for you. The Lord is, always has been, and always will be in complete control of all things. Thank Him for His goodness, for His constant presence, and for being in control of everything that affects your life.

What is the result of your expressions of thanksgiving joined with your specific requests for God to act?

Paul wrote that the result is the "peace of God"—a calmness that far surpasses our human understanding (Philippians 4:7). It is a peace that will guard your heart and mind against any temptation to worry or rely on your own intellect, strength, or skill.

It's only when you and I trust God fully that we can experience true, lasting peace.

4. Refuse to Cherish Your Anger

Some people cherish their anger. They value it. They see it as a mark of strength. They are so accustomed to feeling angry that it becomes part of who they are. A psychologist friend of mine told me about a lady he had counseled for quite some time. No matter what he tried, she refused to let go of her anger. At their final session, he talked with this woman about her unforgiving spirit toward someone and pleaded with her to give it up.

He said she walked over to the window, held up both hands, and cried out, "I can't give it up! I can't give it up! I can't give it up! Because I don't have anything left if I give it up!"

She was captive to her own anger. If she laid it down, she wouldn't have anything else to think about in life. Cherished anger means *I have it, and I'm going to keep it until I die.* Is there something in your life that you can't lay down? The truth is that you can with God's help.

5. Refuse to Self-Medicate Your Anger

One of the worst possible ways people try to control their anger is with alcohol, drugs, or overuse of prescription medication. These substances may mask the anger temporarily or even help keep it at a low boil. But in the end, this self-medicated approach to anger always fails. It more likely will lead to dependency or addiction. And at that point, you have two problems to deal with instead of one.

Choose to let go of your anger rather than mask it.

6. Be Patient

Letting go of anger is not a simple process. It can be a very complicated and difficult progression that takes time. Be patient and be persistent. Now that you have built a foundation for releasing anger, you are ready to begin taking active steps to free yourself from its bondage.

TEN STEPS FOR DEALING WITH ANGER

Step 1: Admit Your Anger to God

A woman once said to me, "I've been angry all my life. I never saw it as something I needed to confess, but one day I realized that my anger was something God could heal." She continued, "I knew that the first step toward receiving any healing is to admit there's a problem. So, I went to God and said, 'I admit that I am angry. I'm not entirely sure why I'm angry, but I know that I am. Please help me.'"

Soon after this woman prayed, the Lord brought to her remembrance three separate and distinct painful experiences from her childhood. As she recalled each of them, she felt intense anger rising up in her. So she prayed, "Lord, help me to release to You all the negative feelings and pain I have right now. Please cleanse my heart and mind of this memory, so that I will never have a strong reaction to that horrible experience again."

She said, "Each time I prayed this, I immediately burst into tears. I sobbed and sobbed until I thought there could be no tears left. I felt a strong release, as if something deep inside me were being dislodged and swept away in the flow of my tears. The sense of release was tremendous. And in the aftermath, I felt so relieved.

"I asked the Lord to fill me with His peace and to remind me of a happy memory to replace the negative one. I chose to recall the joyful experience in vivid detail, even to the point of laughter. As I did this, I felt the love of the Lord pouring into me. I shared my pain with God and allowed Him to cleanse me and renew areas of my soul with His love and joy. It was the most amazing spiritual experience of my entire life."

I asked her, "Were you ever angry after that?"

"Yes," she said, "but it wasn't anger at the same degree of intensity. And it didn't come from a place as deep in my soul. Any anger I felt after that was about other situations or circumstances. It was much more in the moment and didn't involve people or experiences in my distant past."

Then this woman made an amazing statement: "It was as if my anger had become a habit. I responded in anger because I didn't know how else to react. I talked to a wise, older friend about this, and she gave me suggestions about how to respond to negative situations and problems without anger. Over time, I have felt less and less angry. It has been eighteen years since that emotional and spiritual healing, and it really takes something major for me to feel anger now."

I believe it is true for many people that an angry response has become habitual. If this is the case for you, I recommend that you talk to God. Tell Him, "Father, I confess that I don't know how to respond to emotional pain or rejection apart from anger. Show me a new way of handling life's difficult situations. Lead me to the right information and help me to make the changes that I need to make. I trust You to help me break this habit of anger."

This woman's story also illustrates the second principle for letting go of anger.

Step 2: Identify the Source of Your Anger

A person once said to me many years ago, "I thought my husband was making me angry, but then I realized that it wasn't really his actions that were triggering this emotion. It was a memory of my father's actions that had established a pattern of anger in my life." This is true for many people. Something Dad or Mom said in the distant past still rings as criticism in a person's ears. The "tape" goes round and round. It is played, rewound, and played again:

> You are worthless.
> You were never wanted.
> You will never amount to anything.
> You will never have what you dream of having.

Your "recording" could be something your spouse said during an argument or what your teenager said before storming out of the house. The pain of these memories, coupled with a strong sense of rejection, can result in inner turmoil that frequently manifests itself as anger.

When someone is angry with you, you need to consider several things. If you are being accused wrongfully, there is little you can do to calm the person's anger. The angry person most likely does not want to hear your side of the story. He or she may not be willing to listen to any possible explanation or excuse.

Oftentimes, people will become angry about something that has nothing to do with you. But they need to find someone to blame, so they transfer it to you. When that happens, you need to deal with it quickly and properly.

In Matthew 18, Jesus provides very clear instruction on how to deal with conflict: "If your brother sins, go and reprove him in private; if he listens to you, you have won your brother. But if he does not listen to you, take one or two more with you, so that by the mouth of two or three witnesses every fact may be confirmed. And if he refuses to listen to them, tell it to the church" (verses 15–17).

The wonderful thing about this teaching is that it also works in reverse. If you're the one who sinned and someone is justified in her anger toward you, then you need to go to her, confess your sin, and ask for her forgiveness. If she doesn't accept your apology, you may need to try again with the "one or two more" Jesus spoke of at your side.

Whether someone's anger at you is justified or unjustified, you can pray for that person to be healed emotionally and find peace. Ask God to help him or her let go of the anger and focus on positive things. Pray that God will move in the angry person's heart to bring healing and joy. Finally, ask the Lord to bless and restore your relationship with that person.

Step 3: Purpose in Your Heart to Give Up All Rights to Anger

The way you address anger is a matter of your will. You can and must take authority over your emotions and *choose* to release the anger.

Don't try to justify your anger.

Don't make excuses for it.

Don't transfer it to, or blame, others.

Own up to your feelings through prayer: "God, help me to deal with this quickly and effectively. Don't let anger poison my soul."

I once heard a woman describe it this way: "Anger is like spilling something on a clean white shirt or blouse. If you clean it quickly and in the right way, there is a good chance it won't become a lasting stain. But if you ignore it and wait too long to treat the stain, your garment likely is ruined forever." And this does *not* mean spewing it onto the perceived offender right away. That does not solve your anger problem; it inflames it.

"But I have a right to be angry," a person might say. "If I don't speak up immediately, I'll lose my opportunity to let the other person know that I'm worthy of respect."

Or you may hear someone else explain, "I have a right to respond in a way that lets a person know I have a right to my own feelings and to express them in any way I want, including anger."

The truth is that you do not have any of these so-called rights. The rights people seem to think they have fall primarily into two categories: self-defense and self-actualization.

YOU HAVE NO RIGHT TO SELF-DEFENSE

The best defense against hurtful and angry words and deeds is very often doing and saying nothing. Many times and in many situations, God has shown me the tremendous benefits of remaining silent.

Now, if someone is coming at you waving a frying pan, I'm not saying you should just stand still and let her hit you in the head with it. But if a man or woman is screaming obscenities and threatening you, do not shout back. Walk away. If you fight back, you are only fueling the other person's anger. Let God deal with the person and defend you. It's amazing how He can bring just the right individual with just the right words into the angry person's life—confronting him or her with God's truth and love and convicting the angry person of wrong behavior.

"But what about situations in which others are accusing a person publicly or taking them to court?" you might ask. My advice in those situations is to say as little as possible, speak and act as kindly as possible, and resolve the issue out of the public eye and out of the courts if at all possible. Twenty years from now, nobody will care if you were right. But they'll remember if you acted in an ungodly way or allowed yourself to become involved in an ugly, drawn-out battle. Your reputation and legacy are always at stake in public disputes and disagreements.

It is a myth to think that responding in anger is going to cause another person to respect you. The other person may come to fear you but not respect you. That gift is given to people who are prudent, patient, and quietly persevering in godly actions.

YOU HAVE NO RIGHT TO SELF-ACTUALIZATION

There is no right that ensures you can achieve your personal definition of success through your own efforts, intellect, or physical strength. Some of the most brilliant and godly people I know would not be considered successful by worldly standards. They have never prospered financially or materially. But they are doing all that God has asked of them and are succeeding in ways that He values.

The right you do have once you are in relationship with God is rooted in His promises. The more you yield your abilities and desires to His divine will, plan, and purpose for your life, the more God will bless and guide you. He will bring opportunities your way and help identify, develop, and perfect all your God-given talents and spiritual gifts. And you will experience the peace of God (see Philippians 4:6–7).

When you demand to have it your way, you may want something that is 100 percent contradictory to what God desires to do in and through you. I encourage you to ask the Lord to unfold His will, plan, and purpose for you according to His ways and His timing.

I am not suggesting that you suppress or deny all the dreams and desires in your heart. As a believer, you need to set goals and pursue them. I am calling on you to subject your dreams, desires, and goals to God. Ask Him to reveal His definition of success for you and how best to achieve it.

RELINQUISH ALL YOUR RIGHTS

Completely surrendering your anger to God can be very difficult. It means you're giving up your "right" to get even with a person who wronged you or made you angry. You're saying, *I won't try to hurt you or seek payback.* You're willing to forgive no matter what the person did to you. And when you do surrender completely, you'll find that God heals, blesses, and guides you in ways that are truly miraculous.

Step 4: Take a Time Out

I encourage people to develop a certain habit when they feel anger rising up inside them. If you start seeing red, choose to visualize it in the shape of a stop sign. Imagine yourself at an intersection, and come to a full stop. Carefully consider all the directions your anger can go, then respond slowly and deliberately.

Psalm 103:8 says that God is "slow to anger."

James 1:19 encourages everyone to be "quick to hear, slow to speak and slow to anger."

Make sure your response will be a godly one.

Rule your tongue. Don't speak too quickly.

Step 5: Get to the Root of the Problem

In many cases, a person's anger has nothing to do with what you've said or done. He is responding out of frustration, stress, insecurity, jealousy, fatigue, or something else that's entirely unrelated to his interaction with you. It's not uncommon for people to become angry when they allow themselves to get too hungry, too lonely, or too tired.

In my early years as a pastor, when it came to listening to other people's stories, I did not have nearly as much patience as I have now. I thought—as many men, and certainly many pastors, do—that I needed to be a problem solver. Whenever someone began to tell me about a need or problem, I wanted to jump quickly to the solution, especially if I clearly saw the answer in terms of biblical truth. I did not realize the value in letting that person tell me all the details. But now I understand what a tremendous benefit it is to people when they're allowed to share their full story. I have found that I too benefit from catching a glimpse of how God has worked, is working, and will work in someone's life.

When I was young, my mother would say to me, "Tell me what you want me to know." She never pressured me to tell her what she wanted to hear or what she thought she *should* hear. My mother allowed me to say exactly what I wanted to say in my own timing. And, of course, I ended up telling her everything. I find my mother's approach to be a wise one in most relationships.

Step 6: Voice Your Anger to the One Who Can Help You the Most

There is very little value in venting anger just for the sake of venting it. Behavioral scientists have discovered that even after an individual screams into a pillow, most of the feelings of anger that have taken up residence in that person are still there. Expressing anger does not produce healing.

There *is* value in venting one's emotions in conversation with a trusted friend or counselor who can provide valuable insight and help you find rational solutions. It is not always possible, however, to have the right person available at the exact time a listening and caring heart is needed. But there is Someone to whom you always can voice your deepest emotions.

Go to God with your anger. Get by yourself, on your knees, with your Bible open. Ask the Lord to show you why you're angry and what you can do to redirect your negative feelings into positive behavior. He knows why you're angry. He knows your situation and your circumstances. Trust Him to reveal the best way to identify, deal with, and let go of your anger.

As you read your Bible, focus on the words of Jesus in the four Gospels. Or turn to the book of Psalms for encouragement and peace. Practical, how-to advice is found in the book of Proverbs. And for guidance on victorious Christian living, open your Bible to any of Paul's writings, including Romans, Ephesians, and Philippians.

Step 7: Redirect Your Energy

Anger produces energy that can be redirected to countless good behaviors. Use your anger to do something useful and productive.

- Wash and wax your car. If you're still angry after that, clean the interior.

- Clean out a closet, the attic, the cupboards, or any other area of your home or office.

- Weed your flower beds, or till the soil in your vegetable garden.

- Go to the driving range and hit a large bucket of golf balls.

There is something therapeutic and beneficial about engaging in physical activity. It helps you blow off steam. And when you rechannel that negative energy in the right direction, it can prove to be profitable. Just think of all you can accomplish. So get rid of it. Replace your anger with physical activity.

I do not, however, recommend operating heavy machinery or power tools as a way to redirect anger. Careless mistakes occur far more often when a person is angry. The same goes for driving any kind of vehicle. Don't let your car or motorcycle serve as an outlet for your anger.

What about walking, running, swimming, or riding a bicycle? These activities are good for the body, but they do not require your complete attention. You can still stew in anger as you engage in exercises such as these.

What about doing a puzzle or reading a book? These are good for focusing the mind, but they are not activities that release pent-up physical energy. Choose an activity that engages both the mind and body in a healthful, productive way.

Intense anger has an element of confusion to it. In most cases, it is a free-floating emotion looking for a place to land. As a result, people who are angry often want to pound something with their fist or find an object to pick up and throw. Give anger a positive focus. Expend that negative energy in a way that is productive, not destructive.

Step 8: Reset Your Personal Emotional Dial

The apostle Paul challenged the Ephesians to "put away" their anger (Ephesians 4:31). In the Greek, this phrase literally means to strip away or to lift up and toss away. In other words, the Bible commands that we remove anger completely from our hearts.

And if you're a believer, you have the power of the Holy Spirit within you to lay it down. All you need to say is "God, I don't want this anger in my life, and I choose to lay it down by Your grace, love, and goodness."

Now, there are some other things you still have to deal with. That's not the end of the issue. But that's a major part of letting go of anger. You put it down. Get rid of it. Get rid of "bitterness and wrath and anger and clamor and slander . . . along with all malice" (Ephesians 4:31).

And if Paul didn't mean that you actually could "put it away," he would never have encouraged the church to do that. You can do it by the power of the Holy Spirit of God. As a believer in the Lord Jesus Christ, you have the power to lay it down.

In an interesting contrast, what Paul told the church in Ephesus was the exact opposite of what he said to believers in Colossae. To them, the apostle wrote, "Put on a heart of compassion, kindness, humility, gentleness, and patience" (Colossians 3:12). The phrase *put on* literally means to clothe yourself. He's also telling us to wear these qualities and to cover ourselves with them. Paul makes a very strong and very clear distinction between which emotions we need to "put on" and which we need to "put away."

Step 9: Predetermine How You Will Respond in the Future

After any angry encounter, it's wise to decide how you will respond the next time you see that person. You may want to rehearse in your mind what you will say and how you will behave. Envision yourself in a similar situation or circumstance and ask, *What would I do differently? How should I behave the next time something like this comes up?*

You might say, "But I don't know what kind of mood the other person will be in." His or her mood or behavior doesn't matter. What does matter is that you determine in your heart that you are going to greet that person with peace in your heart, a cheerful attitude, and a positive word. Do not let the mood or behavior of other people dictate your responses to life. Choose how you will act.

Always keep in mind that you cannot predict or control what other people will do or how they'll respond in a particular situation. You can only control how *you* will respond. And to a great extent, you can choose in advance how you will respond.

Don't let another person affect the spring in your step or twinkle in your eye.

Don't let anyone rob you of your smile.

Don't let someone else cause you to be discouraged or unhappy.

For decades, sports psychologists and trainers have taught athletes the benefits of visualization. Men and women in solo sports such as diving or ice skating see themselves completing a difficult maneuver in their minds. In team sports like baseball and basketball, players visualize themselves hitting a home run or scoring the winning basket. There is a direct correlation between good rehearsal—mental or physical—and excellent performance in everything from music to public speaking, acting to athletics.

The more you mentally prepare yourself for difficult experiences, the more peaceful you will be in times of anger or frustration.

Step 10: Set Emotional Goals in Key Relationships

Talk about your relationships. You don't need to overanalyze to the point of stifling normal, open communication and interaction. But you also shouldn't neglect to talk with those closest to you about your feelings, hopes, dreams, and desires. And you certainly should spend some time learning about theirs. Find a happy balance.

Spend quality time alone with your spouse, each of your children, and your close friends. Point out positive aspects of the other person's character, attitude, and personality. Reflect on what your relationship has meant to you over the years. Talk about ways you can strengthen your marriage, your parent-child relationship, or your friendship. Express your desire to see the relationship grow stronger.

Ask the person, "How can I pray for you?" and find opportunities to pray together. You can learn a tremendous amount about someone by listening to how he or she prays.

A man once said to me, "I get the barometric pressure reading on my marriage when I hear my wife pray for me. And I thought I was the only one taking stock of what was being said. Then one day she told me, 'I know how you're feeling about me by the things you ask God to help me do.' From that moment on, I began paying attention not only to what my wife was saying but to what I was saying as we prayed together. I gained major insights not only into our relationship but into my own motives and desires."

I'm thoroughly convinced that two people intentionally can decide that they're not going to be angry with each other. Certain safeguards and benchmarks can be put into place to stop a discussion from escalating into an argument. On the other hand, if no intentional decision is made, anger *will* continue to manifest itself. Never assume that all anger will dissipate just because you love each other. Some of the fiercest and most angry tirades occur between people who claim to be in love.

When discussing your relationship with another person, talk about what you can do to help each other confront painful or difficult situations without resorting to anger, bitterness, or resentment. One of the best things you can do to control your own anger is to remain flexible and have a sense of humor about your own faults and flaws.

Learn how to determine what is truly important in life and what's not. Things that are urgent are not necessarily important. Don't get bogged down by trivial things that pull you away from God and His best for your life.

PREVENT WHAT YOU CAN PREVENT

Keep these three principles in mind for dealing with your anger:

- Prevent what you can prevent.

- Learn from what you cannot prevent.

- Ask God to help you lay aside angry responses that do not bring about a positive result.

INVITE GOD TO HEAL YOUR ANGER

Some anger is so deep that only the grace of God can heal it.

The anger has been there for so long and has become such a part of daily life that the person cannot possibly free himself. The good news is that no degree of anger is beyond God's reach. Ask the Lord to prune any anger from your heart.

Decades ago, A. B. Simpson wrote this vivid picture of what it might mean to ask God to heal your anger:

Before the Holy of Holies can be fully opened to our hearts and we can enter into . . . communion of God, the veil upon our hearts must be rent asunder, and this comes as it came on Calvary—by the death of our flesh. It is when we yield our own natural self to God to die and He slays us by the power of His Spirit that the obstruction to our communion with God is removed and we enter into its deeper fullness. The greatest hindrance to our peace and victory is in the flesh. Whenever the consciousness of self rises vividly before you, and you become absorbed in your own troubles, cares, rights or wrongs, you at once lose communion with God, and a cloud of darkness falls over your spirit. There is really nothing else that hurts or hinders us but this heavy weight of evil . . . we can never rend it asunder, but the Holy Spirit can. . . . Bring it to Him, give Him the right to slay it, and the veil will be rent asunder . . . and the glory of heaven will be revealed in your life.

Do you really want all that God desires to give you? If so, ask Him to remove any obstacle that stands in your way. One of those obstacles may be deep-seated anger.

DAILY ASK GOD TO CLEANSE YOU

Every day, ask the Lord to remove any anger, bitterness, or evil thoughts that may have taken root. Pray that God will give you peace, help you forgive, and enable you to let go of that day's anxieties, troubles, hurts, and struggles. Ask Him to fill your mind with thoughts of His goodness toward you. I'm confident that if you make this a daily habit, you'll be surprised at how well you sleep and how refreshed you feel when you awaken each day.

Many times I pray as I go to bed, "Lord, thank You for today. I ask You to take control of my subconscious mind as I sleep and allow the Holy Spirit to continue to work in me even through the night hours. You know what I need and the ideas I must have in order to do the work You have called me to do. I ask You to begin the birthing process of those ideas even as I sleep."

I'm often amazed that my first thoughts after waking up are creative ideas that are exactly what I need for a particular sermon, project, or decision facing me. They are ideas birthed in the peace of the Lord.

At times God will awaken me in the middle of the night with an idea that is crystal clear. When that happens, I write it down immediately, and usually I'm able to go right back to sleep. In the morning, not only am I grateful for the idea on the notepad beside my bed but I also have discovered that those divine interruptions to my sleep never leave me feeling exhausted—on the contrary, I find myself invigorated.

In contrast, if I go to bed troubled about something, my mind continues to churn on that topic while my body is trying to sleep. If I wake up in the middle of the night, I rarely have an answer—my mind is still dwelling on the problem. The more I think about the problem throughout the night, the more troubled my mind will become and the longer it will take to get back to sleep. Rarely do I feel refreshed and thoroughly rested after such a night.

If you're struggling with anger toward another person, or if you have an angry outburst during the day, give that problem to God before you go to sleep. Ask Him to forgive you for the harsh words you said or the anger you expressed in ungodly behavior. Ask the Lord to cleanse you completely from all the negative thoughts you have toward any person or situation. Ask God to take control. Trust Him to work on the solution and the answer while you sleep. Thank Him in advance for giving you His peace and for renewing your ability to love, work with, care for, or otherwise relate to the person who was angry at you or with whom you were angry.

MAKE A CHOICE TO
LIVE FREE OF ANGER

What does it take to make you angry?

Is it taking less and less to make you angry, or more and more?

Years ago, I came upon a sentence that changed my life. The author, whose name I have long since forgotten, wrote: "The size of a man's anger is the measure of that man."

The moment I read that statement, I determined to give up all anger in my life. I would not be ruled by anger, and I would not inflict my anger on others. I certainly didn't succeed right away. But in looking back over my life, I clearly recognize things that once made me frustrated or angry no longer have an effect on me.

That does not mean I, or any other person, can become totally immune to anger. It does not mean that I will not feel twinges of it from time to time. What it means is that I've set my will toward living an anger-free life. And I'm trusting God daily to turn me into an anger-free zone. I know that it's the only way I can be the effective and productive pastor, teacher, and friend I desire to be.

ADMIT IT—DEAL WITH IT

Revisit the prerequisites cited at the beginning of this chapter. As you reflect on the following questions, ask God to reveal the honest answers to you.

1. What excuses for anger are you still clinging to?

2. Why are you finding it difficult to change your attitude or give up worry?

3. Are you still cherishing your anger—nursing it as something valuable?

4. How have you been medicating your anger? Be specific.

5. With whom or what are you struggling to be patient?

6. Ask God to free you from any tendency to be an angry person.

CHAPTER 6

CURE

||||||||||||||||||||||||||||||||||||||||||||||||||||||||||||||||||||||||||||||||||

The Balm for Anger: Forgiveness

A woman once said to me: "The last thing I wanted to do was the very thing I needed to do."

Her statement was referring to the way in which she finally let go of the tremendous anger she had felt toward her former husband.

There was no doubt that this woman had been badly mistreated. Her husband had several affairs before she became aware of his infidelity. One day he simply walked out the door and didn't come home. He left her with two teenagers and very little financial support. She did not hear from him for several months, until she received a letter instructing her to file for divorce.

I invited her to tell me her full story. Here is what she told me.

One day, as she poured out her painful experience to her pastor, he said to her, "You need to forgive your husband, forgive yourself, and open up your life to the future God still has for you."

She said, "I can't forgive."

He replied, "You not only can forgive, but you must forgive."

"Why?"

"Because Jesus commands us to forgive. Forgiveness is not a suggestion. It's a command."

This woman began to discuss the topic of forgiveness with her pastor and realized that she had not really understood the true nature of it.

The misconceptions she had are ones that many people have, so let's set the record straight:

- Forgiveness is *not* saying that nothing bad happened. It is not denial.

- Forgiveness is *not* saying that the injured party felt no pain. In all likelihood, the injured person felt great pain and may still be in pain.

- Forgiveness is *not* saying that there should be no negative consequences for the offending party. Rather, it is trusting God to bring justice and deal with the person in the way He deems best.

Forgiveness is very simply "letting go." It is refusing to hold the person in the prison of your own heart for another second. Forgiveness is releasing everything related to what the offender did and leaving his or her punishment up to God.

LET THE HOSTAGE GO!

In today's world, we are all painfully aware of what it means for someone to be taken hostage. We are outraged when the news of such a crime reaches us. Yet when we refuse to forgive others—or ourselves—it's as if we're holding that person, or ourselves, hostage. Let me explain.

When someone is taken hostage on the international scene, the abductors usually want something. It may be money, weapons, the release of prisoners, or any number of other things. In essence, the message being sent is: *Give us what we want, and we will give you back what we've taken.* There is always some condition—some sort of ransom to be paid.

When you or I refuse to forgive someone who has wronged or hurt us, we are engaging in similar behavior. Until the person we are angry with meets our demands, we withhold love, acceptance, respect, service, kindness, patience, or whatever the person values. The message sent is: *Until you repay me for the wrong you've done, you won't receive anything good from me.*

People who truly forgive cancel all claims of compensation for the emotional wounds inflicted upon them.

DROP ALL CLAIMS

Forgiveness is the giving up of resentment, rage, and anger—including one's right to get even.

Saying "I forgive you" to someone and truly meaning it are two very different things. If you sincerely and completely forgive another person, you give up any "right" you may think you have to get even. In fact, one way to know that you truly have forgiven someone is when you no longer have any desire to seek revenge or payback for what the person did.

Unforgiveness is the refusal to give up anger and vengeance. It is rooted in the idea that "somebody has to pay." What do you think the proper payment or compensation would be for the pain you have endured? If any form of adequate retribution comes to mind, you are harboring unforgiveness.

DROP YOUR "RIGHT" TO UNFORGIVENESS

As I have read through the Bible, I have not found a single book, chapter, or verse that justifies holding unforgiveness toward a person.

No matter how badly I hurt, how many tears I cry, or how desperate I am for Him to resolve a situation for my good, God gives me a vital role to play in His healing and restoring process: I must forgive.

SET YOURSELF FREE IN THE PROCESS

Many people who suffer from an unforgiving spirit do not even know that unforgiveness is the root of their problem. All they know is that they can't stand to be around certain people. They find themselves wanting to lash out when particular subjects are discussed. They feel uncomfortable or uneasy around certain personality types. They lose their temper over little things and constantly struggle with guilt over past sins. But they show little concern about hating people they know they should love. All these feelings and emotions are often woven together into a fabric of unforgiveness. To be emotionally free, you must forgive.

The benefits of forgiveness are primarily for *you*. In many cases, there's really no direct benefit to the person you are forgiving. Your forgiveness may enable her to forgive you, herself, or others. But the greatest benefit is to your relationship with that person. Forgiveness restores

- Your freedom to love

- Your freedom to communicate

- Your ability to associate or work together

CHRIST COMMANDS US TO FORGIVE

Paul wrote, "Be kind to one another, tender-hearted, forgiving each other, just as God in Christ also has forgiven you" (Ephesians 4:32). The apostle was reminding the early church what Jesus had vigorously and repeatedly taught. As part of the Sermon on the Mount, Christ said: "Be merciful, just as your Father is merciful. Do not judge, and you will not be judged; and do not condemn, and you will not be condemned; pardon, and you will be pardoned" (Luke 6:36–37). The word *pardoned* may also be translated "forgive." Note that Jesus' commands are straightforward. There are no ifs, ands, buts, or maybes about them.

The Lord went on to say, "For by your standard of measure it will be measured to you in return" (Luke 6:38). In other words, the degree to which you forgive is the degree to which God the Father will forgive you.

When teaching His disciples to pray, in the sixth chapter of Matthew, Jesus stresses the importance of forgiveness by including it as part of what we know as the Lord's Prayer. He said, "Forgive us our debts, as we also have forgiven our debtors" (verse 12). Jesus explains this issue even further: "For if you forgive men for their transgressions, your heavenly Father will also forgive you. But if you do not forgive men, then your Father will not forgive your transgressions" (14–15).

That is one of the most important statements in the Bible. If you forgive those who wrong you, the Father will forgive you. If you refuse to forgive those who wrong you, the Father will refuse to forgive you. In both passages of Scripture, Jesus makes it our responsibility to forgive others *before* we seek forgiveness from God. Too often, people try to do it the other way around. We ask the Lord for the grace that we have refused to extend to someone else. But Jesus reversed the order. Forgive others, and then ask God to forgive you.

It's important to note that Jesus is not referring to salvation here. The forgiveness of our sins at the time we receive Him as Savior and begin to follow Him as Lord is a onetime event sealed by the power of the Holy Spirit. What Jesus is saying is that my unwillingness to forgive someone else, my refusal to let go, my refusal to lay it all down places me in a position where the heavenly Father will not forgive me of my sin. This has nothing to do with salvation, which is a settled issue. This teaching has to do with your daily walk.

If you and I hold on to anger against someone else, we will not be in right relationship with God, which is a sin. And if I'm deliberately, willfully sinning against Him, all I'm doing is digging myself deeper and deeper into these feelings of hostility, bitterness, and anger. We may try to rationalize it away. But the truth is that unforgiveness is a critical, detrimental, and destructive attitude that absolutely will destroy your life and separate you in your fellowship with God.

Some time ago, I heard an amazing story of forgiveness from a counselor friend of mine. He was trying to help a young woman who had been severely beaten as a child by her father. They were discussing this issue in sessions without complete success. She had been able to disassociate herself from her father but had never been able to fully forgive him. Now she was preparing to have a session that included her mother. The young woman assumed that Mom knew about the beatings and in some way had complied with Dad's behavior, but she didn't know with certainty.

The day before the session was scheduled to begin, a godly friend of this young woman came to town and asked, "Have you forgiven your parents for what happened to you as a child?"

"How can I?" the young woman said. "What happened to me is beyond forgiveness."

The friend left the apartment where they had been talking and returned a few minutes later with two small stones. She handed them to the young woman and said, "Hold one of these in each hand as tightly as you can." Then she waited.

After a few minutes, the young woman said, "Why am I doing this? I'm ready to put down these rocks."

"No," her friend replied. "Keep holding them. It's very important that you don't set them down."

"Well, then," the young woman said, "you are going to have to cut the pie and make the coffee."

"Fine," said the friend. "I'll feed you the pie. But you'll need to hold your coffee cup, even though I know it's not easy with those rocks in your hands. But don't put them down."

After a couple of hours had passed, the troubled woman finally said,

"Okay, I've had enough of this. I'm putting these rocks down, and you are going to tell why you made me hold them for so long."

The friend explained, "Those rocks are like the unforgiveness you are holding in your heart toward your parents. When you refuse to forgive, every aspect of your life is limited in some way. If you want to return to full function and reach your hands toward God to receive all He desires to give you, then you must forgive your parents. The Lord's plan is for you to release them so you can receive from Him."

"How do I do that?" the young woman asked.

"Let's walk down to the pond behind your apartment," her friend said. "Bring the rocks."

The two women made their way down the path to the pond, where they prayed together. The young woman cried out to God, saying, "Heavenly Father, I admit to You that I have not freely forgiven my father and mother for the harm they caused me. I'm holding them in my heart with a desire to see them punished. Please help me set them free and place them in Your hands so that I might receive Your forgiveness in my life. In faith, I give you the worst of my life, believing that You have promised me the best life possible through a relationship with You. Help me to forgive, God. Help me to receive Your forgiveness right now. In Jesus' name, I pray. Amen."

After they finished praying, the troubled young woman, with tears streaming down her face, threw both rocks as far as she could into the pond.

The next day, my counselor friend noticed a change in the young woman's countenance as soon as she walked into his office. During their session, the mother said she was unaware of her husband's actions and asked her daughter to forgive her for failing to protect her.

The young woman smiled and said, "Mom, I already have forgiven you."

Forgiveness is the most positive and productive action a person can take to erase the pain of past hurts. It's also crucial in letting go of anger.

SHED YOUR REASONS FOR *NOT* FORGIVING

Given Christ's command to forgive, and given the many blessings that come with it, why don't we forgive?

Someone might say to you, "You don't need to forgive. You didn't do anything wrong, so just forget it ever happened." There are two things wrong with this type of friendly advice. First, you won't be able to forget it happened *until* you forgive. Secondly, forgiveness will allow you to stop holding anything against the other person. It doesn't matter if the other person is 100 percent wrong and you are 100 percent right. If you are harboring hurt, resentment, or frustration toward someone, you are obligated to forgive that person in order to remain obedient and in right relationship with God.

Through the years, I've heard all sorts of reasons for refusing to forgive. Below are the ten most popular ones I've come across as a pastor. Let me assure you that just as you must shed your excuses for not releasing your anger, so must you put aside all your reasons for refusing to forgive.

Excuse 1: The person doesn't deserve to be forgiven.

The truth is that nobody deserves forgiveness. All true forgiveness— whether granted by God or by another person—is a matter of undeserved mercy. No person can ever do anything to earn or win God's forgiveness. It's a free gift for anyone who chooses to believe in the atoning sacrificial death of Jesus on the cross.

You may think that the person who has hurt you should try to earn your forgiveness. That isn't likely to happen. Even if the person tried to win your forgiveness, there is no precise scale for determining how much groveling or apologizing the person should do. In most cases, the offender will not try to make amends or ask for forgiveness. Ultimately, forgiveness needs to be something you choose to give that person.

Excuse 2: If I don't hold on to the memory of what the person did, nobody else will ever hold this person accountable for it.

God remembers and already holds the person accountable. You don't need to.

You know the truth. But better yet, God knows the truth. And He's all that really matters.

Excuse 3: I can't forgive until I hear an apology.

You may be waiting for the rest of your life. Some people insist that the offender make the first move toward reconciling a relationship. That's plain ol' pride at work. And what about those people who hurt you who have already died? No apology will ever come from them. Genuine forgiveness does not have any prerequisites or make any demands on others.

Excuse 4: If I forgive too easily, people will think I'm weak.

Why do you care what other people think? God commands you to forgive. He is pleased when you obey Him. And He'll honor your forgiveness. Other people will never be able to reward your behavior in the ways God can.

Excuse 5: If I forgive, the person who hurt me will take advantage of me.

Forgiveness does not make you weak or vulnerable. It makes you obedient to God. That is a position of strength and always the right position to be in.

Excuse 6: The person who hurt me isn't ready to receive my forgiveness.

The other person does not have to be ready to receive forgiveness from you. Forgiveness happens in *your* heart and mind. It's not a matter of reaching any kind of agreement with the person who hurt you.

Excuse 7: I have partially forgiven what the person did to me.

There is no such thing as partial forgiveness. If you are holding anything against the other person, you have not forgiven him or her. The concept of "partial forgiveness" is a little like saying you are "partially obedient." And partial obedience is disobedience. Genuine forgiveness is all or nothing.

Excuse 8: I just don't feel like forgiving right now.

Why not? What are you gaining from failing to forgive? If you don't feel like forgiving right now, you may never feel like doing it. Your decision to forgive should not be based on feelings. It should be an act of obedience to the Father. There is nothing to gain from waiting to forgive.

Excuse 9: I tried to forgive, but I just couldn't. I'm a failure at forgiveness.

Try again. This time, ask God to help you to forgive and to let go of any hurt, anger, bitterness, or resentment. People who can't seem to forgive may need an act of God's deliverance. Ask the Lord to intervene and make your forgiveness lasting and genuine.

Excuse 10: I'm not sure the other person's behavior was that bad. I may have deserved what happened to me.

Don't second-guess your emotional pain or attempt to justify the sin of another person. Forgiveness is far stronger and better than justification. By making excuses for what happened, or by taking some of the blame upon yourself, you are allowing yourself to not deal with the real issue. You simply are making excuses not to forgive.

THE PROCESS OF FORGIVENESS

As I mentioned previously, there is no such thing as partial forgiveness. But there often is a process that some people must move through before they can come to the point of forgiveness. Just as there is a process for moving through grief that allows people to become whole again, there is a process toward forgiveness.

Stage 1: Confusion

In the initial moments of an angry outburst, the victim may feel blind-sided to the point of shock and confusion. That person may struggle to find an explanation for what happened and what the consequences of that outburst might be.

Stage 2: Detour

Sometimes the response of one or more people in the aftermath of an argument is denial. This reaction is a detour that diminishes the importance or nature of the impact. Usually, it is either the person who initiated the conflict or the person who became the angriest who takes this approach. The person who was the object of anger tends to take a detour labeled "distancing." This person will try to put some space between him and the argument's instigator.

Stage 3: Discovery

Eventually, suppressed and repressed anger will find a way to express itself. A wise person will attempt to discover what caused the anger and search for reasons behind why it has taken up residence in her or in someone else. Ideally, this stage of discovery will lead a person to seek ways of curbing anger and removing it from her heart and relationships.

Stage 4: Forgiveness

This stage often begins with a person's confessing sinful anger to the Lord and then asking God to cleanse him or her of resentment, bitterness, and hostility. For victims of anger, it involves making a decision to pardon their offenders and freeing them from any threat of retaliation or revenge.

Unforgiveness stops the flow of love in a person's heart—love toward

God, self, and others. It also hinders our capacity to receive love from the Lord and others. Forgiveness enables us to walk in step with our heavenly Father and experience the fullness of an intimate relationship with Him.

If a believer does not feel God's love, she likely is harboring unforgiveness. It could be due to a failure to forgive another person or to forgive herself. Refusing to let go of anger often puts us in a position of feeling unworthy before God. A right relationship with the Father requires us to put away anything that is not consistent with His character, including bad anger.

FORGIVING YET AGAIN

What about when you feel as if you've genuinely forgiven another person, only to find yourself feeling anger, resentment, or bitterness toward the person in the future?

There are times when forgiving a person once is not enough. In Matthew 18, the disciple Peter asked Jesus, "How often shall my brother sin against me and I forgive him? Up to seven times?" (verse 21). Rabbis at that time taught that it was necessary to forgive someone only three times. So Peter must have thought he was being very generous in suggesting seven times.

But Jesus replied, "I do not say to you, up to seven times, but up to seventy times seven" (Matthew 18:22). God wants us to forgive people as many times as they sin against us. We are never justified in saying, "I have forgiven all that I can forgive." If we are reminded of an offense again and again, then we must forgive each and every time we remember it. We must be quick to say, "I forgive. Father, help me to forgive completely."

ASKING FOR FORGIVENESS FACE-TO-FACE

If you believe God is leading you to go to a person and ask for forgiveness, do so with humility. Recognize that in this step, you are taking responsibility for your actions and attitude. Do not try to solicit an apology or repentance from the other person in return for your apology.

FORGIVING SOMEONE FROM YOUR PAST

If you are holding something against a person who is dead or far away, there's a way you can deal with it.

Place two chairs in a room so they face each other. Sit in one of the chairs and imagine the person you are angry with is in the other chair. Have a conversation with that person.

Tell the person you are visualizing in the other chair precisely how he or she hurt you. Say exactly what you would if you were facing the offender. Actually, it's a little easier because the person can't say anything back. And there's no defense—you're doing all the talking. You're free to say whatever you need to say.

Tell whomever it might be: "I had a wrong spirit toward you, and I'm confessing that my attitude hasn't been right. I've held it against you all these years, and I want you to forgive me. I know that my feelings toward you have not been Christlike even though I claim to be a Christian." And once you say and deal with that, and you forgive the person, claim by faith that this is the end of it. You have no reason to do otherwise. You've done everything you can to express your unforgiving spirit, so make that the end of it.

THE CHALLENGE OF FORGIVING YOURSELF

I have met a number of people through the years who have struggled greatly in their attempts to forgive themselves. Some have blamed themselves for an accident that took the life of a friend or family member. Some have held on to guilt over an abortion, a divorce, or something they said that made their teenager run away from home.

The ability and capacity to forgive ourselves is absolutely essential if we are to successfully let go of anger and experience peace. If you fail to forgive yourself, you most likely will

- Punish yourself on an ongoing basis by depriving yourself of things that God intends for your pleasure and enjoyment.

- Live under a cloud of uncertainty, never quite sure of where you stand with God or other people.

- Struggle with feelings of unworthiness and low self-esteem.

- Strive compulsively to be "good enough" to deserve forgiveness from God or others.

If this is your struggle, I encourage you to read and take hold of these words from Psalm 103:

The LORD is compassionate and gracious,
Slow to anger and abounding in lovingkindness. . . .
He has not dealt with us according to our sins,
Nor rewarded us according to our iniquities.
For as high as the heavens are above the earth,
So great is His lovingkindness toward those who fear Him.
As far as the east is from the west,
So far has He removed our transgressions from us.

Just as a father has compassion on his children,

So the LORD has compassion on those who fear Him.

For He Himself knows our frame;

He is mindful that we are but dust (verses 8, 10–14).

God understands your weakness and frailty. He knows your sin and is willing to forgive and forget it. Your challenge is to believe what God says and forgive yourself, while fully trusting Him to forgive you.

God makes it very clear, "If we confess our sins, He is faithful and righteous to forgive us our sins and to cleanse us from all unrighteousness" (1 John 1:9). The Greek word that is translated as "confess" in this verse means "to agree with God about the nature of one's sins." Chances are that you know you have sinned. Simply agree with God that you have fallen short and that your sin has broken your fellowship with Him. Ask God to heal and restore your relationship. He promises to do so in His Word.

FORGIVING AND FORGETTING

People have said to me through the years, "I can forgive, but I can't forget." God has given us memories to help us not repeat our mistakes. We also are able to remember His commands and walk in obedience to Him. But God did not give us memories so we can readily recall the mistakes of others. He does not desire for us to remind people of their mistakes.

The fastest way for a conversation to blow up is for one person to say, "I remember the last time you . . . " or "I'll never forget your . . ." Those statements, and others like them, are rarely productive. And they can lead to other accusatory language, such as "You always . . ." or "You never . . ." Before long, voices are raised, blood pressures rise, and anger is full-blown.

In fact, it may not be physically possible to fully forget something that has happened to you. Scientists who study the brain say that no one is able to forget anything they have experienced, unless they have brain damage. But even if we can't fully forget, we can functionally forget. In other words, we can choose *not* to recall or remember painful emotional experiences in our past.

In her book *Tramp for the Lord*, Corrie ten Boom wrote, "When God forgives your sin, He buries it in the deepest sea and puts up a 'no fishing' sign." When God forgives, He also forgets. His Word tells us, "Their sins and their lawless deeds I will remember no more" (Hebrews 10:17).

Choose to forget what God forgets. Once you admit your sin to Him and receive His forgiveness, ask the Lord to help you enter into His "forgetfulness." Refuse to harbor resentment against another person. Deny any impulse to recall angry exchanges, bitter remarks, and hurtful actions.

SEEK TO FORGIVE AS JESUS FORGAVE

If anyone ever had reason to be angry, it was Jesus at the time of His crucifixion. He was 100 percent innocent of all charges that had been brought against Him. He was spat upon, beaten, flogged, scourged, and had a crown of thorns thrust onto His head. Then He was forced to carry a heavy wooden cross through the marketplace in disgrace. He was a sinless man about to undergo the most torturous form of death known in His time. No one ever had greater cause to be angry.

Yet what did Jesus say when they nailed Him to that cross?

"Father, forgive them; for they do not know what they are doing" (Luke 23:34).

There's no forgiveness to match that. If Jesus can forgive, you and I can forgive. None of us will likely ever experience the torture and mistreatment Jesus endured.

There is no way to rationalize holding a grudge while also claiming to live under the authority of the cross. As a believer, I have a responsibility to forgive—no matter what.

It's easier to forgive others when we remember the enormous blessing that God has given us by freely forgiving our sins. Those who have experienced the Father's forgiveness know the joy and peace that comes when sins and guilt are washed away. If you have difficulty forgiving another person, simply recall what God has done for you. Choose to reflect to others the grace and love that He has shown you. You will never resemble Christ more than when you forgive others as He forgives.

FORGIVING FULLY AND LIVING IN FREEDOM

If you want to forgive but just are not able to do it, ask God to help. Pray:

"Father, I want to be able to forgive the person who hurt me, just as You have forgiven me. Please help me to reflect the attitude of Jesus when He spoke from the cross, 'Father, forgive them; for they do not know what they are doing.' "

I have no doubt that whoever humbly and sincerely prays this prayer will receive God's enabling power to forgive.

How can you tell if you have fully forgiven someone?

The next time you think about that person, you won't feel hurt or anger. You will not go out of your way to avoid him or her. You won't have a problem hearing about someone doing good to that person or learning that the person has prospered in some way. You will live with a freedom that is reflected in your positive attitude and abundant joy.

I was in a restaurant not long ago, and a woman in a booth nearby waved to me, so I waved back. I didn't know her, but she came over to my table and said, "I want to tell you about the impact you had on my life. I heard your sermon one morning on the topic of forgiveness, and both my husband and I felt deeply moved to ask God to forgive us. We received Jesus Christ as our Savior. Then I also felt moved to forgive a woman I had hated. This woman didn't know I hated her, but after I forgave her, I became much more comfortable in her presence. We began to talk more, and I discovered that the two of us have a lot in common. Today we're very good friends. In fact, she's the person I'm having dinner with this evening."

She went on to tell me how her husband was on fire for God and about all the wonderful things that had happened in her marriage and family. "It all began with forgiveness," she said.

The truth is that some of God's greatest blessings, including friendships, start with forgiveness.

ADMIT IT—DEAL WITH IT

1. As you have read this chapter, has someone come to mind whom you need to forgive? Name that person. Are you ready to forgive him or her? If you are, what steps will you take to accomplish your goal?

2. If you don't feel ready to forgive, ask God to show you what is holding you back; then respond to His prompting.

3. Don't read another chapter until you take the necessary steps to obey God's command to forgive and forget.

CHAPTER 7

REBELLION

IIIIIIIIIIIIIIIIIIIIIIIIIIIIIIIIIIIIIIIIIIIIIIIIIIIIIIIIIIIIIIIIIIIIIIIIIIIIIIII

Anger Aimed at God

Have you ever known a person who was angry with God?

Are *you* angry with God?

There are many reasons why people are angry at God. Perhaps a child or another loved one died unexpectedly. Maybe a job was lost or a home destroyed. Perhaps a loved one was severely injured in an accident. Any one of these events (and countless others) could lead a person to cry out to God, asking, "How could You let this happen?"

But what is His response?

First, let me assure you that God can handle any angry outburst. He is not surprised by our anger; He is not disappointed when we are angry at Him; He is not upset by our questions. God is not threatened by our anger.

Second, even though the Lord is able to understand our anger toward Him, it is never justified. In other words, we need to be careful not to make God the object of our anger.

EXPRESS BUT DO NOT NURTURE

While it is acceptable to express your anger to God, be careful not to nurture anger toward Him. It can become a destructive stumbling block—hurting you and others, and grieving God.

In seeking answers to the "why" questions that give rise to anger, take hold of these truths:

- When bad things happen to God's people, He is not punishing them—either as an individual or as a group. The Lord disciplines those He loves (see Hebrews 12:6). God chastises us in order to remove sin from our lives, restore us to right relationship with Him, and lead us into greater and greater blessings. Chastisement is an act of correction. Punishment is an act of consequence and stands in sharp contrast to chastisement. Punishment comes after a person has been judged and found guilty. Chastisement is what a loving father does as a part of the healthy process of training a child to become a godly and loving adult.

- When bad things happen to God's people, you need to remember that we live in a fallen, sinful world. Much of the evil we see, hear, or read about is a result of our Creator's giving mankind free will. When Adam and Eve disobeyed God in the Garden of Eden, their sin set in motion a chain of events that negatively affects our world every second of every minute of every day. Most of the evil and bad things that happen are due to the poor stewardship of our free will.

  But without that freedom, man would not be able to reject Satan and make a choice for good. Our free will enables us to choose God and experience a loving, intimate relationship with Him through His Son Jesus Christ and the power of His Holy Spirit.

- When bad things happen to God's people, we need to recognize that we live on a planet that is filled with disease, severe weather, earthquakes, and other natural phenomena. All those dangers are additional consequences of a fallen world.

- When bad things happen to God's people, we may never know the reasons behind the pain and suffering they experience. There simply are some things in this life that we are incapable of comprehending. We may never know the answer to all our "why" questions on this side of eternity. But what we do know is that God is sovereign and in control at all times (see Psalm 103:19). And He promises to work *all* things "together for good to those who love God, to those who are called according to His purpose" (Romans 8:28).

God sees the beginning and end of your life and the lives of your loved ones. He sees the full context of every situation—past, present, and future. The Lord always has the best plan for you, and He knows exactly how to provide what is necessary for it to succeed.

As a friend said to me one day, "I don't know. But I know the One who knows." And that is sufficient. It is the essence of trust and the way our heavenly Father calls us to live. We must obey God and leave all the consequences to Him.

The key thing we must remember when tragedy strikes is that God's love and justice remain pure and absolute. The Lord is always for us, not against us (see Romans 8:31). He is dependable and fair. His love has been supremely demonstrated in the death, burial, and resurrection of Jesus. Whatever loss we experience can always be held in balance with the hope of a greater and more wonderful eternal blessing.

It is one thing to express your anger to God but an entirely different thing to remain angry with Him and refuse to let go of that anger.

I know a very prominent man who became angry at God when he was a child. This man's beloved younger brother died, and he blamed

God for it. He never stopped blaming God. Whom did this man hurt in the process? Himself! He prevented himself from having a loving relationship with his eternal Father and died holding on to anger and bitterness.

In the Old Testament, we learn that Job had a very different response to trial and heartache. In Job 13:15, he proclaims, "Though He slay me, I will hope in Him. Nevertheless I will argue my ways before Him." A very wealthy man with seven sons and three daughters, Job is described as "The greatest of all the men of the east" (1:3). But after God lifted His divine protection, Job lost everything. His children were dead, his servants killed, and his livestock taken. But the Bible says, "Through all this Job did not sin nor did he blame God" (1:22). Even when covered with boils from head to toe and told by his wife, "Curse God and die!" (2:10), Job refused to sin against the Lord.

Of course, he wasn't happy about what happened to him and certainly didn't think he deserved to be in that situation. So Job spoke to God at length about his pain and adversity. At one point he even wondered, "Why did I not die at birth?" (3:11). Yet after all his suffering, Job still expressed hope and trust in the Lord: "I know that You can do all things, and that no purpose of Yours can be thwarted" (42:2). Ultimately, that hope and trust was rewarded when "the LORD increased all that Job had twofold" (42:10).

We must always come to the same conclusion Job did. There is no benefit to be gained by harboring anger, hostility, resentment, or bitterness against God. He alone can help us endure pain and disappointment and emerge on the other side of those difficulties with a sense of hope and peace.

King David was a man who knew many sorrows. He was angry, frustrated, or disappointed on numerous occasions. He freely expressed all his emotions to God, including anger. However, David always came back to a central truth. God is God, and He is worthy to be praised. One of my favorite passages of Scripture is Psalm 16:

Preserve me, O God, for I take refuge in You.
I said to the LORD, "You are my Lord;
I have no good besides You."
As for the saints who are in the earth,
They are the majestic ones in whom is all my delight.
The sorrows of those who have bartered for another god will be multiplied;
I shall not pour out their drink offerings of blood,
Nor shall I take their names upon my lips.
The LORD is the portion of my inheritance and my cup;
You support my lot.
The lines have fallen to me in pleasant places;
Indeed, my heritage is beautiful to me.
I will bless the LORD who has counseled me;
Indeed, my mind instructs me in the night.
I have set the LORD continually before me;
Because He is at my right hand, I will not be shaken.
Therefore my heart is glad, and my glory rejoices;
My flesh also will dwell securely.
For You will not abandon my soul to Sheol;
Nor will You allow Thy Holy One to undergo decay.
You will make known to me the path of life;
In Your presence is fullness of joy,
In Your right hand there are pleasures forever.

Even as you express your emotions to God, make sure you come to the place where you can say, "Father, I will trust in You, and I will praise You no matter what."

DON'T BUILD A WALL AROUND YOUR HEART

When a person becomes angry with God, he will find it increasingly difficult to hear from Him and can miss His words of comfort and counsel. Think about it. Do you really listen to a person when you're angry, bitter, resentful, or hostile toward him or her? When you're really mad at someone, it's very unlikely that you'll remember anything the person says in the heat of an argument.

The same thing is true of our communication with God. When we're angry at the Lord, we will not be as open to hear His voice or as willing to wait upon Him. It's a sure-fire way to miss just about anything and everything God wants to say to us.

Not everyone who suffers pain and loss becomes angry and hostile toward God or other people. I have witnessed many families who have endured extremely difficult times by steadfastly clinging to God while everything around them raged. And when the storm subsided, they found that trusting in the Lord brought them through it with more peace and joy than they ever thought possible.

Do not build a wall between you and God. You *need* to hear from Him!

DO NOT GET INTO A TUG-OF-WAR WITH GOD

Recognize that when you're angry at God, it's always a control issue.

You may think you're in control of your life. But let me assure you that our heavenly Father is the One in control of all things, at all times, and in all ways.

Man may want to be number one. But God *is* number one.

He should be the focus of all our love, praise, and thanksgiving. You and I may want to have things done our way, but God's way is *always* the best way. It will be accomplished according to His plan, in His timing, and for His glory.

Don't get into a tug-of-war with God. You run the risk of interfering with His will, plan, and purpose for your life, which always is far better than anything you can hope or imagine (see 1 Corinthians 2:9).

THE RUIN OF REBELLION

Give me honest answers.

Is everything in your life going the way you think it should?

Do you find yourself asking God, "Why don't You do this?" Or "Why did You allow that?"

Do you see things working in a way that will bring you earthly blessings and eternal rewards? If not, consider the possibility that you are living according to your own rules and desires rather than God's.

Any time we're pursuing what we want, without regard to what the Lord wants, we are moving away from God. If we are not moving toward Him, we're in rebellion.

In most people's thinking, *rebellion* is a word that describes juvenile delinquents and criminals. But we need to see rebellion in a broader way. Spiritual rebellion is any thought, attitude, belief, word, or deed that is in conflict with God's commandments, His principles, and His nature.

People who are angry are very often rebellious. They're upset that life is not going the way they planned. Rebellious people may be frustrated by their lack of progress toward personal goals. They may be envious or greedy because people around them are doing better than they are. Many rebellious people pursue an ungodly lifestyle. They're interested in doing what feels good rather than what is right.

Rebellious people are often filled with anger and bitterness because they believe they have a right to feel the way they feel and to do as they please. In their resentment, frustration, and sinful attitudes, they distance themselves from God.

One of the most dangerous and costly things you can do in life is to rebel against the will of God. Anyone who has accepted Jesus Christ as Savior and lives by the power of the Holy Spirit can know the Father's will, plan, and purpose for his or her life. And when you knowingly rebel against God, it can have a devastating effect on you and those around you. It will have an impact on your family, your friends, your job—and depending on your position in life—your church, your community, and, quite possibly, your nation. As you look around today, you can find plenty of evidence that the consequences of rebellion against God include tremendous suffering, loss, disillusionment, discouragement, heartache, and pain.

When we rebel, we

- Refuse to do what God has commanded us to do. If the Lord sets a goal before a person and that person rejects it, that's rebellion.

- Pursue those things God forbids us to pursue. If a man pursues another man's wife, that's rebellion.

- Pursue what God allows in a manner that He forbids. If a person seeks a promotion at work and is dishonest about his job performance or slanders qualified coworkers, that's rebellion.

- Pursue what God allows but not in His timing. If a woman writes a bad check to buy a new dress because she can't wait until payday, that's rebellion. When we pursue something too soon or wait too long, we miss God's best.

In His Word, God makes it clear what we are to do and not do. The Bible explains in great detail how we are to live, work, and have relationships. Part of the Holy Spirit's role in a believer's life is to give specific guidance about when to act, with whom to act, and how to respond to specific situations, circumstances, and opportunities.

GOD'S ABSOLUTE LAW OF SOWING AND REAPING

Allow this irrefutable and absolute truth of God to sink deep into your heart and mind:

We reap what we sow,
more than we sow,
and later than we sow.

It doesn't matter if you believe in God or not—His law of sowing and reaping never changes (see Galatians 6:7).

The majority of the people on earth have little regard for God's laws. (They think obeying His commandments is a good idea for other people—just don't ask *them* to do so.) God's laws exist and are absolute regardless of whether or not a person recognizes, agrees with, or obeys them. Let me also assure you that these laws are in place for your good. God did not give us these laws to keep men and women from having fun or enjoying life. He created them for our protection, in the same way a loving earthly father provides boundaries, rules, and limits for his children. God is always looking out for your best interests, and He is always working things for your good.

The Bible gives us many examples of people who rebelled against God. One of the best examples is Saul, the first king appointed over the nation of Israel. In 1 Samuel 15, God told Samuel, the high priest and prophet of that time, that he was going to punish the nation of Amalek. Through Samuel, God gave these specific instructions to King Saul: "Go and strike Amalek and utterly destroy all that he has, and do not spare him; but put to death both man and woman, child and infant, ox and sheep, camel and donkey" (verse 3).

That may sound extremely severe and heartless to you, but this particular group of people had openly and actively attacked the Israelites.

They were not the least bit interested in coexistence. And with their attack, they became the enemy not only of the Israelites but of God.

The Bible tells us that Saul defeated the Amalekites, but he captured Agag, the king of the Amalekites, and kept him alive. Saul also spared the best of the sheep, oxen, and lambs, and anything else that he determined was "good." Israel's king destroyed only those things he despised or counted worthless (verse 9).

Then Saul boasted to Samuel, "I have carried out the command of the LORD." But the prophet replied, "What then is this bleating of the sheep in my ears, and the lowing of the oxen which I hear?" (verses 13, 14). Saul tried to justify his disobedience, saying that he had spared the best of the animals to make a sacrifice to the Lord.

But Samuel rebuked him, saying, "Has the LORD as much delight in burnt offerings and sacrifices as in obeying the voice of the LORD? Behold, to obey is better than sacrifice, and to heed than the fat of rams. For rebellion is as the sin of divination, and insubordination is as iniquity and idolatry. Because you have rejected the word of the LORD , He has also rejected you from being king" (verses 22–23).

Those two verses give a crystal-clear picture of how God sees rebellion. To Him, it is as dangerous and destructive as witchcraft, willful and deliberate sin, and worshipping false gods.

Rebellion also has elements of deception and self-justification. We may try to convince ourselves and others that we're obeying God's laws, but we are not. And deep down, we know it.

"But I go to church."

"I give money to help the poor."

"I take my children to Sunday school."

All these works are like "filthy rags" in God's eyes (Isaiah 64:6 KJV). He wants our full, complete, and total obedience. No matter how big our sacrifice seems to us, it will never compare to what Jesus did at the Cross.

Never lose sight of the fact that rebellion is an act against God's established order and authority. Any time you or I rebel, it's as if we're saying that we know more and know better than He does. Our best choice is to trust and obey our all-loving, all-knowing, and all-powerful heavenly Father in every situation and circumstance of life.

GOD'S LINES OF AUTHORITY

In every area of life, God has established a line of authority. Why? His purpose is not so that one person can rule over another with absolute power. God's lines of authority are balanced. Those in leadership are to serve and care for those who follow them. The people who follow are to comply with decisions the leader makes. All leaders are ultimately under God's authority.

Our heavenly Father has established lines of authority so that families, churches, businesses, and so on can function with maximum productivity and effectiveness. Authority allows for clear leadership and direction, mutual support and respect, and consistent order and stability. Without lines of authority, you cannot have harmony. Chaos rules.

We human beings crave order, whether we know it or not. No home can function without a head of household. No team, sports or otherwise, can win without someone calling the plays. No church can minister effectively without a pastor. No business can perform to its full potential without a boss.

Authority has its place in relationships as well. The roles of a husband and wife, mother and father, parent and child, brother and sister, and others have all been established by God. When these relationships maintain the Lord's established line of authority, love flows and conflict is avoided. When roles get reversed or fellowship is broken, anger can result and confusion will reign.

We have two sources that clearly define the lines of authority: the Bible and the Holy Spirit. God places His Spirit in every believer to give clear guidance about authority and order. His Word imparts knowledge, wisdom, courage, strength, and all the other necessary virtues to live a successful Christian life.

When Jesus went to the Cross, He did so in submission to the authority of His Father. Our Savior fulfilled His purpose willingly—He *gave* His life freely. It was not taken from Him against His will. Yes, Christ endured excruciating pain and suffering. But there also was incredible joy, because Jesus knew He was doing the will of God the Father.

The same is true for us. We may be called upon to do some things that are painful or uncomfortable. But when we yield ourselves to doing God's will His way, we also will find purpose and joy.

Rebellion Can Be Rooted in Doubt

Some people rebel against God because they doubt His existence or His goodness. Others turn away from the Lord because they blame Him for something. They may doubt that God loves and cares for them or question that He is actually in control. If any of these are your reasons for rebellion, I invite you put away your doubt and embrace the truth.

Those who do not believe God exists are fooling themselves. Many atheists reject the idea of a divine Creator because they want to be in control. They are unwilling to surrender their lives to Him and admit that they cannot live victoriously in their own strength.

Those who doubt God's goodness haven't really encountered God. To know Him is to know His love, mercy, grace, favor, forgiveness, and blessing. People who blame God for the evil in their lives do not understand Him. The Father cannot produce evil, nor does He ever tempt people to do evil.

Still others believe in God's authority but do not want to be "fenced in" by His laws and commandments at this particular time in their lives. They want to "enjoy life" and wait until they are old to give their lives to Christ. I pray that they don't wait too long, because none of us is promised tomorrow.

The Bible says, "Behold, now is 'the day of salvation'" (2 Corinthians 6:2).

If you haven't surrendered to Jesus Christ, then you're not a Christian. Don't wait another minute to get on your knees and ask Him to forgive your sins, cleanse your heart, and save you. When you trust Jesus as your personal Savior, immediately the Holy Spirit comes into your life and seals you as a child of God. You can remove any doubt about where you'll spend eternity by accepting Christ today.

THE ULTIMATE ROOT OF REBELLION

The ultimate root of rebellion is pride. Ever since the fall of Adam and Eve in the Garden of Eden, mankind's basic nature includes a desire to live by our rules, pursue our goals, and fulfill our desires. Rebellion totally ignores the truth that God is the ultimate authority over *all* creation, including us. Rebellion refuses to recognize that God is sovereign over the entire universe—He is omnipotent, omniscient, and omnipresent. His nature is love, goodness, mercy, and justice.

Because God is all-knowing, all-loving, and all-powerful, He knows what's best for His creation. Your heavenly Father knows what's best for you today, tomorrow, and forever. God desires to give you His best by pouring His blessings into every area of your life.

God has given mankind free will so that you and I can make a personal choice to obey or disobey Him. We can choose to develop a relationship with Him or reject Him, to love Him or hate Him.

When we make a personal choice to disobey the Lord, we sin against Him. And a holy God cannot tolerate, excuse, or associate with sin. We become separated from God in our disobedience, and we no longer are able to enjoy the fullness of His presence and provision.

Pride ultimately leads us to believe that we know better than God. Don't be fooled! Put your pride aside and follow Jesus Christ.

TWO MAIN MANIFESTATIONS

Generally speaking, people rebel against God in one of two ways. First, a person may totally disregard God's commandments, God's people, and God's principles. Second, a person may align himself with a rebellious person or group. Both of these manifestations of rebellion were evident in the Garden of Eden.

In Genesis 3, the devil came to Eve as a serpent. He tempted her with the forbidden fruit and she ate. She took the fruit and ate it because the devil told her it would make her "like God, knowing good and evil" (verse 5).

The forbidden fruit was from "the tree of the knowledge of good and evil" (2:17). It was the only tree in the garden that was off-limits to them. The serpent, however, deceived Eve to the point that she rebelled against God's clear command not to eat the fruit from that tree: Genesis 3:6 tells us, "When the woman saw that the tree was good for food, and that it was a delight to the eyes, and that the tree was desirable to make one wise, she took from its fruit and ate; and she gave also to her husband with her, and he ate."

From one perspective, you might assume that Adam was an innocent party in this—he was just eating food his wife gave him. But whether he knew what the fruit was or didn't bother to ask, Adam chose to eat it. He aligned himself with a rebellious person, and in so doing, he committed the sin of rebellion too.

Both Adam and Eve rejected God's established lines of authority. Eve should have submitted to her husband, and Adam should have surrendered to God. As a result of their rebellion and disobedience, God banished Adam and Eve from their garden paradise. The consequences of their sin brought pain, suffering, and death to all mankind.

But God will forgive us when we turn to Him, admit our rebellion and sin, and ask Him to cleanse us. There may still be consequences to pay here on earth, as Adam and Eve discovered. But we are eternally secure the moment we trust Jesus Christ to save us.

Rebellion cost King Saul his throne.

Adam and Eve lost their garden paradise home.

God may not spare us pain, suffering, or heartache when we willingly choose to live outside His will, plan, and purpose. But the Father's forgiveness does allow us the privilege of His help and guidance as we walk through any consequences we must face. Always remember this absolute truth taken from the Word of God (see Galatians 6:7):

We reap what we sow,
more than we sow,
and later than we sow.

JUST SAY NO
TO REBELLION

There is a simple formula for dealing with any temptation to rebel:

- Say yes to God.

- Say no to Satan.

- Walk away from any person who tries to lead you to sin.

Don't give in to the devil's temptations to disregard God's Word. Be careful not to fall into snares set for you by rebellious people. If someone is trying to lure you into sinning against God, that person does not deserve your time or attention. Choose to be around people who want to obey God and serve Him. Ask the Lord to point out and protect you from any rebellious person in your life who, knowingly or unknowingly, may threaten your relationship with Him.

SURRENDER FULLY TO GOD

If you are living obediently before God, you will have a sense of contentment and joy within you. As a believer, you will experience hope that cannot be shaken and peace that "surpasses all understanding" (Philippians 4:7 NKJV). You will not envy what other people have or seek to be like them. You will "cease striving" for things that are not of God and will completely rest in Him (see Psalm 46:10). You will discover the Lord's will, plan, and purpose for your life—and in doing so, you will find lasting contentment and fulfillment.

To what degree have you surrendered your will to God?

To what degree would you say that you are living in obedience to Him—not only in your outward behavior but in your inward desires, attitudes, and emotions? Fifty percent? Are you living His way half the time and your way half the time? Is it more? Or . . . is it less? Are you living for God at all?

God calls us to be 100 percent committed, 100 percent surrendered.

Is there *any* area of your life where you say to God, "Hands off!"? If so, then you are in rebellion. If you are setting aside any habit or desire and not giving God full authority over that part of your life, then you are establishing a "red zone" of rebellion.

Psalm 107 offers a stern warning (verses 17–18):

Fools, because of their rebellious way,
And because of their iniquities, were afflicted.
Their soul abhorred all kinds of food,
And they drew near to the gates of death.

The rebellious are very often afflicted with a wide variety of problems, torment, and struggles. A person can have no desire to eat, which is another way of saying the rebellious become weak and are in poor health. Verse 18 says those in rebellion are in a state of dying—not only physically but emotionally and spiritually as well.

If there is any rebellion in your life, you need to admit and confess it. When you do, God's Word promises that He'll deliver you from it (verses 19–20):

Then they cried out to the LORD in their trouble;
He saved them out of their distresses.
He sent His word and healed them,
And delivered them from their destructions.

If you are in rebellion, do not wait to cry out to the Lord for His forgiveness and mercy. Recognize that the afflictions in your life may be the result of your rebellious ways. Trust God to save you from your distresses, heal you of any suffering, and deliver you from your rebellion.

The Lord may still require you to face some of the consequences and penalties, but He can and will heal any pain associated with your rebellious behavior. God also will grant you renewed fellowship with Him and will walk with you through whatever difficulties lie ahead.

The only solution for rebellion is to lay it down. Surrender to God, cry out to Him, and receive His forgiveness and help.

ADMIT IT—DEAL WITH IT

1. Are you angry with God? Why? Have you told God you're angry?

2. Ask Him to help you release that anger.

3. When does anger at God become rebellion against God? Have you rebelled?

4. Go to the Lord today and ask Him to forgive you, restore you to a right relationship with Him, and have mercy on you.

5. If you are in a relationship with a rebellious person, what steps will you take to confront the rebellion or distance yourself from that person?

CHAPTER 8

PEACE

||||||||||||||||||||||||||||||||||||||||||||||||||||||||||||||||||||||||||||

Establishing Personal Peace in an Angry World

W hat comes to mind when you think of an oasis?

Do you envision a place of refuge and peace in the midst of a barren desert?

Take a moment and imagine what it would feel like to be at an oasis.

Throughout the Middle East, you still find many oases, with small groves of date palms in the midst of what appears to be desert wasteland. These palms are watered by the fresh water of artesian springs. The environment of an oasis is cool due to the shade from the palms. An oasis is a refreshing place of restful peace. An oasis is also nourishing, especially when the dates are ready for harvest.

In Israel, the oasis at Ein Gedi is filled with date palms and life-producing fresh water, only yards away from the mineral-laden, lifeless waters of the Dead Sea. These two environments, which are so close to each other, could not be more different.

The challenge we all face is to make our personal spaces life-giving oases of rest, refreshment, and nourishment in the midst of chaos and confusion. No matter how many angry people are around us, God can make our lives oases of peace.

RETHINKING YOUR PERSONAL SPACE

The good news always is that nearly every person has control over his or her thoughts and emotions. For the most part, we choose how we feel, what we think, and what we believe. Each of us also has a great deal of control over our personal space.

Your personal space radiates from you like the rings created when a pebble is thrown into a pond. Let's say the first ring is everything within arm's reach. If you stretch out your arm and turn around 360 degrees, that is your primary personal space. It is always there whether you are standing, sitting, or lying down.

The second ring of personal space is everything within the normal conversational tone of your voice. Without raising your voice, who can hear you and understand what you are saying? This ring usually extends out about twenty feet from you.

The third ring of personal space is everything within the sound of your raised voice. When I was a boy, my mother would sometimes call me in to dinner from the front door of our home. No matter how many other moms were calling their children, I never confused those voices with my mother's. I could hear her even through the noise of traffic or friends at play. This third ring of personal space might extend as much as one hundred feet outward from your body.

The farther out the ring of personal space, the less authority you and I have over that area. We may control very few things in our environment, and even less in our world, but we do have at least some degree of influence over the area that makes up our personal space. And when you join with like-minded individuals who stand with you physically, spiritually, and/or emotionally, your combined influence can be great, indeed!

FIVE AREAS OF AUTHORITY

You have at least five areas of authority over your personal space.

People

You control which people are allowed to enter and occupy your personal space. They include your immediate circle of family and friends, coworkers, and, in particular environments, total strangers. When you fly on a plane or sit in a movie theater or church, people you don't know can occupy your personal space. You may not have total authority over what people do in your personal space, but you do have some degree of influence. You have the freedom to move away from those who violate what you have established as the rules governing your personal space.

Be careful not to allow angry or violent people into your personal space, and do your best not to display angry behavior toward those you have welcomed in.

Messages

You have authority over what you allow to be seen and heard in your personal space. This includes messages from radio, television, print media, and the Internet.

Think about the music you listen to. Pay attention to the movies and TV programs you watch. Consider the sites you and your family members visit on the Internet. As a parent, you have authority over what your child sees and hears in his or her bedroom. Closely monitor what your children watch on television, where they go on the Internet, and what they listen to on their iPods or MP3 players. As a parent, you have full authority over your kids as long as you are fully responsible for their physical, emotional, material, and spiritual needs.

In recent years, programs on broadcast and cable television networks have become increasingly:

- *Violent.* A person can hardly watch television without seeing or hearing about a murder or assault.

- *Sexual.* From situation comedies to police dramas, sexual innuendo and immoral sexual behavior run rampant.

- *Disrespectful.* Even programs about law and order often have storylines that are rooted in disrespect for authority.

- *Dishonoring.* Increasingly, the media seeks to ridicule Christians and others with traditional values while applauding those who live sinful and aberrant lifestyles.

These same messages are seen and heard by children and teenagers through various websites and song lyrics. Scientists and researchers are still studying and debating the short- and long-term effects on individuals of violent and pornographic messages. Many argue that there is no connection between what we see and hear and what we do as a result. They claim that what we're exposed to through media does not lead to violent or sexually deviant behavior.

But it seems only commonsensical to me that what a person sees and hears is eventually internalized in some way. If a person does not have a solid foundation of faith or a deep sense of security with which to filter the media messages, there is likely to be a negative impact from seeing or hearing too much violence. At the very least, a person will become desensitized to violence. Pornography produces intense sexual desires that can manifest themselves as lust, fornication, adultery, and sexual abuse. Proverbs 4:23–27 offers these words of warning and encouragement:

Watch over your heart with all diligence,
For from it flow the springs of life.
Put away from you a deceitful mouth,
And put devious lips far from you.
Let your eyes look directly ahead,
And let your gaze be fixed straight in front of you.
Watch the path of your feet,
And all your ways will be established.
Do not turn to the right nor to the left;
Turn your foot from evil.

I'm convinced that a steady diet of violent or sexually explicit messages will create deep feelings of frustration and make the presence of sin that much greater in your life. We live in a "noisy" world filled with unholy, ungodly, and unacceptable music, movies, television programs, magazines, books, and websites that will destroy your peace and undermine your relationship with Jesus Christ. If a message or media has control of your life, ask God to deliver you, guard you, and grant you His peace. Pray for His strength and help to put aside whatever is keeping you from walking and living in right relationship with Him.

Conversations

You have authority over the way you allow others to routinely speak to you and the conversations you have. This includes profanity and other foul language, filthy stories, and dirty jokes.

People used to refer to that kind of lewd conduct and conversation as "smut." It's not a word we use as much today. In fact, most people don't even know its origin. Actually, smut is a parasitic fungus that leaves sooty black spores on leaves and other parts of plants. This is also what happens to the soul when it becomes covered with the "fungus" of obscenities, vulgar stories, and pornography.

You are entirely within your rights to ask other people *not* to swear or use foul language in your presence.

A surgical nurse told me recently that when the doctors she works with begin to use foul language, she doesn't even need to say anything. She just raises her eyebrows and gives them her what-would-your-mother-think look. These surgeons no longer use foul language or tell dirty jokes in her presence. They respect her for her work and her character. In fact, they request her to be their surgical nurse. Why? Because the respect she demands is the respect she gives to others.

A person is rarely angry with those he or she respects and admires. The use of profanity and vulgar language is rooted in disrespect. Using it will harm your relationships with others and damage your walk with the Lord.

Material Possessions

You have authority over the contents of your refrigerator and the various cabinets and drawers of your home. I am continually amazed at the number of people who make alcohol and prescription medications easily accessible to their children and teenagers.

Not long ago I watched a father express intense sorrow over the death of his sixteen-year-old daughter. She had been killed in an automobile accident involving alcohol. He said, "I never made any connection between the alcohol in our home and my daughter's driving habits. I feel guilty about having made it so easily accessible to her." Let me assure you that if you have alcohol in your home, your children are very likely to find it and experiment with it.

Prescription medications are another danger to your kids. Make sure there are no leftover pills in your cupboards or medicine cabinets that might attract a curious child or teenager. Whether you have children or not, my advice is to remove all alcohol and unused prescription medication from your home.

Attitude

You have authority over the prevailing attitude of your home—never lose sight of that, especially if you're a parent. Ask yourself, *Is my home filled with peace? Is it a place of beauty and quiet rest?*

Many homes today are filled with chaos and noise.

What is the attitude of the people in your family? Are they angry and disrespectful or happy and obedient?

What is *your* attitude?

The attitude you display is usually the one that others will reflect back to you. Make sure yours is positive, encouraging, and godly. Confront any negative attitude you sense in your spouse or children. Feelings give rise to actions sooner or later. A hostile, resentful, or bitter attitude *will* produce angry behavior.

DISTANCE YOURSELF FROM FIVE TYPES OF PEOPLE

In your home, workplace, and any other area of your personal environment, choose to distance yourself from people and activities that display these characteristics:

- Violence

- Vengeance

- Vindictiveness

- Vacillation

- Violation

DISTANCE YOURSELF FROM
VIOLENT PEOPLE AND SITUATIONS

Violence is the use of physical force to injure someone or to compel someone to do something. It often results in significant damage to people, property, or both. Violence tends to occur quickly and with devastating force.

Anger is at the root of all violent behavior and is often the only clue that violence will erupt. I encourage you to distance yourself from

- Individuals prone to swearing as a routine part of their communication.

- People who constantly ridicule or intensely criticize others, whether individuals or groups of people.

- Those who make demeaning statements about any person or group that reflect prejudice or bias on the basis of color, race, culture, age, or sex.

Listen to what a person says and to the tone of voice he or she uses. Don't dismiss someone's choice of words by thinking, *He doesn't really mean that* or *She doesn't really think that*. The truth is that people nearly always think and mean what they say, at least to some degree.

A year or so ago, I heard about a woman who was married to a military officer. This man was prone to angry outbursts that caused his wife and children to wither in his presence. This woman feared that one of her husband's outbursts might turn physical. So she waited for a good time to discuss this with him. When that day came, she said, "I want to say something to you in as loving a tone of voice as I can. Please take what I'm going to say as something important and something that I believe is for the good of our family. I'm asking you to deal with your anger—not only for the children's and my sake but for your sake."

She went on to say, "You do not need to raise your voice to make us respect you or to do what you ask. Your anger makes us afraid of you and avoid you. I also want to tell you that if you ever lift a hand against me or our children, I will walk out the door of our home and never return. I will also do my best to keep our children from having any further contact with you."

This man was stunned, but he knew his wife was serious and that she was a woman who stood by what she said. He responded by doing just what she asked. He confronted his anger and changed the way he spoke to his family.

All this occurred more than sixty years ago. This husband and wife are in their late eighties today. This man's children love him dearly and enjoy being around him. The same can be said for his wife. He is one of the most respected members of his community. In fact, few people would believe that he was once a man filled with anger.

Can people prone to violence change their attitude and deal with their anger? Absolutely.

What can you do about the intrusion of violent people into your life?

- Refuse to live under a threat of violence.

- Refuse to get into a car with anyone who is extremely angry or who has displayed road rage in the past.

- Refuse to serve on a committee with a person prone to angry outbursts.

- Refuse to allow a violent person to introduce a debate or discussion in your home.

- End any debate or discussion simply by changing the topic.

- As lovingly as you can, tell angry people that you like them a great deal more when they are *not* angry. Then inform them that you have zero tolerance for violence. If such people respond to your words in an angry or violent manner, do what you can not to associate with them.

Do Not Remain in a Violent Atmosphere

A friend of mine recently went to a post office after dark to see if he could purchase a newspaper from a vending machine there. As soon as he reentered his vehicle, the female passenger with him said, "Let's get out of here! NOW! NOW! NOW!" She spoke with such uncharacteristic urgency that he immediately put the car in reverse and roared out of the parking lot.

As they drove down the street, his friend explained how she had noticed two other cars pulling into the post office parking lot. When she saw those vehicles preparing to park on either side of them, this woman sensed grave danger. Thankfully, they escaped without harm. But the next day, they heard on the radio that a violent incident involving a drug deal gone bad had occurred in that very parking lot.

If the Holy Spirit or common sense tells you to leave a situation, get out as fast as you can. Don't dismiss God-given signs and warnings. Flee from violence.

I know another woman who went to graduate school in an unfamiliar city. Her new roommate was the friend of a friend, and she found an apartment for them prior to the start of the semester. But this roommate did not make a wise choice. When the young woman arrived in the city, she sensed immediately that the apartment was not a good place for them to live. Within a week, this woman and her roommate found a much nicer place for just a few dollars more a month. When they told the manager that they would be moving at the end of the month, he said, "I didn't think you gals would stay long."

"Why not?" one of the young women asked.

"Well," he said, "I figured you'd get word that we've had two rapes and a murder in this building during the last six months. And I could tell you weren't the kind of women who would want to live in a building like that."

The other young woman responded, "Why didn't you tell me that when I first applied to rent an apartment?"

The manager just shrugged. People who are willing to accommodate violence in their lives rarely want to admit that they do so.

Commit this truth from God's Word to your memory and recite it often: "If possible, so far as it depends on you, be at peace with all men" (Romans 12:18).

DO NOT ASSOCIATE WITH VENGEFUL PEOPLE

Vengeance involves making enemies and punishing them. In most cases, vengeance is a long-standing and seemingly endless cycle.

Just look at the Middle East. One side does something the other side doesn't like, and there's retaliation. And then there's retaliation for the retaliation. And so it goes—year after year, decade after decade.

This same cycle is evident between individuals and in many families. Those with a vengeful spirit have a strong desire to hurt someone, usually to a level that's beyond what they've experienced themselves.

How can you identify a vengeful spirit? Listen to what a person says. Does she make threats? Does he talk about harming others? Is she hoping that something bad happens to a person she knows? Watch out for people who say things like "That person *needs* to be punished." Or "I'd like to give that person a dose of his own medicine."

Confront people who seem to take delight in having enemies or who seem to create enemies at every turn. Refuse to participate in anything that involves getting even, payback, or revenge. Do not seek or take part in vengeance.

God's Word tells us, "Never take your own revenge. . . . 'Vengeance is Mine, I will repay,' says the Lord" (Romans 12:19).

DO NOT BEFRIEND THOSE WHO ARE VINDICTIVE

A vindictive spirit is a close cousin to vengeance. But the difference is that vindictive people are always on the defensive. They constantly blame someone else for their pain. Bad things in their lives are never their own fault, and they're quick to lash out at the people who, they say, owe them something. It may be a company, a former employer, a family member, a community official, or even society as a whole.

A college student told me recently that he felt as if nobody in his dorm liked him.

So I asked him, "Who do *you* like in your college dorm?"

"Nobody," he said.

Well . . . there's the problem. Vindictive people rarely make good friends or establish strong, positive relationships with those around them. They view others with suspicion and doubt—and they are constantly looking for ways they can "even the score" against people who don't respect or include them.

To some vindictive people, everyone is their enemy. Run from people like that. Call on others in positions of authority who may be able to intervene and help that person. Because vindictiveness and anger go hand in hand, people who harbor that spirit can become a danger to themselves and others.

Do not allow yourself, your family members, or your friends to ever have a "me against the world" attitude. Remember the apostle Paul's words from Romans 12:17: "Never pay back evil for evil to anyone. Respect what is right in the sight of all men."

DO NOT ALIGN YOURSELF WITH VACILLATING PEOPLE

The word *vacillate* means "to be indecisive . . . to sway from side to side." There is no sense of security in an atmosphere of vacillation. Those types of environments are marked by shifting sands, unsteady footing, and constantly changing beliefs and opinions. If you allow people into your personal space who are constantly vacillating, you can become so frustrated that you begin to feel anger.

These are some of the characteristics of a vacillating person:

- They love you today but not tomorrow.

- They want things done a certain way this time but a different way the next.

- They believe one thing on Sunday and a different thing on Thursday.

- Their demands change from hour to hour, day to day, or week to week.

- They think something is "wrong" or "bad" one day but not the next.

You do not need to pursue or to continue relationships with people who are full of indecision or lack strong moral fiber. The vacillating person has no anchor—he rides the waves of whatever he sees, hears, or experiences. Such a man or woman is extremely prone to frustration, anxiety, and anger.

Continually speak truth back to vacillating people. Focus on sharing the truth of God's love, concern, and presence. Hold these individuals accountable for what they say and for discrepancies between what they say and do. God's Word tells us that a "double-minded" person is "unstable in all his ways" (James 1:8).

DO NOT STAY ASSOCIATED WITH A PERSON WHO VIOLATES YOUR PERSONAL BOUNDARIES

Avoid people who do not honor your personal boundaries or the "rules" you have established for your own personal space. "Violators" do not respect you. And if a person does not respect you, he or she is likely to hurt you—emotionally, materially, or physically. Distance yourself from these people.

TAKE A NEW LOOK AT YOUR PERSONAL SPACE

Many years ago now, a Christian man who worked in the entertainment industry in Hollywood said this to a friend of mine: "It is very difficult to be a clean drop in a dirty pond."

It is not only very difficult, it's impossible!

Be very aware that your environment will change you if you don't take charge of it. You must be focused and intentional if you desire a personal space that reflects the nature of Jesus Christ. Maintaining an atmosphere of peace marked by spiritual refreshment, nourishment, and shelter requires constant decision making and oversight. You cannot live in a personal environment that is filled with anger, violence, vengeance, vindictiveness, or vacillation and remain sweet, calm, and loving.

YOUR PERSONAL SPACE GOES WITH YOU

Your personal space is like a bubble around you. It goes with you wherever you go. This truth directly relates to how you can and will influence the larger environments of your family neighborhood, city, state, and world. What you do in your personal space is the primary way you will impact your home, your workplace, your community, and your church.

With very few exceptions, you *can* control these ten aspects of your life:

1. You can control where you go—including the route you choose to get there.

2. You can control where you work. It may take some time to make a change, but you *can* choose your employer.

3. You can control where you go for recreation or fun. You decide the movies you see, the museums you visit, and the clubs or gyms you join.

4. You can control where you attend church and your various ministry activities.

5. You can control who you choose to associate and have fun with.

6. You can control, to a large degree, what you take into your body. You choose what you will eat and drink, the quality of air you breathe, and the medications or supplements you take.

7. You can control what you allow to take root in your heart and mind. You may not be able to avoid seeing or hearing everything you find offensive, but you can keep those negative images and messages from taking up permanent residence in you.

8. You can control, at least to some degree, the noise level of the world around you. You can request that certain music not be played or that the volume be turned down.

9. You can control what you speak up for or speak out against. Verbally or in written form, you can send messages that make a difference.

10. You can control your behavior and attitude toward others. Small acts of kindness can make a difference. Sharing a smile, a look of affirmation, or a short but sincere compliment can make another person's day. And let's not overlook the importance of good manners and generosity. Opening a door or yielding to another car in traffic can influence your world in a positive way.

All these things are under your control every day. And each of them can greatly impact your efforts to make your life an oasis of peace. Keep in mind that exercising control of your personal space need not be done in an ungodly, rude, or angry way. But if you do not speak up for a more peaceful, calm, loving, and godly environment in the world around you, others may create the environment they want—and they are not likely to be your brothers and sisters in Christ.

You are the only one who can take charge of your personal space. Nobody else can do it for you. And it's your responsibility to positively influence the world around you. The good news is that God promises to help you with both!

ADMIT IT—DEAL WITH IT

1. Whom have you allowed to repeatedly violate the personal boundaries you set?

2. With what positive or negative images and messages are you filling your mind and heart?

3. Are you engaging in conversation or listening to language that leaves you feeling dirty or angry?

4. What unhealthy substances have you allowed in your home? What will you do to get rid of them?

5. Who seems to have the most influence over the attitudes in your home? What are those attitudes?

6. What can you do to make your life an oasis of peace in a barren and ungodly world?

7. In what ways might you take greater control over your personal space?

CHAPTER 9

RELATIONSHIPS

Living with Angry People—or Not

Few things in life are more troublesome than a relationship infected by anger.

Who in Your Immediate World Is Angry?

Without a doubt, John was one of the angriest men I have ever known. I never heard him say a positive word to me or anyone around me. I did my best to avoid him whenever possible, and I said as little as possible when I was in his presence.

Unfortunately, he was impossible to avoid or ignore completely. John was my stepfather.

My father died when I was a baby. I have no memories of him and know only what my mother and aunts have told me about him through the years. My mother raised me as a single mom until I was nine years old. I asked her shortly before she died why she had married when I was that age, and she replied, "I thought you needed a father as you approached your teenage years."

From my perspective, Mom and I were getting along just fine. We had our struggles—most of them financial. But we were doing okay, and I never doubted that my mother loved me. In countless ways, she supported me emotionally and provided for me physically. She had only a sixth-grade education but insisted that I diligently attend school. If I brought home grades that were not all A's and B's, her only concern was whether or not I had done my best.

I have vivid memories of coming home from my afternoon paper route to find my dinner set out on the table for me. My mother had prepared it before she left for work. I had a constant assurance that I was always on my mother's mind and was loved by her completely.

Most important, my mother gave me a firm foundation spiritually. We read the Bible together. We knelt in prayer together. And every Sunday, we went to church together.

It's possible that John had a spiritual life in the years we lived under the same roof—I know he had one in the last couple of years before he died. But when all you see and hear from a person is anger, it's hard to discern any other aspect of the person's personality.

John never struck me, but he certainly wounded me emotionally. He belittled me constantly, letting me know that he didn't think I was worth the air I breathed. He especially belittled my desire to someday preach the gospel. He thought I should get a real job, which, in his opinion, meant working in the textile mill where he and my mother worked. I do not recall a single word of praise, encouragement, or approval from him.

John's anger at my mother went a step further. I clearly recall the day when I saw him with his hands around her throat. I threw my full body weight against him to knock him away from my mother, and I let him know very clearly and forcefully that I would defend my mother no matter what I had to do to him. And when he held a knife in a way that threatened me, my mother came to *my* defense. She let him know that if he ever harmed me in any way, he'd have to go through her first. Can you begin to imagine the tension in the house from the day John walked in until the day I walked out to attend college?

As difficult as living with an angry stepfather may be, it is even more difficult to be married to an angry person or to have an angry child. When a person's home is not a haven of peace, there are few places where he or she can find contentment and feel safe.

I know a man who lived with an angry wife for more than two decades. Nothing this man did or said seemed to appease her, although he asked repeatedly what he could do to help make her less angry. She had no answer, and he eventually concluded that she wasn't really angry with him but was likely angry with herself or with God. However, that didn't make life any easier.

This man repeatedly shared about his unhappiness with his marriage. He said, "I dread going home. When I touch the doorknob to enter our house, I pray for strength. I never know what mood my wife will be in. I can almost guarantee that before the evening is over, I will have said or done something that will trigger a major outburst. Her temper will flare, she'll raise her voice and slam doors, and I will be left alone in the living room trying to figure out exactly what happened and why."

The truth is, there's little rationale behind most angry outbursts. No predictable pattern reveals what triggers the anger, so there's no way to avoid it.

A person once said to me, "I decided the best way to keep my spouse from being angry was to do anything and everything he said as quickly and quietly as I could."

I asked, "Did your total-compliance policy work?"

"Almost," she said.

"What does that mean?" I asked.

She explained, "We went for months without any sarcastic angry tirades. Then suddenly, one day, my husband seemed to explode. And you won't believe what he said to me."

"What?" I asked, almost afraid to hear.

"He said, 'I'm sick and tired of your walking on eggshells around me and doing anything you can to please me! I'm sick and tired of your doing whatever I ask you to do without ever questioning or arguing with me.' I don't mind telling you, Dr. Stanley, I was stunned at what he said *and* how he said it. I had never heard so much anger in his voice."

"I would have been stunned too," I said.

She continued, "He agreed to seek counseling shortly after that outburst. And as I heard him tell the counselor about this episode, I suddenly realized that my husband actually enjoyed arguing. He saw it as a sign of a healthy relationship. His family frequently engaged in heated debates. My family, on the other hand, rarely had disagreements about anything. We had very different communication styles."

I asked her, "Did the arguments in your husband's family produce clear-cut winners and losers?"

She replied, "That's exactly what the counselor asked. The simple answer is no. My husband's family just enjoyed venting opinions. They liked to boss one another around and goad each other. But nobody really changed any behavior. They just shouted like two teams playing a game. And when it was over, everyone went out for pizza together."

It took more than a year of counseling for this couple to realize that they needed to come up with a mutually acceptable form of communication. The husband had to learn to value his wife's reluctance to argue, and she needed to accept the fact that her husband didn't always mean what he said. She admitted to me later that the effort they made to communicate better was hard work on her part and less than satisfying on his part. But they did manage to make a go of their marriage with fewer angry outbursts. They did so primarily for the sake of their children.

Countless people might respond to an unhappy marital situation by saying, "You need to see a counselor." As much as I believe in the value of solid counseling from a genuine Christian who has the best interests of his clients at heart, not every marriage problem can be solved through counseling. Many of the struggles that husbands and wives encounter are deeply rooted in one of the marriage partners. Unless—and until—those personal problems are addressed and resolved, genuine peace and harmony in their relationship is unlikely.

If you are in an unhappy marriage, I certainly advise you to explore your situation with a Christian counselor to get the help you both may need. Should your counselor recommend individual counseling for your spouse before you go as a couple, you must understand that you cannot insist he or she go. You can recommend it, but you can't put pressure on your spouse. People benefit from counseling only to the degree that they recognize a change is necessary. A person must want personal and marital healing *and* be willing to do what it takes to be healed. Even if your spouse will not agree to seek advice about managing his or her anger, you may find that personal counseling helps you learn how to cope with your angry spouse.

The best counseling is premarital counseling. Did my mother know John was such an angry man when she married him? I don't think so. In fact, I know she asked John's family about his character before becoming his wife. They either didn't know about his anger problem or didn't bother to share that information with my mother. Perhaps they thought she could help him.

Let me assure you that I do not believe an angry person can be turned into a peaceful one solely through the help of another human being. Removing anger from the human heart is a spiritual process that must involve God's direct intervention. But you can learn the signs of an angry person whom you need to avoid in the first place.

AVOIDING AN ANGER-FILLED RELATIONSHIP

Not only are you wise to avoid marrying an angry person, but you also need to avoid friendships and business relationships with those who cannot control their anger. The Bible very clearly teaches that we are *not* to be in close relationship with certain types of people, including

- *A gossip.* The apostle Peter added "troublesome meddler" to a list that includes murderer, thief, and evildoer (1 Peter 4:15). A gossip can destroy a person's reputation. Having a gossip talk about you behind your back can easily stir up your anger. A gossip is always disloyal and seeks to hurt someone else in hopes of building up himself or gaining the favor of a third party. God's Word says, "He who goes about as a slanderer reveals secrets, therefore do not associate with a gossip" (Proverbs 20:19). The Bible also says, "A perverse man spreads strife, and a slanderer separates intimate friends" (Proverbs 16:28).

- *A quick-tempered person.* The perpetually angry person eventually will cause you to be the same way—and that anger will be a stumbling block to you. It will keep you from seeing good in others, from quickly and freely forgiving others, and from offering the "fruit of the Spirit" (love, joy, peace, patience, kindness, goodness, faithfulness, gentleness, and self-control) to others (Galatians 5:22–23). Proverbs 22 tells us, "Do not associate with a man given to anger, or go with a hot-tempered man, or you will learn his ways and find a snare for yourself" (verses 24–25). This is also a warning not to be or act that way ourselves.

- *A rebellious person.* Rebellion is not only anger at God; it is a quiet, willful resistance that manifests itself as discontentment or disloyalty against those in authority. The rebellious person chooses not to obey and is pulled in various directions by his own lusts and desires. He is not committed to God, nor is he likely to be committed to any person in leadership. A person who is loyal only to himself cannot be counted on to be loyal to a friend. The first chapter of Isaiah clearly explains the blessings of obedience and the consequences of rebellion: "If you consent and obey you will eat the best of the land; but if you refuse and rebel, you will be devoured by the sword" (verses 19–20).

- *A self-indulgent person.* Self-indulgence may manifest as gluttony (consistent overindulgence in food and drink), immoral behavior (actions taken to satisfy fleshly and lustful desires), or greed (relentless desire for more and more wealth and possessions). The self-indulgent person may be power-hungry or manipulative. He is always seeking what he wants when he wants it with little or no regard for the needs and concerns of others. If you form a friendship or work relationship with such a person, he or she will attempt to consume your time, your resources, your energy, and if possible, the time, resources, and energy of those around you. God's Word warns: "He who keeps the law is a discerning son, but he who is a companion of gluttons humiliates his father" (Proverbs 28:7).

- *A sexually immoral person.* The Bible is very clear on the issue of sexual immorality. No one is to engage in premarital or extramarital sex. There are no exceptions. Sexual intimacy is reserved for marriage alone. This stance is 180 degrees in opposition to our culture. Movies, music, television programs, and the Internet are full of sexual content—from innuendo passed off as humor to outright immoral behavior. Advertising on everything from billboards to magazines constantly and unashamedly uses sex to sell products. This constant bombardment has led to an epidemic of unplanned pregnancies, which can lead to abortion and unloved children, and sexually transmitted diseases, which can result in persistent, recurring illness and even death.

  The Bible clearly shows us the path to purity and righteousness and teaches us how to walk in it. Either we're moving toward fulfillment of our fleshly desires without regard to God's wisdom, or we are moving toward His will, plan, and purpose. The easy way is the way of the world. The disciplined, obedient way is the way of the Spirit.

  If you are friends with a sexually immoral person, you will eventually begin to compromise your own values and standards. The compromise may be subtle at first—perhaps a change in the way you dress, the words you use, the jokes you tell, or the things you watch and listen to on TV and radio. Don't start down that slippery slope.

- *A fool.* We tend to think of fools as silly or frivolous people. But the Bible takes a much more serious approach. Twice the psalmist calls fools "corrupt" and says "there is no one who does good" (Psalms 14:1, 53:1). Fools arrogantly choose their own way over God's. They push Him out of their lives and refuse any and all direction, discernment, or wisdom offered in His Word.

  The book of Proverbs describes fools as unwise, unteachable, lacking honor, slanderous, lacking self-control, deceitful, mocking sin, arrogant, careless, undisciplined, and ill-tempered (1:7; 24:7; 3:35; 26:1; 10:18; 12:16; 14:8; 26:1; 14:9, 16; 15:5; 16:22; 29:11). Such people are incapable of truly developing the bonds of genuine friendship or marriage. It is impossible to form or maintain a good, mutually beneficial relationship with a person demonstrating any of the above character flaws.

It is natural to feel some degree of anger toward a person who slanders, gossips about, manipulates, uses, or lies to us. Being in relationship with any of the six types of people listed above can be a more subtle snare, leading you to become angry with yourself for getting involved with him or her.

CONSEQUENCES OF ANGER-FILLED RELATIONSHIPS

Most of us know and enjoy the benefits of healthy relationships. However, becoming involved with a constantly angry person can have strong negative consequences. An angry and emotionally troubled relationship with a spouse, child, friend, or coworker can:

- *Disappoint you.* One morning, you may awaken to find that your angry friend or spouse has walked out. A number of years ago, I was close friends with a person who suddenly, and without any explanation, withdrew from our relationship. To this day, I do not know why this happened. He never offered an explanation, and I remain disappointed to this day.

- *Distress you.* You may feel deep concern, knowing that your friend is making unwise choices or is rebelling against God.

- *Drag you down.* You may find that you are increasingly fighting feelings of inadequacy, fear, depression, frustration, or discouragement.

- *Destroy you.* An unwise anger-filled relationship can draw you away from Christ. It can damage your physical and emotional health, your career, and other relationships that are supportive and valuable.

In each of these cases, it is easy for a person to feel twinges of anger in the midst of constant doubts and questions: *Why is he/she acting this way? What went wrong? What can I do? What should I do? How did this happen?*

The anger you feel may not totally be directed toward the other person. As I have indicated previously, you could be mad at yourself. It takes two people to establish a relationship. But very often, it takes only one person's anger or emotional troubles to end it. Don't blame yourself entirely for the failure of the relationship. But do explore what went wrong so you might learn from the experience. And, when possible, attempt to reconcile or rebuild relationships that you consider vital to your life and family.

If your relationship with an angry person is producing any of the four results above, it's time to reevaluate. Reflect upon *why* you've chosen to remain in the relationship. Ask yourself what you hope to gain by sustaining it. Are you emotionally dependent on the angry person, or have you allowed him or her to become emotionally dependent on you? Are you being forced to stay in the relationship through emotional or even physical abuse from the person? If you've struggled with these feelings for a number of years, it's easy to fall into a mutual pattern of anger, bitterness, or depression and to stay there.

The health of your adult relationships is very often directly related to the health of your family during your childhood. If, while growing up, your family life was marred by poor communication, power struggles between your parents or siblings, angry outbursts, fear, or withholding of affection, you likely will be prone to develop adult relationships that exhibit the same patterns.

There are no perfect friendships or relationships, because there are no perfect people. There are, however, mature, godly, mutually rewarding and satisfying marriages, friendships, and working relationships. These tend to be ones in which both parties are seeking to become mature, godly, wise, and supportive individuals. In choosing relationships, ask God to bring people into your life who aspire to live by the same values that you do.

HOW TO TELL IF ANGER IS DAMAGING A RELATIONSHIP

Periodically evaluate your relationships—especially the ones with people you know have anger issues, including an angry spouse. You can tell if the relationship is becoming impaired or harmed if

- You stop spending time together.

- You stop talking to each other.

- You become reluctant to share your joys and sorrows—you stop laughing and crying together.

- You no longer say thank you or do other thoughtful things for each other.

- You lose your warmth, affection, or appreciation for each other.

- You become increasingly critical of each other—less tolerant of each other's errors, less appreciative of each other's efforts, and less accepting of each other's weaknesses.

- You build a wall and no longer share your life freely with each other—one or both of you holds things back and conceals motives, feelings, and thoughts.

- You are not honest with each other about what either of you may be doing, thinking, or feeling.

- You stop trusting each other.

IDENTIFY WHAT IS STOPPING
THE FLOW OF LOVE

One of the root causes of anger between two people can be placed under an umbrella labeled "lost love." We tend to be disappointed if we believe a loving relationship is deteriorating beyond our control or that we are being rejected unfairly or without warning. But we also tend to become angry at the person for not holding up his or her end of the love relationship.

Consider these five possible attitudes and behaviors that can stop the flow of love between two people, result in anger, and steal their peace.

Selfishness

When a person begins to focus on self rather than considering the other person, the relationship begins to suffer. Selfishness often manifests itself as busyness. When someone becomes extremely preoccupied with what she is doing, becomes singularly intent on reaching her personal goals, or becomes focused solely on what she wants to do and where she wants to go, the other person in that relationship is going to feel neglected. If the other person senses that his needs, wants, or desires no longer matter in the marriage or friendship, the hurt person may walk away.

Manipulation

If one person begins to control the other, the relationship will develop cracks that can damage or destroy it. Manipulation takes many forms—including verbal taunts or abuse, playing mind games, withholding what is promised or needed, and making threats in order to control behavior. With manipulation, one person becomes "master" and the other becomes "slave." The relationship is no longer marked by shared concerns and goals, but rather, becomes a dictatorship. When that occurs, love cannot flow freely between two people.

Jealousy or Covetousness

When someone becomes so jealous that he or she refuses to allow the other person to spend time with friends or family members, the relationship begins to disintegrate.

Jealousy is holding on to something that you believe is rightfully yours—in a marriage, *someone* who is rightfully yours. The issue with jealousy is the degree to which one person holds on to the other. In any healthy relationship, each person needs the freedom to form and voice personal opinions, to pursue and develop God-given talents, and to create and strengthen other godly relationships. Husbands should have like-minded and supportive male friends; wives should have like-minded and supportive female friends.

Envy or covetousness differs from jealousy in that it is the desire for something that rightfully belongs to someone else. Envy is to want what another person has or is. It may be a physical trait such as beauty or strength, a possession, a talent, a spiritual gift, an ability or skill, a relationship, or any number of other things. A person may covet another's reputation, fame, or position of authority. It is impossible to sustain a healthy relationship with someone who wants what you have or desires to be who you are. Friendship and marriage both require mutual respect and admiration for what the other person has, does, and is.

Constant Criticism

When one person constantly disapproves of the way the other person looks, talks, or acts; continually disagrees with the other's choices and decisions; or consistently degrades someone else's value or worthiness, the relationship begins to come apart at the seams. Certainly a constructive, helpful suggestion from time to time is warranted between friends, spouses, and coworkers. But nonstop criticism about another person's perceived faults, failures, or mistakes is deadly to a relationship.

Inappropriate Sexual Intimacy

Friendship and marriage are two entirely different relationships when it comes to sexual intimacy. The lines have become blurred in our society, but God's Word is clear—sex outside of marriage is sin.

Sexual intimacy has no place in friendship. It is something our Creator reserved solely for a husband and wife. Certainly a friendship can grow to the point where romance blossoms and marriage results. But even then, sexual intimacy needs to be reserved for *after* the "I dos."

When sex is introduced into a friendship, the nature of that relationship automatically changes. Sexual intimacy does not add to a friendship. Nothing that is contrary to God's commandments can build up a relationship.

CONSIDER THE NATURE OF THE RELATIONSHIP

A key question to ask yourself if you experience ongoing, near-constant conflict with another person is *What is the nature of the relationship?*

Relationships tend to come in three varieties.

For-a-Reason Relationships

God may send a person into your life for a specific reason. Perhaps you are called to meet a need in his life, or he's called to meet a need in yours. Some relationships seem designed specifically to help us through a difficulty, to provide guidance and support for a God-appointed task, or to help us physically, materially, emotionally, or spiritually. In turn, the Lord may lead you into a relationship to help another person through a difficult time, to provide support or guidance, or to help that person in a physical, material, emotional, or spiritual way.

Sometimes, through no fault of either person, the relationship comes to an end in a peaceful, agreeable way. Perhaps one person dies or moves away. Maybe the purposes for the relationship are accomplished, and encounters between the two people become less frequent. The work is done, the prayer is answered, or the need is met. Whatever the reason, God decides the time has come for both people to move on.

For-a-Season Relationships

At times God sends people into our lives for a season—usually for mutual sharing, growth, and learning. The season may be defined by external circumstances. For example, you may be assigned a roommate in a college dorm, or you may meet a person whose child is on your daughter's sports team or in your son's preschool class.

Seasonal relationships usually bring mutual peace, comfort, and companionship. The relationship is real, and it is valuable. But it lasts only for a set period of time. There is usually sadness when a seasonal relationship ends because the ties are deep and strong. Still, seasons change, and so do our life experiences. Children graduate, families move, companies go out of business, and people retire.

Lifetime Relationships

Other relationships are intended for a lifetime. These relationships help teach us lifelong lessons about commitment, friendship, loyalty, and love. A lifetime relationship touches the deepest feelings and the deepest beliefs in a person. A lifelong friend has the historical context of your relationship against which to weigh your behavior and give advice. He or she also has a deep understanding of who you are as a person. A lifelong friend should help give you a glimpse into your purpose on this earth from a godly perspective.

We are wise to cherish and value each of these types of relationships. We should not minimize the worth or impact of a friend who is in our life for only a reason or a season. Every relationship deserves our best effort and our highest expressions of care, kindness, and love.

If you are planning to make a commitment to a friend, be certain that you both understand what that truly means. I'm not referring only to the commitment between a husband and wife, although that is certainly needed in every marriage. I encourage you not to promise to be another person's friend for a lifetime if you can see that the relationship is likely to be only for a reason or a season. Do not make a long-term commitment in business, counseling, or caregiving if you suspect that the person may be in your life for a limited time or in limited ways.

MAKING THE DECISION TO STAY OR WALK AWAY

Not every relationship can be salvaged or repaired if emotional pain and anger have occurred continually over an extended period of time. Intense circumstances also can make reconciliation difficult. The apostle Paul knew this when he wrote, "If possible, so far as it depends on you, be at peace with all men" (Romans 12:18). The truth is, sadly, that it is not always possible to be at peace with everyone. You may feel at peace toward someone and still lose the relationship because that person is not at peace or is unwilling to reconcile with you.

And there are times when we must walk away from a relationship. Perhaps the other person is walking on a path of outright rebellion against God. Maybe he or she has threatened to hurt you, become abusive to you, or put your relationship on unhealthy or sinful ground. God *will* step in at times and say, *No more.*

When that is not the case, we should do our best to restore or reestablish a broken relationship. We need to seek the Lord for direction about how to rebuild it to a point of strength and happiness.

If God is telling you not to restore a damaged relationship, do your best to end it in peace. If you agree to withdraw from each other, you may be able to simply let the matter lie. But if one person wants to sustain and repair the relationship and the other does not, you are going to find yourself in conflict. You most likely will be uncomfortable in the other person's presence unless and until you find a way of resolving the situation. I encourage you to invite God to bring you both to a place of forgiveness and peace. Do not delay in this. The longer you wait to bring the relationship to a resolution, the stronger the pain one or both of you is likely to experience.

If two people truly want to heal a broken relationship, take heart. Almost any damaged friendship can be repaired if both those involved are committed to healing it. Restoring the relationship will take an intentional, dedicated effort with lots of patience and clear communication. But, through prayer and persistence, it *is* possible.

FIVE STEPS TO HEALING A DAMAGED RELATIONSHIP

If you are in a relationship that has been damaged by either your anger or another person's, there are four basic steps you must take to heal it.

1. Apologize to each other.

If the relationship is worth saving, each person should be willing to apologize for his or her part in any breakdown, misunderstanding, or outburst. A broken friendship is rarely the result of just one person's words or actions. It takes two to argue! There is nearly always something that each person said or didn't say, did or didn't do, that contributed to feelings of anger, hurt, or bitterness. Genuinely choose to forgive each other for the pain of the damaged relationship.

2. Identify constructive positive steps each person can take.

Deal in specifics. Focus on observable, definitive behaviors that can be readily changed or adjusted in the near future. For example, if you agree that you need to spend more time together, set a date and location. Plan an event or vacation that will result in time spent working on and talking about your relationship.

3. Make a mutual commitment to rebuild.

Agree to work on the relationship. If one person says, "I'm gone, I'm finished," recognize that you cannot force him or her to stay or to have the kind of relationship you desire. You can't make another person love you or be your friend. As in marriage, friendship is a choice—an act of will.

4. Agree to move forward and let the past be the past.

Refuse to harbor blame or resentment. Don't bring up old hurts. Don't let your mind dwell on the frustration, sorrow, discouragement, or disappointment you have felt in the past. Face the future with optimism. Be confident that you will be able to restore your relationship and that bright days lie ahead for you both. Think and act positively. Ask God to heal your relationship and make it stronger than ever.

5. Pray together.

If at all possible, pray together—as often as possible. Ask God

- To show you how to help each other grow spiritually.

- To show you how each person needs to change his or her character, attitudes, and behavior.

- To heal your emotional wounds.

- To reveal how you can become better friends or better spouses.

The good news is that when God is invited to reconcile and heal a relationship broken by anger, abuse, or conflict, He renews it. The Lord doesn't merely restore what was—He makes the relationship better than it ever was!

ADMIT IT—DEAL WITH IT

1. If you are in a relationship with an angry person, how has that affected your love for the person? Your health? Your peace?

2. What might be the root of the person's anger?

3. What strategies have you tried in dealing with the person? Note which ones have been productive and which ones have not helped.

4. Which strategies from this chapter have you been unwilling to try? Why? Are you ready to do whatever God leads you to do to find peace, even if it means breaking off the relationship?

CHAPTER 10

CHARACTER

||||||||||||||||||||||||||||||||||||||||||||||||||||||||||||||||||||||||||||||||||||||||||||||||

Establishing Peace in Yourself and
Training Your Children in Love

Training children to develop godly character is one of the biggest responsibilities a parent has. And one of the best ways to do that is to model such character, bearing witness to the presence of God in their lives.

Character is closely linked with integrity—which the Merriam-Webster dictionary defines as "firm adherence to a code of especially moral or artistic values." Both character and integrity are at the core of a person's reputation. And ultimately, that reputation is the person's lasting legacy.

The New Testament teaches Christians how to develop the character of Jesus Christ. He is our role model, and we are to seek to be like Him in thought, speech, and action. Part of the Holy Spirit's function in our lives is to help us become more and more like Jesus every day we're on earth. The specific traits associated with the character of Christ are described by the apostle Paul in Galatians 5: "The fruit of the Spirit is love, joy, peace, patience, kindness, goodness, faithfulness, gentleness, self-control; against such things there is no law" (verses 22–23).

In these two verses, we find the template for good character! The person who bears these traits will be considered "good" in every culture of every nation on earth. As Paul wrote, no one is going to pass a law against these qualities. Furthermore, few people will disagree with behaviors that are firmly rooted in love, joy, peace, patience, kindness, goodness, faithfulness, gentleness, and self-control. These traits describe the way each of us would like to be treated. They are terms that should be our goals when it comes to character development or character training.

The apostle refers to them as "the fruit of the Spirit." It's what God develops in a person who is seeking to "walk by the Spirit" (Galatians 5:16) and be "led by the Spirit" (verse 18). In other words, if you desire to have a close relationship with the Lord and are trusting the Holy Spirit to lead and guide you daily, this "fruit" will be developed in you and lead you to act more like Jesus. If you are not trusting the Holy Spirit to lead and guide you, then you are going to "carry out the desire of the flesh" (verse 16). Your resulting behavior is likely to include "immorality, impurity, sensuality, idolatry, sorcery, enmities, strife, jealousy, outbursts of anger, disputes, dissensions, factions, envying, drunkenness, carousing, and things like these" (verses 19–22).

Godly character produces godly behavior.

Ungodly character produces ungodly behavior.

It's as simple and straightforward as that.

Obviously, anger is not a good character trait. And the "fleshly deeds" of enmities, strife, disputes, dissensions, and factions all have an element of anger associated with them. Anger starts as a bad attitude that eventually can turn into bad behavior. The combination leads to ungodly character. There's no getting around the fact that anger and good character do *not* go together.

Also, if you are a believer, God will not allow you to harbor anger, resentment, bitterness, or hostility without confronting you about seeking to rid it from your life. If you desire to live a godly life, then the Lord will continually come against the anger in you and convict you about the need to remove it.

Why is God so intent on removing anger from your life?

Because you cannot hold bitterness, resentment, or hostility toward another person and still expect to have a good relationship with God. Jesus said, "If someone says, 'I love God,' and hates his brother, he is a liar; for the one who does not love his brother whom he has seen, cannot love God whom he has not seen" (1 John 4:20).

You cannot be angry and love freely and fully.
You cannot be angry and joyful at the same time.
You cannot have peace when you are angry.
You cannot be patient when you are angry.
Your kindness is not evident when you are angry.
Your goodness is swallowed up by anger.
Your faithfulness suffers when you are angry.
Your gentleness is overshadowed by anger.
Your self-control is undermined by anger.
Anger is an enemy to your walk with God.

TRAINING YOUR CHILD IN PEACEFUL, GODLY BEHAVIOR

The Bible commands parents: "Train up a child in the way he should go, even when he is old he will not depart from it" (Proverbs 22:6).

Training goes beyond teaching. Teaching is the presenting of concepts, rules, and principles. It is the conveying or sharing of information. Teaching is largely a function of telling a person what he or she needs to know.

Training involves the practical application of what's learned through discipline and instruction. It is a matter of giving your child opportunities to witness and display godly behavior over and over. Repeatedly exposing him or her to a life that overflows with the fruit of the Spirit will make your child sensitive and obedient to God's voice.

If you want your child to show love to others, then you must train your child to be loving. To do that, put your son or daughter in situations that provide opportunities for giving, sharing, and caring. Model the appropriate ways to show love, and then praise your child when you see him or her acting in a loving manner.

If you want your child to have peace, then train him or her to be peaceful. How? Give your son or daughter opportunities to be a peace-maker, and teach your child how to resolve conflicts without violence.

Each of the character traits listed as "the fruit of the Spirit" is subject to training opportunities. But it's not the school's responsibility or the church's responsibility to train your children. As a parent, you are responsible for training your sons and daughters to develop godly character. It will take dedication and commitment on the part of Mom and Dad. The church is there to reinforce the parents' training, and your child's school can provide backup support. Just make sure that your church and the children's school have leaders and teachers who—by what they say and how they live—reflect the values you are instilling at home.

As you and your children encounter opportunities to display joyful, kind, good, and gentle behavior, you will be training them, in their thoughts and actions, to be in line with God's desires and standards. Deuteronomy 6 provides invaluable insight regarding why we must train our children to know and obey God's law:

> *Now this is the commandment, the statutes and the judgments which the LORD your God has commanded me to teach you, that you might do them in the land where you are going over to possess it, so that you and your son and your grandson might fear the LORD your God, to keep all His statutes and His commandments which I command you, all the days of your life, and that your days may be prolonged (verses 1–2).*

His commandments are not intended to be learned, tucked away in our memory, and never applied. God's law is meant to be lived out and applied to everyday circumstances and interpersonal relationships.

Obeying His commandments, statutes, and judgments is associated with promises of great blessing throughout the Bible.

God's people were told very clearly that they were to teach these commandments thoroughly and continually: "You shall teach them diligently to your sons and shall talk of them when you sit in your house and when you walk by the way and when you lie down and when you rise up" (Deuteronomy 6:7).

Parents were to teach when the family sat in their homes, when they walked around the community, when the children did their chores, and so on. God's law was to be taught from morning to night.

His people were to teach their children the ways in which the Lord had led and blessed them in days past and how to trust Him for provision and protection in the future. Above all, they were to teach their children to worship the one true, living God and to worship Him only.

THE BEST LEARNING PROGRAM

When you are continually following God's law, habits are established that actually become both your attitude and your motivation. In the end, doing what you know is right in His eyes will form who you are. Godly habits become godly character.

Now, what does this have to do with anger?

It is your responsibility to develop a godly character that eliminates anger as a habitual response to the challenges, trials, and difficulties of life. And it is also your responsibility to teach your children why it is right to demonstrate godly character traits and *not* right to display anger and other ungodly behaviors. They must know God's truth about anger and about the Lord's desire for His people to live in peace. Even as you teach God's commandments and principles, you must present opportunities for your children to settle arguments, resolve differences, make decisions, and state their opinions and desires without anger. This is the best way to train a child.

RELIANCE UPON THE HOLY SPIRIT

The apostle Paul stated clearly in Galatians 5 that you must want the Holy Spirit to lead and guide you in order to develop godly character—what he called "the fruit of the Spirit." This is perhaps the best way you can train your child.

Continually, consistently, and thoroughly encourage your son or daughter to trust God and leave all the consequences to Him. They will need His guidance throughout their entire lives. Children can begin to learn this from the time they understand the difference between right from wrong.

Let your children know that one day they will be totally responsible for their own lives. We all are accountable to God for what we say and do. Train your children to accept responsibility for their thoughts, beliefs, and actions—along with their personal relationship with Jesus Christ.

Pray with your children for God's help and His guidance.

Let your children hear you pray and express your reliance upon the Holy Spirit for daily direction. Let them hear you talk to God as you ask Him for specific guidance to resolve specific problems and to meet specific needs.

PROTECTING YOUR CHILDREN
FROM ANGER AND VIOLENCE

Good parents must be the enemies of anyone who seeks to harm their child. If your son's or daughter's school is an unsafe place for him or her, you must act to protect your child. If your child is being bullied, it is your job to be his or her defender and to make sure the bully is punished and removed from his or her life. If your child is being abused, it is your job to make sure he or she is moved to a place of safety and the abuser is apprehended and punished.

Part of protecting your children means shielding them from experiencing anger and violence. This includes controlling what they see and hear in your home. You need to closely monitor the messages you, your spouse, and other family members are sending. And be careful to limit and monitor your children's exposure to television, radio, the Internet, and other media.

MODELING GODLY CHARACTER

The primary way children learn is by copying the behavior of their parents. If you are angry, you are modeling anger for your children. So it should come as no surprise that your son or daughter displays anger the same way you do.

Your children are watching you, listening to you, overhearing you, trying you, and testing you at all times. That's part of the growth and development process. Your anger not only impacts those who *hear* you but also those who *overhear* you. Whether it's your child in another room or a coworker at the desk next to yours, those who overhear you most likely have no involvement in the issue that has made you angry.

When children see their parents argue, a feeling of confusion and insecurity sets in. They don't know which parent is right or whose side they should take. Children will question their parents' love for each other, and out of that, they may question their parents' love for them.

Your child is studying you constantly—learning about treating others, resolving conflicts, overcoming temptation, and forgiveness. You are your child's living textbook for how to pray, how to find answers in God's Word, and how to live by faith. You are your son's or daughter's number one teacher when it comes to all matters pertaining to character. It is from you that your child learns about love, joy, peace, patience, kindness, goodness, faithfulness, gentleness, and self-control.

My mother was a wonderful example of such a role model. She did not have a tremendous knowledge of the Bible, but she insisted that I read the Bible and attend church with her. We prayed together every night until I went to college. Whenever I came home from school, we would pray then too. And if my mother did not have an answer for a problem I had, she and I explored the Bible's answer together. On countless occasions we went to the little concordance in the back of her Bible to find a topic. Then we would look up the verses listed to get God's solution.

My mother's main message to me was "Charles, obey God." Those three words were drilled into me. They echo in my heart and mind to this day. She trained me to follow God. She trained me to show love and respect to others. She trained me in how to be a faithful person who knows true joy and peace.

Above all, my mother modeled love to me. I had absolutely no doubt that Mother loved me every day of my life. A child who grows up knowing he is loved is a young person who knows confidence and security. That child not only knows what love feels like, but he understands how to share it sincerely and deeply.

A child who does not have the unconditional, abiding love of a parent is a child who feels frustrated and anxious and is prone to anger.

We see reports frequently about children who are starving physically. Let me assure you, there are millions of children in our world today who are well fed but are starving emotionally and spiritually. They do not know what it means to be loved unconditionally by their parents, nor do they know that God loves them with unconditional love.

HALLMARKS OF A LOVING PARENT

How do children learn they are loved? Let me share ten ways to be a loving parent.

- *Spend quality time.* Loving parents give their child quality time—which usually includes a significant quantity of time. But make no mistake. These two concepts are not the same thing. Three hours spent *watching* your kids at the playground will not have the same lasting, positive effects as spending thirty minutes *playing* with them there. A child needs the security of knowing that his parents are available to him and ready to help whenever he needs it.

- *Lend a listening ear.* A loving parent listens to a child carefully. When my children were young, I made it a point to stop what I was doing and listen to them with singular focus. I knew that if I wanted Andy and Becky to listen to me when I had something important to say to them, I needed to listen to them when they had something to say to me.

- *Admit when you are wrong.* No parent is right all the time. A loving, godly parent admits when he is wrong and lets his children hear his confession. There's no better way to model the accessibility of God's love and forgiveness to a child than by admitting faults and failures. Doing so gives your child permission to admit his or hers too.

- *Ask for forgiveness.* If you are wrong and admit it, you also may need to ask your child to forgive you. When necessary, let your son or daughter hear you ask for forgiveness from them and from God.

- *Discipline your child with a motive of protection.* A loving parent does not discipline out of anger. Correction and punishment must stem from a genuine desire to protect the child and to help him or her understand what is beneficial, acceptable, and helpful in life and what isn't.

- *Encourage your child to pursue excellence.* The loving parent wants the best for his child. I instilled in my children: "Look your best. Do your best. Be your best." If they heard me say that once, they heard it ten thousand times. Encouraging your child in this way sends two unspoken messages. The first is "I believe you can achieve great things." The second, "You are worthy of God's best—not just some of the time but all the time."

- *Lead your children to accept responsibility for their walk with God.* As a child grows and develops, he needs to be taught that he is responsible to God. Don't tie your son or daughter to your apron strings when it comes to accountability. A child needs to learn that God requires certain things of him and that ultimately, he is accountable to Him for his choices, decisions, and behavior.

Very often when my children came to me with a problem or decision, I said to them, "Go talk to God about that." This is risky, to a degree. If you have not taught your child the truth of His Word or you have not trained him to pray, then he may not be able to receive or understand God's guidance. I made it a point to teach my children the truth of the Bible and to train them in praying and listening to their heavenly Father.

There are times when my children came back to me, saying, "Dad, you decide."

I'd respond, "What did God say?" They didn't want to tell me. It was obvious what had happened. The Lord had said no and they didn't want that answer. They wanted me to say yes so they could have my permission instead of God's. I wasn't about to fall for that. I'd simply say, "Go talk to God about it again."

- Make your child's relationship with God the most important relationship in your child's life. All parents want the love and devotion of their children. But mothers and fathers must always regard their son's or daughter's relationship with God as the most important relationship that he or she can ever develop. Your children will learn this as you show them that the most important relationship you have is the one with your loving heavenly Father. Your closeness with God is not a threat to your child. Rather, it is a point of security. Your son or daughter will understand that if God and Dad, or God and Mom, are in close relationship, then the Lord will influence the parents to always do what's best for the child.

- Spend time daily in God's Word and in prayer. Encourage your child to read God's Word every day. Buy a version of the Bible your child can read and understand. Let your son or daughter see you reading Scripture and overhear your conversations with God. Encourage your child to pray—both in your presence and alone. You do not need to have a formal Bible study in your family, or a set time for prayer, but you can certainly do that if you feel the Lord is directing you that way. In modeling prayer and Scripture reading for your child, you are showing him or her how you receive guidance in your life. You will be giving your child a compass he or she can trust for the future. And that is an extremely loving and valuable thing to give a child.

- *Encourage your child to discover God's plan.* God has a will, plan, and purpose for every child (see Jeremiah 29:11). It doesn't matter whether the parent "wanted" a child. God "wants" every child who is conceived. Every child is born with a built-in set of talents, skills, abilities, and gifts. God has a job for your child to do, a way for her to serve others, and a way for her to invest her time and spiritual gifts to bring glory to Him. Help your child discover the Master's plan.

  Do not call upon your child to fulfill your unrealized dreams, and do not force him to follow a plan you set before him. Yes, children must be responsible to obey their parents (see Ephesians 6:1). But in that same passage of Scripture, moms and dads are commanded, "Do not provoke your children to anger; but bring them up in the discipline and instruction of the Lord" (6:4). Your goal for your child should be for him to set his own goals according to God's will, plan, and purpose for his life.

As part of helping your child discover her part in the Lord's great plan, encourage her to pursue God wholeheartedly with total trust in Him for help, direction, and guidance. Teach your child to obey God and leave all the consequences to Him. You can start saying this to your child even before she can talk. Train your sons and daughters to obey and trust their heavenly Father, and they will thank you forever.

THE LINK BETWEEN CHARACTER AND ANGER

How does all this advice and teaching relate to the issue of anger and character development?

No child will ever be persistently or deeply angry at a parent who does the ten things listed above with consistency and genuine love. Have you ever heard of a son or daughter being angry at Mom or Dad for giving quality time, for encouraging him or her to trust God, or for listening closely and carefully? I haven't.

On the other hand, I've heard about many children who are extremely angry at their parents for not giving them enough time, not encouraging them to trust God, and not listening to them.

A child who grows up in a home where the parents display love in these ten ways is going to be fully equipped to cope with life's challenges. The son or daughter who is shown love in these important ways will feel very little frustration or anger. He or she will experience very little bitterness or resentment toward people in the world outside the home. When difficult times arise, the child is going to have a depth of character that will enable him or her to face the problems or crises. He or she will also have an inner strength and courage to take on problems and find solutions.

Finally, the child who is shown love in these ten vital ways is going to be an outstanding role model for parenting. He or she will find it easy to develop a close relationship with God and is going to display good character in the best ways possible.

ADMIT IT—DEAL WITH IT

1. What issues are impeding your own character development?

2. Write down one thing you can do right now to improve your own character, and then do it.

3. In what way might you better model godly character to a child you love—as either a parent, family member, teacher, coach, or friend? Take steps to do it.

4. What one thing can you do to express love to your child in a better, clearer way? Then take steps to share that love.

5. If you need to apologize to your child or ask his or her forgiveness for something, do it today!

CHAPTER 11

CONFLICT

*Confronting Conflict
in a Godly Manner*

Jesus taught His followers to settle their disputes before they went to the temple to make their offerings or sacrifices. The pattern was not "get right with God and then get right with other people." Jesus wants us to get things right with others before we even think about going to the Father about a situation. In teaching this, Christ was acknowledging, in part, that conflicts do exist. Indeed, they are unavoidable in life.

All of us would like to live in a totally conflict-free world. Even people who say they love vigorous debate or enjoy spirited competition will say that at the end of the day—or perhaps at the end of all their days—they want peace. A world without criticism, differences of opinion, or heated arguments would be a paradise to many. But I assure you, such a world is not going to be established this side of heaven.

THE TRUTH ABOUT CONFLICT

I have identified six universal truths that will help you identify and deal with conflict.

1. Conflict Can Be a Learning Opportunity

God never promises anyone a life free of conflict. But He encourages us to learn how to respond to it in a godly way. Jesus said in Mark 9:50, "Be at peace with one another."

2. Conflict Is Not Inevitable

Even though conflict cannot be fully avoided, it also is not inevitable. Competition between two people can often result in conflict, but that doesn't always have to be the case.

In the early days of our nation, two giants of the faith, John Wesley and George Whitefield, led major revival movements that resulted in thousands of people accepting Jesus Christ as their Savior. These two men disagreed doctrinally and really didn't like each other. But they refused to engage in personal attacks or public disagreements.

One day a man asked John Wesley if he thought he would see George Whitefield in heaven. Wesley replied, "No, I do not." The man asked, "Are you telling me that you don't believe George Whitefield is a converted man?"

Wesley replied, "I do not believe that I will see him in heaven because he will be so close to the throne and I will be so far away that I may never see him."

Two New Testament saints were also in conflict at times. In the second chapter of Galatians, Paul writes about how he opposed Peter "to his face" for refusing to associate with Gentile converts in the presence of his fellow Jews (verses 11–12). Cephas, as Paul refers to him in the text, was afraid the Jews in Antioch would reject him if he was seen eating with Gentiles. Paul rebuked Peter's hypocrisy "in the presence of all" (verse 14), saying that as believers in Christ, we are no longer bound to Jewish laws, customs, or traditions:

For through the Law I died to the Law, that I might live to God. I have been crucified with Christ; and it is no longer I who live, but Christ lives in me; and the life which I now live in the flesh I live by faith in the Son of

God, who loved me, and delivered Himself up for me. I do not nullify the grace of God; for if righteousness comes through the Law, then Christ died needlessly (verses 19–21).

This confrontation was necessary because Peter's conduct led the church into error. But there is no evidence that he was angry at what Paul said. By accepting the rebuke and not replying to it, Peter avoided conflict.

3. Some Conflict May Merely Be Different Interpretations

Conflict often arises because two people hold different interpretations of what is right. In those instances, believers must immediately go to the Bible. Read it with an eye toward the most direct and simple interpretation possible. If God's Word says "don't," then don't. If Scripture says "do," then do.

Christians can have healthy disagreements about how to interpret various biblical passages. Some of the longest and most interesting debates I had in college involved end-times prophecy and the assurance of eternal life.

Sometimes people have different interpretations about how a Christian should live, who is qualified for leadership in the church, or what's right in another person's life, career, or relationship.

A number of years ago I was harshly criticized publicly by the leader of a prominent ministry. His comments about my personal life were very hurtful to me, and I struggled with some angry feelings because I felt there were certain things he should have done:

- He should have behaved differently toward me.

- He should not have said what he said—and certainly not on a public broadcast.

- He should have checked his facts and drawn different conclusions about my personal life.

- He should have kept his opinions to himself.

- And, most important, he should have come to me first with his criticism before going public.

I called this man to let him know how he had hurt me with his comments, and I quickly realized from our conversation that he didn't know the facts about my situation. He had drawn conclusions that were unfounded. When I asked him why he didn't come to me to say he felt offended, he had no answer. Also, he expressed no regret whatsoever for the pain he caused me personally and professionally. I hung up the phone disappointed and, frankly, a little stunned. I knew that if I did not deal with my feelings immediately, I could become even angrier and perhaps more bitter toward him.

I made a conscious decision not to retaliate. I would not make any attempt to justify myself. I would not publicly point out his error or even tell others he had made an error. In fact, I decided that I would refuse to tell who he was, what precisely he said, or discuss the situation that prompted his criticism. I have stayed true to those decisions for many years.

I went to God and said, "I release this man from my concern. He is now Your concern! I trust You to deal with him in whatever way You choose." In making that statement, I let go of the anger, frustration, and hurt I felt. Even as I share this incident in hopes that it will help you, I feel no anger toward him.

4. Not All Conflict Is Willful

Conflict sometimes arises through simple neglect or an innocent mistake. Not all disagreements and differences are rooted in intentional behavior.

5. Some Conflict Can Produce Good

As people discuss the reasons for their conflict, more understanding and appreciation for each other can develop. New creative approaches and processes can be identified as people share different perspectives and ideas. The Bible says, "As iron sharpens iron, so one man sharpens another" (Proverbs 27:17). When two pieces of iron rub against each other, it makes both of them sharper. In the same way, an honest, friendly debate or discussion makes everyone involved more knowledgeable and better informed. Friends, family members, and coworkers can challenge you to grow in faith, be bolder in your witness, and pursue a greater degree of excellence. And you can do the same for them. Conflict can produce positive results—without anger.

6. Some Conflict Arises from Poor Communication

Conflict is often rooted in a failure to communicate. When I really want to make sure that I've been heard correctly, I will ask the person, "What did you hear me say? What do you think I meant?" Very often, the person will say something back to me that is not exactly what I said or meant. I have found that it's far better to clear up any miscommunication or misinformation immediately, so that people do not form incorrect conclusions and opinions.

If you have any doubt about what you think another person meant by what he said, get clarification right away. It's possible you may not have heard him correctly. Sometimes miscommunication occurs as a result of a hearing problem or noise that disrupts the conversation. Language, cultural, and generational barriers are additional threats to clear communication. You simply may not have the same definition for a word or phrase that the person you're talking to has. If you don't know or understand what someone said or meant, simply ask him or her, "How do you define that?" or "What does that word mean to you?" This type of miscommunication occurs frequently between people from different countries or if the language one person is speaking is not his or her mother tongue. It also happens when people use technical terms or words that are unique to their experience, education, or career.

Another barrier to clear and accurate communication is a lack of information and/or context. You may not have heard everything you need to in order to draw an accurate conclusion. Not long ago, I heard about a woman who described how a particularly harmful rumor began circulating in her workplace. She said, "I was sitting at lunch with a group of women, telling them about a friend of mine. She and her husband had gone on vacation to a spa resort. I said, 'They both came home saying it was their last resort.'

"A woman at the next table heard only that last sentence. She assumed that the person I was talking about—who was someone she knew—had a major fight with her husband and their marriage was on the rocks. She began to spread the rumor that this woman could be headed for divorce.

"But if she had waited to hear my next sentence, that rumor would not have started. I went on to tell the women at my table, 'They called it their last resort because it was so wonderful, they said they'll never need to try another one. They liked it so much that they hope to go back twice a year for the rest of their lives.'"

Make sure you heard something correctly, in full context, and that you truly know what was meant by what was said.

Finally, make sure that you aren't extending a person's comments to cover all of life, all the time. Keep a person's comments in their proper perspective. Consider the circumstance and setting in which they were made and draw your conclusions accordingly. If someone says to you, "Did you hear what I said?" don't assume automatically that the person is saying, "You never listen to anything I say" or "You never pay attention." The person simply may be saying, "I'm not sure I spoke loudly or clearly enough for you to have heard me correctly." We run into problems when we take one comment and assume it's a definitive opinion or statement for all time.

On the other hand, even if you're seeking clarification for a hurtful comment, don't feel the need to push that issue in each and every instance of communication. Some statements are likely to be ones you are wise to let slide right on by. Wait until you see a clear pattern of repeated negative statements before you stop ignoring what's being said.

Consider the man who says to his wife, "Your hair looks very nice today, honey." But instead of receiving her husband's compliment, she snaps back, "What does that mean, 'Your hair looks nice today'? Are you implying that it didn't look nice yesterday or the day before?" That poor guy is in the middle of an argument he didn't even see coming.

Sometimes miscommunication is actually a lack of communication. It is difficult to find common ground with a person who walks away in the middle of a discussion or hides behind a newspaper rather than answering a difficult question.

Perhaps the worst type of bad communication is name-calling. When people are angry, they frequently engage in personal attacks. This is just plain bad communication. Refuse to get caught up in name-calling.

It is possible to share the fact that you're disappointed, concerned, upset, or in pain without raising your voice, digging up the past, or attacking another person's physical attributes. You can always choose to voice your emotions without commenting on someone's appearance, desirability, race, age, cultural background, family history, intelligence, or past failures.

Making personal attacks in the heat of an argument almost always damages the other person's confidence, self-image, and self-worth. The hurt can be so deep that it marks the end of all love, trust, and respect in the relationship.

PRINCIPLES FOR RESOLVING CONFLICT

Make it your goal to be an agent of healing and peace. When conflicts arise, don't immediately take one side or the other. And resist a win-at-all-costs mentality. Take the lead in seeking resolution for the disagreement. The moment conflict erupts, immediately ask God to give you an attitude of humility and to help you become a genuine peacemaker.

Through the years, I have been amazed at the people I've encountered who argue so loudly and vigorously for "peace." They are sometimes so angry as they talk about peace-versus-war issues that they turn red in the face and can hardly speak coherently. They are quick to blast away verbally at any person who disagrees with them, and they apparently see no problem or contradiction with getting violently angry in their pursuit of "peace." You cannot be a good advocate for peace among nations—or among your fellow citizens—if you do not seek it in your personal relationships.

Please understand that I am not advocating a "live and let live" mentality when it comes to speaking out from a godly perspective about important social issues. What I'm saying is that even if you disagree philosophically or theologically with others, you can seek to engage them in debate or encourage right behavior before God without resorting to anger or violence. In the long run, the calm, peaceful way is nearly always the most effective.

There are several principles to resolving conflict in our lives.

Assess the Effect on Your Emotions

Be realistic about how conflict affects you. Assess the personal impact and your normal emotional response to conflict. Do you wither in the face of disagreement? Do you cringe at the very idea of having an argument? Would you rather suffer in silence than make your opinion known?

If you lose an argument, do you criticize yourself for not being able to make your point effectively?

If you win a heated debate, do you gloat?

The apostle Paul was discouraged when he learned that some people were preaching the gospel with a wrong motive (see Philippians 1:15–17). Even so, he chose to see the big picture—the gospel was being preached! He wrote, "I rejoice, yes, and will rejoice" (Philippians 1:18). Regardless of how he may have felt personally, he chose to maintain an attitude of contentment, gratitude, and joy.

That's a good perspective for most people to adopt in the aftermath of a conflict. Look for the good that may come from the incident. If you spoke truth, rejoice that it was shared, even if you have little confidence that it was truly heard. God can bring about results you cannot envision or understand.

I once heard a woman say, "I'd rather have my husband home debating an issue with me than down at the local bar giving his opinions to a woman bartender."

As you assess your emotional response, keep in mind that conflict always exposes some problem, disagreement, or issue in at least one person's life. If you can keep your eyes on the root problem rather than what was said, who said it, and how he or she said it, you will be in a position to bring peace and healing with your emotional health intact. It may not occur at the moment of the conflict, but God can cause it to happen somewhere down the line. As much as possible, put your emotions into neutral so you can more objectively assess what is really taking place. Then you will be better able to address the underlying issue, or issues, in a calm manner.

Identify the Trigger

Something always triggers a conflict. There's a difference between the deeper root cause of a conflict and the surface issues that might set off an argument. Ask yourself:

- Was it something one of us said?

- Was it the tone of voice we used?

- Has there been a breakdown in communication?

Conflict is triggered by a difference of opinion, a lack of shared perspective, or a disagreement about how to proceed in a matter. Some conflict involves differences in style—one person likes one thing, the other person likes something else. Many times it involves a difference in mood or personality—one person is laid-back, the other is combative.

Conflict also can occur when one or more of the people involved is physically exhausted, emotionally drained, or stressed out. A physician friend of mine strongly believes that at least half of all conflict is triggered by low blood sugar. If you can isolate what sparks it, conflict can usually be defused quickly or prevented from happening entirely.

Identify the Cause

The root cause of a conflict often is not easily identified. It may be jealousy, envy, anger, hurt, or any number of emotions and factors. To explore the reasons behind a past or present conflict, try to determine:

Is the disagreement rooted in a deep emotional problem or need the other person has? Consider his or her personal history and life experience. If a person has grown up in an abusive environment, he or she is likely to respond to conflict very defensively. Any statement that sounds like one of the hurtful messages heard as a child is likely to be met with anger, resentment, or fear.

Is the conflict the result of one person's unrealistic expectations? Some people cannot accept anything that is less than perfect. They cannot stand to admit they are wrong or made a mistake. Conflict tends to make a perfectionist frustrated, irritated, and angry.

Is the root of the conflict pride? There's nothing wrong with being wrong occasionally. But a proud person cannot admit he made a mistake. Pride often prevents someone from saying, "I'm sorry. I was wrong. Please forgive me." A proud person feels compelled to defend, justify, and maintain a belief that whatever happened wasn't his fault. This lack of responsibility, accountability, and remorse almost always leads to conflict and anger.

Once you've identified the root cause of a conflict, remember that you cannot help a person who doesn't want to be helped. And even if a person wants your help, you cannot heal her emotional pain—only God can do that. You can provide a listening ear, a comforting and loving heart, and even wise counsel. But healing must come from the Lord.

Neither can you force a person with unrealistic expectations to lower them or compel a proud person to become humble. You cannot insist that someone lay down resentment, hatred, or bitterness. You cannot require another person to forgive. In the end, you cannot erase all causes of conflict. But rather than become frustrated, I encourage you to focus on what the two of you can do to move forward together in a peaceful way.

TEN THINGS YOU CAN DO PERSONALLY

You may not be able to avoid a conflict, but you are responsible for how you respond. Some situations cannot be avoided, nor should you ignore them. Sometimes you will be at the receiving end of another person's anger, hostility, or resentment. But you can always choose what your reaction will be.

Here are ten things you can do to create a positive outcome to a conflict and set the stage for a peaceful resolution. And you can do all these things without any participation from the other person involved.

1. Refuse to respond in anger.

Choose to adopt and maintain a quiet spirit. No matter what another person says or does, refuse to speak in anger or frustration. Nobody can force you to argue or get angry. How you respond is your choice.

2. Make no attempt to defend yourself verbally.

You may need to walk away from an explosive situation in order to avoid emotional pain or physical injury. But make no attempt to explain yourself or respond to an accusation until the outburst is over. There may be a time later when you need to state your case. But until that time comes, keep quiet. God's Word says, "Set a guard, O LORD, over my mouth; keep watch over the door of my lips" (Psalm 141:3).

3. When the time comes to speak, ask God to help you with what to say.

Determine in advance what you truly desire or need. Identify clearly how you want the other person to treat you, the change you want made, or the problem that needs to be addressed. Spend time in prayer, asking God to reveal His desires for you, the other person, and your relationship. Listen in silence until you have an understanding of the Lord's will and His direction. You will know that it is God's way when His peace fills your heart. The Father's solution benefits everyone involved, not just you. Jesus promised His followers, "For the Holy Spirit will teach you in that very hour what you ought to say" (Luke 12:12).

4. Explore what you might do to help a person with needs in his life that may be the underlying cause for the conflict.

Discernment is a spiritual gift that the Holy Spirit imparts to every Christian who requests it (Proverbs 2:3). Too often, we jump to our own conclusions and generate answers and solutions out of our own experience and limited knowledge. Instead, we need to wait on God with an open heart and an open Bible to discern what He desires to heal or the ways He desires to bring about reconciliation. Ask the Lord to guide you and to reveal to you what you need to know. Let me assure you, God has a solution for every conflict. Your responsibility is to discover it.

5. See the conflict as coming from God.

Please understand that I'm not saying God sends or causes conflict. Rather, the Father allows it for a purpose, which He ultimately will use for your good. If you see conflict as having godly purposes, you are going to be far less likely to get angry and lose control in the midst of it. You will be slower to react and more willing to change your attitude and behavior when necessary.

After hearing me teach this concept, a man said to me, "You mean to tell me that I am supposed to see my wife's nagging as coming from

God? It's not coming from Him. It's coming from her! And if the nagging isn't coming from her, it's coming from her mother!" I told him, "God is allowing your wife and mother-in-law to speak to you. There's something in what they say that you need to learn. The Lord may be telling you to change an aspect of your life that makes your wife's—or your mother-in-law's—anger justified. It also is entirely possible that the nagging has nothing to do with you. A situation or circumstance outside your marriage may be causing her to react negatively toward you. In this case, ask God to help make you a better husband by loving, supporting, and praying for her."

You can learn one of two things from a person—what to do or what not to do.

6. Identify your part in the conflict.

Ask God, "Is this my fault?" Reflect upon the situation and identify any part you played in bringing about the conflict or escalating the argument. If you recognize that you are at fault in any way, accept responsibility, admit your fault, ask for forgiveness, and make a commitment to change your conduct.

7. Begin to treat the other person with genuine kindness and tenderness.

Look for a way to express love to him or her. Speak well of the person to others. Pray for him or her, and remember the words of the apostle Paul: "Be kind to one another, tenderhearted, forgiving each other, just as God in Christ also has forgiven you" (Ephesians 4:32).

8. Choose to make necessary changes.

Learn any lessons you can from the conflict as quickly as possible. Be open to changing whatever you need to about yourself without requiring the other person to do the same. Every conflict has a seed of potential in it for your personal and spiritual growth.

9. View the conflict as an opportunity to respond as Christ would.

Jesus is every believer's role model for all aspects of life. Ephesians 5:2 tells us, "Walk in love, just as Christ also loved you and gave Himself up for us, an offering and a sacrifice to God." You and I need to remember what the Lord would do when deciding how we respond to conflict.

10. Make a decision about how you will respond to future conflict or criticism.

Your behavior is always subject to your will. The same goes for your attitude. You can choose what to think and say long before a conflict. Decide that you will respond slowly and wisely, rather than instinctively and rashly. Make a commitment to pursue God's wisdom in the midst of conflict.

TWO RESPONSES
TO END CONFLICTS

I have discovered two responses that go a long way toward ending an argument peacefully or defusing a conflict calmly.

First, if a person is venting at me in anger, the wisest response I've found is to let the person have his full say. And when he pauses, as if waiting for me to reply, I say very calmly, "I am grateful that you told me how you're feeling and had a chance to express your opinion. You've given me some things to think about. I'm going to evaluate what you said and go before God with it. I will ask Him to confirm if I have been wrong and to show me how I need to change. Now, is there anything else you want to point out that will help me improve my character or change my ways?"

Such a response usually stuns a person so much that he or she has little more to say. My purpose is not to shock the other person. Rather, it's to call him or her to more rational and calm communication. If there's good information to be given, I want to hear it. But if he or she has nothing positive to share, I want the other person to recognize that too.

Responding in this way can also lead to a change in attitude. Asking for suggestions that may lead to my improvement shifts the focus away from my perceived faults and flaws—and that's a step in the right direction. If a person truly has a helpful recommendation, I respond, "Thank you. I'll try that" or "I appreciate your advice and will consider it."

The *second* response I have found helpful in resolving conflict is asking the other person, "Can you suggest something to help me avoid creating a situation like this in the future?" Then I give the person an opportunity to speak fully, and as he does, I listen closely. There may be a nugget of valuable information in what is said. Again, this shifts the argument away from venting and fault finding to conflict resolution and problem solving.

These responses will work to resolve conflicts in your marriage, parent-child relationships, friendships, and at work. Try them.

A QUIET SPIRIT AND MEASURED RESPONSE

I went into a business meeting one time, and as soon as I sat down, a man came into the room and launched a scathing verbal attack against me. His tirade lasted almost fifteen minutes, but I did not say a word or try to stop him. And taking their cue from me, no one else in the room tried to stop him either.

When the meeting ended, a pastor friend said, "Charles, I have never seen such a totally unmovable face or expression in my life. You never budged. You didn't reveal anything about how you were feeling—and you stayed that way for fifteen minutes!"

I knew there was no point in trying to defend myself. The other men at that conference table knew me, and they knew the truth about the accusations he was making. That man was succeeding only in destroying himself and his reputation, the longer he ranted at me.

On another occasion, I was scheduled to face a group of news reporters and editors. But I sensed that some of those present were going to do their best to trick me into saying something I would regret later.

So I got a small notecard and wrote on it, PAUSE BEFORE SPEAKING. Then I tucked the card among my notes for the news conference. I knew that I would need to listen closely and think carefully before I responded to any question. This card served as a mental reminder to me even though I didn't look at it once during the interviews. The principle of "pause before speaking" is a good one to remember in any conflict.

When you pause, pray silently that God will give you wisdom about what to say and when to say it. Ask Him to guard your tone and keep any sarcasm or cynicism out of your voice.

One of the questions I was asked at the news conference was what I would do if I didn't win an election for a denominational leadership position. I paused and then responded, "Well, I can't lose." The reporter followed up by asking, "What do you mean, you can't lose?"

I said, "If I win the election, I win. If I lose the election, I still win because I'm obeying God by accepting the nomination. He is in control and will reward my obedience in whatever way He chooses." There was total silence in the room after I said that. No one knew what to do with my answer.

ADMIT IT—DEAL WITH IT

1. Recall the last time you had a conflict with someone. What happened? How did you respond?

2. After reading this chapter, is there anything you might have done to prevent the conflict? To keep it from escalating? To better resolve it?

3. How would you change the way you responded to that person?

4. What might you do to prepare yourself for a conflict in the future?

CHAPTER 12

PURPOSE

||||||||||||||||||||||||||||||||||||||||||||||||||||||||||||||||||||||||||||||||||||||||||||

A Case Study of God-Engineered Conflict

E arlier in these pages, we established that there was such a thing as righteous indignation or good anger. So, then, there must be such a thing as righteous conflict. Right?

Absolutely.

The angriest and most prolonged conflict of my life happened more than forty years ago, but I still remember the entire experience vividly. It marked a turning point in my life and ministry. These events also changed the way I regard anger and conflict. The irony of the situation is that the angriest experience of my life happened in church, not in a secular environment.

I have come to regard it as a "God-engineered conflict" that was rooted in righteous indignation. I know without a doubt that the Lord engineered this trial for the greater purpose of bringing more souls to Himself and to establish more of His glory on the earth.

In 1969, I was called by the executive committee of the First Baptist Church in Atlanta, Georgia, to be the associate pastor. When I arrived, however, I discovered that very few people in the church knew I was coming. I was introduced on a Sunday morning by a man who said simply, "I want you to meet our new associate pastor, Charles Stanley. He's going to preach for us this morning." The brevity of his introduction did not bother me at all. I just stood up and preached.

During the first year and a half I was in Atlanta, apart from Sunday-morning services, I saw the senior pastor only three times. The executive committee ran the church.

The day came when the senior pastor invited a man to preach a weeklong revival at the church, but no revival occurred. Now, this was a Baptist revival, so surely somebody ought to have come forward to receive Jesus as Savior! Even on Sunday morning, nobody came forward after the senior pastor preached. He said, "This is so sickening, I can't stand it!" He threw down his microphone and walked out. A short time later, he resigned.

As associate pastor, I had the primary responsibility of preaching on Sunday nights. But with the senior pastor gone, I was asked to preach also on Sunday mornings. Well, things started happening. More and more people began coming to the church, and a new atmosphere began to take hold as people accepted Christ and joined our fellowship.

I met with the executive committee on an unrelated business matter a short time later and said, "We need to ask God about this decision," referring to the matter at hand. The businessmen on that committee looked at one another, and then one of them said to me, "Let's leave God out of this. This is business." I said, "Oh, we can't do that." That was perhaps the first sign they saw that I was not going to be easy to control. But it was unthinkable to me to leave God out of a church-related decision.

The pulpit committee responsible for selecting a new senior pastor had forty members. But it was run by a core group of seven who were among the most influential and wealthy members of the church. These seven decided they couldn't handle the idea of my ever becoming the senior pastor. So they began to lobby the other members of the pulpit committee to reject me as a candidate for the position.

It took me about three months to realize fully what was happening. As you might imagine, all of this provided plenty of dry tinder to start a small fire of anger in me. I knew that I could either retaliate directly, or I could pray. I chose to pray. I had a certainty in my heart that I was called to be the senior pastor of the First Baptist Church in Atlanta.

In the midst of all this, I traveled to West Palm Beach to preach a revival. It was Friday afternoon, and I was praying, when I got a very strong sense that God was speaking to my heart. *Here is what I am going to do,* the Lord said to me. Then He outlined His plan.

It is one thing to know God's will and another thing entirely to do God's will in the face of opposition from people. In my situation, this created an environment primed for conflict.

I spent a great deal of time in the church's prayer room those days. And each time I thought about the situation, I'd say, "God, there's no way." And time and again He'd speak back to my heart, *Just trust Me. Don't look around. Trust Me. Don't listen to what people are saying. Trust Me!* There was no response to that except to say, "God, I trust You!"

The main accusation against me seemed to be that I preached salvation, the Holy Spirit, the second coming of Christ, the inerrancy of the Bible, and Scripture's relevance to our day and time. From my perspective, if you take these things out of a church, you don't really have a church. You have a social club. That is what had developed and what was at stake. It was a spiritual conflict.

A person once asked me, "Weren't you angry with the devil?" My general approach to Satan is to ignore him whenever I can. I don't waste time or energy on the devil. I resist him, ask God to rebuke him on my behalf, and go on doing what the Lord has called me to do. If I must deal with Satan, I choose to quote God's Word to him. Jesus used that approach, and I see no evidence in the Bible that Christ ranted or raved at the devil. The Lord told him, "Go!" He also "rebuked" demons and commanded unclean spirits to "come out" (see Matthew 4:10, 17:18; Mark 1:25, 5:8, 9:25; Luke 4:35, 8:29, 9:42). But there's no indication that Jesus ever was violent or angry. So I choose to make Christ my role model.

At the outset of my conflict in Atlanta, most of the congregation were not aware of the false accusations being spread about me. But slowly, the opinions of the core group on the pulpit committee infiltrated the greater membership. I remember one man who stood one Sunday and said as a word of testimony, "I've learned more about the Word of God in the past six months than in my entire life." The following week, this man wouldn't even speak to me. People who greeted me warmly one Sunday wouldn't even look my way the next.

The entire situation baffled me. I could not figure out why those who opposed me on the pulpit committee didn't just go out and find another person to be senior pastor. Instead, they spent a great deal of time and energy defaming me in hopes that at least twenty-one of the forty committee members would not vote for me (simple majority ruled). Technically, I was still the associate pastor. I was taking on the role of senior pastor only on an interim basis because there was nobody else to do it. The only attempt the core committee made to find a different senior pastor was to talk to a man who was extremely liberal in his theology. They promised him the moon if he would agree to come to Atlanta. When word got out that he had been contacted, the rest of the committee members came unglued over what they perceived had been done behind their backs and without their approval.

The next tactic of the core committee was to take me to lunch one day and suggest that I leave on vacation and never come back. In essence, they were asking me to resign. I said, "I didn't come to this church solely because you called me to be your associate pastor. I came because God called me to come here. I'll be happy to resign the minute He tells me to leave."

Then one of the men on the core committee quietly offered me a large sum of money to resign quickly and quietly. I said, "If you don't know me any better than that after these two years I've been with you, then you *really* don't know me. You couldn't stack up enough money on this table to cause me to deliberately and willfully disobey God."

The conflict went on for ten months. Much of that time, I came to the church each day feeling like a stranger among the staff members and congregation.

Those who opposed me wore constant frowns. You could see criticism and anger in their faces, hear it in the tone of their voices, and sense it as they walked across a room. They seemed to go out of their way to avoid me, and rarely would they make eye contact when they spoke to me. Yet through God's grace, I felt totally free and liberated in their presence and had no problem looking my critics in the eye.

I'm sharing all these details with you to make a point. There may be times in your life when conflict makes your life difficult and challenging, but you know you need to stay in that situation. The conflict may be long, and it may be intense. But if it is God-engineered, you don't dare walk away—no matter what.

While I was away from the church, preaching at a college in Tennessee for a week, the pulpit committee decided to make a negative recommendation to the congregation at the next Wednesday-night service. For some reason they determined they should have a *no* vote on me before they could seek a senior pastor. That gave me one more Sunday to preach before the Wednesday recommendation.

But, surprisingly, I returned from Tennessee with no sermon idea. That had not happened to me before, nor has it happened since. God did not give me a message until after the Sunday-morning service began and the choir had finished singing. I walked to the pulpit and let my Bible fall open. It landed on Proverbs 3:5–6, which says:

> *Trust in the LORD with all your heart,*
> *And do not lean on your own understanding.*
> *In all your ways acknowledge Him*
> *And He will make your paths straight.*

For the next forty minutes, God's words on the topic of obedience streamed out of my mouth. I had no notes, but I could hardly catch my breath between sentences. I gave an invitation to come forward for salvation, and people began getting up and walking down the aisle to receive Jesus. But at the same time, people in the choir began walking out the side exits, and some other people were heading toward the back door. It was quite a sight to see. Those walking out of the church were passing the people coming forward to receive Christ.

It was a total division of the church. This was not a conflict I had directly initiated or desired. But it was definitely one that God had engineered.

Yes, our heavenly Father does send conflicts. In those cases, it is the truth of God's Word that triggers it. And the purpose of the conflict is so that His power and presence will be established in a relationship or in a situation that needs His power and presence.

Righteous indignation, or good anger, can and does produce righteous conflict.

On Wednesday afternoon, just hours before the congregation was to vote on whether I should be fired or become the next senior pastor, three attorneys came to see me. They told me why I couldn't be the senior pastor, how the church would never accept me, how my future as a minister was over if the church voted me out, and how I'd never get another job. They bluntly told me that the only way to resolve the conflict was for me to resign and leave quickly.

I said to them, "You are asking me to make a decision I have to live with for the rest of my life. I'm putting that decision back on you and the congregation. You and they are going to have to make a decision that you will live with for the rest of your lives. I'm willing to abide by your decision, because I know God will take care of me. But I can't disobey God and leave this place until He tells me to go. I'm willing to live with my decision if you are willing to live with yours. If the people in this church vote to fire me, that's fine. But that will be their decision, not mine."

Through the years, I've talked with a number of people who have told me about similar showdowns in their lives. A spouse may have said, "I want you to agree to a divorce." The other party's answer has been similar to the one I gave: "I'm not going to agree to a divorce. That is a decision I'm not prepared to live with. If you want a divorce, you will have to pursue it on your own." In many cases, taking this stance prevented a divorce. It is not a position that works in all cases, but it does work in some.

I have talked with people who have had similar showdowns with their children or colleagues. One mother said to me, "My son and I had a clash of wills at my house last night!"

"Who won?" I asked.

She replied, "I did. I told my grown son that I would not tolerate his behavior. I said, 'Allowing you to continue sinning blatantly in my home is the same as my agreeing to or participating in it. And I do not agree with your sin. You will need to change or move out.'"

"What did he do?"

She said, "He moved out, calling me all kinds of names as he packed his bags and stomped out the door. I made it clear that the decisions he was making were his decisions and he would have to live with them. I told him in clear terms that I was willing to live with my decision. As he left, I said, 'Your decisions today go far beyond our relationship as mother and son. They are reflecting your choices to disobey God. Are you really prepared to live in disobedience to Him?'"

"How did he respond?"

"He slammed the door on his way out," she replied. "But three months later, he came back apologizing. He told me that what I said forced him to do some serious thinking. He didn't ask to move back in, and I didn't offer it. After all, he is twenty-six years old. It's time for him to develop a life of his own and take responsibility for supporting himself. But he did ask if he could go to church with me the next Sunday. You can't imagine how that pleased me!"

I said, "Oh, yes, I can!"

I would like to have imagined such a positive resolution to the conflict I was experiencing at the church.

On Wednesday night, I slipped in through a side door and sat in the back of the main church auditorium. I went unnoticed as I watched silently with my Bible opened to Isaiah 54:17:

"No weapon that is formed against you will prosper;
And every tongue that accuses you in judgment you will condemn.
This is the heritage of the servants of the LORD,
And their vindication is from Me," declares the LORD.

The chairman of the board of deacons, who had voted for me to leave, said as part of his opening remarks that the church would vote by secret ballot. A man stood up toward the back of the main auditorium and said, "No, we're not. Tonight we are going to find out where everybody stands. I make a motion that we vote by standing vote on every measure." His motion passed.

The meeting went on for three hours. Finally, Mrs. Sauls—a lovely woman who had been a nurse for some fifty years—stood and said in her sweet Southern drawl, "Mr. Chairman, I call for the question." When the vote was put to the two thousand people present that night, about two thirds stood in favor of my being the pastor. About a third stood in opposition. The result was a clear majority decision in my favor.

After the vote was taken, a man noticed I was present and asked me to come down to the platform. I acted as if the vote had been unanimous in my favor and said, "I appreciate your confidence. I'll give you my answer in two weeks."

I spent the next two weeks in prayer to make certain that the Lord's word to me in West Palm Beach was still the same. With full confidence that it was, I accepted the call to be the senior pastor at the First Baptist Church in Atlanta, Georgia.

The people who had opposed me so vigorously never came back to church. They began to meet in a medical building a couple of blocks away. A number of them came to Sunday school. But as soon as class ended, they'd walk down the street to their church. Some came on Wednesday nights to eat in the dining room. But after supper, they refused to come to prayer meeting.

This went on for three months. Then one day in January, I felt especially drawn to Psalm 64:7, "But God will shoot at them with an arrow; suddenly they will be wounded."

I certainly had no intention of seeking vengeance. God was making it clear to me that He, and He alone, would deliver my vindication. The next Wednesday night, at a church business meeting, I asked the membership to give my Sunday-school superintendent and me the full authority to appoint all the deacons and church officers. A member of the original opposition group stood, came to the platform, and gave a speech about how he and other good people were being run out of the church. He said to me, "If you don't watch what you are doing, you are going to get hurt." And then he hit me in the face with the back of his hand.

A woman in the audience stood and shouted, "How dare you hit my pastor!" Another person, a former boxer, rushed up to the platform. Even though this man was about seventy years old, he held out his cane and said, "You're not going to hit my pastor!" Another man jumped up and escorted away the person who had hit me. I didn't say a word. I didn't even react. This man's actions made the entire opposition appear to be a group that couldn't control itself.

Some of the people in the congregation began to cry. When the vote was taken, my request to name the deacons and officers of the church passed.

The next Sunday, as we began singing the first song, a man came rushing up to the platform, pushed away the song leader, and said, "Today you haven't come to hear a sermon. You've come to witness a funeral."

I motioned to our television cameramen to turn off their cameras, which were broadcasting the service live. The man continued to talk, but as he did, three people stood and began to sing "Onward, Christian Soldiers." Very quickly, the rest of the congregation stood and joined them in singing. The man left, and the people remained standing like a solid wall.

A woman who had been watching us on television saw the man rush up to the pulpit before the cameras went to black. She called the police and said, "There's a long-bearded hippie trying to take over the service at the Baptist church." Several police cars soon arrived at our doorstep. It was quite a morning!

The next night, thirty of the church's sixty deacons resigned. On Tuesday morning, all the women's missionary union leaders and more than half of the Sunday-school teachers resigned. After they all left, the rest of the church had a party to celebrate.

The opposition even threatened the television station that aired our live broadcast. They promised that every Sunday-morning service would be interrupted unless they took us off the air. The station bowed to their threat, and for exactly one year, we were off television.

What happened in the year that followed the opposition's leaving was nothing short of a miracle. The church began to grow rapidly. And when our services did go back on the air, we returned with programs on two stations. Those programs were in color, while our previous broadcasts had been in black-and-white. It was as if all the deadwood had been cut away and pruned back so the church could explode with growth and spiritual blessing.

PRINCIPLES FOR DEALING
WITH PERSECUTION

It is easy to feel anger in the midst of ongoing, intense persecution.

There were countless times during that period of conflict when I felt as if I was in spiritual battle, not only for the future of the church but for my own peace. I knew the attack was coming from the Enemy. But I also knew that God was with me. I believed He was going to win the war. Even so, I was in a real fight to overcome anger, resentment, and bitterness. It would have been very easy to hold ill feelings toward those who were trying to destroy my ministry.

I learned five vital lessons in how to walk through God-engineered conflict, which I share with you here.

1. Keep your eyes on the Lord.

Any time I got my eyes off God and onto my persecutors, I felt anger rising up in me. But when I saw my adversaries as part of a greater lesson that God was teaching me, and part of a greater work that He was doing in and through my life, I felt peace. It may sound odd to you now—and it was odd to me then—but I actually felt love toward those who were opposing me so vigorously. I wanted God's best for their lives. And I knew that if they would only turn to receive His best, everything would be resolved for them, for me, and for the entire church.

On one occasion as I was praying, God spoke to my heart: *If you see this as something I'm allowing in order to make you an even stronger, more victorious person, then you'll come out of it better, not bitter.*

My response to Him was "I will choose to see this through Your eyes."

Some people see all forms of persecution against them as coming from the devil. In one sense, they are correct. God does not instigate, authorize, or promote the persecution of His people. On the other hand, the Lord does allow persecution to come our way. And in allowing it, He enters the situation with us and will work it for our good. I call it God's supernatural engineering.

Engineering involves the design, construction, and maintenance of a process or function. It includes creativity, innovation, and ingenuity to generate a system in which all components function in proper relationship with one another. Only God can truly engineer a successful outcome for a righteous conflict. Only He can cause "all things to work together for good to those who love God, to those who are called according to His purpose" (Romans 8:28). Man often turns good situations into evil, but God has the greater wisdom in knowing how to bring good from evil.

In nearly every incident of persecution I have experienced personally or witnessed close up, I have seen God work in much the same way. As long as the persecuted remains faithful to the Lord and refuses to sin, God brings victory. The power and influence of the enemy is diminished in the person's life, and a greater strength emerges. This affects not only the persecuted person but also those who witness the God-engineered consequences, resulting in tremendous blessings and impact.

2. Ask the Lord to strengthen and sustain you.

The Bible has a lot to say about those who endure persecution.

- A crown of victory awaits those who run the race faithfully to the end. (1 Corinthians 9:24–25; James 1:12; Revelation 2:10)

- God's strength and protection are given to those who withstand evil. (Psalm 21:11; Romans 12:21; Ephesians 6:13)

- God's blessings are granted to those who overcome and stand firm in their faith. (Jeremiah 1:19; John 16:33; Revelation 3:12)

If you are experiencing persecution or conflict, ask God to sustain you in it, to help you not to sin by becoming faint-hearted or fearful, and to show you how to respond so that He receives glory and honor.

3. Recognize that you are fighting a spiritual battle.

To withstand conflict, you must know with certainty that the battle is the Lord's. Be sure that you are being persecuted for the cause of Christ, not simply for your own foolishness, error, or stubbornness.

Ask yourself:

- Has the Lord really directed me to take the stance for which I am being persecuted?

- What's at stake here? Will a victory advance the kingdom of God, or will it only benefit my career, reputation, et cetera?

- Who will get the credit? God must be the only One who receives glory and honor for a victory, especially if the conflict is one that He is allowing and engineering.

Any time you find yourself in a spiritual conflict, remind yourself of the apostle Paul's words to the Ephesians:

Finally, be strong in the Lord and in the strength of His might.
Put on the full armor of God, so that you will be able to stand firm against the schemes of the devil. For our struggle is not against flesh and blood, but against the rulers, against the powers, against the world forces of this darkness, against the spiritual forces of wickedness in the heavenly places. Therefore, take up the full armor of God, so that you will be able to resist in the evil day and having done everything, to stand firm. Stand firm therefore, HAVING GIRDED YOUR LOINS WITH TRUTH, and HAVING PUT ON THE BREASTPLATE OF RIGHTEOUSNESS, and having shod YOUR FEET WITH THE PREPARATION OF THE GOSPEL OF PEACE; In addition to all, taking up the shield of faith with which you will be able to extinguish all the flaming arrows of the evil one. And take the HELMET OF SALVATION, and the sword of the Spirit, which is the word of God.

With all prayer and petition pray at all times in the Spirit, and with this in view, be on the alert with all perseverance and petition for all the saints (Ephesians 6:10–18).

As you stand in the face of conflict or persecution, you must arm yourself with

- *Truth*. Be sure you know the facts of the situation from God's perspective.

- *Righteousness*. Make certain you are in right standing with God and that you are living a blameless life before your persecutors. Their actions give you no license to sin.

- *God's peace.* Make reconciliation with the Father your goal for everyone involved. Always use God's Word to speak encouragement to your persecutors.

- *Faith.* Keep your focus on God.

- *Confidence.* Be sure of your salvation and deliverance through God's hand. Expect Him to work on your behalf to ensure a victory that is consistent with His purposes.

- *God's Word.* Be quick to quote Scripture in the midst of your persecution. Let God's Word encourage you and do your talking for you.

- *Prayer.* Call out to God on behalf of those who are angry with you. Pray for the people who are persecuting you. Ask Him to move on their hearts and to make them more open to His presence in their lives. Pray for your fellow believers that God will strengthen them as they stand with you in your time of persecution.

- *Perseverance.* Don't give up. Stay fully armed. Commit to prayer.

Hundreds of years ago, when great ships sailed the oceans of the world, predicting storms was not done with the use of satellite photos or weather radar. Ships frequently were engulfed by fierce storms. Crewmembers would bind themselves to the ship's masts to keep from being swept overboard. Many sailors rode out storms that way, trusting God to deliver them from the raging sea.

When the storms of anger, conflict, and persecution bear down on us, you and I need to bind ourselves to the mast of the Lord Jesus Christ.

Then we must hold tight, trusting God to silence the winds and the waves that rage against us, to preserve our lives, to strengthen us in His goodness, and to keep us strong in our faith.

4. Continue to Forgive—No Matter What

Throughout this conflict, God provided me with countless opportunities to forgive. I knew in my heart that I had no right to harbor unforgiveness. And when I chose to forgive, I was sure that God would show Himself strong on my behalf.

In forgiving, I did not deny that I felt hurt.

I did not convince myself that the matter was not important.

Rather, I chose to turn everything over to God. I released the people who spoke or acted against me into His hands. It's one thing to have a bad attitude when you hand over a person to the Lord: *Here, God. You deal with them. And, if possible, deal with them in a way that punishes them severely.* It's an entirely different thing to turn them over in an attitude of prayer: *Here, God. You deal with them in whatever way You think is best for their lives.* Praying for another person to receive the fullness of God's grace and mercy can be difficult, but it brings the greatest release and reward for everyone involved.

I also discovered that the sooner I forgave those who were trying to get rid of me, the sooner I could receive God's healing for any pain or sorrow that resulted from their persecution and anger.

Be quick to forgive. Then forgive freely and fully.

5. Keep Looking for the Victory

There's a reward to be gained through persecution. Don't lose sight of it. In the Sermon on the Mount, Jesus taught us:

> *Blessed are those who have been persecuted for the sake of righteousness, for theirs is the kingdom of heaven. Blessed are you when people insult you and persecute you, and falsely say all kinds of evil against you because of*

Me. Rejoice and be glad, for your reward in heaven is great (Matthew 5:10–12).

Persecution and conflict are for only a season. As painful as the experience may be, the glory of eternity will heal the pain of harsh words and the anger of evil deeds. Ultimately, God wins. And because you are living life in and through Him, you win too. There is no persecution that compares to the eternal rewards promised to you from your loving heavenly Father.

Even while we remain on earth, conflicts we experience can

- Strengthen us in our faith.

- Toughen our resolve to influence others for God and for good.

- Refine our character.

- Give us greater cause to thank and praise God.

Always remain on full alert for what the Lord is doing in your life. Be aware of the lessons He is teaching you, the experiences He is using to conform you to the image of His Son, and the victories He is engineering so you might bring more honor and glory to Him.

ADMIT IT—DEAL WITH IT

1. Have you ever experienced a God-engineered conflict? What happened during the conflict? What was the outcome?

2. Are you still dealing with negative feelings from that conflict, such as unforgiveness, toward anyone involved? If so, what can you do today to forgive that person (or persons)?

3. If the conflict did not end the way you believed God wanted it to, what might a healthy and godly attitude be, moving forward?

4. Are you still angry or resentful long after the conflict was seemingly resolved? Admit it to God and ask Him to free you from it.

CHAPTER 13

OPPORTUNITY

|||||||||||||||||||||||||||||||||||||||||||||||||||||||||||||||||||||||||||||||||||||||||||||||||

The Potential for Personal Growth

One of the things that people often say when they're angry is "I don't deserve this."

They're right. Few people deserve anything that comes their way—good or bad. The number of things in life that have nothing to do with achievement or accomplishment represents a very high percentage.

You didn't "deserve" to be born into your family—whether it's a wonderful, godly family or an awful, ungodly one.

You didn't "deserve" the neighborhood in which you grew up—rich or poor, peaceful or violent, clean or dirty.

You didn't "deserve" most of the opportunities you've been given.

You didn't "deserve" the majority of critical comments leveled against you.

We live in a fallen world, and bad things do happen to good people.

A wiser and more mature approach is this: I need to learn what God desires for me to learn from every situation, and then I must take the action He desires for me to take.

As I have written repeatedly in this book, God is—and always will be—in control of everything. If the Lord has allowed something unpleasant, painful, or seemingly unfair to happen to you or those important to you, He has a reason for it. Ask God about the situation. Talk to godly friends. Seek wise counsel.

What can you learn? What changes should you make in the way you process information, communicate with others, or establish healthful emotional boundaries? What is the "call to action" that God is speaking to your heart and mind? If the Lord wants you to right a wrong or solve a problem, He will provide both direction and resources to bring you to a godly response.

In all negative situations, there is something to be learned. Jesus said to His followers, "Blessed are you when people insult you and persecute you, and falsely say all kinds of evil against you because of Me" (Matthew 5:11). Open your Bible and read it. In a concordance, look up a keyword related to your situation and study what God's Word says. Look for stories in Scripture that involve people who faced a difficulty similar to yours.

LEARN A NEW HABIT
OR RESPONSE

Very often, an angry response becomes a habit in a person. The good news is that all our habits have been learned, so they can be un-learned too. Anyone can choose to reverse persistent anger in his or her life.

First, make a choice to think about things that are positive and beneficial. The apostle Paul encouraged the Philippians, "Whatever is true, whatever is honorable, whatever is right, whatever is pure, whatever is lovely, whatever is of good repute, if there is any excellence and if anything worthy of praise, dwell on these things" (4:8).

Can a person *choose* what to think?

Absolutely.

Refuse to nurse negative and hurtful thoughts. Don't reopen emotional wounds. Reject any thoughts of revenge. Choose instead to think about those things related to the goodness and greatness of God. Ultimately, all things that are true, honorable, right, pure, lovely, of good repute, excellent, and worthy of praise are found in Christ. So, rather than think about the person who hurt you, think about Jesus. Rather than focus on the issue or circumstance that made you angry, focus on the One who died for you.

Second, choose to become involved in positive activities that require your full attention. Make new decisions about how you will spend your time, money, and mental energy. Choose to associate with people who are pursuing positive goals. The apostle Paul wrote to the Colossians, "Set your mind on the things above, not on the things that are on earth" (3:2). In other words, focus on those things that last beyond your lifetime and extend into eternity.

Third, ask God to help you monitor your own thoughts and speech. Countless people wander through life, not really paying attention to what they're thinking and saying. They are just going with the flow, thinking about whatever captures their attention at the moment, visually or verbally, and saying anything that comes to mind. Choose to take charge of what you think and what you say.

Anger is fueled by negative thoughts and negative words. Turn off the fuel pump! Recognize that you have the choice not to dwell on what you happen to see and hear. You can choose how you will process and react to what you're exposed to on a daily basis. You also are in control of what you say to yourself . . . about yourself.

The person who is most influenced by a negative comment is the person who makes the comment. Your ears are usually the ones closest to the words coming out of your mouth. Don't become a victim of your own negativity.

Any time you hear yourself say something critical or harsh about yourself or another person, immediately take these steps:

- Ask God to forgive you for belittling or diminishing the value of a person He created and loves, as He loves all people, infinitely—including you.

- Immediately say something positive about yourself or the other person. Share a genuine compliment or word of appreciation.

- Thank God for His ongoing work in your life and in the life of the other person. Openly and verbally acknowledge that you and everyone else are "works in progress" and that the Holy Spirit is present and active in the life of every person who has accepted Jesus Christ as Savior.

LEARN MORE ABOUT YOURSELF

Choosing to deal with anger presents you with an excellent opportunity for personal evaluation, healing, and growth. Ask yourself these five questions:

1. Are you blaming the wrong person for your pain?

Are you angry at your spouse or a friend for a past hurt that did not even involve either of them? Were you abused or abandoned as a child or teenager? Were you deeply mistreated, betrayed, rejected, or harmed by someone in your past?

Emotional pain has no expiration date. Very often, a person carries old hurts into new relationships. Search your past and change old patterns of responding or reacting.

2. Are you projecting your flaws onto people around you?

It takes a great deal of personal objectivity to answer this question honestly. We usually do not see our own failures, flaws, or weaknesses with clarity. Rather, we tend to project onto other people the thoughts and feelings that we secretly hold about ourselves. This is especially true when it comes to our *negative* thoughts and feelings.

If we are stingy, for example, we tend to criticize another person's lack of generosity. If we are harboring anger, we often will criticize someone else's bad temper. If we see ourselves as having little value, we tend to treat other people as if they are not valuable. If we are failing at some task or behavior, we often will be quick to point out the failures of others.

Take a long, hard look at any criticisms you are leveling at another person. Are those actually areas in which you fear that you are coming up short? Are you pointing out another person's sins without recognizing that you are guilty of committing the same ones?

3. Are you afraid of intimacy?

Are you reluctant to have close relationships? Do you seek more personal space than other people? Do you feel uncomfortable when a person gets to know you too well? Are you suspicious if a person seems to like you too much?

The old saying is true: *It is better to have loved and lost than never to have loved at all.* It is better to have a close friend and lose him or her than never to have had a friend.

Full intimacy with Christ means laying down your life to Him. Jesus called for our total surrender when He said, "He who has found his life will lose it, and he who has lost his life for My sake will find it" (Matthew 10:39). We will experience God's best only when we are fully submitted to Him. Take the risks associated with personal and spiritual intimacy. You will not be disappointed.

4. Are your expectations for the relationship unrealistic?

Do you want more than the other person is able to give? Are you expecting something from someone who has no clue about what it is you are expecting?

Some people have a tremendous amount of love to give. They are quick and generous with their warmth, compassion, and kindness. But others have very little to give and are slow and reluctant to express love.

Men and women with abundant happiness and peace in their lives are very confident in establishing and developing relationships. Those who are angry, hostile, and resentful do not work, play, or interact well with other people.

If you know how to show love in good, appropriate, beneficial ways, God will give you plenty of opportunities to be loving, generous, available, and transparent. And He will bring people into your life who are the same way.

Be realistic. It is far easier to adjust your expectations than to change the other person. If you choose to establish a relationship with someone who has less emotional maturity or depth than you, then you likely will have to love more, forgive more, and communicate more than he or she does—especially at the beginning of your relationship.

5. Are you feeling rejection or low self-esteem?

Are your emotions related to the actions of another person? Or are you struggling with a sense that you don't deserve to be accepted and loved? Some people have such low self-esteem that they do not believe anybody is capable of loving them. They build a wall of unworthiness around themselves. But they don't see that wall; they think other people are rejecting them by remaining distant or inaccessible. The truth is that the people outside the wall have no way in! Be honest with yourself. Are you capable of receiving the love someone else desires to give you?

AN OPPORTUNITY TO GAIN A NEW PERSPECTIVE

Most of the situations that create an angry response are trivial, external, or momentary. In addressing anger, choose to gain a more realistic perspective about the true nature of those circumstances.

Trivial

People often allow the most petty, insignificant comment to trigger their anger. Our culture has become so preoccupied with hurt feelings. What is it that hurts your feelings? In most cases, it's a word spoken in passing. Sometimes the person speaking doesn't intend to cause pain. And he or she may not even be aware that what was said has been hurtful.

Through the years, a number of people have come to me and said, "Dr. Stanley, I want to ask your forgiveness." I've learned that the best response I can give is "You are forgiven, and you don't even have to tell me what you did." They rarely leave it at that, of course. They feel a need to tell me why and how they have wronged me. Sometimes this man or woman includes a statement about what they perceived I said or did.

Not long ago one person said, "Something you said made me so angry that I decided to quit coming to church. It happened five years ago, and now I'm back."

Did I intend to make that person angry? Absolutely not. I may have been telling a large audience to turn away from ungodly behavior to pursue righteous living. But I certainly do not direct my sermons at any one person. Also, my intent is always to motivate change through the power of the Holy Spirit, never to trigger anger.

I have learned that when people get angry over something they think I said, or they think I mean, or they think I aimed directly at them, they are nearly always wrong about at least one of those conclusions. People tell me all the time about things they heard me say that I never said. I can prove it with transcripts and recordings. Still, they heard something from somewhere inside their minds or hearts—a message they attribute to me that convicts them of negative behavior or sin.

When they finally get over their anger toward me, they return to the church, to listening to me on radio, or watching on television. Who was hurt by their anger or by their leaving? They're the ones who experience loss. In the case above, this person had lost five years of instruction and encouragement from God's Word.

If your feelings are always getting hurt by someone, or by people in general, you need to find out why. What has made you so sensitive that you respond so strongly to the slightest provocation or misunderstanding? Why do you have such a short fuse?

A man once said to me, "I've always had a quick temper. My dad had one. My grandfather had a quick temper. It's genetic."

Genetic? No. It is a learned behavioral habit that was passed on from one generation to the next.

We learn our emotional responses. If you have a short temper, it's likely that somebody in your early life, perhaps unintentionally, taught you to have one. Or, if you're quick to take offense, you learned that response too.

The good news is that what you have learned, you can unlearn. It takes effort and consistent awareness, but you can unlearn harmful emotional responses and establish new behavioral habits. Ask God to show you what needs to change from His perspective. If He doesn't consider something important, it doesn't have to be counted as important by you.

External

Many of the things that trigger anger are external. Some potentially stressful and volatile situations in your life may be related to a large group of people or to the nation as a whole. They are not situations that are limited to you individually or to your immediate family members, friends, or coworkers.

This is not to say that the larger situation has no impact on us. It does. But we need to understand that we are not alone in many of the circumstances we face. It's very likely that many other people are feeling the same way we are.

I have known people to get very angry when gasoline prices go up ten cents per gallon overnight. I wonder if these folks are joyful to the same degree when they see gasoline prices drop.

Other people get mad at rush-hour traffic on the freeway. Still others become angry over home mortgage interest rates; the way a war is being fought overseas; or how their federal, state, or local government is being run. Turn on talk radio for a few hours, and you'll hear plenty of people angry over these external issues.

I'm not saying you should turn a deaf ear to these situations and circumstances. In fact, some of these issues may require us to exercise our righteous indignation. What I want you to recognize is that a personal outburst of anger will do little to nothing to solve a greater problem or stop a trend.

Do you tend to see yourself being personally persecuted when you are simply part of a group experiencing a negative situation? If you are upset about something that is happening in society or in the political realm, you can take positive actions. Call or write an elected official, a prominent businessperson, or some other person you know who can make a difference. Explain specifically what you want to see done. And make sure you understand the issue well enough to know how you want your elected representatives to vote on it.

You may want to consider joining or starting a group dedicated to resolving an issue in your community. Recognize that there is little chance that you can take on the problem alone and be successful at resolving it. External situations require a communal response.

Don't stew over negative things that are happening in the world around you. There's absolutely nothing to be gained by screaming at the TV set or venting your anger at your spouse. Redirect that negative energy into positive actions for change.

Momentary

A large number of things that trigger an angry response are temporary and fleeting. Hurtful words are often spoken impulsively and without much thought or consideration about their impact. Pause before, during, and after anger wells up inside you. It's possible that by the time you express your feelings, the person will be gone, the situation will have changed, or the problem will have been resolved.

Do you become enraged when someone cuts you off in traffic?

"She could have hit me!" you may say.

But she didn't.

"He was rude!" you say.

So? All people are rude sometimes, and some people are rude all the time. And most likely, you are rude sometimes too.

"They had no right to do that!" you say.

True. But what does getting angry accomplish? *Their* blood pressure won't be affected. *Their* stomachs aren't going to be tied up in knots.

In the traffic situation, you may be delayed in your arrival at work or home by a minute or two. Use that extra time to quote a verse of Scripture to yourself or to thank God for helping you avoid an accident. Redirect your angry response, and turn it into something that has the potential for long-lasting good.

ADJUSTING EXPECTATIONS

Anger sometimes surfaces because a person's expectations are not being met. If you are expecting perfection in behavior or total consistency in performance from someone, you are going to live in a constant state of disappointment. And that can lead to feelings of frustration or resentment. Be open to adjusting expectations for yourself and others as a way of avoiding bad anger.

Perfect Behavior and Perfect Performance Are Not Humanly Possible

Do not expect perfection from others or from yourself. It is simply not possible in human beings, no matter how diligent or persistent they may be in their pursuit of perfection. Why? Because we live in a fallen world. Our physical bodies and fleshly desires remain, even if we have an intimate relationship with God. The world is filled with trouble, tragedy, and trial. Relationships have countless opportunities for miscommunication or misinterpretation of both words and actions. And no matter how hard we try or how skilled we may become, we still make errors, miscalculations, and mistakes—even in those areas where we excel.

What *is* possible? To look your best, do your best, and be your best. To this day, I can still hear my mother's constant words of encouragement, "Do your best, Charles." God expects us to give our best effort all the time, no matter what.

"But," you may say, "the Bible tells us to 'be perfect.'" It's true that Jesus said as part of His Sermon on the Mount, "Therefore you are to be perfect, as your heavenly Father is perfect" (Matthew 5:48). This statement, however, must be seen in the context of the Lord's greater message. Jesus was teaching that we are to love our enemies and pray for those who persecute us. He said,

> *For if you love those who love you, what reward do you have? Do not even the tax collectors do the same? If you greet only your brothers, what more are you doing than others? Do not even the Gentiles do the same? Therefore you are to be perfect, as your heavenly Father is perfect (verses 46–48).*

The perfection Jesus is calling for here is a perfect, godly love for all mankind. God loves those who have yet to express any love for Him. He hears prayers of repentance from all people regardless of their race, culture, age, gender, or nationality. Jesus commanded His disciples to love the same way He did: "A new commandment I give to you, that you love one another, even as I have loved you, that you also love one another" (John 13:34).

We also must not expect perfection in terms of *our* behavior. The truth is that human emotions fluctuate dramatically and frequently. You may feel closer or more distant from a person on an hourly, daily, weekly, or monthly basis. Our feelings ebb and flow. You may change your mind in light of updated circumstances, which lead to new choices or decisions. You may alter your opinion after being given additional or more accurate information. Just because something was one way in the past does not necessarily mean it will stay that way in the future. And nothing can maintain a superior quality or consistency without a significant amount of time, attention, and effort.

A man once said to me, "When I was hired by my company, I thought I'd always work there. It never dawned on me that after thirty-three years of loyalty and good work, they'd eliminate me in a so-called downsizing. My termination was part of a move my employer made so it could hire younger workers at lower salaries. I was bitterly disappointed and angry at what the company did to me."

"Are you still angry?" I asked.

"No," he said. "I have come to feel relieved and actually blessed by what happened. A wise friend had a deep and long conversation with me one day. I learned three great truths. First, nothing is certain except a person's relationship with God. Second, nobody is irreplaceable except Jesus Christ. And third, anything that we hope will last requires diligent and ongoing effort.

"The interesting thing is that my friend is neither a psychologist nor a member of the clergy."

"Who is he?" I asked.

"He's a physicist! He talked to me in terms of inertia—and how something in motion must have a continual application of energy to remain in motion. He talked about the continuing changes that occur all around us. Nothing is in a totally steady state. All living things are in some state of growing or dying. New emerging cells and old, dead cells exist in all living things at all times. He also talked about predictability and concepts related to random occurrence."

"I would like to have been part of that conversation," I said.

"It was fascinating and deeply encouraging," he continued. "I came away from that discussion with a strong realization: The only reliable thing in life is God. I also learned that rather than being surprised by change, I should expect it."

"That is a wonderful truth to have learned," I said. "What has happened since then?"

"I decided to start my own business. For years, I have enjoyed two great hobbies: fishing and photography. So, I began to advertise that I was willing to serve as a guide and take people into the countryside to fish, take photos, or both. Some of these trips were overnight excursions and others were one day only. I have received a tremendous response and am making as much money as I did in my old job. Plus, I'm having a lot more fun and made dozens of new friends. We talk about geography, ecology, fishing techniques, types of fish, photography techniques, and many other outdoor topics. But almost every conversation eventually turns to the subject of faith as we discuss the One who created all that we see and enjoy in nature."

This man learned a tremendous lesson that everyone is wise to take hold of. The only constant in life is the God who creates all things, knows all things, and governs all things. The Bible describes our Creator in these terms: "Every good thing bestowed and every perfect gift is from above, coming down from the Father of lights, with whom there is no variation or shifting shadow" (James 1:17). In these few words, the truth is presented that God does not waver in any aspect of His goodness or greatness. He is never less than perfect—never inconsistent, faltering, wavering, or unreliable.

What God says, God does.

What He is, He remains and will always be.

And we are promised the same thing about God the Son. The apostle Paul wrote, "Jesus Christ is the same yesterday and today and forever" (Hebrews 13:8).

Only God is omnipresent—eternal and timeless, with absolute consistency.

Only God is omniscient—knowing all things at all times, wise in all judgment and decisions, and with full and perfect insight into all situations.

Only God is omnipotent—all-powerful and capable of controlling all things at all times in a way that impacts every individual with a perfect purpose.

Only God is without change—totally good and perfect in His love, totally without variance in His perfect character.

Do not expect any of these marks of absolute perfection and consistency from yourself or others. In plain and simple terms, you are not God, and neither is anyone else.

Be Realistic in Your Expectations of Love

Many people seem to assume that if two people are "in love," then they will never hurt or become angry with each other. That's unrealistic—and very likely impossible. Difficult situations and circumstances come up, unwise choices and decisions are made, stress runs high, and energy runs low. Before you know it, anger erupts and love is called into question. Even the most loving and faithful husband and wife disagree from time to time.

The good news is that genuine love between two people goes a very long way in keeping anger at a minimum. Love is essential to overcoming anger, resolving differences of opinion, and continuing to live in peace.

Don't become overly emotional at the first sign of disagreement or conflict with your spouse. Don't harbor tiny faults, errors, or mistakes and nurse them into giant offenses. Don't assume that one conflict over one issue signals the end of your relationship.

Many things in life should be allowed to pass without comment. Many "issues" should never be given "problem" status.

I have met young women who are expecting to find husbands someday to fill their lives with romance, shower them with affection, and be physically and emotionally available to them at all times. I believe, and I tell them, that they are setting themselves up for disappointment.

I have met young men who are hoping to find wives someday to fill their lives with tender loving care, make lots of home-cooked meals, and be available to satisfy all their emotional and physical needs. I believe, and

I tell them, that they too are setting themselves up for disappointment.

I certainly am not trying to disparage love and marriage. They are wonderful gifts given and ordained by God. But I have lived long enough to know that there are down moments in any relationship—no matter how great the love between the two people. The good news is that, as with all other things subject to change, a marriage or friendship can be renewed. It takes effort to keep any relationship strong and vibrant. Many times, both people involved are called to change in ways that enhance rather than detract from the marriage or friendship.

A woman told me not long ago that she finally came to an understanding about her fault in a failed marriage. Up to that time, she felt that her husband's infidelity and irresponsibility had been the sole causes of their divorce. But after reflecting on what her role in the breakup may have been, she said, "I came to an awareness that my fault in the relationship was complacency."

"How were you complacent?" I asked.

"I made a bad assumption. I thought that because we had been married for more than twenty years, we would always be married. I didn't think I needed to do anything to keep my husband interested. I failed to do my part to plan things we could do together that would build new bonds and create new memories. I wrongly assumed that our children would bind us together. In the end, we drifted apart, and I wasn't even aware we were drifting."

"How did you feel once you came to that awareness?"

"I was angry!" she said. "But I was not angry with my husband, as I had been in the past. I was angry with myself."

"Have you forgiven yourself for your complacency and your anger?"

"Yes," she replied. "And it was a wonderful release to finally understand my part of the problem and then to finally forgive myself. I made a vow to never take a relationship for granted—including my relationships with my children and grandchildren, and also my relationships with friends. Every relationship needs work."

How right she is!

The only true Prince Charming a woman will ever know is the Prince of Peace, Jesus Christ. And the only true fulfillment a man will find for every area of his life is in our Lord and Savior.

If you find yourself frequently feeling angry toward your spouse, ask yourself if your anger stems from expectations that one or both of you have set too high. Love covers a multitude of flaws, failures, and sin. Choose to love your spouse through the rocky, turbulent times.

A man once told me, "I don't like arguing with my wife or feeling angry toward her. So we always kiss and make up on the same day we have a disagreement. We have made a decision to go to bed happy with each other."

That's not only good marriage advice; it's biblical wisdom.

Be Realistic in Your Expectations of Loyalty

No matter how much a spouse, friend, or coworker wants to be loyal to you or fulfill your mutual goals, he or she *will* disappoint you from time to time. People make mistakes. And sometimes those mistakes negatively affect our relationships in some way.

Some time ago, one of my friends developed an inappropriate relationship. He put both his marriage and his career in jeopardy. Because people knew he and I were friends, some suggested that I break all ties with him. They said, "He has jeopardized your reputation." But I refused to listen to their advice.

I took a different course of action and confronted my friend about his behavior. I pointed out that he had been disloyal not only to his wife and family but to me as well. As we talked, it became obvious that he had not faced the full extent of the consequences related to his behavior until that moment. While he insisted that the relationship was innocent, he also acknowledged that it could be regarded as inappropriate. He asked, "Can we still be friends?"

I said, "Yes." While his loyalty to me is something I *cannot* control, my loyalty to him is something I *can* control. So I explained, "I will be your friend, but I must also tell you that I can no longer trust you in certain areas or with certain information, as I once did."

Trust is always broken when a person steps beyond the boundaries of loyalty or faithfulness. But anger does nothing to resolve a breach of trust. It only creates a wider breach.

If you believe someone has been disloyal or unfaithful to you, there is nothing to be gained by silence or denial. If the offense is minor, you may be able to resolve the issue in conversation. It's possible the offending person did not realize he was being disloyal. Maybe he did not know that his behavior was unfaithful. If the offense is major, you most likely will need more than talk to repair the relationship. Sometimes the only solution to broken trust is to sever ties with the person. Before you decide to repair or end the relationship, I encourage you to pray, meditate on God's Word, and seek wise counsel about how you should do it.

There are a number of behaviors that can be classified as disloyal. They include

- Adultery or an act of infidelity

- Dishonesty in business dealings

- Public accusations or criticism

- Attacking a person's actions or accomplishments after having supported them in the past

Right and wrong in these situations sometimes get out of focus. The disloyal person may claim to have a good motive for what he's done. Judas no doubt thought he was justified in handing Jesus over to the religious authorities in Jerusalem. The disciple may have been trying to help speed up the timetable for Christ to be revealed and declared the Messiah. But Judas' actions betrayed Jesus. His deeds were acts of disloyalty.

If a friend or spouse tells you that he or she is feeling betrayed by something you said or did, be quick to apologize. Express your sorrow and repent of any disloyal action or behavior. Ask for forgiveness. Do not attempt to justify what you've done or diminish the extent of the harm caused. Do what you can to heal the hurt the other person is feeling.

LOOK FOR THE GOOD
THAT CAN COME

Throughout these pages, you have read the encouraging words of Romans 8:28: "And we know that God causes all things to work together for good to those who love God, to those who are called according to His purpose." The Bible promises believers that there is a peace to be gained and a godly response to be made in every difficulty, hardship, and trial.

A Peace to Be Gained

No matter how negative the circumstance, how intense the outburst, or how severe the threat, a person in an intimate relationship with God can experience a peace "which surpasses all comprehension" (Philippians 4:7). Jesus said, "Peace I leave with you; My peace I give to you; not as the world gives do I give to you. Do not let your heart be troubled, nor let it be fearful" (John 14:27).

Jesus certainly did not deny that some situations and circumstances would be difficult or challenging. Nor did He promise His followers that they would be free of problems and hardship. On the contrary, Christ said clearly, "In the world you have tribulation, but take courage; I have overcome the world" (John 16:33).

Every hurtful or unpleasant experience can be regarded as a faith challenge. It can be approached as an opportunity to trust God in greater depth or in new ways. It can be viewed as a call to begin intense prayer for a person or group.

Ask God to give you His peace and to help you have the calm, quiet confidence that comes from total trust in Him.

A Godly Response to Be Made

Before he came to a saving knowledge of Christ, the apostle Paul was a murderous persecutor of the church (see Acts 8:1–3). But after his encounter with Jesus along the road to Damascus (see Acts 9), Paul was transformed into a man of peace.

The apostle wrote to the early church in Rome, "Never pay back evil for evil to anyone. Respect what is right in the sight of all men. If possible, so far as it depends on you, be at peace with all men" (Romans 12:17–18). He also encouraged believers, "Do not be overcome by evil, but overcome evil with good" (Romans 12:21).

Paul was also a very practical man who recognized problems and received godly insight to solve them. To deal with people who are angry or hostile toward you, he wrote, "If your enemy is hungry, feed him, and if he is thirsty, give him a drink, for in so doing you will heap burning coals on his head" (Romans 12:20). But Paul was not only talking about blessing our adversaries with physical food and drink; he also meant that we should give encouragement and praise and offer spiritual truth. In this way, we might cause them to become convicted by the Holy Spirit and compelled to accept Jesus Christ as their Savior and Lord.

If a person or group is persecuting, hurting, or rejecting you, God has a reason for their behavior. Ask Him to show you what it is and how to accomplish His will, plan, and purpose for it.

In Romans 12:20, Paul was making the point that you can bless, benefit, or help your enemy to the point that frustration, irritation, aggravation, or confusion will generate a sense of remorse or repentance in him. But there's an even deeper truth being expressed in Paul's metaphor.

In the Old Testament, a situation arose in the days of Moses that involved outright rebellion. A group of Israelites rose up against Moses in an effort to remove him as leader and take over (see Numbers 16:41). So God sent a plague into the camp to "consume them instantly" (verse 45).

But Moses did not sit idly by. He wanted to spare his enemies from the wrath of God. So Moses called for Aaron to take incense from the altar fire and "make atonement for them" (verse 46). Aaron did as Moses said and "ran into the midst of the assembly" (verse 47). The Bible says Aaron "took his stand between the dead and the living so that the plague was checked" (verse 48). This act was the equivalent of drawing a spiritual line in the sand. The plague stopped at the exact spot the burning incense was poured out.

When we do what is right in a negative situation, our actions can put an end to a plague of anger, bitterness, and resentment. And when we speak God's truth in love, our words are able to stop the cycles of revenge and retaliation.

Good *can* overcome evil. But for that to happen, our best intentions must produce good and practical actions that bring real benefit to everyone involved.

As you confront anger in your life, look for the good you can do. Make prayer your first "good deed" toward a good goal.

ADMIT IT—DEAL WITH IT

1. What one lesson have you learned about dealing with anger, yours or another's, and put into practice?

2. What further lessons are you going to try to learn? What resources will you use to help this learning process?

3. What one thing can you do to stop dwelling on some hurt you don't "deserve" and achieve a measure of peace?

4. How can you change your expectations, for yourself or the other person?

5. Write down three positive things you can do to turn bad anger into good anger. Start doing those things today.

IF YOU ARE NOT A CHRISTIAN . . .

I have been a minister of the gospel of Jesus Christ for more than fifty years. I have been a Christian since I was twelve years old. This book has been written entirely from a biblical perspective, and the truths in it are firmly rooted in the Word of God.

If you are not a Christian, you may have wondered as you read this book: How is any of this possible? How can I let go of my anger? How can I forgive? How can I respond in peace and love to someone who's angry at me?

I do not believe it's possible for you to forgive without first knowing that God has forgiven you and that you are no longer in bondage to sin. If you want God's forgiveness, admit that you're a sinner, and tell God that you believe Jesus died on the cross to pay your sin debt in full. Ask God to forgive you for your sins, and He will answer your prayer, write your name in the Lamb's Book of Life (see Revelation 13:8), and forever call you one of His children.

Not only that . . . but the moment you receive Jesus as your Savior, God will seal you with His Holy Spirit. Jesus called the Holy Spirit our "Helper" (John 14:26). The Holy Spirit will enable you, strengthen you, and teach you how to live the Christian life. The Holy Spirit will reveal to you the truth of God's Word as you read your Bible. He will prompt you to do and say the right things to overcome your anger or to deal with the anger of others around you. He will enable you to forgive things you never thought you could forgive. And the Holy Spirit will help you be a godly man or woman and bring honor to Him by the way you live your life.

Without God, you cannot completely control anger.

With God, you can.

Make the choice right now to invite Jesus into your life. Through the power of the Holy Spirit, God will heal any and all of the emotional wounds you suffered in the past and will help you live with courage and peace. I encourage you to call on Him today!